THE BONDS OF LABOR

The BONDS
of LABOR

German Journeys to the Working World, 1890–1990

CAROL POORE

WAYNE STATE UNIVERSITY PRESS
DETROIT

Kritik: German Literary Theory and Cultural Studies
Liliane Weissberg, Editor
A complete listing of the books in this series can be found at the back of this volume.

Library of Congress Cataloging-in-Publication Data

Poore, Carol.
    The bonds of labor : German journeys to the working world, 1890–1990 /
Carol Poore.
        p.   cm.—(Kritik)
    Includes bibliographical references (p.) and index.
    ISBN 0-8143-2897-0 (alk. paper)
    1. German literature—20th century—History and criticism.   2. German
literature—19th century—History and criticism.   3. Labor and laboring classes
in literature.   4. Social problems in literature.   5. Labor and laboring classes—
Germany—History.   6. Germany—Social conditions.   I. Title.   II. Kritik (Detroit, Mich.)
    PT405 .P59 2000
    830.9'3520623—dc21   00-010461

Contents

Illustrations

Acknowledgments

At the completion of a long project, it is a pleasure to express my gratitude to all those who have helped to sustain my work over the years. I was able to devote long periods without interruption to writing thanks to a fellowship from the American Council of Learned Societies, a grant from the Friends of the University of Wisconsin–Madison Libraries, and the generous support of the Brown University Graduate School and Dean of the Faculty Bryan Shepp at Brown University. The outstanding collections of the University of Wisconsin–Madison Memorial Library were my main source of research materials, and the Interlibrary Loan Office of the Brown University Library handled my many requests with good-humored speed.

Friends and colleagues who read and critiqued my manuscript at various stages include Steve Brockmann, Vicki Caron, Bill Crossgrove, Vicki Hill, and Fred and Ursula Love. I am especially grateful to Arthur Evans, the director of Wayne State University Press, as well as two anonymous readers, for invaluable guidance and suggestions. I thank Liliane Weissberg for including my book in her series. David Nelson put much effort into creating the computerized manuscript. Jonathan Lawrence was the most perceptive, painstaking copy editor I could have wished for. Needless to say, any flaws in the book are my sole responsibility.

Others were there for me from beginning to end in a variety of essential ways: Dennis, Emily, and Lucas Hill, Margot Jones, Ed and Micheline Rice-Maximin, Waltraud Tepfenhardt, and Max. I would also like to name here the generation of my parents and their brothers and sisters, those who have passed away and those who are still with me: Charles and Lillian, Hugh and Laura, Drayton and Jan, Edna and Hale. Workers and farmers all, their values have provided a foundation for my life in many unforgettable ways. Finally, I am not the first of his former students, and will hopefully not be the last, to dedicate my book to Jost Hermand, teacher and friend.

Introduction

But what is knowable is not only a function of objects—of what is
there to be known. It is a function of subjects, of observers—of what
is desired and what needs to be known. A knowable community is a
matter of consciousness as well as of evident fact.

—Raymond Williams[1]

In the fall of 1997, seven years after German unification, the leading news
magazine *Der Spiegel* featured a cover story about growing social and
economic inequalities in this, Europe's wealthiest country. Captioned "The
rich are getting richer, the poor are getting poorer—and why work is worth
less and less in Germany," the cover illustration depicts this country as
divided today not by a wall but by an abyss.[2] On one side stand the well-
dressed members of the business and financial elite, with their briefcases,
cellular telephones, champagne, dalmatians, and golf clubs. On the other
side of the gaping, unbridgeable chasm stand figures representing increasingly insecure and marginalized groups: manual laborers, the working poor,
the unemployed. In the accompanying article, *Der Spiegel* documented the
German repercussions of the historically unprecedented upward shift in
accumulated wealth which is an intensifying global trend today. Specifically,
experts from across the political spectrum pointed to the growing numbers
of both the super-rich and the working poor and welfare recipients as
evidence of a serious breach between the worlds of the more and less
privileged.[3] And furthermore, they voiced their fears that the experience
of work was no longer serving as a reliable unifying factor to bring citizens
from most income levels into some form of functioning social whole.

While these structural economic changes are a worldwide phenomenon, they have given rise to particular anxiety in Germany, with its

11

history of extreme political ruptures. For in this country, perhaps more than in others with a much longer and more stable history of national cohesion, the experience of work, along with ideological assertions of its importance, has been central to the building of national identity. And in particular, the identification of work with supposedly universal goals has been an essential part of all efforts to integrate the industrial workforce—indeed, all manual laborers—into the nation. To recall the most obvious examples of this tradition, one need only think of pre-1914 glorifications of "German" work, of the fascination with "production" during the Weimar years, of National Socialist notions about the "social honor" of labor, of the East German emphasis on performance in the service of the socialist community, and of the West German "economic miracle."[4]

Within these broad cultural discourses on work, the division between mental and manual labor and the place of the industrial working class in a hoped-for national consensus have been problems of especially acute significance. To be sure, the more privileged were always confronted with the "lower classes," an amorphous group composed not only of those who worked with their hands but of all poor and marginalized inhabitants of the social abyss. Yet since the nineteenth century, it has been the industrial working class that mounted the most serious efforts to lessen and even abolish socioeconomic inequalities through its trade unions and its Social Democratic and Communist politics. This meant, in turn, that all debates and policies regarding the "social question" necessarily had to concentrate on defining the place of those whose "strong arms" kept the wheels of industry turning, as Georg Herwegh wrote in his anthem for the General German Workers' Association in 1863.[5] Since that time, the most bitter political struggles have been waged over determining the place these particular workers were to occupy within the nation. The anti-democratic traditions of the Wilhelminian period, which excluded industrial workers and manual laborers from full social and political participation, continued to operate fatally during the Weimar Republic to exacerbate class divisions. As soon as the Nazis came to power in 1933, they brutally repressed workers' organizations in a terroristic drive to create a racially defined "national community." After 1945, the "Workers' and Peasants' State" of the German Democratic Republic (GDR) was not able to gain the loyalties of many of those whom it purported to represent. In the Federal Republic, it appeared for a time that the economic boom associated with reconstruction had solved the social question by enabling workers to participate in general prosperity. However, after the oil crisis of 1973, and increasingly so after unification in 1990, a renewed uneasiness over the social divide arose in Germany.

Interlaced throughout these political, social, and cultural developments are striking expressions, originating from every possible perspective, of the extreme difficulties in bridging gaps between social classes, between above and below. And such perceptions have often been coupled with a strong sense that the world of factory workers, manual laborers, and the poor is an unfamiliar, even hostile realm to those outside it; a "foreign" territory to be explored, controlled, or ignored; the dark "souterrain" existing right underneath the feet of those walking in the light above.[6] In a book review entitled "Bericht aus dem Unbekannten" (Report from the Unknown), for example, published in the first issue of the journal *Der Klassenkampf* (The Class Struggle) on October 1, 1927, novelist Arnold Zweig called attention to the chasms separating the well-educated bourgeoisie from the working classes in Germany. Speaking with the greatest urgency, he predicted that entrenched traditions of class privilege would lead to political and human disaster if they were not replaced by more social justice and equality:

> In England, America, and France, not to mention Russia, deeply moved ambassadors of the bourgeoisie have constantly gone down to the exploited, whom they viewed with amazed understanding. . . . But since the Wars of Liberation in Germany, the rift between those who work with their hands and those with a higher education has become an institution which separates the Germans more deeply from each other than any kind of geographical or political divide. Members of the German bourgeoisie know much more about French or English middle-class ladies (Madame Bovary, the Forsythes) than about the thoughts, moods, and needs of their own employees: the workers who bake their bread or build their houses, who drive their streetcars and dig their graves, who connect the electricity to their houses and who drill for their water. . . . It is a cause of great harm for all people that the entire burdens of a society are laid onto one class; that talents are pressed down into this mire and suffocate there; that millions of hopeful young people decay and go to ruin in everyday life.[7]

What Zweig captured so well in this statement was the persistence of older hierarchical, nondemocratic structures that entrapped both workers and the poor at the bottom of the social pyramid. And to his mind, this state of affairs made Germany still appear backward by international comparison, whether with Western industrialized countries or with the young Soviet Union.

Yet even in Germany, there is of course a long tradition of

"ambassadors of the bourgeoisie" going down to explore in a multitude of ways what Zweig termed here the world of the "lower classes crushed by the burdens of society." From Georg Büchner to Bertolt Brecht and beyond, writers in the progressive, democratic, and leftist traditions have depicted sympathetically the groups Zweig called the "least known and most exotic of all subjects."[8] More specifically, however, since the late nineteenth century writers and others from the middle or upper classes have set out for the most varying reasons to enter into the world of manual labor by becoming workers themselves for a time. And they have produced a wide variety of texts, both fictional and nonfictional, that circle around this experience of traveling down into an unfamiliar world to share in its travails. While literary historians have devoted much attention to topics such as the image of work and workers in literature and to the efforts of writers and other intellectuals to find a place in working-class movements, these journeys to the working world have not been investigated in any coherent way. Yet these texts comprise a century-long literary tradition that expresses in particularly concentrated form an entire spectrum of political and cultural responses to the division of labor and to the social question.

In the first instance, reformers or leftists have willingly entered into the working world in order to investigate what Friedrich Engels termed the "condition of the working classes." Their exposés comprise a subgenre of the much larger category of works devoted to exploring all the dark areas of the social abyss. However, many journeys into the unfamiliar realm of manual labor were involuntary, such as those which impoverished German students were compelled to take during the period of inflation following World War I. Texts that portray this kind of experience are concerned less with reporting on the workplace than with attempting to make sense of being thrust into an unfamiliar, generally oppressive milieu. Finally, calls for all Germans to journey into the working world by temporarily performing manual labor have been central to both right-wing and left-wing political programs in the course of the twentieth century. The Nazi Labor Service can only be described as pure coercion, which its propagandistic texts sought to justify. However, efforts in the socialist GDR to expose all citizens to some type of manual labor were a much more entangled mixture of the voluntary and the involuntary, and in turn, writers there created much more complex depictions of this experience.

Rather than holding up some version of the reality of workers' lives as a way of evaluating these journeys, my project here is to focus on how specific autobiographies, reportages, essays, films, and novels represent the unfamiliar experience of becoming a manual worker, with particular attention to texts that provoked public debates and to the notable intersections here between discourses about class and race or ethnicity. This literary tradition illuminates the concepts and fantasies of work and workers held by writers and others who left their more privileged positions to become engaged with efforts to create a society that would allow for more liberty and equality, for those "on the bottom" to have a greater chance to express and satisfy their own needs and desires. But of course it was by no means the case that these sojourners in the world of labor always set out with emancipatory intent. On the contrary, their journeys often had the goal of gaining knowledge for the sake of strengthening control over those below.[9] Consequently, these texts are just as much about the intricate "bonds" of domination over those who worked with their hands as about the "bonds" of fraternity between those who renounced privilege and those who hoped to rise. My study of this rich yet well-defined body of material thus seeks to augment both historical studies of class relations and the labor movement as well as literary studies of themes and images by exploring the cultural history of responses to social inequities.

All the approaches to journeying into the working world can be characterized as facets of a mentality of awakening—that is, the awakening of those with relatively secure economic and social status to the existence of another social reality around them. Experiencing voluntary or involuntary arousals from periods of relative blindness to social injustice, those undergoing these shifts in consciousness often hardly seemed aware of their forerunners, of their place in a tradition. Thus, the cultural history of this repeated process, in which individuals or groups suddenly set out to explore or were more or less forced into unknown yet proximate worlds, does not present itself as continuous over the past century, but rather as a series of explosion-like periods of discovery or rediscovery—some quite short-lived and others of somewhat longer duration. As a consequence, bringing the obscured phenomenon of journeys to the working world to light involves two things: first, keeping in mind its location as one variant of the broader tradition of social exploration; and second, focusing on the points where these journeys became most visible and urgent, where they attracted the most attention and provoked the most public debate. Accordingly, the chapters of this book are meant to function as a series of spotlights illuminating this century-long tradition of descending into the unfamiliar world of manual labor.

After establishing the context of nineteenth-century explorations of the social abyss, the first chapter presents three early approaches to journeying across the social divide that anticipate later developments. The first German journey to the working world is a text by a young Protestant theologian named Paul Göhre who worked in a factory in Chemnitz for three months in 1890. Göhre's project was a semi-ethnographic investigation that sought to give middle-class readers a picture of all aspects of workers' lives from the perspective of covert participant observation. By becoming a worker for a time, Göhre desired to learn more about this world in order to be able to resist more effectively the Social Democratic leanings of his future working-class congregations and steer them in a more conservative direction. The heated debates his book occasioned only intensified when Göhre—transformed by his experiences in the factory—soon left the Church and became a Social Democrat himself. From a different perspective, to the left of Göhre, the Austrian Social Democrat Max Winter reinvented the neglected genre of social reportage in the late 1890s. Winter appears to have been the first journalist to take on various jobs doing manual labor for a short time and then to publish exposés of onerous working conditions in trade union and Social Democratic newspapers. Here, entering into the working world meant that Winter attempted to renounce privilege, listen to the voices of workers, and join them in their efforts to abolish the most oppressive sides of manual labor. Finally, resonating to some extent in Göhre's writings but becoming much more intense in right-wing circles after the turn of the century were volkish stirrings that sought increasingly to bring German workers into a national consensus. When confronted with the chasm between social classes, representatives of these groups did not respond at first by descending into the world of manual labor. Rather, they called for all "Germans" to unite against supposed domestic and foreign enemies. This trend is well exemplified in *Wolf Eschenlohr*, a novel written by the volkish author Walter Flex in 1917, which is structured around the confrontation between a student and a factory worker. Although the student does not actually become a manual laborer in the novel, Flex evokes a vision of national unity across social classes that prefigures later right-wing and National Socialist calls for this very step to be taken.

The second chapter traces conservative, right-wing trends during the Weimar Republic which culminated in National Socialist paeans to the "Worker" and the institutionalization of the Nazi Labor Service. The chapter begins with an overview of the phenomenon of student workers in the early 1920s, when, for the first time, significant numbers of middle-class students were compelled by financial necessity to work as manual laborers. Their experiences are recorded in collections of autobiographies, and a number of other texts also take up the theme of the working student or the mediator between classes. A few of these remained on the level of vaguely worded calls for "brotherhood," such as Fritz Lang's film *Metropolis* (1927). For the most part, however, novelistic depictions of entering into the unfamiliar working world promoted the idea of a volkish German community that would transcend class differences by closing its ranks against Jews, Bolsheviks, and foreigners. The chapter discusses these sources as part of a much broader debate about introducing a national labor service that was to unify the "workers of the mind and workers of the hand." These advocates of the nationalization of work called for utilizing hard manual labor as a potent social leveling force. They did not propose journeys down that might support workers in their efforts to rise up, but rather aimed at keeping workers in their place through measures ranging from false promises of unity to sheer terror. And just as importantly, they supported the compulsory Reich Labor Service as a way to subject non-working-class Germans to anti-intellectual discipline. Of course, what all these right-wing voices generally distorted or ignored was the oppressive aspect of brute manual labor. Many writers and theorists on the left, however, who sought to keep their focus on the concrete effects of socioeconomic power relations between above and below, opposed plans to use a national labor service as a force for social leveling. The chapter concludes with a discussion of a novel by the Communist writer Karl Grünberg and a scene from a drama Bertolt Brecht wrote in exile, both of which use journeys to the working world to unmask right-wing Nazi rhetoric about class reconciliation through shared manual labor.

Although labor service advocates gained the upper hand in Germany, writers who continued the tradition of literary reportage undertook very different kinds of journeys to the working world during the Weimar Republic. Like Max Winter, these writers sought to travel across class boundaries in ways that furthered workers' struggles for emancipation, and their reward after 1933 was to be forced into exile or the obscurity of "inner emigration." Trying to find lasting rather than temporary brotherhood, they rejected all right-wing tendencies to glorify physical labor and its use as a disciplinary tool. On the contrary, they kept their sights on how unremitting manual labor diminished and stunted workers' lives—that is, on the world of class relationships. Chapter 3 tells the stories of three such writers on the left who came from the upper or middle classes and who entered into the worlds of manual labor and poverty, attempting to relativize their own more privileged positions for the sake of a greater liberation. This chapter focuses on texts by Alexander von Stenbock-Fermor, the "Red Count" who began as a right-wing work student and reported later on proletarian life as a member of the League of Proletarian-Revolutionary Writers (BPRS); Maria Leitner, a socialist journalist who traveled through the United States doing manual work and reporting on it and on American race relations for the German press; and Lili Körber, whose reportage deals with her experience in a factory in the Soviet Union.

When writers began to enter the working world again in both German states after the war's immense destruction, they were often hardly aware of the efforts of their forerunners—so thoroughly had the traces of these earlier journeys been erased. This meant that postwar authors had to rediscover for themselves some of the methods their predecessors had used. Or, they had to find new ways of "going down" that were more appropriate to their changed historical situation. Chapter 4 traces journeys to the working world in selected novels, short stories, and reportages of the GDR. In this state, under the auspices of the Bitterfeld Program, it was official cultural policy for a number of years beginning in 1959 to encourage writers from non-working-class backgrounds to develop close connections to factories or agricultural cooperatives and to incorporate this subject matter into their artistic production. These contacts were one aspect of much broader efforts to reshape traditional divisions between mental and manual labor, to break down the traditional privileges of the wealthy, and to create more opportunities for the formally disadvantaged—efforts that also entailed restructuring the educational system and reorganizing the workplace. Before 1989 it was mainly in works of GDR literature where voices could be raised that problematized these efforts to establish a "socialist community" and which kept alive more emancipatory visions. My analysis begins with earlier texts that thematize hopes of learning from the working world, traces writers' growing skepticism about this process, and moves on to later works where such journeys appear to be either ways of dropping out of the performance-oriented "socialist community" or even punishments. As an alternative to depictions that either continued to highlight the educational, disciplinary function of manual labor or presented it as an apolitical sphere of refusal, the chapter discusses several texts by Volker Braun. These are more successful at relativizing privilege in both their content and their narration, and they continue, even after reunification, to voice a wish for connection across the social divide.

During the years of reconstruction in West Germany, the pervasiveness of the ideology of social partnership meant that the world of manual labor hardly figured any longer as a locus of fundamental resistance to unsatisfactory conditions. Consequently, it was only in the early 1960s, when this ideological consensus began to face more serious challenges, that a small number of outsiders began to journey once again into the working world there. Chapter 5 focuses on the two ways in which writers and other intellectuals chose to participate in manual labor as a way of resisting the ideology of the "classless society." First, journalist Günter Wallraff recuperated the tradition of oppositional social reportage by investigating working conditions in factories and allying himself in ways aiming toward social change with the workers whose world he entered into briefly. Second, a number of radical students made their way to the working-class "base" in the declining years of the student movement around 1970 in an effort to break out of existential isolation and find meaningful political involvement. For these students, entering into the world of manual labor meant leaving the ivory tower with romantic hopes of becoming a new revolutionary avant-garde. The chapter closes with a discussion of Wallraff's last extensive project: that of disguising himself as a Turkish foreign worker and recounting his experiences with prejudice and discrimination as well as with manual labor. Crossing the demarcation lines of ethnicity and the barrier of social class introduced a whole new set of problems and dynamics. In contrast to his earlier reportages, where his journeys to the working world were connected with efforts of West German workers to organize themselves, Wallraff was able to imagine the resistance practiced by the new ethnic minorities only in the form of ineffective minstrelsy. His controversial best-seller thus unintentionally exposed hidden and not-so-hidden preconceptions about ethnicity and race, as well as about privileges of representing the "non-Germans" within Germany's increasingly transnational labor force.

What all the journeys to the working world discussed here had in common in the most basic way was a search for community. These writers, theorists, and politicians either experienced or evoked situations in which people from the most diverse socioeconomic backgrounds were working and living together. Yet they diverged fundamentally in their conceptions of the form that any community created like this should take. Would it be a social order founded on coercion, more of a "prison than a haven," in which manual labor would function as a punitive leveling factor?[10] Or was there a possibility for more democratic directions, whereby those who descended into the social abyss would enter into emancipatory coalitions with those below? This was the alternative that confronted those entering the working world from the beginning of their journeys, and it is one which still confronts us today. Consequently, the conclusion of this book reflects on the apparent end of this tradition after 1990 and offers some conjectures about the forms such journeys might take in the future.

1
In Darkest Europe and the Ways Out, 1890–1918

The Context of Social Exploration

In its premodern variations, the tradition of traveling down into the "world below" reaches back into the misty realms of fairy tale, legend, and myth. In these stories, gods became mortals, kings and queens slipped into peasant garb, and nobles moved as ordinary travelers along dusty roads—either as punishment for their misdeeds or as a means of gaining access to worlds and knowledge previously inaccessible to them. These fantasies, romances, and quests gradually yielded, however, to a more modern, prosaic kind of journey, that of "social exploration," which developed in the nineteenth century with the growth of industrialization and the urban working classes.[1] Most generally speaking, the breakdown of older paternalistic, hierarchical social structures, which went hand in hand with the relocation of increasing numbers of people from the countryside to the cities with their factories, became an unavoidable concern for members of the upper and middle classes, whose reactions to this process ranged from alarm and fear to engaged interest in solving the social question. Accordingly, in the course of the nineteenth century and afterward (and even more so in countries such as England, France, and the United States than in Germany), "social explorers" set out to investigate in various ways the strange nether worlds occupied by the poor and the working classes, worlds of darkness underlying the supposedly secure foundations of their own societies. These were travelers who, rather than journeying outward to faraway lands in search of adventure, exoticism, or escape, headed down into the depths close at hand. Often disregarded by the more well-to-do, this "souterrain" was nevertheless accessible and visible to those who made up their minds to enter it. And so, like Friedrich Engels, they studied the "condition of the working classes"; like novelist Eugène Sue, they delved into the underworld "mysteries of Paris"; like Salvation Army founder William Booth, they investigated "darkest England and the ways out"; like naturalist playwright Gerhart Hauptmann, they recalled forgotten histories of oppression and revolt; like Upton Sinclair, they entered into the "jungle"; like Jacob Riis, they wanted to expose "how the other half lives"; like Jack London, they journeyed into the "abyss"; like George Orwell, they reported on how it felt to be "down and out in London and Paris."[2]

Broadly speaking, travelers to society's depths up to the late nineteenth century usually set out to enter into the world of the urban poor. This included the industrial working class, but it also encompassed others on the margins of society—the shifting groups of the lumpen proletariat, poor women and children, the homeless, tramps, the unemployed, criminals.[3] In attempting to imagine whether and on whose terms these outsiders could ever be integrated into their respective societies, social explorers offered a range of solutions and programs that spanned the entire spectrum of cultural, religious, psychological, and political perspectives and were intertwined in the most convoluted ways. Some viewed the social abyss as an uncanny, brutal world, as the abode of unabated misery or exotic wildness, and emphasized its separateness from the realms above. Others took these groups as potential objects for Christian charity or middle-class social work, hoping to care for and improve the lower classes, and thereby to control, discipline, and domesticate them. And still others attempted both to engage themselves more seriously with the lower classes' own struggles to rise and also to uncover how obstacles to their advancement and happiness had been created by the upper and middle classes themselves. As examples, several early texts may be highlighted here that set many of the parameters for subsequent journeys to the social abyss and the industrial working world.

The first of these is not a German novel, but a French one that inspired imitations in many countries, including over one hundred in Germany: Eugène Sue's *Les Mystères de Paris* (The Mysteries of Paris).[4] In this phenomenally successful, sensationalistic novel about the Paris underworld, first published in serialized form in 1842–1843, a grand duke disguises himself in the "mask of the people" in order to gain access to the world of poverty and misery in Paris and to atone for his own attempted crimes by trying to help the needy and pursue evildoers.[5] In his own preface, Sue referred to American author James Fenimore Cooper and his portrayals of "savages" and "barbarian tribes" and promised that in his novel, he would expose the reader to the lives of "other barbarians" who were just as far removed from "civilization" as those whom Cooper had depicted so well. However, the great difference between Cooper and himself, Sue maintained, was that he had no need to travel to faraway lands and distant peoples to do this. For, as he told his readers enticingly, "the barbarians of which we speak are in our midst."[6] This motif of traveling to the domestic abyss in order to step outside "civilization"—rather than to the mysterious Muslim lands or the Orient, to the last frontiers of the globe such as the North Pole, or to "savage" peoples supposedly living in "darkness"—is continuous in the fiction and nonfiction of social exploration since the mid-nineteenth century.[7] In countless texts written during this period of colonialism and, later, imperialism, the discourse of class intersects with those of Orientalism, of exploration and the conquering of nature, and of race to create images of a nether world teeming with lowly, inferior beings.

In Germany, these motifs are densely concentrated for the first time in the works of many naturalist authors of the 1880s and early 1890s. Often basing their writings on personal observations, these writers sought to expose the social and economic misery of their time by bluntly depicting the unadorned truth.[8] To be sure, this ideological and political intent was often infused with real sympathy for the lower classes.[9] However, since many of these writers concentrated almost solely on the deformations they uncovered in the social abyss, they created a host of what have been termed "gruesome images" to depict the world of the poor and the urban working class.[10] Typical of this approach are the reportages by Karl Böttcher, who invited his readers in 1888 to "come along, I will lead you to where the masses live in our big cities, to the absolute depths of poverty, to the people whose clothes are torn and whose consciences are in shreds, to the dregs of society."[11] Such metaphors of beastliness, filth, unrelieved misery, and inherited defects among the lower classes abound in much of naturalist literature. However, these images generally block out the fact that many of these very residents of the social abyss had long been involved in political activity and cultural production on their own behalf.[12]

The second approach to social exploration that developed in the course of the nineteenth century was social work, which sought to care for, but also to control and domesticate, the lower classes.[13] Two aspects of this effort to master the social question stand out as relevant here: the method of case studies of the pauperized population, and the perspective of Christian charity, which was often coupled with insistence on strict order and discipline. Particularly striking illustrations of this approach are the numerous nineteenth-century accounts of the milieu of itinerants, vagabonds, and journeymen, often by writers who had some theological training or other religiously motivated interest in establishing hostels for this footloose population. These include, for example, Clemens Theodor

Perthes's *Das Herbergswesen der Handwerksgesellen* (Hostels for Journeymen, 1855); Carl Vocke's *Erzählungen aus der Herberge: Eine Volksschrift* (Tales from the Hostel: A Popular Account, 1857); D. Rocholl's *Dunkle Bilder aus dem Wanderleben* (Dark Pictures from Life on the Road, 1855); and the minister Friedrich von Bodelschwingh's *Meinen lieben Brüdern von der Landstraße* (To My Dear Brothers of the Highways, 1902).[14] Evoking panoramic images of masses of homeless, rootless people who endangered social stability through the hostile distance they kept from state and Church institutions, these advocates of moral uplift emphasized strict religious indoctrination and hard work in the hostels they founded for transients, the poor, and workers.[15]

This approach to providing for the unruly lower classes grew as a cornerstone of Christian social work and political activity in the course of the nineteenth century in Germany, as many who were involved in these projects of domestic missionizing also became active in political organizations—some of an increasingly volkish cast. These included groups such as the Christian Socialist Party (founded in 1878 by the conservative, anti-Semitic Protestant court chaplain Adolf Stoecker), the Christian Socialist Congress (founded in 1890 by the ministers Stoecker, Friedrich Naumann, and Paul Göhre, among others), and Naumann and Göhre's National-Social Union (founded in 1896).[16] Claiming to speak for the fluid population of workers and other poor people who were the objects of their ministry, these organizations pursued an increasingly nationalistic politics of class integration. And in doing so, they focused obsessively on counteracting what they viewed as the heathen, unpatriotic influence of Social Democracy on the inhabitants of the social abyss.

In contrast to such an approach, which was fundamentally one of social pacification, other writers and theorists went further, striving to renounce some of their own class privileges and to ally themselves with budding emancipation movements from below. In reportage, articles and reports, and political manifestos, these social explorers attempted to develop concrete, radical proposals for practical action on behalf of disadvantaged groups. The beginnings of these activities in Germany lie in the years immediately preceding the 1848 revolution. Reflecting the heightened social awareness characteristic of this period, a noteworthy group of writers set out to document the misery and injustice they saw around them in an effort to enlighten their readers. Some of the best examples include Bettina von Arnim's *Dies Buch gehört dem König* (The King's Book, 1843; based on Heinrich Grunholzer's case studies of poor people in Berlin), Wilhelm Wolff's *Das Elend und der Aufruhr in Schlesien* (Misery and Revolt in Silesia, 1844; one of the most important historical sources on the Silesian weavers' revolt); and Ernst Dronke's *Berlin* (1846;

which weaves chapters on social abuses into an encyclopedic panorama of the city).[17]

Of the texts of social exploration from the 1840s that take this approach, two stand out for their consistent shift of focus from the failings of those below to the culpability of those above. The first is Georg Weerth's *Skizzen aus dem socialen und politischen Leben der Briten* (Sketches from the Social and Political Life of the British), which was initially published as a series of letters from Bradford, England, to the *Kölnische Zeitung* (Cologne News) in 1843 and 1844. In these sketches, which have been called the first German social reportage, Weerth set out to explore what he termed, with a nod to Sue, "the mysteries of Bradford."[18] However, unlike Sue, in his journey to the souterrain Weerth sought to combine more general historical, theoretical, and factual material with true accounts of how poor people and workers lived. But he soon realized that he needed access to their private lives in order to see more than was readily apparent on the surface to a middle-class outside observer. Finding that the workers' distrust of strangers was an insuperable obstacle, Weerth decided to assume a role they would accept and persuaded a physician friend to introduce him as his assistant while making rounds through workers' households. Unlike his contemporary Sue and many of the later naturalist authors, however, Weerth did not confine himself to depicting only unrelieved misery and indignity. Rather, he also wrote movingly about these workers' efforts to create spaces for beauty and refinement in their lives.[19] Maintaining that the bourgeoisie was blind to these desires emanating from below for something higher and better, Weerth concluded that the human potential of the people he visited was being crushed by a brutal economic system. As potential solutions, he pointed to struggles by various reform groups and the Chartist movement to rectify the exploitation he saw.

Like Weerth, Friedrich Engels also refused to view the differences between the "known" world of the upper and middle classes and the "unknown" world of the poor and the emerging working class as due somehow to fate or to the "nature" of those on the bottom. In *The Condition of the Working-Class in England* (1845), Engels produced a study replete with dates, facts, and statistics that set out to expose class structures in the quintessentially capitalist city of Manchester as the causes of the overwhelming poverty and misery there. Dedicating his book to the "working-classes of Great Britain," Engels legitimated his approach rhetorically by claiming that it was founded on knowledge he had attained through renouncing his privileged position: "I forsook the company and the dinner-parties, the port-wine and champagne of the middle-classes, and devoted my leisure-hours almost exclusively to the intercourse with plain Working-Men; I am both glad and proud of having done so."[20] Engels was concerned above all with exposing how the propertied classes kept the lower classes in a subordinate position; that is, rather than envisioning a strange, uncanny nether world or a world in need of discipline and middle-class guidance, he emphasized the role of the bourgeoisie in creating this world, focusing particularly on urban geography.[21] Asserting that in general, poverty had a "separate territory . . . assigned to it in the great cities, where it struggles along removed from the sight of the happier classes,"[22] Engels bolstered this statement with detailed descriptions of Manchester's layout. From the design of thoroughfares to the locations of factories and shops that blocked the passerby's view of the slums—all these things sufficed, Engels wrote, "to conceal from the eyes of the wealthy men and women . . . the misery and grime which form the complement of their wealth."[23] In his approach to journeying into the everyday world of the poor and the working class, then, the social critic Engels sought to uncover the strategies of containment directed against the inhabitants of this world, and to hold metaphors of visibility and invisibility up to the light of political and economic analysis. After the failure of the 1848 revolution, however, this kind of social analysis and reporting disappeared for the most part in Germany for next fifty years. It survived only in abbreviated form in articles about workplace conditions and everyday life in the Social Democratic press, and in different guises in naturalist literature.[24]

Of course, social explorers continue up to the present day to journey down into the worlds below them out of the most varying motivations. However, by the end of the nineteenth century in Germany, one particular sector of the social abyss was becoming a special source of fascination and alarm to those above. This was the class of industrial workers who intermingled with the poor and the outcast, but who were also becoming increasingly successful at organizing themselves politically to challenge established power relations and economic structures. Faced with these threatening voices arising from below, travelers from the upper and middle classes made the industrial working world a site of intensified focus for their social explorations. In fact, as one historian has noted, empirical social research in Germany in the second half of the nineteenth century grew largely out of a "concern with working class people and their problems." Carried out by groups such as the highly influential "Verein für Sozialpolitik" (Association for Social Policy) and various religious organizations, such research "was essentially motivated by the need for action and reform" and was often intended to counteract more radical, Social Democratic alternatives.[25] And furthermore, feeling the cold winds from below that were beginning to blow through the cracks and fissures in their more sheltered lives, a few social explorers even set out to journey into the working world by living as manual laborers for a time. With their claims to authentic experience, they asserted the authority to present and define this world to a middle-class reading public.

The Christian Socialist Paul Göhre and His Imitators

'Twas a great success: the book was read and even passed from hand
  to hand,
For it gave a different picture than the newspapers of our land.
Amazement was great. There was no denying what we had never
  imagined before:
The reproach that we now set out our own people to explore.
You know about the blacks, who revel in the harsh glare of tropical
  light,
But you know nothing at all about your own people and their plight!
—Rudolf Lavant, "Drei Monate Fabrikarbeiter"
(Three Months in a Workshop, 1891)[26]

The literary tradition of journeys to the industrial working world in Germany begins in 1890, a year which—if not a true turning point—nevertheless marked the beginning of a brief period of social and political thaw. The great miners' strike of 1889, the electoral success of the Social Democrats in the spring of 1890, and the impending expiration of the Anti-Socialist Laws in the fall placed the social question squarely at the forefront of public debate. Yet while the future role of Social Democracy was the most immediate challenge to the established order, it was also only one aspect of the broader question of what place workers and their world were to occupy in German society. Hardly a homogeneous group, the industrial labor force was differentiated in many ways—according to gender and family situation, social origin (e.g., whether workers came from urban or rural areas), mobility versus permanency of employment, the skilled or unskilled nature of their work, religion, nationality (e.g., Germans and Poles in the Ruhr and Upper Silesia), and innumerable differences of cultural and regional milieu.[27] However, in spite of all this variety, those factors still predominated which linked workers together as a social class with common bonds. Most workers had firsthand experiences with being at the mercy of employers' whims, suffering from impoverished, unstable living conditions, teetering on the brink of financial ruin, living together in fairly well demarcated areas of cities, and associating and socializing primarily with others from the same social group.

Furthermore, along with these shared life experiences, workers also found themselves frequently excluded from bourgeois society. As many historians have shown, German workers' negative relationship to the state was often strengthened by their perception that institutions such as schools, the military and police, and the courts, among others, were there to serve the more privileged, but not themselves.[28] Similarly, workers often took other powerful institutions such as the churches to be allied more closely with the circles above them than with their own interests. Politically, the three-class electoral system, which was in effect in Prussia until 1918, placed workers at a very concrete disadvantage, denying them an equal franchise. And even though the intense repression of their organizing activities during the twelve years of the Anti-Socialist Laws (1878–1890) was the bitter experience that indelibly molded Social Democrats of that generation politically, most workers had suffered in many ways from denigration, humiliation, and exclusion, no matter what their ideology.

Consequently, in spite of the heterogeneity of the working class, the many ways in which workers often took over elements from bourgeois culture and values,[29] and a variety of efforts at introducing social reforms before 1914, the situation of workers during this period was still so different from that of the classes above them that they felt themselves consigned to the margins. However, they were unwilling to resign themselves to this inferior status. Since the 1860s, they had countered the repression directed against them by creating their own cultural and political organizations, particularly within the framework of the Social Democratic and trade union movements. And in spite of censorship, exile, and imprisonment,[30] Social Democracy had succeeded in consolidating and broadening its influence among the working classes, becoming a permanent force on the political scene. With this threat to the status quo weighing on his mind, one contemporary observer from Christian Socialist circles formulated the most burning problems of 1890: "Will it be possible to eliminate the class struggle by means of generous social reforms, and to lessen the social conflicts between workers and employers? Will it be possible, if not to overcome Social Democracy, then at least to divest it of its hostile attitude toward the state, to make it into a workers' party which is friendly toward the state, or to create a national workers' party alongside it?"[31] That is, the issue that the Social Democrats' successes had brought to the center of political contestation was whether workers would have the power to transform society on their own terms or whether they would be integrated somehow into the existing social and political system.

It was in June of 1890, shortly after the Social Democrats' electoral gains and just before the expiration of the Anti-Socialist Laws, when theology student Paul Göhre set off on what he termed his "journey into the darkness" to work in a Chemnitz machine tool factory for three months.[32] According to contemporary reports, this first German journey to the working world, published as *Drei Monate Fabrikarbeiter und Handwerksbursche: Eine praktische Studie* (Three Months in a Workshop: A Practical Study, 1891), attracted "enormous attention" and generated controversies both within and outside Church circles.[33] In his preface to the 1895 English translation, Richard T. Ely, professor of economics at the University of Wisconsin, described the impact of this "simple story": "The book was greeted by the wealth and culture of Germany like a revelation. As one of the most conservative newspapers of Germany put it, it was as if someone had returned from the heart of Africa and described the ways of a strange and hitherto unknown nation, so great had been the actual separation of classes. The book was never more timely than today, and it is as instructive in England and the United States as in Germany."[34] Ely emphasized Göhre's ethnographic approach, which sought to give a picture of all aspects of workers' lives from the perspective of covert participant observation. However, Göhre did not enter into the working world in order to acquire knowledge for its own sake, but rather with a particular religious and political agenda of his own in mind. His project was rooted in the context of Christian social work, which sought to domesticate and improve the lower classes and which was sometimes open to limited social reforms.

Little is known about Paul Göhre's (1864–1928) early years, except that his father was a court clerk and other family members were craftsmen and workers.[35] With this background, the thoughts that Göhre expressed in letters to close friends for some time before 1890 do not seem so surprising. Here, he toyed with the idea of becoming a worker for good after completing his theology studies in order to missionize other workers by setting before them a living example of Christian charity and self-sacrifice.[36] Soon abandoning this plan, Göhre decided to enter a factory for three months in the summer of 1890, between completing two years as a minister's assistant in an impoverished Saxon weavers' village and taking a position as a minister in Frankfurt an der Oder.[37] In the first chapter of his book, entitled "My Path," Göhre explained his reasons for undertaking this expedition.[38] Saying that he had been concerned for some years with the social question from a religious standpoint, he still felt very unfamiliar with the actual condition of the working classes. Realizing that workers were increasingly rejecting the Church, and maintaining that— like everyone else—they showed only their best sides when they came into contact with clergymen like himself, Göhre decided that the only way to discover what they were really like was to live "among them as one of them" for a time.[39] Furthermore, desiring to know "the full truth about the attitudes of the working classes, their material wishes, and their spiritual, moral, and religious character" (2), Göhre, as an aspiring minister, was particularly interested in finding out for himself how the "materialistic, atheistic" worldview of Social Democracy had influenced workers and whether they still had religious needs that he could address.

Unlike some of the later sojourners in the world of work, Göhre was not particularly concerned with describing his own existential, psychological responses to the temporary metamorphosis he had undertaken or to the experiences of unaccustomed physical labor and a strange milieu. In recounting his transformation ("Last year at the beginning of June I hung up my scholar's gown and became a factory worker"), he was content to note that he put on old clothes and set off with some apprehension into the unknown of Chemnitz (1). Beyond mentioning a few times how hard the manual labor was for him and asserting that his pursuit of such a difficult project demonstrated the "bitter seriousness" of his endeavor (10), he hardly remarked at all on his subjective responses. Rather, his main concern was to explore working-class life from as many angles as possible, to do research, as the subtitle of the book suggests, through a "practical study." Göhre emphasized from the beginning his efforts to avoid false generalizations and to be open-minded and "objective." Accordingly, given his consciousness of some of the methodological problems in his undertaking, it is all the more striking to see how his own religious and political motivations shaped his study in more subtle ways. In particular, his agenda led him to emphasize certain aspects of working-class life and to select from a storehouse of familiar metaphors to create images of the unknown world he had entered.

Göhre's procedure in collecting his information was as follows. Having selected Chemnitz because it was Saxony's industrial center as well as a center of Social Democracy, he tramped into the city on foot, lodging at first in the hostels there. Claiming to be an unemployed clerk who wanted to try his hand at factory work, Göhre thus entered into the milieu of journeymen, the unemployed, and all the down-and-out men who were on the road. And, as they commonly experienced, his efforts to find work on his own proved unsuccessful due to the prevailing high unemployment in the region—an initial brush with hardship. Consequently, in order to carry out his project, Göhre decided to reveal himself to the director of the Kappel machine tool factory, who was willing to hire him as a simple laborer and not let anyone else in on his secret.[40] Assigned to doing odd jobs in a tool-and-die section of the factory, Göhre lent a hand wherever extra help was needed and so came into contact with many of the approximately 120 men in his department. He noted that he also spent all his free time with his fellow workers: eating his noon meal at the local pub, visiting his neighbors and his co-workers' families, going on excursions and to Sunday dances with them, and attending meetings of the local Social Democratic election association.

During these three months, Göhre was open about his religious beliefs, which always provoked the kind of discussion he was looking for;

nor did he totally conceal his education. Nevertheless, he maintained that no one suspected his real identity while he lived the life of a worker: "It did not occur to the people—and it was probably simply unimaginable to them—that an educated person could voluntarily renounce all comforts, his profession, and his high social status, even temporarily, for their sakes" (10). One worker in the factory did recall in 1896 that Göhre had seemed unusual somehow and gave this cameo portrait of him: "This new worker stood out quite a bit because of his personality. Of course, like everybody else, he was wearing a workshirt belted around his waist, a dirty old pair of pants, and a beat-up hat. But the way he acted and appeared, and his bold, fearless look, gave away the fact that he was really something different from the common, average laborer. . . . He gave the impression of being a genius who had come upon hard times."[41] But this man also went on to say that any suspicions the workers might have had about Göhre were put to rest by his explanation that he was trying factory work because he had ruined his eyes as a clerk.

In accordance with his ideological project, Göhre was not only interested in the manifold effects on workers of the actual experience of difficult manual labor itself. Consequently, only two of the book's eight chapters deal with the material situation of the workers and their jobs in the factory, while the others are devoted to "Social Democratic Agitation," the "Social and Political Opinions" of the workers, "Education and Christianity," and the workers' "Morality." In preliminary remarks, Göhre was careful to stress that he intended his observations and conclusions to apply only to men like his particular group of co-workers, who were for the most part highly skilled, relatively well paid, and—living as they were in "red Saxony"—well organized as Social Democrats. He noted right away that his fellow workers treated him well, describing them as cheerful, friendly men who filled in their breaks with gossip, jokes, and more serious conversations about topics ranging from family matters to religion, economics, and politics.

Establishing in this way for his middle-class readers that these men were many-sided "human beings" rather than mere "work animals," Göhre focused in his chapter entitled "Work in the Factory" on what he viewed as the main drawback of this kind of toil: the division between mental and manual labor which prevented these workers from developing all their human capacities. While noting that machinists were often performing highly skilled work, Göhre also wrote quite insightfully about the deadening effects of boring repetition, of concentrating on small parts rather than on a whole project, of having little personal interest in what happened to products once they left the workshop, and of being subjected to draconian rules of conduct. With dismay and a certain sense of outrage, he reported that workers had few opportunities to use their knowledge, to make decisions or improvements, to demonstrate carefulness or industriousness, or to identify closely with their work—that is, to bring their human, mental capacities to bear on brute manual labor. He concluded, however, that this constant stifling of their abilities led workers to concern themselves in a grandiose manner with matters lying beyond their limited sphere of knowledge, such as politics. This ideologically tinged characterization clearly contradicted his initial, positive image of his fellow workers (55).

In succeeding chapters, Göhre set out to investigate the effects of Social Democracy on his workmates, and specifically, how this movement had influenced their attitudes toward politics, education, religion, and morality. In other words, what he sought to comprehend was the mentality behind a statement he reported having heard more than once on the factory floor: "One day Bebel and Liebknecht will replace Jesus Christ" (109). Convinced that the perspectives of Social Democracy would never again disappear totally from the world, he attempted to ascertain his workmates' familiarity with these ideas by attending meetings of the local Social Democratic election association. While deploring the "dreadful ignorance" some of the workers displayed, he was deeply impressed for the most part by their serious efforts to learn and by their willingness to debate late into the night after a long, strenuous day in the factory. After hearing some of their clear, insightful speeches, Göhre wrote that he was filled with a sense of "admiration and shame" upon listening to "these simple weavers, mechanics, and manual laborers" who could have held their own with people far better educated than they (82).

Basically sympathetic toward these workers' efforts to exercise their intellectual capacities, Göhre reacted quite differently when writing about the Social Democratic presence in the workplace. He had gone to work when the Anti-Socialist Laws were still in effect and when factory rules strictly prohibited Social Democratic organizing. Nevertheless, he maintained that his co-workers generally viewed the Social Democrats as their legitimate representatives, and that there was quite a bit of political activity going on behind the scenes. In this part of his analysis, Göhre distinguished sharply between what he termed the "elite" Social Democratic leadership and its "masses" of followers. Maintaining that only a miniscule number of workers understood the program of Social Democracy, Göhre painted a picture here of a workforce that was basically gullible and easily led astray by political agitators. In his chapter on workers' political opinions, Göhre presented his workmates as for the most part rather satisfied with the given order of things if only a few improvements could be made in areas such as wage levels. Along these lines, he quoted a worker approvingly who had asserted that men like himself were not seeking equality with the upper classes, for "there will always have to be rich and poor" (114).

This tone of rather patronizing support for a basically settled, passive workforce found its complement in the intensely negative metaphors Göhre used to describe the activities of the "elite" Social Democrats. In one characteristic example, he denounced the personal influence of Social Democrats on politically uncommitted workers as "so to speak, the flesh of the monster of Social Democratic propaganda, whereas the Party's overall organizing campaign is the bones" (104). Above all, Göhre directed his most bitter invectives against the internationalist tendencies in Social Democracy, maintaining that the masses of average workers were rather positively inclined toward the fatherland and its representative, the kaiser. In his view, they did not share what he termed the "miserable, treacherous political convictions of the Social Democratic elite, whose blathering about humanity leads to the weakest kind of cosmopolitanism and thus to devaluing and proscribing everything which is truly patriotic" (117). Accordingly, Göhre concluded that with respect to their political and social opinion, this workforce was like a huge pyramid held together by the mortar of Social Democratic agitation, with the "elite" leaders at its apex. Its broad base was composed of the "chaotic mass" of those who simply wanted to vote for one of their own, for a Social Democratic workers' candidate. It is in these sections of his book that Göhre's efforts to be "objective" and to learn from what he saw and experienced collide most strongly with his preconceived notions about the nature and goals of Social Democracy. In other words, when he set out to write about everyday working conditions, he expressed a good bit of sympathy toward his fellow workers. However, when these very same workers began speaking together in challenging voices through an organization that Göhre considered subversive, his resistance stiffened against the idea of social change originating from below, against disruptions of social pacification and harmony.

But Göhre was not only concerned about the alternative economic and political program of Social Democracy. He was perceptive enough to understand that more was at stake in the central social conflicts of his time. For Social Democracy was not only a new political party, but it also advocated a new worldview that sought to transform the educational goals, spiritual life, and moral standards of the working classes. In the final chapters of his book, Göhre reported on conversations with his fellow workers about these topics. In these discussions, he argued from the basis of his religious beliefs, which his co-workers opposed for the most part by appealing to scientific facts. Based on these encounters, Göhre concluded that the goal of Social Democracy, whose worldview many of his co-workers had adopted, was to replace Christian teachings with a belief in a merely natural world order, moral law with utilitarian habits, and Christian love with a calculated feeling of solidarity (154). Here again, his daily experiences with his fellow workmen, which had led him to describe their lives, their abilities, and their intellectual potential quite positively at certain points, were overshadowed by these direct challenges to his deeply held beliefs. Writing about the substitution of "vague Social Democratic notions" for "eternal truths," Göhre now described the great majority of his workmates as living impoverished, empty lives, "without joy, without hope, without help" (156–57). Concluding that the influence of the materialist worldview had been nowhere so pervasive as in sweeping away traditional religious beliefs among these workers, Göhre gave the following characterization of the cold, desolate world he had entered "down below": "Now a world without God is growing up from down below. It is constantly expanding and forcing into its icy orbit those who are still struggling, hesitating, and vacillating, who are basically not interested in the bleak articles of faith of the materialist worldview. Abandoned by their own church with no help, enlightenment, leadership, or comfort, and inescapably surrounded by the atmosphere of socialist ideas, they are all dying a slow, often tormented spiritual death" (190). In such passages, Göhre returned to his notion that most workers were basically passive and thus ripe for manipulation by the more active Social Democrats. However, in other sections he balanced out this more condescending view with assertions that everything done for the workers and in their name ought to be done in cooperation with them (215). Recalling again the centrality of the division of labor to the social conflicts and problems he was encountering, Göhre stated emphatically that factory workers wanted greater respect and recognition, not just higher wages; that they were not mere tools or machines, but human beings; that they were not only "hands" but also "heads" (212). And in his view, Social Democracy was also an expression of such ideals of improvement and uplift, in spite of its "lack of conscience" in emphasizing only the "useful" rather than the "good" (194).

Fundamentally, Göhre concluded from his three months in the workshop that certain reforms the Social Democrats advocated, such as a shorter, eight-hour working day and higher wages, were necessary and justifiable. He insisted, however, that these reforms could be carried out by appealing to the self-interest of employers, without the need for any more far-reaching social transformations. The nationally oriented, religious nature of his alternative to Social Democratic perspectives comes through most clearly in his concept of work. While almost overwhelmed from the first by the darkness, dreariness, and noise of the factory, Göhre nevertheless apotheosized his workplace as shining in the light of "poetry and nobility," meaning by this "the poetry of a grandiose, interlocking mechanism" and the "nobility of human labor" (44). Evoking an image of the factory as an organic whole in which everyone had his proper place, Göhre hoped that the work being performed there could also serve something higher, musing: "And what the dirt-blackened men in blue overalls were creating there—wasn't it also an act of worship, of service to God? Couldn't it at least become such a thing?" (42).

Göhre was convinced that the heretofore unknown division of labor brought forth by capitalist production was the main source of his fellow workers' dissatisfaction and unrest. Accordingly, he proposed that the only way factory production sites could truly become places of human, moral uprightness and service to God was if all those connected with them, from high to low, could have similar opportunities for using their mental abilities and thus developing their personalities within the "factory organism" (87). If social revolution and chaos were to be avoided, he proposed, workers would have to give up their utopian dreams (read: Social Democratic leanings), and factory owners would have to correct voluntarily some of the most blatant inequities at the workplace "for the sake of the fatherland and the Volk, for the sake of morality and religion" (87). This would be in the employers' own interest, Göhre maintained, because it would enable them to cultivate "a much more settled, and thus a much more conservative stock of workers" (116). In this process of channeling social unrest, Göhre proclaimed, educated men should follow his example and descend "from their professorships to the people" in order to counteract the subversive, destructive influences of Social Democracy (217). Accordingly, in the book's closing words, he borrowed from the contemporary vocabulary of colonization to express his missionizing goal: "to train, refine, and Christianize Social Democracy, which is still wild and heathen today, and to annihilate its anti-Christian, materialist worldview" (222).

The publication of Göhre's book in 1891 created quite a controversy, provoking responses from both inside and outside Church circles.[42] In these debates, the two main points of contention centered around his assertion that it should be somehow possible to combine Christianity and social reforms, as well as around the validity of the observations he made on the basis of having become a worker himself for a short time. Göhre's book appeared at a moment when rapid social transformations were pressuring members of the clergy to make their Christian beliefs more relevant to the world of industrial labor.[43] The most stubbornly conservative theologians, of course, denied any need for change. They sermonized, as one minister did in 1891, that "the leader of the Social Democrats is not Bebel, or Liebknecht, or Singer; the leader is the Devil."[44] However, there were other, more moderate circles in Wilhelminian Protestantism who, uneasy about prevailing social inequities, were somewhat more open to proposals for reform.[45] In these groups, calls were often heard for monied interests to become more socially responsible and to think more about sustaining moral values rather than only about amassing wealth.

The group most relevant for understanding the controversy Göhre's book caused was the Christian Socialist Congress, founded in 1890 by a heterogeneous collection of clergymen ranging from the anti-Semitic conservative Adolf Stoecker to the more liberal Friedrich Naumann. Göhre became its first general secretary, a position he held from 1891 to 1894. At the end of his book, he mentioned this as the church-related political organization through which he hoped both to work toward finding a solution to the social question and also to counteract the influence of Social Democracy. As one historian has noted, Naumann and other liberals involved in this group realized that "evangelism or church charity no longer sufficed" and "called upon academic youth to give new meaning to the term 'brotherhood of man' and to reach out to the working class with 'practical help.' "[46] When this Congress split up in the mid-1890s over disagreements between its liberal and conservative factions, Göhre and Naumann, along with Max Weber and others, went on to found the National-Social Union. This organization, which has been described as the "first movement to attempt to combine volkish ideas with the interests of the workers' movement," advocated a greater degree of social justice and a "social empire" while hoping to influence the working class to turn in a more nationally oriented rather than Marxist direction.[47]

When Göhre's book appeared in 1891, then, it was immediately perceived to be taking sides on contemporary issues of the utmost importance in a unique way that demanded a response. The best example of the debate over the book was carried out in the pages of the journal *Christliche Welt* (Christian World), whose editor, the liberal Protestant minister Max Rade, had first published Göhre's study in serialized form shortly before it appeared as a book. In this journal, articles by a Greifswald theology professor named Hermann Cremer, by Rade, and by the young Max Weber expressed sharply diverging opinions about Göhre's method, about his efforts to combine Christianity with some elements of Social Democracy, and, in the broadest sense, about the position of the industrial working class in German society. The conservative professor Cremer complained that he deeply regretted the publication of Göhre's study, saying that "as far as I can judge the effect of the book, almost nothing has harmed the charitable work of the ministry so much recently as this *Drei Monate Fabrikarbeiter*."[48] To support such a serious accusation, Cremer ridiculed Göhre's method, maintaining that his journey into the factory had brought nothing new to light and only served to create more mistrust toward the clergy among the working classes. In this theologian's opinion, those from "above" could best get to know workers' worlds by regarding them with charity. According to this point of view, Göhre had proposed a course that was too intellectual and modern and which sought to replace faith with mere reason.

In response to Cremer's attacks on Göhre in the pages of his journal, editor Max Rade invited Max Weber to write an article in his support, declaring that young theologians who were interested in contemporary social questions found it difficult to thrive within the Church. Obliging Rade's request with an article entitled "Zur Rechtfertigung Göhres" (In Defense of Göhre), Weber—calling himself "Göhre's friend" and a "layman" far removed from Church life—concentrated on two points.[49] First, disagreeing with Cremer, Weber emphasized the intellectual legitimacy of focusing on one specific local group of workers. To be sure, probably with Eugène Sue in mind, Weber poked fun at the "philistine idea that dark, mysterious forces are at work in the laboring classes which need to be 'exposed.' " He asserted, by contrast, that the main impression Göhre's book gave the reader was that these workers were "also human beings with flesh and blood"—perhaps a revolutionary enough idea for the time.[50] In Weber's opinion, the value of Göhre's approach to journeying into the working world lay in the access it could give to spheres inaccessible to cold statistics, to the "imponderables" of the workers question, to human reactions and psychological moments that could be best recounted in the kind of narrative Göhre was able to write after his three months in the workshop. Accordingly, Weber summarized the worth of Göhre's undertaking as follows:

> The book is less interesting for its scholarship than for its practical, sociopolitical significance. It must be judged according to its intention: whether it has brought the class it treats and the class it addresses closer to each other. *This is undoubtedly the case* [Weber's emphasis]. If the esteemed critic [i.e., Cremer] deems it "bad enough" that many circles, as he himself thinks, only learned through this book about numerous external and internal living conditions of the working class, others will find this only all too understandable.[51]

Here, while leaving aside the question of the book's usefulness for workers themselves, Weber pronounced Göhre's project successful in informing its readers about a world relatively unknown to them. After defending Göhre's method in this way, Weber went on to assert that modern workers had no need or desire for Cremer's patronizing brand of theology.[52] They had become emancipated intellectually from such traditions, Weber declared, and their insistence on equal rights was totally justified. In this vein, taking to task all those who were still bent on treating workers and the poor with condescension, Weber wrote: "Workers do not demand alms or relief through charity for their dire economic situation. Rather, they are claiming the right to a larger share of the earth's riches."[53] To Weber's mind, Göhre's main accomplishment was actually to have accepted this fact. He praised Göhre for trying to grapple as a theologian with the questions of how workers' rights could be better secured and how poverty could be mitigated through better social organization and legal guarantees.

If these two responses to Göhre's book highlight the clashing perspectives on the social question of conservative theology and liberal reform thought, the Social Democratic response concentrated on somewhat different aspects of Göhre's project. There are no substantial sources that hint at what workers themselves might have thought about Göhre's method or his conclusions.[54] However, the Social Democratic journal *Die Neue Zeit* (The New Age) was quick to print a long review of Göhre's book immediately after it appeared, written by Max Schippel, one of the journal's regular contributors.[55] Schippel did not criticize Göhre at all for entering into the factory milieu as an outsider. Rather, he commended him for his sincere efforts to get at the truth and for the accuracy of many of his observations about working-class life. However, he had nothing but scorn for many of Göhre's conclusions. For this Social Democrat, it was nothing but an odd theologian's notion that work under the exploitative capitalist system could ever be carried out "in the service of God." Furthermore, he dismissed Göhre's calls for factory owners to reform the system voluntarily from above as mere idealism. Schippel's own perspective on the social question reflected the mechanistic thinking common within Social Democracy at the time, for he viewed the technological development of the means of production as inevitably bringing about progressive changes for the working class. On the other hand, writing after twelve years of the Anti-Socialist Laws, he also maintained that workers had been excluded from political participation to such an extent that the gap between social classes seemed unbridgeable by peaceful means. And in his view, it was this extreme separation between social classes that made it so difficult for even a sensitive observer like Göhre to overcome bourgeois prejudices and blind spots.

Paul Göhre remained a controversial figure long after the debate over his book died down, due to his own further development and also because his project gave rise to several imitations. In a surprising turn of events after his three-month sojourn in the factory, Göhre went on to become a Social Democrat himself, leave the Church, and edit the first workers' autobiographies shortly after the turn of the century. In spite of the seemingly drastic nature of this metamorphosis, however, Göhre described the path he had taken as consistent with both his Christian beliefs and his understanding of what true patriotism really meant. Having left the Christian Socialist Congress in 1896 because of its domination by ultra-conservative, property-owning interests, Göhre had joined Friedrich Naumann's National-Social Union in that same year.[56] In 1899 he explained why he was now resigning from this organization as well, claiming that it had become nothing but a bourgeois, nationalistic group that was no longer focused on workers' concerns. In the following year, he explained "how a parson became a Social Democrat" in a speech given before his new "party comrades" in Chemnitz.[57] Disenchanted with Christian Socialist organizations, he now believed that he could work most effectively toward social justice within the framework of Social Democracy. In a ringing conclusion, Göhre promised that from then on he would stand in the front lines of Social Democratic struggles.

It would be more accurate, however, to say that he wound up in the rearguard of Social Democracy in his further activities. Perhaps the best illustration from the cultural sphere of the limits to Göhre's transformation is to be found in the prefaces he wrote to the series of four workers' autobiographies that he edited, beginning with the two volumes of Carl Fischer's *Denkwürdigkeiten und Erinnerungen eines Arbeiters* (Reminiscences and Memoirs of a Worker) in 1903 and 1904.[58] Fischer had sent his manuscript to Göhre because he was so impressed with the theology student's account of working in the factory.[59] Yet Göhre sentimentalized this man's sober depiction of his wretched life to such an extent that it seemed as though "he had never seen the inside of a factory" or experienced the hardships of life on the road.[60] Göhre presented Fischer here as a simple, pious, anonymous man of the people—a perspective that fit smoothly into the volkish, neoromantic program of the publisher of the autobiographies, Eugen Diederichs. Yet although Fischer was by no means a Social Democrat, his precise, clear account of his life, which had been spent almost entirely at hard physical labor, reveals a high degree of consciousness about the exploitation he experienced. Consequently, while Göhre provided Fischer and several other workers an opportunity to reach a reading audience, he also sought to quash their distinctive voices and their potentially alternative, disruptive consciousness.[61]

Nevertheless, there was room for a man like Göhre within Social Democracy. As "the party's most celebrated convert from the ranks of the academically educated during the late nineties,"[62] Göhre served several times as a Social Democratic deputy in the Reichstag between 1903 and

1918. In this capacity he was frequently attacked by left-wing leaders such as Franz Mehring and August Bebel for his insistence that socialism was merely a "political and economic program" that could coexist peacefully with both Christianity and the monarchy. After serving in the military in World War I, he represented his party in several positions as an undersecretary in the Prussian government. Having joined forces with what he had described earlier as "wild, heathen" Social Democracy, the limited nature of his metamorphosis found its counterpart in the rise of tendencies toward compromise and national orientation within the party as a whole. As one commentator had already remarked in 1899 about the prospect of Göhre's new party affiliation: "In that event it would be just as correct to say that Social Democracy has become Göhrisch, as to say that Göhre has become a Social Democrat."[63]

While *Drei Monate Fabrikarbeiter* expresses an unresolved tension between Göhre's feelings of sympathy for his co-workers and his plans for manipulating them, his immediate successors or imitators were more obviously one-sided. Generally located within the sphere of middle-class social work, they were concerned primarily with improving the inhabitants of the social depths, which often meant gaining tighter control over them.[64] In the preface to his study, Göhre had already urged others to follow in his footsteps. Immediately after his book appeared, women's rights advocate Minna Wettstein-Adelt set out to beat him at his own game, publishing her *Dreieinhalb Monate Fabrikarbeiterin: Eine practische Studie* (Three and One-half Months in a Workshop: A Practical Study) in 1893. Naming Göhre as the "pioneer" who gave her the idea of living "as a worker among workers,"[65] Wettstein-Adelt secured jobs briefly at four different factories in Chemnitz—a stocking and glove factory, a weaving mill, and two spinning mills.

In contrast to Göhre's Christian Socialist perspective, this traveler to the working world was not religiously oriented and also was not particularly interested in the influence of Social Democracy. Rather, her primary concern was the emancipation of women, and her goal was to extend this movement into the lower classes. On the one hand, this focus enabled her to bring out certain topics that Göhre had neglected. She inquired about birth control, wrote sympathetically about the double burden of women workers with families, and dealt repeatedly with sexual harassment and prostitution. On the other hand, her exclusive preoccupation with moral uplift also led her to utilize metaphors that were much more negative than Göhre's to describe the milieu she had entered. In a manner reminiscent of naturalist depictions of the social abyss, she described her co-workers as "beasts" and even "reptiles" who could not possibly improve themselves (75, 80). Rather, the solution she advocated for their plight was that women from the upper classes with a "sense of order and discipline" should attempt to better the lives of their sisters down below. Accordingly, she urged her female readers, whom she imagined as the "upper ten thousand," to become factory supervisors. In her opinion, this would be to the benefit of all concerned: the upper-class ladies would have a worthwhile occupation; the factory owners would be able to rely on them; and the women workers would no longer be harassed by male superiors (23). In this capacity, women like herself could teach efficiency, order, and thriftiness (36), and they could bring enlightenment "into the miserable rooms of these deplorable creatures, who live like animals in a stall" (107). In the end, Wettstein-Adelt shifted her attention away from how working women themselves might have defined their own needs to what women from the upper classes could provide to them through engaging in social work.[66]

Göhre's appeal to others to follow his example was also heeded in the circles closest to him, among Christian Socialists. These brief journeys to the social abyss and the working world are less significant in themselves than for the disproportionate reaction they provoked, which extended into high levels of the Protestant church and the government. In 1892 a theology student named Theodor Wangemann, who had worked in church-run hostels, decided to explore this milieu from the inside by posing as an unemployed journeyman. After traveling for three months through the Rhineland, Westphalia, and Hannover, he published a series of articles entitled "Aus meinem Wandertagebuch" (From My Diary of Life on the Road).[67] Wangemann claimed to have been assimilated fully into the life of the unemployed and to have learned to regard the world through their eyes. In actuality, however, he argued mainly for a stricter police system and a better-organized network of hostels that would discourage unearned charity and compel vagabonds to work for their daily bread.

Yet even such a tentative effort to bridge the social abyss called forth a hostile reaction. The Protestant High Consistory reprimanded Wangemann, forbade him to carry out any more such journeys, and made inquiries among the regional churches about the extent of such activities.[68] While there were few if any reports of other disguised theologians following in Göhre's and Wangemann's footsteps, the High Consistory nevertheless issued statements against the dangerous, un-Christian practice of directing "tendentious" accusations against entire social classes.[69] Viewing such journeys to the abyss as the "explosion points of existing tensions" in their highly polarized class society, Church leaders called for ministers to preserve the appearance of impartiality.[70] Such pronouncements show that although voices oriented more toward social justice had been somewhat stronger within religious circles only a few years earlier, the highest Church councils had soon turned against clergy who still tried to focus on such concerns.

There is one other example from Christian Socialist circles of a traveler to the working world who was clearly following in Göhre's footsteps. Early in 1895, schoolteacher Elisabeth Gnauck published her "Lieder einer freiwilligen Arbeiterin" (Songs of a Voluntary Worker) and "Erinnerungen einer freiwilligen Arbeiterin" (Reminiscences of a Voluntary Worker) in Friedrich Naumann's journal *Die Hilfe* (Aid).[71] In these brief texts, Gnauck described her sojourn as a trainee in a paper carton factory in Berlin. Here, she utilized metaphors that recall those found in other journeys to the social abyss, drawing analogies between the working world and exotic, indigenous peoples. In this vein, she depicted her entry into the world of women factory workers:

> And so I went to them. It was a new world into which I entered, a *foreign* world [emphasis in original]. What a reproach this word contains! The work was just as foreign to me as the leisure; the opinions, needs, and customs of the inhabitants of this world were unknown to me. I actually had a clearer idea about the igloos of the Eskimos and the wigwams of the Indians than about the homes and workplaces of the proletarian women who were members of my Volk. In school we had learned about every continent— only not about the world closest at hand. Now it was my task to learn to comprehend this strange world by living in it.[72]

Like Wettstein-Adelt, Gnauck overcame this sense of strangeness somewhat by identifying with the special problems female workers faced on the job. However, like Göhre, she also suggested that social change should come only from above, that the "propertied classes" should take Christianity more seriously and strive to improve economic conditions, and that these measures would perhaps win workers back to religion.[73]

As was also the case for Wangemann, this account of a brief journey to the working world is less notable in itself than for the ways in which the antagonistic reactions to it brought out the fault lines of social class in Germany. In a lively debate in the pages of *Die Hilfe,* readers from a conservative professor to a woman factory worker clashed over the accuracy of Gnauck's observations about the prevailing unacceptable conditions down below.[74] Gnauck's journey to the working world attracted notice even in high levels of government. Immediately after her articles appeared, a representative in the Prussian Diet commented on them in a debate about the Protestant Trade Unions:

> And this is in a newspaper edited by a Christian minister! (Hear! hear!). The author is an offshoot of Mr. Göhre, the student who also disguised himself as a worker and produced

a book which is brimful of erroneous opinions. This "female Göhre," who meddled around with women workers, apparently saw the world through their eyes, too. But gentlemen, as long as we still have not found the prescription for eliminating all want and misery, it is sinful to agitate like this. It is sinful for a Christian minister to publish such things in his journal, things which only serve to promote social revolution. (Strong applause).[75]

That such relatively minor texts could attract this kind of attention serves to confirm the statement from the Protestant High Consistory that these journeys to the working world were tapping right into the center of "existing tensions." In spite of Gnauck's timid recommendations and her hopes for bringing workers back into the fold of religion, then, even her extremely measured identification with them was too much for this political representative and his cohorts. It was their conviction that the Church had to remain above the fray of class confrontations.[76] But when religious leaders agreed with such calls for impartiality, they were simply mirroring the policies of the kaiser and his government, who were steering a firm course against Social Democracy and its sympathizers.

It is striking that when Göhre and his imitators described their journeys into the working world, they compared their projects to expeditions into the "darkness" and the unknown realms of indigenous peoples. And furthermore, when commentators of all political stripes from conservatives to Social Democrats drew analogies to Göhre's journey, they all utilized the vocabulary of global colonization, referring most frequently to Africa. As the colonial powers expanded their conquests ever farther in the course of the nineteenth century, the image of Africa as the "Dark Continent" had become firmly entrenched.[77] The quintessential statement of this myth, of course, was Henry Stanley's *In Darkest Africa*, which appeared both in the original English edition and in German translation in 1890, the same year Göhre entered into the "darkness" of the factory. For Stanley, the evocation of darkness served to justify imperialist domination over "uncivilized" peoples abroad. However, by the latter part of the century such references had also become ubiquitous in the literature of social exploration of the domestic abyss, especially in Victorian England.[78] Along these lines, for example, Salvation Army founder William Booth's *In Darkest England and the Ways Out* (1890) and Margaret Harkness's novel *In Darkest London* (1891) depicted expeditions to the world of the "inferior" lower classes in the heart of the Empire.[79]

Although Germany had entered belatedly into the rush to divide up the world, it had recently acquired its own colonies in Africa when

Göhre set out to enter the factory. Accordingly, the political stage was set in this European country, also, for stereotypes of "primitive peoples" to be intertwined with those of class in ways that buttressed domination over the working-class majority. In Göhre's journey to the working world and the imitations and debates it provoked, metaphors of "darkness" serve several functions that indicate seismographically the diverse approaches to the "social question" at this time. First, wherever workers are compared to "animals" living in moral darkness and Social Democrats are labeled "wild and heathen," the analogy to European perceptions of black Africans functions in a racialized way to categorize the lower classes as "naturally inferior" in a social Darwinist sense. In other instances, writers referred to the domestic Dark Continent less as a site of the "primitive" than as a site of the unknown.[80] The conservative newspaper *Die Kreuzzeitung*, for example, discussed *Drei Monate Fabrikarbeiter* on June 19, 1891: "We are sure . . . that Göhre's book reveals an entirely unknown world to many people. And the fact that his book exists is more troubling to us than anything which it contains. Just think: in the German Empire there is a class of the population which is so separated from the national community that an adventurous *expedition, like going into Africa,* and a long 'travelogue' are necessary in order to find out something authentic about these people [emphasis in original]."[81] To this reviewer's mind, it was a matter of the utmost urgency for the upper classes to gain knowledge about the dark working world below in order to stave off unpredictable threats of social upheaval and revolution. Similarly, in his poem "Drei Monate Fabrikarbeiter" (1891), Social Democrat Rudolf Lavant claimed that Europeans knew more about the depths of Africa than about the world of their own factories that Göhre had brought to light. However, he took the tack of reproaching the upper classes for their disinterest in the domestic abyss, implying that they would only have themselves to blame if revolution erupted.[82]

In his journey to the working world, Paul Göhre himself drew on racialized metaphors of darkness that highlighted both the extreme differences between social classes and the unruly forces threatening to erupt from below. However, much of the blatant racism so integral to imperialism held it to be impossible that the peoples to be conquered could ever become the equals of Europeans.[83] Göhre, by contrast, believed that the workers he met in the factory could indeed be lifted up both from material deprivation and also from the "darkness and icy desolation" of their spiritual lives. This would be possible, in his opinion, because his fellow workers were Christian souls who had merely been led astray by Social Democracy, and also because they belonged to the German Volk. Through the knowledge he gained from his ethnographic study of the working world, Göhre intended to speak in the name of workers about their interests to the upper classes, to encourage a nationally oriented partnership between workers and employers, and to counteract political tendencies among workers that appeared to separate them from the interests of the nation and organized religion. Consequently, the thrust of Göhre's study goes mainly in the direction of hoping to overcome class divisions by promoting the national unity of all Germans in a volkish sense.[84]

And yet it would be a mistake simply to view Göhre as a forerunner of later volkish ideologues who called for incorporating the "dark world" of manual labor into the nation by stressing its anti-intellectual, disciplinary aspects. Unlike these theorists, Göhre evidences no fascination with the male body's brute strength and issues no calls for utilizing manual labor to toughen the "soft" upper classes. His frequent references to the detrimental effects of the division of labor are proof enough of this. Rather, as Max Weber pointed out, Göhre had enough respect for workers as fellow human beings that he viewed hard, repetitive manual labor as a humiliating restriction of their abilities. In *Drei Monate Fabrikarbeiter* and his subsequent utterances, Göhre called for the human consequences of this social evil to be mitigated as much as possible by integrating workers into the existing religious order and socioeconomic system. Yet in spite of this somewhat sympathetic attitude, he had little patience for working-class organizing efforts that sought to shift focus from improving those below to breaking down the hegemony of those above. This Christian Socialist who became a Social Democrat located Germany's "darkness" almost solely in a nether realm that was to be penetrated and illuminated from on high, by travelers to the working world like himself.

A Social Democrat in Darkest Vienna: Max Winter's Journeys to the Depths of the Habsburg Empire

Experience teaches that capitalism only reluctantly allows us a glimpse of its workplaces. The bosses do not like it when Social Democrats stick their noses into everything because they think this can only lead to "unrest" among the workers. . . . The bosses do not hear the quiet sighs and the loud curses which are drowned out by the roar of the workplace, and they do not see the enslaved hands which are hidden but clenched into fists. . . . But one of these evil Social Democrats sees them if he goes to the workers as a worker, and he hears the sighs and curses. And so I chose this path.

—Max Winter[85]

While Paul Göhre never explained precisely what he revealed about himself in order to be hired, the fact that he secured his temporary position with the knowledge and aid of his employer shows that he was by no means

Max Winter sitting at his desk, ca. 1900. Verein für Geschichte der Arbeiterbewegung, Vienna.

viewed as a disruptive rabble-rouser. For Max Winter, a committed Social Democrat and Viennese journalist who also began writing in the 1890s, the path into the working world and the world of poverty was a different one. In contrast to Göhre, Winter was not seeking to expand his knowledge in order to integrate workers more securely into the nation and defuse their threatening potential. Nor did he aim only to enlighten the upper classes about the abuses he uncovered in the social abyss. Rather, Winter intended to ally himself with workers' own organizational activities by journeying into their world and reporting on it in ways that supported their efforts to challenge established power relationships. In over one thousand reportages written for the Austrian Social Democratic press and collected into as many as fifteen books, Winter recounted in vivid detail the condition of the lower classes in Vienna and the surrounding areas. Furthermore, he was the first leftist journalist to take the approach of going to work briefly himself in order to gain access to otherwise impenetrable sites of exploitation.

Max Winter, the son of a railroad official, was born in Tárnok, near Budapest, in 1870 and grew up in Vienna.[86] In 1895 he was asked by Victor Adler to join the editorial staff of the *Arbeiter-Zeitung,* the official newspaper of the Austrian Social Democratic Party—a position he held

VISITE PORTRAIT

Max Winter in the role of a "sewer scavenger" (1905). Verein für Geschichte der Arbeiterbewegung, Vienna.

until 1930. It was for this newspaper, as well as for many other Social Democratic and trade union publications, that Winter wrote most of his reportages. In addition to his prolific journalism, Winter also became active in politics and was elected as a Social Democratic representative to the *Reichsrat* from 1911 to 1918. After the end of World War I, he was a member of the city council and a vice mayor of Vienna and from 1925 to 1934 a member of the *Bundesrat*. Along with journalism and politics, Winter—whom his contemporaries sometimes called a "socialist of the heart"[87]—was also keenly interested in children's welfare and education. He was active in the "Friends of Children" movement, which—as a part of Social Democratic workers' culture—sought to provide for poor children's needs. A glance at the titles of some of his books indicates the wide range of his interests. His reportages appeared in collections such as *Im dunkelsten Wien* (In Darkest Vienna, 1904), *Im unterirdischen Wien* (In Underground Vienna, 1905), and *Die Blutsauger des Böhmerwaldes: Bilder aus dem Leben der Holzknechte* (The Bloodsuckers of the Bohemian Forest: Pictures from the Life of the Woodcutters, 1908). Other writings by Winter include *Das Kind und der Sozialismus* (Children and Socialism, 1924) and *Die lebende Mumie: Ein Blick auf das Jahr 2025* (The Living Mummy: A Glimpse of the Year 2025, 1929)—the latter a utopian novel about a man who sleeps for a century and awakens in a socialist Vienna. In 1934, when the authoritarian *Ständestaat* banned the Social Democratic Party and its affiliated organizations, Winter, who had already planned a lecture tour abroad, decided to go into exile, traveling first to South America and then to the United States, where—like so many other émigrés—he settled in Hollywood. For three years he tried to write filmscripts, gave lectures about early childhood education, and wrote reportages about California farmworkers for the exile press. Alone, impoverished, ill, and expatriated by the Austrian government, Winter died in Hollywood in 1937. His funeral in Vienna later that year was the occasion for one of the last large gatherings of Austrian Social Democrats before the Anschluss.[88]

Like many other Social Democrats, Winter wrote reportages that were reminiscent in many ways of those published during the turbulent period of the 1840s by writers such as Bettina von Arnim, Ernst Dronke, and Georg Weerth.[89] Just as these earlier social explorers had investigated conditions among the lower classes with the goals of enlightenment and emancipation, activist intellectuals and writers such as Winter descended into the world below decades later to produce exposés about exploitation and poverty with the hope of rousing workers to organize. A few examples of reportages by some of the most well-known Social Democrats of the time may stand for a host of others: Minna Kautsky's "Was der Staat seinen Salinenarbeitern alles zumutet" (What the State Expects Its Salt-Mine Workers to Endure, 1885), Victor Adler's "Die Lage der Ziegelarbeiter" (The Situation of the Brickmakers, 1888), and August Bebel's "Hofgänger bei der mecklenburgischen Getreideernte" (Farmhands at the Mecklenburg Grain Harvest, 1896).[90] The majority of Winter's reportages were similar to these, although he by no means limited himself to reporting on the industrial workers toward whom Social Democrats directed most of their organizing efforts. Rather, with a broad concept of social change in mind, he also wrote frequently about the ravages of poverty among the lowest of the low: the unemployed, the homeless, street children, and criminals.

In order to enter even deeper into the most hidden areas of the social abyss, Winter sometimes took on another identity as a worker or social outcast. By doing this, he could investigate workplaces, milieus, and experiences that were generally barred to someone of his background and convictions by all those who continued to benefit from established power relations. In several instances, Winter disguised himself in some way or went along with a guide to a specific location without actually performing the particular work in question. For example, in the reportage "Bei den Sklaven der 'Alpinen': Eine Nacht im Schwechater Werk" (Among the Slaves of the "Alpine": A Night in the Schwechater Factory, 1900/1901), Winter pretended to be a reserve worker in order to investigate this ironworks. In "Wien I: In Diensten des Herrn von Wittek" (Vienna I: Working for Mr. von Wittek, 1902), he donned a railroad worker's uniform to explore the railway yards. And in "Kanalstrotter" (Sewer Scavenger, 1904) he accompanied through the sewers of Vienna a man whose only income came from the lost coins and saleable objects he found there.[91] In other reportages, however, Winter recounted what happened when he actually worked or took on another role, as in "Ein Tag Lagerhausarbeiter" (A Day as a Warehouse Worker, 1900), "Vor und in der Wärmestube" (Outside and Inside the Shelter, 1901), "Eine Nacht Polizeihäftling" (A Night in Police Custody, 1904), and "Eine Nacht im Asyl für Obdachlose" (A Night in the Homeless Shelter, 1905).[92]

While Winter used basically the same method of covert participant observation in these brief journeys to the social abyss as did Göhre and his imitators, there were fundamental differences between his projects and those that were more conservative or reform-oriented. His perspective on social change emerges most clearly in his ability to register and interpret perspectives arising from below and in the ways he intended his exposés to be used. The reportage entitled "Ein Tag Lagerhausarbeiter" provides a particularly good illustration of his approach. As a Social Democratic journalist, Winter often searched out or was invited by local activists to workplaces where organizing was going on or where a strike was imminent. It was such a situation that provided the occasion for this reportage. The workers in the municipal warehouses in Vienna had begun to voice their grievances and were gravitating increasingly toward Social Democracy. Since their employer was the city government, Winter's reportage about their working conditions was directed against the ruling Christian Socialist Party and its most prominent member, Karl Lueger, the anti-Semitic mayor of Vienna. After deciding to investigate this confrontational situation for himself, Winter first had to find a way into this workplace. Realizing that the warehouse administration would never allow a Social Democrat like himself to spend time there as a worker among workers, Winter presented his solution like this: "If I wanted to learn what things are like today, I had to go to the Christian Socialist administration as a—Christian Socialist. That's easier than one might imagine."[93] And so, Winter simply appeared at the warehouse, claimed to have been sent there by the Christian Socialist head of the city employment office, and was immediately hired.

After these preliminaries, the reportage concentrates on giving brief sketches of the workers, describing conditions in the warehouse, and making suggestions for improvements. Due to the unskilled nature of the work (loading and unloading grain and other staples), many of the men had been hired as day laborers like Winter and most appeared to be quite poor. While some were bright and alert and filled as much time as possible with conversation and various subterfuges to snatch a few minutes of rest, Winter described others as worn down to a state of passivity and dullness. The work they were required to perform was tiring, unhealthy, and dangerous, and the day laborers, in particular, were often pushed to exhaustion by the foremen, mostly members of the Christian Socialist Party.[94] To make these working conditions come alive for the reader, Winter described his own reaction to the unaccustomed manual labor:

> At the beginning I did all right. I was rested, and the sacks which four of us had to lift together only weighed fifty to sixty kilos. But when my "helper" said jokingly about nine A.M.: "Today it feels like five o'clock won't ever come!" I thought to myself that he was right. For my part, I had probably lifted about three thousand kilos already in this first hour, and I had earned the respectable sum of thirty hellers for this. My back and stomach muscles were already hurting from the constant bending and lifting. The last sacks in the freight car got heavier and heavier. Each one weighed eighty to one hundred kilos. It makes you sweat to grab and lift two of them every minute. I was getting dangerously hot even though it was by no means warm in the big, unheated, drafty hall which was open on all sides.[95]

As is evident here, Winter, in contrast to Göhre, wrote much more concretely about the extreme physical exertion necessary to perform this kind of labor, about low wage levels, and about uncomfortable, dangerous conditions in the warehouse. These included the lack of ventilation and masks to protect workers from the huge amount of dust in the air, inadequate sanitary conditions, extremes of heat and cold, slippery floors caused by spilled grain, and the lack of break rooms and a satisfactory canteen. He noted that during his day in the warehouse his co-workers often criticized their employers and supervisors for these reasons but were afraid of being fired if they complained too loudly. The reportage concludes by urging workers to continue organizing to improve their situation, implying that Christian Socialist employers and governmental officials would not improve these conditions without strong, concerted pressure from below. By publishing this reportage in the Social Democratic press, Winter intended to publicize these workers' struggles to others in similar situations and to strengthen the ties between workers and his political party. In other words, Winter, a Social Democrat who was concerned with strategic questions of organizing, wrote the account of his journey into the working world for the workers he was writing about, and it was meant as an operative tool for them to use in challenging established power relationships.

As is also the case in the texts by Göhre and his imitators, metaphors of darkness abound in Winter's writing. However, in an ironic reversal of perspective, when Winter polemicized against "black Vienna" he meant the Christian Socialist Party of Karl Lueger, with its hostility toward Social Democracy and workers' demands. His collection of reportages entitled *Im dunkelsten Wien* obviously invokes the myth of "darkest Africa" although it contains no direct reference to that continent. Here, the metaphor of darkness implies that it was not necessary to leave central Europe in order to find poverty and misery. Above all, however, Winter presented the gloomy hopelessness of the social abyss, or, recalling Sue, "the mystery of underground Vienna,"[96] as caused mainly by the darkness falling from above. By this he meant the benighted policies of employers who put profits ahead of everything else and of the government that failed to provide an adequate social net. From his perspective, those above were also living in darkness, for their privileged positions usually made them blind to conditions in the real world around them. Thus, Winter often described his reportage as having the purpose of making his addressees see, as in the following passage from 1905 about women working in cottage industry around Vienna:

> Then I would like to make the blind man see. I would
> like to take him by the hand and lead him from mother to

mother, from family to family, in Ottakring or Meidling, in Brigittenau or Favoriten, from house to house, each one a workshop, each one a home of sorrow and misery, of work's torments and life's burdens. I would like to take him to the women cottage workers in Vienna, to these women who are often blessed with far too many children, and the blindfold would have to fall from his eyes. You proletarians, enslaved workers, and disinherited ones know how things are, but the others, what do they know? What does the fashionable lady know as she fans herself after an exciting dance? What does she know about the woman who made her fan?[97]

In describing these souterrain milieus, Winter, like Göhre and his imitators, also characterized the poverty, unhygienic conditions, and crowded living quarters he found there as realms of darkness. However, the more reform-oriented travelers to the working world had not turned their critical eye on the powerful in the same way that Winter did. Rather, desiring to prevent structural socioeconomic change, they applied their metaphors of darkness almost solely to the lower classes whom they sought to "improve." By contrast, while Winter certainly understood Social Democracy as a movement of uplift, he generally presented the people who were the subjects of his reportages as desiring something better for themselves and their children. Their dream, which he tried to express, was for an end to poverty and dulling manual labor. But from Winter's perspective, this could not be attained within the prevailing economic and political system.

In addition to his reportages on the working world, Winter had an eye and ear for the human needs and longings of even those who were at the absolute bottom of the social abyss. For example, in a piece about hostels entitled "Eine Nacht im Asyl für Obdachlose," Winter recounted setting out to share the experiences of those who were unemployed, homeless, and hungry.[98] In contrast to the approach of many who were involved in the profession of social work among such outcasts, Winter did not enter into this world with the goal of developing more effective means of disciplining and controlling the members of these social groups. Rather, he set out to record detailed conversations with homeless men in hostels that brought out their life stories and especially some of the causes for their miserable condition.[99] In this reportage, written mostly in the first-person plural, Winter emphasized his identification with the unemployed men, released prisoners, and runaway apprentices who were all seeking a temporary shelter. He presented the hostel operators in a negative light because of their rough, unfeeling treatment of the men. And in one particularly moving passage, as a small example of what he thought worthy of noting,

Winter recounted how the men told stories before going to sleep in an effort to entertain and comfort each other.[100] In other words, Winter chose to stress the humanity, rather than the depravity, in the world down below which he had entered.

In some instances, however, Winter did locate the darkness he sought to banish within the inhabitants of the worlds to which he was traveling. To pinpoint his attitude in this regard, it is helpful to look more closely at how he reported his interactions with workers and the poor. Winter was so highly regarded by many of these people that they sometimes sought him out to request that he continue writing and speaking for them, in their interests. They were more than willing to furnish him with material for his reportages by showing him new instances of suffering. For example, in a reportage entitled "Hotel Ringofen" (Hotel Brick-Kiln, 1905), Winter told about talking to men in a pub who recognized him and wanted to show him some of the worst places where the homeless took shelter in Vienna: "Soon everyone in the pub knows who the solitary guest is. And now I also find old friends, proletarians and lumpenproletarians, who have read my earlier depictions of misery and now ask me directly if I'm the one who was in the 'workhouse' and who was recently in police custody."[101] Believing that Winter was writing about their lives with sympathy and incisiveness, these men—unemployed workers for the most part—were eager to lead him deeper into the darkness of Vienna. In the middle of the night, they took him into a huge abandoned kiln where almost one hundred homeless people were sleeping amidst piles of bricks and debris. Winter described his reaction to this shocking sight:

> I am overcome with horror. Are you still human beings? This is your destiny? Hounded, pursued, whipped on by a loathsome fate, you hole up here to find rest and warmth for a few hours—rest and warmth which the world outside denies you and steals from you. And you submit to your fate with servile indifference! You are glad if you can rest here, at least. You are so dulled to life's hardships that you only fear being disturbed by the police. . . . A crowd of miserable shapes surrounded me and snatched greedily at the cigarettes I brought them. They couldn't make head or tail of the person who appeared suddenly in the night and fog among them as their friend—among them, among these people who only have enemies.[102]

Certainly, this passage is a strong expression of sympathy with people who were so downtrodden that they appeared almost like hunted animals hiding from their tormentors. At the same time, Winter also separated himself here from the people whose identity he had taken on at other times. In this description, they are hardly "human beings" any longer; they are indifferent to their own fate; they are "miserable creatures" with inherent failings. In short, they are shown as needing the consciousness and the enlightenment that Winter, their unexpected ally, could bring them.

Here and in similar passages in other reportages where Winter expressed frustration and anger with the people down below, a slippage occurs with respect to both his perception of himself and also his intended addressees. In such passages, he abandoned his usual insight that these people could be capable of thought and action (after all, in this instance he had been led to the kiln by men very similar to the people sleeping in it). As a result, his own narrative voice is brought more into the foreground as part of the forces that claimed the mission of castigating these people and rousing them to action. At such points, Winter spoke as an intellectual political activist who was hard put to cope with the backwardness of the people he wanted to raise up and improve, and who was addressing himself more to those who might commiserate with this point of view than to the people he was writing about.[103] Like many naturalist authors, he had traveled into the souterrain and was now drawing back in horror from the "gruesome images" he discerned there.

However, these occasional points of exasperation were on the whole not characteristic of Winter's reportages. For the most part, he presented the inhabitants of the social abyss as human beings whose capabilities were being suffocated by repressive circumstances but who repeatedly mustered up the energy to resist what was being done to them. In contrast to Paul Göhre and his imitators, however, Winter believed that something more than stopgap measures would have to be undertaken for the abuses he was exposing to be overcome. And until the end of his life in exile, he pursued his efforts to ally himself with the people whose worlds he entered in ways that were useful to their struggles for equality and justice.

Volkish Fantasies of Unity: Walter Flex

During the years when Paul Göhre and Max Winter were undertaking their journeys to the working world, increasingly strident voices were arising from volkish groups that responded to the social question by calling for German workers to be brought into a national consensus. These demands for unifying Germans of all social classes in pursuit of nationalistic, imperialistic interests represented a shift in perspective within the loosely constituted Volkish Opposition. Heretofore, the representatives of this political and cultural trend had tended mainly toward social Darwinism and were strongly influenced by Nietzsche's concept of the *Übermensch*.

Accordingly, they had tended to regard the lower classes as mere "proles" and "subhumans" whose main function was to put their labor power into the service of their superior leaders.[104] But in the course of the industrial boom period that developed in Germany after 1890, volkish theorists attempted to counteract the challenge of Social Democracy and its hated internationalism by proposing to honor manual labor and incorporate workers themselves into the German nation.[105] Such writers and commentators disregarded the negative effects of the division of labor and of poverty. They did not care to test, let alone revise, their perceptions of the working world by "going down" into factories or other sites of labor in the social abyss. Rather, in their exhortations to national unity, they held up mythical images of the future volkish German community, the *Volksgemeinschaft*.[106] And in a new enthusiasm for technological progress, they began to dream of the indivisibility of the German people in an impersonal, gigantic system of production, or, somewhat later, in the German war machine. But no matter how idealistic their pronouncements were, these advocates of the oneness of all social classes, of work in the service of the nation, were objectively furthering the interests of big industry, which was expanding at the time and, after the turn of the century, gearing up more strongly for war production.

As we have seen, travelers to the working world frequently invoked metaphors of darkness to characterize their experiences of crossing class barriers. For some, the darkness was located solely in the uncanny, brutal, or desolate world below, and they saw it as their own task to bring illumination from above. For others, the darkness lay mainly in the blindness and arrogance of the powerful toward the souterrain's inhabitants' struggle to rise. For the Volkish Opposition, the "darkness" they sought to vanquish and destroy came to be located mainly in the groups they defined as lying "outside" the German *Volksgemeinschaft*. Consequently, after the turn of the century, these theorists began to replace the "proles" with the Jews as the "real enemies" of racially defined national unity. Around this time, as one cultural historian has explained, "all such ideologies began to shift in an explicitly antisemitic direction."[107] Now, these advocates of racial purity called fanatically for eliminating the "Jewish parasites" who were "sucking the blood" of the German people and attributed Germany's social problems to the Jews of the "Red" and "Gold" Internationals, thereby seeking to divert anticapitalist protests into anti-Semitic hostility.[108] This hatred of the Jews was the most virulent element in the enmity toward all whom these volkish circles deemed to be "non-Germans"—a hatred that only grew as the nation moved into war and which was complemented by exhortations to reject all subversive tendencies. In 1916, for example, writer Jakob Kneip exhorted his fellow Germans to defy all outside forces seeking to destroy the fatherland by honoring everyone who had spilled a drop of blood for them: "the farm youth, the mineworker, the clerk, the student, all your brothers."[109] Such glorification of comradeship among all social classes on the battlefield was characteristic of all those who dismissed socioeconomic conflicts in favor of conjuring up visions of national cohesion in wartime.

One of the best examples from the war years of such an evocation of the "false collective of the *Volksgemeinschaft*"[110] is to be found in a novel fragment by the volkish writer Walter Flex entitled *Wolf Eschenlohr* (1917).[111] Flex (1887–1917) was a tutor of Bismarck's grandchildren, an author of widely read works that hailed the war as Germany's great cultural mission, and an officer who was killed in the line of duty. In this novel fragment, written shortly before he died, Flex created a fantasy of unity between above and below, personified here in the two figures of a student and a worker who become military comrades. As the novel begins, the student Wolf Eschenlohr is meditating on the glorious struggles of his fraternity in the past for a united German Reich and wondering what will be demanded of his own generation. Not quite a "man" yet, he is still floating in a state of boyish indecisiveness. All this is changed, however, by the appearance of one of the "old boys" of the fraternity, the elderly Kant specialist Professor Wachsmuth, who comes to search out Eschenlohr at this fateful hour. On his way, Wachsmuth has walked by the "fraternity houses and military barracks" where, he tells Eschenlohr, he heard "students and soldiers singing of war" (194). The irrational bonds that the professor invokes begin to work their spell on the student, and the young man is carried away by martial enthusiasm. Later on, Eschenlohr and his fellow students celebrate their brotherhood by drinking the night away in their garden. Eschenlohr is filled with intoxicating sensations of pleasure and oneness with the other young men who are soon going to fight together for their nation: "He sought their hands, their eyes. He felt himself united and one with them, one in pleasure and laughter, one in will and love, one in emotion and devotion" (200).

But as the students greet the dawn with their songs, the erotic mood of unity is destroyed when groups of workers appear, making their way past the students' garden to the factories. Eschenlohr spies one, Karl Igelshieb, whom he knows slightly from the courses for workers which the students have occasionally offered, and vague pangs of guilt befall him.[112] Overcome by the warm feelings of the hour, and calling Igelshieb in thought his "worker comrade" and his "war comrade from now on," Eschenlohr offers the worker a glass of wine (203). Disdainfully pushing the glass aside, Igelshieb goes on to work. He leaves Eschenlohr to realize that he has insulted the worker by treating him patronizingly, and that Igelshieb was right to mistrust this gesture from one of the "students with colorful caps"

(205). Another student, who has observed the strained encounter, offers the following observation about the difficulty in spanning the gap between student and worker: "The abyss between these two worlds cannot be bridged with a dancer's leap. Many good boys from good families who fill the alleys with raucous merriment at German universities have no idea how the echo of their light-footed steps sounds in the attics where their poorer brothers are sitting and listening in silence" (204). The rest of the novel is structured around Eschenlohr's fantasies of incorporating the hostile worker into an unbroken circle of German men and around invocations of the desire for uniting the German Volk through the experience of war. First, Eschenlohr dreams that he and Igelshieb are comrades in battle, but the dream dissolves, leaving Eschenlohr to puzzle over the lack of connections among "students, workers, soldiers, laborers" (209) and to wonder how their brotherhood can be strengthened. Not concerned with uncovering possible socioeconomic causes of these class conflicts, Eschenlohr's mentor, the old professor, convinces him that "reconciliation" between the "unequal children of Eve" can be achieved only by the common task of going into battle together. Accordingly, at the farewell celebration for the fraternity brothers before they enter military service, the volunteer Eschenlohr has the following vision while the professor is addressing the young men:

> He saw the circle of intertwined men and youths open up as if in a vision. They shoved and pushed themselves in among the black velvet of the students' jackets and the gray and light blue Bavarian uniforms: shirtsleeved workers, blacksmiths in blue linen overalls, laborers in gray workclothes . . . More and more . . . They pushed forward in countless numbers . . . The unequal children of Eve . . . They had come from the factories and from the fields . . . Their arms lay on the shoulders of the singing fraternity brothers . . . They sang along . . . Karl Igelshieb had also forgotten the insults which he had received and given . . . His arm lay heavily around Eschenlohr's neck while they sang. (212–13, ellipses in original)

Here, then, the student does not go to the worker, but rather in fantasy he compels the worker to come to him to complete the unbreakable bond of German men preparing to go to war.

Eschenlohr's dreams of unity are realized when he sails through the military's physical examination thanks to all his fencing and dueling and joins a group of recruits described as "thirty young people from all classes in one room" (223). The drill officers put them through almost unbearably rigorous exercises and daily regimens in order to strengthen their will and forge bonds of comradeship, and these tactics succeed. The narrator emphasizes the pleasure the young volunteers take in coalescing into one "mass" beyond all differences of social class and origin: "None of the wealthier volunteers thought about having an extra coat for himself. They did not want to have any advantage over their poorer comrades. They wanted to blend totally into the mass of the unified Volk, whose rights and duties were equal and the same" (223). Furthermore, the recruits are shown as desiring oneness not only with each other, but also with their officers, in an unbroken chain of command and obedience.

The unity of German men would appear to be complete in the novel if not for the Jewish character, Moritz Hirschberg, a schoolboy friend of Eschenlohr's and now also one of the new recruits. Unlike the other young soldiers, Hirschberg is portrayed as continuing to think independently, as pointing out to Eschenlohr that many powerful people will benefit from the war and profit from death. At the same time, however, the narrator pulls out all the anti-Semitic stops to discredit this perspective and locate Hirschberg outside the circle of German comrades. Accordingly, Hirschberg is characterized as feminized and ugly, as physically inferior to the athletic Eschenlohr, and as constantly analyzing and thinking too much rather than simply yielding to pure emotion. And so Eschenlohr contrasts himself with Hirschberg: "It was . . . more refreshing to sense beautiful, immortal life in blood and soul than to capture it in words as if in fragile glass" (228). In sum, then, this novel disposes of the conflicts between students and workers, between social classes, and between leaders and led by conjuring up a homoerotically charged unity of German men in military service and war. And furthermore, it places any arguments that might question this unity into the mouth of a Jewish character who is seen as excluded by definition from the Volk community.[113]

Flex was not at all concerned with social reform, and so there is no indication in this novel that the student characters have any desire to learn about, let alone enter into, the worlds of the workers who appear. The ideology of this writer is therefore significantly different from that of even a reformer such as Paul Göhre, whose goal of creating national unity across class boundaries also had volkish overtones. Göhre's experiences in the Chemnitz factory left him with an indelible impression of the oppressive, dulling effects of manual labor. He believed that his fellow workers suffered from these conditions, and he called for limited reforms that would enable them to make more use of their human, mental abilities. Above all, he did not extol brute manual labor as a tool of social control, but rather he hoped it would be possible to overcome its most negative aspects. By contrast, although Flex never described the world of manual labor, the entire thrust of his novel is to glorify an anti-intellectual pleasure in bodily strength and prowess. Eschenlohr leaves behind the university and the life of the mind in order to join a military community where all submit voluntarily to strict physical drill and only the Jewish outsider retains traces of intellect. On the one hand, then, Flex depicted a student who seemingly relinquishes privilege by choosing to lead a hard life in the military. But on the other hand, Flex actually retained the privilege of representing those who had always had to perform physical labor—whether in the military or in the workplace—because there is no indication at all here that such a hard life could be a source of discontent.[114] Yet a novel such as *Wolf Eschenlohr* only foreshadows much more serious, drastic developments. For soon after the war, these authoritarian visions were to become a central feature of right-wing, prefascist texts that advocated subjecting Germans of all social classes to the leveling discipline of manual labor.

2
The School of Labor: From Weimar Work Students to Nazi Labor Service

Weimar Work Students in Autobiography

The work student is a "capitalist of the spirit" who has the prospect of returning sooner or later to his own milieu.

—J. Hermann Mitgau[1]

Before the end of World War I and the ensuing years of economic chaos in Germany, which culminated in the inflationary spiral of 1922–1923, it was almost unheard of for German students to find it necessary to work in order to finance their studies. To be sure, there were some before 1918 who gave lessons as private tutors, and others studying technical subjects for whom practical work or laboratory experience was a requirement. Nevertheless, the vast majority of prewar German students were able to enjoy relatively carefree lives. While other young Germans from less fortunate socioeconomic backgrounds were already spending long days at work, German students, who came almost without exception from families who could afford to support their children during their studies, were generally able to live off the allowances they received from home. As a result, given their relatively secure economic circumstances and their certainty of moving into appropriate professions upon completing their examinations, German students could remain largely insulated from those who worked with their hands for a living.

In 1925, J. Hermann Mitgau introduced his book-length collection of *Erlebnisse und Erfahrungen Heidelberger Werkstudenten* (Experiences of

Cover illustration from *Erlebnisse und Erfahrungen Heidelberger Werkstudenten*, ed. J. Hermann Mitgau, (1925).

Heidelberg Work Students) with the following reference to Paul Göhre's project and to the chasm between the worlds of students and workers:

> Between 1890 and 1920 one could read books or essays entitled "Three Months in a Workshop" and so forth. Here the authors depicted their experiences in the land of the German worker, which the German intellectual had not yet discovered. And all of these authors wrote with the same pleasure about their discoveries as Hedin did of Tibet or Nansen did about the North Pole. Soon afterward, monographs by German workers appeared, just as newly discovered monographs from faraway times are published. And, sitting in their studies, German intellectuals read with great interest the reports from a world which was entirely foreign and closed to them. Then they went to bed in their warm, six-room apartments, but not without that fearful, eerie feeling which even the mere word "socialism" had evoked before the war. (M, 9)

But now, however, it was no longer possible to relish from a bastion of economic security the titillation of such descriptions of expeditions into unknown worlds right next door or underneath one's feet. For since the end of the war, many German students had been compelled by economic necessity to enter into the previously unfamiliar world of work if they wanted to continue their studies. The independently wealthy student of the prewar period had gone through his service as a "war student"[2] to emerge—perhaps after a brief stint in a Freikorps as a "Noske student" putting down workers' rebellions (M, 174)—as a "beggar student." And students were now to overcome this humiliating status, pulling themselves up by their own bootstraps, by supporting themselves as work students.

The drastic nature of these changes in German student life is indicated by statistics from 1924–1925 on the socioeconomic background of German university students. According to historian Michael Kater, "27.4 percent were children of higher state officials and independent professionals; 19.5 percent were children of industrialists, owners of large businesses (merchants), managers of industry; 27.6 percent were children of intermediate state officials, teachers, intermediate managers of industry; 21.5 percent were children of petty officials, petty merchants and tradesmen; 7.0 percent were children of petty farmers and laborers."[3] Before the war, almost all of these students would have been supported by their parents. However, in the early years of the Weimar Republic, the inflationary spiral that reached its apex in 1923 made it impossible for the first time for many families with middle-level incomes to continue sending their children allowances from home. Still hoping, nevertheless, to enter into the professional careers that a university degree had always guaranteed, many students resolved to help themselves by becoming work students, by being willing to take any jobs where they might earn enough money to finish their studies. As Kater has noted, work students were first observed in German universities in the summer of 1920. By 1921 the annual convention of the national student organization, the "Deutscher Studententag," recognized the accomplishments of the work-student movement and organized the coordination of university placement services with the national student self-aid agency ("Wirtschaftshilfe der Deutschen Studentenschaft").[4] Although the number of work students is difficult to determine from existing statistics, particularly since differentiation was rarely made between numbers working during the semesters and during the holidays, Kater offers the following figures. During the summer of 1920, only 9.0 percent of the German student body were working; by the summer of 1921 this had increased to 32.5 percent. In 1922, 26.7 percent worked during spring holidays, 13.7 percent during the summer semester, and 43.0 percent during the autumn break. In 1923, at the height of the inflation, contemporaries estimated that up to 60 percent of German students were working. According to Kater, if this is divided up more carefully between semesters and holidays, the figures are somewhat lower: the summer semester of 1923 found 24.2 percent of university students and 19.6 percent of students from technological institutes working, whereas the corresponding figures during the following holiday months were 49.8 percent and 65.0 percent.

After the stabilization of the mark in 1924, the number of work students dropped noticeably to about 15 percent during the summer semester, and during the semester break to 32.6 percent of university students and 53.6 percent of students at technological institutes. Numbers continued to decline throughout the remaining years of the Weimar Republic. This was due in part to improvements in the living standard of some middle-class Germans after the monetary stabilization. But it was also caused by the rationalization of labor and the accompanying rise in unemployment among workers, especially after 1929, which effectively shut out of the labor force many students who still might have wanted to work.[5] The number of students working also varied markedly according to social origin and field of study. Two to three times as many students from the lower end of the economic ladder as from its upper rungs found it necessary to work. And, for example, about three times as many philosophy students as medical students took jobs as work students, reflecting the wealthier background of the latter group.[6] The kind of work the students did was also quite varied. Some students, especially those in technical fields, were able to secure employment in areas related to their chosen professions, such as in laboratory or engineering positions, or in workshops the students set up and ran themselves. For example, Paul Rohrbach's book on *The German Work Student* (1924), published in English in order to try to raise money abroad for needy German students, contains photographs of students busy in their own bookbinding, printing, typing, and shoemaking workshops, as well as of students gardening and of women students at work in a university ironing room in Tübingen and in the kitchen in a Jena dormitory. Although this was unaccustomed work to most of these students, to be sure, in these jobs they still remained largely among themselves or among others of their own social standing. However, one- to two-fifths of the work students took jobs in agriculture (digging potatoes, harvesting grain), heavy industry (mining, factory work), or other areas (lumbering, digging peat) where they experienced—usually for the first time in their lives—both strenuous manual labor and also close contact with factory workers, day laborers, and farmers.[7]

Unlike Paul Göhre and his imitators or the Social Democrat Max Winter, who set out voluntarily on their expeditions into the unknown, these Weimar work students were compelled by economic circumstances totally beyond their control to enter into the working world for periods of varying length. And some even had to give up their studies altogether because they were unable to juggle both full-time work and full-time study. Many examples from Mitgau's collection of reports give an idea of the extreme dislocations experienced by Heidelberg work students. An economics student and member of a fraternity sold newspapers at a train station. A student of Germanic philology worked in a fish canning factory, on construction sites, and as a German language tutor in Iceland. A woman student who was the daughter of a state official and hoped to become a journalist worked in the packing department and the office of a factory making hospital equipment. Another philologist harvested grain in East Prussia. A student of political science, the son of a state official, worked on construction sites and at a sawmill. A woman philologist worked in a cigar factory. A law student who was an army veteran worked as an unskilled laborer in a coal mine. A medical student worked at a blast furnace during the French occupation of the Ruhr. A geology student drilled for oil. A theology student worked in a machine tool factory. A law student, son of a mid-level state official, worked in the packing department of a chemical factory. A chemistry student, the son of a teacher, worked as a boilermaker's assistant in a sugar refinery. Another chemistry student, who had been wounded in the war, worked in the office of a tobacco company—and so the examples continue.

The aforementioned books edited by J. Hermann Mitgau and Paul Rohrbach are the two main collections of autobiographical statements by

Frontispiece from Paul Rohrbach's *The German Work Student* (1924), urging foreign donors to contribute money to impoverished German students.

German work students. Their usefulness as sources must be qualified by the volkish leanings of Mitgau[8] and even more so by the openly nationalistic and imperialistic views of Rohrbach, a prolific popular writer on politics and economics.[9] Given their political tendencies, these two men would

Students in a mine near Clausthal, Harz Mountains. Rohrbach, *The German Work Student* (1924).

have presumably censored statements by work students who might have indicated liberal or leftist sympathies. If we keep their biases in mind, however, these books are still valuable sources for learning about how a group of more or less conservative, right-wing students presented both their own images of working-class life and their experiences of giving up a "bourgeois milieu" for the world of manual labor.[10] That is, these reports can be used as a source for studying the mentality of these students as representatives of their classes of social origin. Compelled by financial need to enter into strange worlds, they came with all the predispositions, prejudices, and blinders of the environments where they had grown up. What struck them most about workers and working-class life? To what extent did they try to hold on to their former beliefs, and to what extent were they open to being transformed by these new surroundings? Where do cracks appear in their conservatism, their rigidity, their intellectual and emotional defenses against giving up positions of privilege and hegemony? They were pushed into the working world, but how far were they willing to go, and at what points did they turn away, withdrawing to the citadels of privilege which they had unwillingly left for a time?[11]

In the early 1920s, it was common to find want ads such as the following in German newspapers: "Cry of distress! Academic (philologist,

Female students in ironing room, Tübingen. Rohrbach, *The German Work Student* (1924).

22), stately appearance, refined manners, speaks French and English, seeks immediate evening job as a doorkeeper or waiter in a fine restaurant or as a servant in a high-class home."[12] But even if this young philologist and his fellow students were fortunate enough to find such temporary jobs, they were by no means assured—due to the unprecedented inflation—of being able to make enough money to cover even their most basic needs for food, clothing, and shelter, much less to save for financing further semesters of study. The pictures in Rohrbach's book of "poor students' huts" give an idea of the minimal housing many students had to endure, and the autobiographical statements are full of drastic descriptions of the students' poverty. For example, a report on student life in Berlin mentions cases such as the following. One student who was a veteran worked at loading carts, lived on only two bowls of soup a day, suffered fainting spells due to war injuries and malnourishment, failed his examinations, but still tried to continue his studies. A female student who contracted tuberculosis due to malnourishment had to quit her tutoring job, thus sinking even deeper into poverty. And students were frequently forced to sleep in sheds, garages, and waiting rooms of train stations (R, 22ff.). Contemporary observers often remarked on the poor health of many German students at this time, and specifically, with respect to the increase in tuberculosis among students, some medical professionals noted that they had never seen such extreme cases among patients from this social background. Along these lines, a professor who established a special tuberculosis clinic for students reported:

"I saw things like this twenty years ago in the working-class districts of Berlin and Leipzig, but never before at a university. Therefore, it is not surprising that the ability to perform mentally is also gradually declining."[13]

Nevertheless, students were working, after all, in order to keep on studying. Consequently, there are also many instances in the autobiographical statements where the students mentioned trying to balance out these two worlds by saving enough money during a semester break of work to finance another semester of study, by trying to work full time at night and go to lectures during the day, or by working full time and at least doing some reading in their fields of study in their off hours. For example, one zoology student who had to spend the summer of 1923 harvesting and gleaning grain poignantly described his efforts to continue preparing for his examinations: "It is true that I am not without hours of depression, in which the longing arises once more to have all the fine summer free to devote to my scientific work. . . . Sometimes there are rainy days, and then I can sit at my beloved microscope, but as soon as the sun shines the ears of corn or the potatoes left lying in the field call me out again; microscope and drawing-pen must be put aside" (R, 57). Or another student, a state official's son who worked at various office and construction jobs, resolved at first to read sociology in the evenings but came back to his room at night "half-dead" from working and unable to think clearly. "I feel an indescribable physical exhaustion and a total inability to think," he complained in August 1922 (M, 93). A few months later, in December, this student was still living in the same untenable situation, and his bitterness and disgust had evidently grown. After loading boards in a lumberyard all day, he would drag home a bag of wood scraps every evening "in order to immerse myself in Richard Wagner and Kleist while the fire roared and my stomach growled—a life not fit for a dog!" (M, 113–14). Such extreme disparities between the students' chosen fields of interest and the milieus they found themselves in both reflect the chasm between university life and the working world and also give a good indication of the hardships the work students were willing to endure in order to complete their studies.

In their autobiographical statements, all of the students, without exception, mentioned financial necessity as the overriding reason they had to go to work. Living under the shadow of growing poverty and deprivation, most of them expressed similar feelings upon having to leave their familiar surroundings, feelings that indicated the depth of the gulf between social classes that they saw themselves bridging, or violating. Almost all of them spoke of the uncertainty and apprehension they felt upon entering into a world they knew little or nothing about. Those doing manual labor—which most of the reports in fact describe—frequently voiced their surprise and shock at the exhaustion that rapidly overcame them and at the slow passage of time during the boring, repetitious, strenuous work they were performing. They often wrote of not being able to imagine that they could hold out, of tuning out all thought, of feeling reduced to mere working bodies, of becoming cogs in a production machine with no room for individuality or freedom—in short, of being compelled to carry out "soulless labor."

In telling their stories, with the threat of imminent pauperization and the shock of unaccustomed manual labor as common ground, only a few students assumed a neutral tone, simply recounting the bare facts of working hours, money earned, or expenses paid out.[14] The extremity of their circumstances and the unavoidability of taking sides in the social conflicts of the time apparently did not allow for much "objectivity" or matter-of-factness. Rather, there were two main ways in which these students wrote about their reactions to their difficult situations, two main directions that their ideological assessment of their changed circumstances took. First, there were those who expressed more or less openly both their bitterness and resentment over their severely restricted options and loss of status, and also their disdain for the people from the lower classes with whom they were forced to associate. Second, especially in the early years of the work-student movement, there were those who voiced a more idealistic perspective. If they had to labor alongside workers and farmers after the lost war, they reasoned, they would try to view this as a contribution to rebuilding both the destroyed infrastructure of Germany and also the "lost" unity of the German people.[15]

A good example for the first tendency is the reader of Wagner and Kleist mentioned above, Wilhelm Wernet, who kept a diary of his experiences as a work student from February 1921 until February 1923 (M, 83–115). Born in 1901, the son of a state official whose savings had been eaten away by inflation, Wernet was forced to take a position as a correspondence clerk in the office of a life insurance company before beginning his university studies, thereby entering what he termed the "office proletariat" of low-ranking white-collar workers (M, 87). After only a few days, he had seen enough to realize that this job consisted of nothing but dull, monotonous paper-pushing. Emphasizing that all his plans for future study were aiming toward developing a free personality, he asserted in his diary that students could never identify with this type of activity. Rather, he wrote in disdain, the work student would only be a disturbing element among the mass of well-trained office workers because he would be unable to submit to the merciless division of labor there: "He [the work student] invades the carefully delimited jobs of his colleagues like a wolf invading a herd; he rouses a well-disciplined army of subordinates up from the measured uniformity of their work; he sows discord and creates revolution" (M, 87–88). But, Wernet continued, if the student's material need was great enough, he would have to bow his head and give up his freedom—apparently Wernet's own situation, as he worked for the life insurance company for over a year.

In the summer of 1922, however, Wernet wrote that the wages for office work were falling in contrast to those of manual labor, with the result that a mason was now earning twice as much as a mid-level state official. Consequently, if he did not want to give up altogether his hope of studying, Wernet now believed that his only alternative was to earn money as a manual laborer. Through the student employment office of a technological institute, he arranged to begin working as an unskilled laborer for a marl quarry. His ideas about the working world he was going to enter and the workers he was about to meet are evident in his description of how he went about preparing himself for his first day on the job. In order to outfit himself as a "proletarian," he decided to leave his glasses at home, put on his oldest, most ragged clothes, and try his utmost to conceal his real identity: "I had resolved to lose myself entirely in my role and in no way to betray my origins and where I belonged. . . . I didn't want to think at all at first; I just wanted to be a worker" (M, 94). But his plan of becoming a simple "work animal" among others went awry immediately, for of course the "real" workers recognized him right away as an "intruder" and had their own opinions about this new situation (M, 93). Since the workers were not at all the unthinking machines that the student had imagined, he immediately became disoriented, not being able to adjust his worldview to his new experiences. He could only view the workers as a hostile mass, an attitude that strengthened his own feelings of enmity toward them and of displacement from his rightful social position. The tension between Wernet and the workers almost exploded already on the first day because of his clumsy attempts to mix cement:

> After a while I noted a lively exchange of glances and incomprehensible remarks, the content of which became unmistakably clear by the malicious, insolent, cowardly expressions on their faces. The foreman ordered me to bring cement. Spiteful grins. I took the wheelbarrow and rolled the heavy sacks up about two hundred meters. In no time I was covered from head to toe with blue-white cement dust. Like a biting wind, the atmosphere was filled with suspicion, malice, hostility, and hatred. What had I done to these people? Suddenly I understood the real meaning of the term "class struggle." (M, 95)

Such descriptions of the animosity students encountered on the job, as well as the ill-will and bitterness that they felt in return, appear frequently in these autobiographical statements. And like Wernet, students often responded by stubbornly resolving to stick things out to the end, to show the workers that they would not give up. Another example of a situation in which a student described settling down to work "like a machine" appears in the report of Erich Brautlacht, who was able to finish his studies and become a village judge during the Nazi period.[16] Like Wernet, Brautlacht became an unskilled laborer, and his job was to work with a gang of men shoveling concrete along boards into a limekiln. He described the work rhythm as follows:

> The workmen saw that I was getting tired. They laughed and went on working twice as hard as before. I clenched my teeth: "Keep it up! Is it sympathy you want? Are you not glad for once to get out of breath?" The man that stood at the bottom had a red pock-marked face and red hair. He was the strongest of the workmen. His shovelful was a double load. After filling up the board of the man in front of him, he would sit down on the wooden beam beside him and grin at me from ear to ear. I hated the man from the moment that I first saw him. It was an inborn hate, blood against blood. When I looked at him I redoubled my strength. My board remained clean. (R, 49)

Remaining a manual laborer for the duration of his time as a work student, Brautlacht maintained that with his strong constitution he could actually take some pleasure in the work—even including in his report a little poem written in a naively ecstatic tone: "Exhausted and thirsty I sank / Only to rise up again, / Meek in my power, / Trembling once more to the strain / And crying for work!"[17] But the student Wernet was fortunate enough to be able to trade in his shovel for an office job already at his construction site, a job keeping track of statistics on wages and hours worked. Returning to "mental labor," picking up his beloved pen again in his stiff hand, he expressed his feelings of joy at this moment: "It meant that I had returned to a beloved country from which I had been forcibly expelled" (M, 103). However, he found that the hatred of the workers was directed against him in his new capacity in an even more extreme way. Now he believed that the entire workforce was against him, and he reported that when he walked through the construction site, workers whispered behind his back, pretended to work harder than they actually were doing, and even threw stones at him now and then (M, 103).

For work students like these, who came to their jobs with perceptions of class divisions so rigid that they sometimes tended toward racialized views ("blood against blood"), there could be no question of even the most tenuous rapprochement between social classes. In spite of the hostility and extreme rebelliousness that Wernet said he encountered from the workers, then, his main conclusion from all his experiences was not that the workers might have had some justified grievances that needed to be rectified, but rather that these simple people had a natural need for authority. And so, in turn, he proposed that students, as future supervisors, could play an essential role in exercising this authority over workers due to their "intellectual, technical, and moral superiority" (M, 107). Not having had any success with this approach in his actual working experiences, however, and not prepared to engage with workers in any kind of dialogue, Wernet could only look forward to being able to escape from both mentally dulling office work and exhausting manual labor, from what he saw as the tortures and mockery inflicted on him by sadistic foremen and workmates: "When I enter the lecture halls in Heidelberg, I will be certain that this is my right, and that I have worked harder than others to earn it" (M, 97). That is, Wernet and other work students like him could only hope for the day when they would be able either to get control of the workers or to get away from them.

Another group of work students, especially in the early years of the Weimar Republic before monetary stabilization, wrote in more idealistic ways about their experiences in this new milieu. These students, many of whom were veterans and former officers, often reminisced about the war as a time of "comradeship" between German men of all social classes and tried to justify their economic need to work as a contribution both to rebuilding Germany after the war and also to cementing the "unity" of the German Volk. This perspective was stressed in a statement issued by the national student convention held in Erlangen in 1921: "The path to reconstruction entails creating the national German Volk community. For students, a means to this end is practical manual labor."[18] A specific example of this type of thinking can be found in the report by Hans Maier entitled "The Work-Student System, a Way to Social Labor" (R, 71–75). In April 1920, shortly following the Kapp Putsch, Maier had been a member of a Freikorps of students from Tübingen, "called by their old army leaders" to the Ruhr, fighting "shoulder to shoulder with the Defence Force of the State," he wrote, "till order was again restored"—that is, until the general strike in the Ruhr area was crushed.[19] Eleven months later, when he realized that he needed to work during his vacation, Maier actually returned to the same factory in Dortmund that he had occupied as a member of the Freikorps "to investigate that riddle that had then so powerfully urged itself on me in this place," he stated, the riddle of "class war." Writing in 1925, Maier presented himself as having been part of a "pure and idealistic movement" which had, however, lost some of its "social will" in the meantime. He justified his decision to work as follows: "The German war-student, when, in spite of bitter experiences he yet returned from the field with a burning desire for a social settlement among all ranks of his fellow-countrymen, had the will to employ himself socially, to learn to understand the workman and to be understood by him, and for this reason he became a working-student." In many of the reports that voiced this more idealistic perspective, other students spoke similarly of a vague desire to "understand" workers, to get to know them, to delve into their "psyches." Accordingly, in contrast to students like the above-mentioned Wernet, a student like Maier wrote rather positively of his relationship with the workers, in spite of the fact that he had helped put down their strike only a few months before. He encountered no hostility at first, he maintained, only shyness and reserve, and he was not particularly aware of being an outsider: "Men belonging to different worlds and separated by an endless gulf toiled together at the same work," he recalled. Maier did not find the experience of manual labor to be a hateful leveling factor that he, as a privileged student, wanted to escape as soon as possible. Rather, he viewed it as means of creating a "common pulsation of souls."

Of course, work students like Maier who emphasized their experience of "comradeship" were not conceiving this as a dynamic that might enable workers to find ways of having access to the students' realms of life. Rather, they were thinking along the lines of a one-way street, of breaking out of what they described as their own "isolation," of having the opportunity to learn from "life" rather than merely from dusty books, of combining mental and manual labor. Theology student Fritz Schiele, for example, expressed these desires in his report on working as a farmhand in Pomerania, entitled "My Course as Work-Student—From Cowherd to a Consumptive":

> The work-student is a type that does not owe its existence solely to students' material distress. He is supposed to counterbalance the over-emphasized theoretical studies by practical work. Life itself with its manifold forms and puzzles is to take the young student into its school, teaching him much by its rhythm of laborious active work. We are fighting against the narrowing bar of that education which confounds character with knowledge, stamping physical (menial) work as something degrading. And in such a spirit the "Work-student" takes up work on the land and in a mine, in the factory and office—seizing work of all description. (R, 22)

Or, to cite another example of such an idealistic expression of longing for connections between study and life, between intellectual and physical activity, one doctoral candidate said that his motive for becoming an agricultural worker was "to connect mental and manual labor with each other in a lasting way. For I believe that this is not only appropriate to our economic situation, but also beneficial for mental labor, since it can be liberated thereby from its isolation" (M, 202).

These musings on mental and manual labor and on the new "comradeship" these students thought they had found with workers tended in two contradictory directions that were typical for this more idealistic group of work students: class abdication and, even more so, the reassertion of class domination. These two tendencies appear clearly in the report by the former Freikorps member Maier, who wrote that "the academician had lost touch with the life of the people," and that therefore "the present task of the students is to recover this" (R, 74). On the one hand, a student like Maier actually seemed receptive to learning some things about workers that he did not know before—he visited fellow workers in their homes, saw how they lived, and concluded from this that students had no right to think of themselves as better than workers who were citizens just like the students, "equally free and independent." Maier formulated his new, positive insight: "The working-student's labour is not a descent to the life and mode of work of a lower class of humanity, but a fellowship with brothers who, at greater risk to their humanity, are similarly situated" (R, 74). Such warnings against behaving condescendingly toward workers appear in many reports, indicating the difficulty many students undoubtedly had in treating workers as their equals on any level. For example, a student of Germanic philology who worked on a large landed estate at harvest time described his fellow work students most critically with respect to this dynamic:

> We were four students: a Russo-German, totally useless, and unwilling to do any kind of practical work, an object of derision for most of the workers; then a little Baltic aristocrat, well-suited and willing to work, but easily distracted by other things; and a completely down-and-out first-semester law student, who managed not to lift a hand for days, to leave behind a debt of 70 marks, to get drunk every night, or to have a good time in some ditch by the roadside. . . . And the social perspective of this student was just as impossible: he looked down on the workers as "rabble" and thought of himself as too good for this kind of work. (M, 74–75)

Even where these students actually expressed some sensitivity toward workers' situations, however, they were generally responding to individual life stories rather than to the condition of workers as a group. So, for example, a female philology student who worked in a tobacco factory wrote sympathetically about the exhausted, sickly women she met there: "Confronted with their misery, I forgot my little bit of discomfort" (M, 124). Partly because of her own receptiveness and partly because of working at a job where it was possible to carry on conversations most of the time, this student became acquainted with many facets of her co-workers' private lives. Accordingly, she wrote that she took along from her stint in the factory "a colorful, varied image of these people"—quite an unusual statement in these autobiographical reports (M, 125). Even this student, however, who was unusually sensitive on a personal level, did not choose to reflect on how the workers' situation as a group might be improved. A business student who worked in a lignite mine in 1923 remained an extremely rare exception to this individualistic perspective. He noted that the miners were probably so "left-radical" because of their desperate situation, remarking that "in general, wages are too low in relation to what is demanded of the worker" (M, 187).

The limits of these hopes for "getting to know" the workers, and thus the basically conservative, anti-intellectual direction of these statements about social reconciliation, can be seen especially clearly in the way students kept their distance when they encountered the organized workers' movement—whether in the form of unions or of political parties. In other words, whereas these students may have been open to some extent to registering the effects of hard, monotonous labor upon themselves and even on workers, they were generally not at all prepared to "get to know" much about workers' efforts to improve their situations in ways that would entail challenging the hegemony of the social classes from which the students came. One of the most striking things about these autobiographical statements, then, is the fact that even though all the students remarked in various ways on the onerousness of their jobs, almost none of them went on to express any sympathy for efforts to improve working conditions.

With respect to the organized workers' movement, the decision work students often confronted was whether they would have to join a union. A number of the reports note that because of personal connections with employers or simply the employers' preferences, students were actually given jobs in some instances where workers had been dismissed. In situations like this, the presence of work students brought about complaints from the shop's union and even strikes over the issue of their employment (M, 36). As one theology student wrote: "The workman sees in the working student a possible strike-breaker. Often enough it has happened that the workmen go on strike for the sole reason that they are not willing to work with students" (R, 35). When students commented on this situation in their reports, they generally wrote about their efforts simply to get along with their more obliging, apolitical workmates, whom they tried to play off against the "works committee" or the "union" with their "agitation" and "grumbling" (M, 35–36). For example, a law student who worked in a pension office in 1922 characterized the committee representing the white-collar workers as made up of lazy, cigarette-smoking types who were always in meetings and who constantly complained about the boss. At his next job, in a rolling mill, where he had been hired at a time when many workers had been laid off, he reported that the works committee had protested his hiring, whereas his workmates accepted him cheerfully (M, 35–37). Or, the student Wilhelm Wernet mentioned above, who clearly suffered from the unaccustomed physical labor at the quarry, described his confrontation with workers after he refused to join their union:

> During the noon break a guy told me in a cynical way that I had to come to the barracks. Another fellow who overheard advises me in a kind way to give in. I go along, determined not to do it. Over there a larger group greets me with curious silence and eloquent glances. I give up struggling. . . . So I said: Give me a piece of paper, and I signed it. . . . I went back to my work and my dirt with the feeling of having suffered a defeat which was more than only a personal one. (M, 96)

Wernet explained in his report that he needed to save every penny for his studies and that union dues would have been a burden to him. On the other hand, the workers, in trying to protect their interests, threatened to strike if he was allowed to work without joining the union, and so he gave in. However, the significant thing here about the dynamic between the student and the workers is that Wernet expressed no willingness at all to imagine why the workers were so intent on acting in unity and solidarity with each other. On the contrary, he could only view them as "cynical" and as a potentially violent mass against which he, as a solitary individual, had no power. This hostile and even fearful attitude toward workers who were organized as a group to attain their own goals appears like a red thread in reports by students who were suddenly confronted with workers expressing their own demands. The philology student Johanna Merker, for example, who was hoping to become a journalist, described the election of the works committee in the factory where she had a job packing hospital equipment: "In the canteen we sat crowded on a bench all the way in back in the corner, where there is no light, air, or sunshine. All around us were broad male figures with excited, angry faces which looked distorted and uncanny in the gloom. . . . Finally, because of all the yelling, we couldn't hear a thing that was being said" (M, 70–71). The metaphors here of darkness, claustrophobia, and threatening violence underscore the unthinkability of bridging the gap between social classes. Consigned to the depths of society, these workers were not supposed to be able to speak for themselves. And when they did, they often seemed "uncanny" and incomprehensible to their student observers who were hardly thinking of renouncing any of their own privileges for the sake of real dialogue with those below.

Consequently, even for the students who seemed more willing to adjust somewhat to their changed situation, who expressed a longing to learn from practice, and who evidenced some sensitivity to workers' claims for equality, their exhortations to brotherhood only went so far. Former Freikorps member Maier made these limits quite clear in his report: "For the students who by their higher education and training are called upon to take an active and leading part in the great tasks of the time it is of immense worth to become, through his [*sic*] own experience as a working-student, acquainted with the deep material needs of men" (R, 72). Other work students were even more explicit when writing about what they hoped to gain from their temporary "fellowship" with workers. Thinking that they now had a deeper understanding of the workers' psyches, they dreamed of becoming more effective supervisors, directors, and academically trained "leaders of the people" (M, 145, 175). Or, as one student from Tübingen put it: "The students . . . will know how to lead with the same clear awareness which they gained while being led."[20] The "comradeship" of which this group of students so idealistically wrote, then, tended mainly in the direction of fantasies of forced unity of mental and manual labor at the production site, in which old, traditional hierarchies would prevail, or in which the future leaders would actually have a strengthened hand over the workers who had been their "brothers" for a short time. For after all, as Mitgau wrote in the introduction to his collection of reports, these students still clung to the hopes of returning to their own milieu, of retaining the traditional privileges of their own classes. In the end, they remained *Geisteskapitalisten,* as Mitgau described them, "capitalists of the spirit" (M, 18).

Descents to the Working World in Film and Fiction

During the early to mid–Weimar Republic, a number of novels and at least one well-known film appeared that focused on students or other figures from "above" who enter the world of manual labor. While relatively few in number, these texts are nevertheless unique indicators of larger cultural and political confrontations over class relationships and visions of the German nation. First, in a more abstract sense, the "mediator" from above who seeks to bridge the chasms between high and low is a significant figure in cultural expressions of class conflicts during the Weimar Republic. To be sure, these mediator figures generally are not workers themselves, and thus fall outside the specific focus here.[21] However, there is a particularly well-known instance in which the "mediator" actually descends to his "brothers" down below and briefly takes the place of one worker at a machine: Fritz Lang's film *Metropolis* (1927). The scene in the film where the son of the master of Metropolis becomes a worker is pivotal for locating the film within contemporary controversies about class differences.

Second, there is a group of novels that allude approvingly to authoritarian, militaristic experiences in dueling fraternities or in the Freikorps and glorify the shift—to use Gottfried Benn's words of 1933—"from the economic to the mythical collective" of all Germans.[22] Composed more as political tracts with clumsily constructed plots than as aesthetically sophisticated fiction, these works provide examples in concentrated form of a mentality on the rise—that of National Socialism. As in Walter Flex's *Wolf Eschenlohr*, fantasies are invoked here of a militarized social and national unity of Germans—specifically, students and workers—across class barriers, and strong anti-foreign and anti-Communist resentments are mixed in with Flex's anti-Semitism. In contrast to Flex, however, who was fixated on the idea of German men from all social classes being united in military training and on the battlefield, the focus here is on student characters from the upper and middle classes who actually enter into the working world for a time. However, in the visions of these conservative, right-wing authors, the world of work remains fundamentally a backdrop against which students— as vehicles of the authors' propagandistic goals—can test themselves or experience ecstatic feelings of grandiosity.

THE MEDIATOR: FRITZ LANG'S *METROPOLIS*

Metropolis centers around the figure of the "mediator" between above and below in a highly abstract, mythico-religious, futuristic, science-fiction setting. Ever since the film premiered, most critics have agreed that its content with regard to class relations, culminating in the slogan that the "heart must mediate between the hand and brain," is sentimental, inconsistent, and reactionary, prefiguring, as Siegfried Kracauer pointed out, Goebbels's statements about the "art of modern political propaganda."[23] Taking this evaluation as their point of departure, recent discussions of the film have concentrated more on its heretofore neglected portrayal of the interrelationships among gender, sexuality, and technology, and by doing so, have brought out key dimensions of both the visual content and also the enduring fascination of the film.[24] However, the film's schematized, abstract depiction of social class, of worlds of light and darkness, continues to be central to its impact on audiences. Specifically, the portrayal of Freder,

Freder comforts a worker in the machine room. Fritz Lang, *Metropolis.*

who is called the "mediator" in the film, resonates in many ways with the cultural preoccupation during the Weimar Republic with forced or voluntary journeys to the working world. And by examining carefully the scene in which he becomes a worker for one ten-hour shift, it becomes possible to situate the film within larger, ongoing controversies about "brotherhood" between social classes. As for any interpretation of this film, the accompanying novel by the filmscript writer, Thea von Harbou, can be drawn upon to explain some of the incoherence in the film's plot after its drastic cutting, although to be sure, the novel has more than enough of its own inconsistencies.[25]

The city of Metropolis, ruled over by Freder's father, Joh Fredersen, is constructed in four levels. From highest to lowest, these are, first, the surface world of light, futuristic skyscrapers including the New Tower of Babel with Fredersen's office, and the pleasure gardens for the sons of the city's masters; second, underneath this, the hellish machine rooms powering the city, where workers toil like robots; third, the workers' city, even farther down, with its dismal, totally functionalized dwellings; and fourth, at the utmost depths, the catacombs, the City of the Dead, upon which Metropolis is built and where Maria preaches her message of patience

Freder completes his shift at the Paternoster. Fritz Lang, *Metropolis*.

and pacification to the workers. At the beginning of the film, Maria has made the journey from the depths to the heights, bringing the poor, ragged workers' children into the pleasure gardens and announcing to the sons of the masters of Metropolis, including Freder, that these are their "brothers." After the servants hustle Maria (the "daughter of a worker") and the children away, Freder runs after them and down into the hall of the great machines, where he witnesses an industrial accident as a hallucinatory vision of Moloch. His first brief visit to this level of the workers' world concludes with Freder rushing back upwards to his father, explaining to him that he wanted to see what his "brothers" looked like, and expressing his fear that the "hands" may turn against his father someday.

After Fredersen insists that things must stay as they are, Freder announces: "I have far to go today—alone—to my brothers," and enters the machine room again, where worker No. 11811 (Georgi in the novel) is carrying out automaton-like motions at a machine shaped like a huge clock. In the novel, this machine—called the "Paternoster"—drives the elevators that are constantly circulating up and down through the levels of Metropolis. Rather than having a functional clock shape, it is described as being small, evil, and unrelenting in its perpetual motion, and as sucking out the "unsubdued, thinking brain" from its human attendant (23). The novel's personification of the machine as more alive and conscious than the workers and its repeated analogies between technology and mythico-religious realms underscore the visual depictions in the film of brute physical labor that remains unchanged throughout the ages. In the novel, Freder finds Georgi working at the Paternoster and babbling about Joh Fredersen, "who is the father of us all." Freder then replies: "Therefore I am your brother," and exchanges clothes with Georgi, saying that he will take his place at the machine (22). The film presents this scene by having Freder hold the exhausted, fainting Georgi in his arms and having him declare, as if in solidarity with his worker brother: "I will stay at the machine." Freder then exchanges his white silk clothes for the dark blue linen of the worker and begins to perform the repetitive motions that the machine requires.

While Freder is working at the Paternoster, the film cuts back and forth between him and the house of Rotwang, who is telling Fredersen that he has invented machine-men, the workers of the future, and explaining to him that the crude maps circulating among the workers are guides to the catacombs beneath the workers' city. In the meantime, Freder finishes his ten-hour shift with the last ounce of his strength, crucified on the hands of the Paternoster clock and still focused on his father, saying: "Father, I did not know that ten hours could be torture." The novel makes it even more explicit that Freder's stint at the machine has not propelled him farther into the workers' world, but rather pulled him more inextricably back into the world of his father. Here, Fredersen pushes the button that signals the end of the shift, eliciting this reaction from his son: " 'Thank you, father!' said the mangled soul before the machine" (40). That is, Freder has internalized obedience and subordination to his father's will, rather than developing a son's spirit of rebellion against the oppressive manual labor that underpins Metropolis.

After his shift at the Paternoster, Freder staggers down into the catacombs with the workers, who are going to hear Maria speak, while Fredersen and Rotwang watch from a hiding place above. Freder goes along, the novel's narrator explains, because "he wanted to get to know the ways of those who walked, as he, in blue linen, in the black cap, in the hard shoes" (41). However, all he really "gets to know" is Maria's message to the workers that they should be patient and endure. Upon listening to Maria, Freder is filled with the grandiose, Christlike hope that he will become the savior, the "mediator" between hand and brain that she is announcing. Yet his promise to Maria in the novel that he will always wear the workers' blue uniform only lasts momentarily, until he goes back up to his father's world once again. From then on, for the rest of the film, Freder is dressed in the clothes of the masters. In his first appearance in white silk again, he joins the dark-clad workers who are listening to the False Maria, the female robot, as she incites them to violence and destruction.

She clearly represents the world of light above, his father's abode, and Freder, in contrast to the dark mass of workers who are enthralled by her, recognizes immediately that she is not the real Maria.

Throughout the tripartite but circular structure of Freder's journey from son of the master to worker and back again, the themes of seeing, of learning, and of speaking and acting on the basis of this knowledge are central. Like some of the work students discussed above, Freder "wants to see" what his brothers down below look like; he wants to "get to know" their ways; and he "learns" that mindless physical labor can be torture. However, also recalling the mentality of these conservative students, there is another kind of knowledge that Freder rejects. Almost in spite of themselves, the film and the novel hint in brief flashes at an alternative consciousness: that of workers attempting to speak and act independently, in their own interests. There is a subterranean perception of danger to Metropolis arising from the fact that the workers are not merely unthinking appendages of the machines, in spite of the panoptical control exercised from above. First of all, those in power are clearly afraid that the "hands" may turn against them someday, and this is the quite believable motivation behind Fredersen's request for machine-workers from Rotwang. To justify this fear, the film presents Maria's story of the Tower of Babel, using shots of brutish, enslaved masses who finally revolt and destroy the Tower. After she then exhorts the workers to wait patiently for their mediator, one worker speaks up with an angry look, saying, "We will wait, but not for long." Such a threatening statement, together with the workers' secret visits to the catacombs, indicates the presence of a potentially rebellious consciousness that has not yet been totally crushed. Consequently, when the False Maria stirs up revolt and destruction with parodies of some of the most widely known slogans from the workers' movement ("Who keeps the machines going?" she asks, and the workers shout back: "We do!"), her appearance as an eroticized, evil machine-woman makes her, in Freder's eyes, into an uncanny embodiment of the workers who are suddenly speaking up for themselves in ways that can no longer be controlled by those from above who wear the white silk.[26] After this point, the workers' revolt is depicted as mindless, brutal anarchy, in which their drive to destroy is so powerful that they even forget the consequences for their own children.

The one worker who appears to be an exception to this general characterization is Grot, the foreman and keeper of the central dynamo room, who is described in the novel as "loving his machine" and wanting to stay with it at all costs (117). His symbiotic attachment to the machine is emphasized less in the film, but he is still the informer who is funneling news about the workers' secret plans and their destructive actions to Fredersen. It is Grot who reminds the workers briefly amidst their anarchistic rioting that their children will be killed by the floods they have unleashed, but his internalized blinders only permit him to see that in destroying the machines, they are destroying themselves. Wanting to put an end to the workers' uncontrollable actions, he thus calls for killing "the witch" who is to blame for all this, and captures the False Maria, dragging her to be burned at the stake. After this climactic sequence, the spirit of rebellion has been exorcized from the workers—for the time being, at least. When they appear in the film's final scene, they are walking again in disciplined, militarized rows, with their heads bowed, beaten down, like tamed wild beasts. Without even one angry voice arising from their ranks, they stand before the triad of Maria, Fredersen, and Freder, the daughter, father, and son, who are about to bring Grot into their orbit.[27] At Maria's urging, Freder brings together the hands of the Master of Metropolis and Grot, thus choosing as his "brother" the informer, the submissive son rather than the rebellious ones, for after all, the other workers never accepted Freder as one of their own, even when he was wearing the blue linen. The evocation of brotherhood and sisterhood here at the end, then, is that of an organic, naturalized whole weighing down on the smoothly functioning realm of labor, in which all threats to this prison of unity have been quashed. Far removed from all concepts of fraternity that would make room for diverging voices and entail shifts in the balance of power, the film holds up a dystopian dream of inescapable wholeness. It resonates with the master's fears circulating in the realms of light of those who dwell far below, in a darkness portrayed here as unchangeable.

RIGHT-WING WORK-STUDENT NOVELS

> We make all the educated people plow through Homer. Force them into the coal mines. Show them industry, show them labor, and this will create the race we need.
>
> —Hans Richter, *Hochofen I*[28]

In contrast to *Metropolis,* the group of novels by right-wing writers about journeys from above to below refer explicitly to the contemporary political situation in Weimar Germany by focusing on students who enter into the world of manual labor. Among these novels, the one that most clearly picks up on Walter Flex's militaristic mentality by melding the Freikorps and work-student milieus is Hugo von Waldeyer-Hartz's *Werkstudent und Burschenband: Roman aus dem deutschen Studentenleben der Nachkriegszeit* (Work Student and Fraternity Sash: A Novel of German Student Life after the War, 1924). Born in 1876, Waldeyer-Hartz was a naval commander and the author of several other novels as well as naval and colonial histories. He depicted the dueling fraternity here as an allegory of the kind of Germany he wished for: an authoritarian, hierarchically structured nation with no room for dissenting voices or outsiders—whether working-class radicals, Jews, or foreigners.[29] The novel's central character, Dieter von Raynach, is a veteran first lieutenant from the landed aristocracy who decides rather halfheartedly after the war to study political science. Once at the university, he joins the Corps Vandalia, a dueling fraternity, and finds his true home, not in intellectual pursuits, but rather in the company of his Corps brothers, with their emphasis on discipline, tradition, unity, conviviality, and manliness. In the first developments of the plot, this circle of young men seems complete in itself, with little connection to the outside world.

However, the values and resolve of the Corps brothers are soon put to the test in several confrontations with workers. First, the students—many of whom are former officers—decide to build a war memorial for their fallen comrades in the center of their university town. When local workers call a general strike in protest over the construction jobs they are losing to the students, shutting off the town's electricity and gas, the students rise to the occasion. Shouting "Everybody help! We're going to show the workers!" they race to shovel coal at the power plant, allied with engineers, other former officers, and businessmen (93). They are even joined by one worker, who finds his way there because the head engineer had been his adored commander in the navy. During the strike, which is soon crushed, Dieter mulls over the power of ideology to undermine the *Volksgemeinschaft* that he believes he experienced in the army and which he longs for Germany to re-create in order to oppose the hated French.

This invocation of German unity rooted in the war experience as the solution to the nation's problems and this projection of challenges to social pacification onto hostile enemies sets the pattern for the rest of the novel. In the next encounter between the students and the working world, Dieter, who needs to make money to finance his studies, decides to become a work student in a machine tool factory. Here he meets a constellation of characters who are used to elaborate further the view of the German national community being set forth in the novel. Greeted at first with curiosity and hostility by the workers, Dieter is finally able to gain the respect of some of them because of his manly strength and energy. Those workers who never accept him are characterized for the most part as the politically organized ones. Of these, the most negative stereotype is reserved for "Black Gustav," the "Bolshevik," who is outfitted with qualities that make him the antithesis of a dependable, subservient laborer: he is lazy and spends his time drinking, smoking, gambling in pubs, and chasing women. As Dieter's period of factory work draws to a close, he concludes that he has hardly gotten to know the workers better. However, he feels no hostility toward them, since after all, he points out,

"They're Germans like me." His hatred and bitterness are aimed against the "Bolshevik." As Dieter explains: "He's the one to hate, because he's a harmful vermin among the people!" (161)

After an interval fighting as a member of a Freikorps against the Poles in Upper Silesia in 1921, Dieter undertakes another stint as a work student, this time digging peat. As in the novel's earlier passages, it is hardly the working world that is the focus here, but rather the students' perceptions of ideological confrontations. Most of this section is taken up with the description of a mass meeting conducted by the student Feddersen, who is traveling around the country preaching a message of social pacification. Earlier, this Feddersen had already declared to Dieter as a work student in the machine tool factory: "It's almost more important to me than money . . . that I come closer to the workers' souls and preach the peace of God to them" (155). Consequently, his message to the peat diggers in his speech at the mass meeting—attended by the other work students as well to support him against the "radical rabble"—is one of learning to obey unquestioningly, to bow one's head, and to bear life's burdens patiently.[30] Feddersen expresses the mission of students who have experienced briefly the world of manual labor: "We students at German universities who are forced to live as workers among workers, we are not lowering ourselves, but raising ourselves up. For each of us in his place is a pioneer on the road to Germany's recovery, a leader in his own small sphere, a preparer of the way" (371). The political dimension of this message, like that of Maria's speech in *Metropolis,* lies in its emphasis on staying in place: the workers in theirs down below, and the students on top as potential leaders and formulators of ideology, as spokesmen for a silenced working class.

This novel is constructed in such a way that all opposing voices and disruptive figures in the emerging volkish national community are crudely expelled at the end. First, a "radical" worker calling for "freedom" who threatens Feddersen at the meeting is thrown out by the crowd, thus removing the political opposition. Then, in a closing scene in Berlin, Dieter recounts an incident he observed in the streetcar. There, a French officer had behaved so arrogantly to the conductor that the passengers forced the officer to get out, in this way removing the foreigner from the community of Germans. The conductor then uttered an ominous prediction: "It's going to happen—the foreign rabble will be chased barefoot out of Berlin" (372). What remains at the end of this novel, then, is an image of the dueling fraternity as a model for Germany: a group in which the connections between all its members and between all generations of Germans should be an unshatterable whole with no place for foreign or dissenting elements (238). The rigidity of the ideological perspective here means that—in spite of some nods toward viewing manual labor as nothing shameful—the working world that these student characters enter remains shadowy and without substance, a mere backdrop for fantasies about German national unity.

In contrast to other novels of the Weimar Republic that pick up on the theme of the work student, it appears that Waldeyer-Hartz's unmitigated affirmation of traditional hierarchical structures was too out-of-date even for other right-wing writers. Although they, too, generally sought to create representations of workers whose voices and actions were controlled by others, they paid more attention to depicting their student characters in working situations, to advocating some sort of partnership between students and workers, or to asserting with varying degrees of enthusiasm their longing for a national community of all German mental and manual laborers. In the earliest of these novels, *Stehkragenproletarier* (White-Collar Proletarian, 1920), about a student who must give up his studies for good, the working world is also hardly depicted. But in contrast to Waldeyer-Hartz's novel, the student character here undergoes certain changes due to his contact with this unfamiliar milieu. The author, Felix Riemkasten (1894–1969), was the son of a skilled worker and a prolific writer of novels, books for young people, and novellas published in soldiers' pocket editions during the war. Although he had some vaguely Social Democratic leanings, his Weimar novels such as *Der Bonze* (The Boss, 1930) and *Genossen* (Comrades, 1931) became increasingly anti-Communist, and the beginnings of this political tendency can be discerned clearly in *Stehkragenproletarier*, his first novel. As the tale begins, Hermann Schwarz—veteran, Berlin law student, and member of a dueling fraternity—is traveling by train to a remote village shortly before the end of the war. He huffily tells an older man in the train compartment—who is blathering on about the honor of sacrificing for the fatherland—that because his parents have lost their wealth, he has been forced to give up his studies and take a position as a clerk for an insurance company. He is trying to get as far away as possible from Berlin, he asserts, because of the shame he feels: "Am I supposed to let people see I'm a worker in the same city where I lived for so long as a fraternity student?" he asks in horror.[31]

Upon settling down to work in the office, Schwarz finds on the one hand that the regimentation of military and fraternity life has prepared him for the workplace chain of command, but he also chafes under the "indignity" of having others constantly tell him what to do. Unlike the protagonist in one of his favorite novels, Wilhelm Raabe's *Hungerpastor* (The Hunger Pastor), Schwarz is unable to find peace and contentment in simple, modest village life. In the evenings, he starts to have regular conversations with a group of men from a local workers' educational society, and this contact with a previously unknown world begins to transform him. Framing his new desires to ally himself somehow with the poor in sentimental and nationalistic phrases, he thinks to himself—recalling the words of the older man he rejected on the train: "We are brothers and Volk comrades, . . . we have bled together for Germany, and *we,* all together, are Germany" (56). Consequently, Schwarz decides to return to Berlin and begins to write articles for the Social Democratic press, where he advocates moderation rather than the "revenge" and "hatred" which he thinks the increasingly radical left wing of the party is promulgating. The novel comes to its melodramatic ending in Schwarz's newspaper office. When striking workers break in to close down the paper, one of their leaders blames Schwarz for harming their cause, and the workers attack and kill him.

In this novel, as in Waldeyer-Hartz's, the working world itself hardly figures as a setting. However, against the background of being compelled to work at a job far beneath his expectations, the conversations Schwarz has with workers open his eyes to the poverty and injustice he has never noticed before. Undergoing a political transformation from disillusioned veteran and conservative fraternity member to sentimental Social Democrat, Schwarz chooses to give up his class privileges to an extent and contribute his ability to write to his new political cause. After he leaves the village for his newspaper job in Berlin, however, little further mention is made of interaction between him, the producer of ideology, and the workers who are members of the Social Democratic Party. Rather, the partnership depicted here upholds established distinctions between mental and manual labor. Furthermore, because Schwarz has been depicted as a martyr to the cause of class reconciliation and harmony, his death functions in the novel to silence effectively the voices of the more radical workers as well.

In two other Weimar novels that focus on the working student, the experiences of hard physical labor and contact with the workplace milieu receive much greater attention and play a central role in the worldview unfolding here. The first of these, *Hochofen I: Ein oberschlesischer Roman* (Blast Furnace I: A Novel of Upper Silesia, 1923), was written by the popular author Hans Richter, who published more than forty novels and young people's books before his death in Poland in 1941, including several written after 1933 that recall nostalgically the former German colonies in Africa or portray approvingly the incorporation into the "Reich" of ethnic Germans from Poland. In this novel, Richter depicts a group of Freiburg students who decide to go to work in the mines and ironworks of Upper Silesia. He utilizes this plot as a way to spin out his resentments against intellectuals and groups he perceived as hostile to Germany, as well as his fantasies of seeing heavy industry run by an alliance of managers, intellectuals steeled by physical labor, and cowed workers.

At the beginning of the novel, a student of economics named Achim Wolfing attends a meeting of Freiburg work students and is immediately impressed by their intense struggle to learn from daily life. Trying to explain to another student what they might gain from practical experience, Wolfing enthusiastically maintains that a judge who has sold herring or a theologian who has worked on the assembly line would be better outfitted in his later career to understand the psyche of the masses than the young man who spends his time reading the "stock market report" and "sniffing cocaine." Gripped by the idea of forging a new type of man in this way, Wolfing impulsively decides to go to work in the mines of Upper Silesia. By doing so, he aims to put himself through a difficult test: "For the economist, the world of iron and steel is simply the university which he attends. Pale theory becomes practice. Whoever wants to be a leader must not hesitate to commit his entire being. I want to complete a practical semester down below."[32] Furthermore, Wolfing plans to acquaint himself with the mentality of workers who, with their socialist or communist ideologies, represent a potential threat to the state: "I'm going into the midst of the masses, to those who have their hands around the throat of the state, as it says so clearly in their political programs. The coal mine is where I want to go" (67).

Once on the job loading coal in the mine, Wolfing is almost overwhelmed by the strenuousness of the work. However, he is helped by paternal advice and support from the old miner Schneider, a simple, kind-hearted, deliberate man who—like Gerhart Hauptmann's Hilse or the foreman Grot in *Metropolis*—only wants to go about his work and has no use for agitators bent on overturning the given order of things. Also, Wolfing is sustained in the face of unaccustomed challenges by the strength of his inner convictions. These may be summarized as his desire to "help" the miners somehow, his resolve not to abandon his job working alongside them "down below," his readiness to learn to look at life differently than he did when he was a student, and his belief that the "new age" to come would have to develop out of the mentality of workers themselves, rather than be dictated by arrogant "professors" from the ivory tower (94).

However, as was also the case in the work students' autobiographical statements, this seeming willingness to learn from practice and find a place as a former "man of letters" among the workers develops in an anti-democratic direction. This becomes particularly evident in the way the novel portrays the students' confrontation with both the outer enemy of their German outpost (i.e., Poland) and the inner enemies of social harmony (i.e., striking workers). At one point, for example, another work student—this one an engineer—gazes out over the new blast furnace and thinks: "Look, down there lies Silesia, our land. Here we stand at the front, and over there, where the dark clouds are gathering, stands the enemy. . . . Here is German land, here German work prevails. . . . A strong race must stand here, brave, fearless, and loyal!" (182). Consequently, caught up in such hostile projections, these students can only understand any challenge to the unity of all Germans as the work of outside agitators rather than as efforts of German workers to voice their own demands, to speak for themselves. As was also true for Waldeyer-Hartz, the negative stereotyping at work here is most blatant in the novel's depiction of the Communist. This character is a man with the Polish name of Woczek who is calling for a strike to improve working conditions. However, in the eyes of Wolfing and the other work students, Woczek and his comrades are nothing but fanatical troublemakers who have an uncanny power to manipulate the gullible workers and turn them into a frightening, hate-filled mass. In spite of the students' claims, then, that they want to learn about the workers' "ways of thinking," they are in fact receptive only to workers like Schneider who are content and passive, rather than to others who are dissatisfied and politicized.

The best illustration of the limits of the students' perceptions, and thus of the narrator's prejudices, comes in the student Karin's description of a mass meeting of striking workers which she observes. Listening to the speaker and the crowd's response, she can hear only "roaring" and "elemental screaming"—the message is incomprehensible. And even when she does make out words like "exploitation," "starvation wages," and "injustice," she simply dismisses these accusations as an "old litany." Visually, she registers the angry faces, so distorted that she describes them as "beasts" and "wildcats," noting that women are also in the crowd to heighten the disgusting picture. The strikers do not appear to her like human beings, but rather as a threatening mass. Like Grot in *Metropolis,* she can only respond by running to warn the engineers about the "animals" threatening them (213–14).

After the strike is broken, when the "outside agitators" have been arrested and the workers' voices silenced, Wolfing has no thought of returning to his studies at the university. Rather, he comes into his own as a "cultural leader" of the vanquished workers, along with an architect who sets out to spruce up their little houses. Wolfing assumes his new responsibility by organizing and playing in the new workers' band and chorus—all these activities with the goal of awakening a sense for "beauty" in these benighted people. As ridiculous as this conclusion may seem, it is related in important ways to the concepts of work and of aesthetics underlying this novel's pre-fascist worldview. From his first day in the mine, Wolfing views the hard physical labor required of the workers as changeless and unchangeable and is only interested in proving that he is strong enough to perform it. As the narrator describes his thoughts: "The student dreamed about how the coal had enslaved the people" (80). Here, the "coal" is personified and mystified as the timeless force that keeps the workers in chains, rather than the economic relations of production that some of the workers are in fact attempting to change. At the end of the novel, when these dissenting voices have been crushed and when only the students, engineers, and managers are speaking, they are able to voice, without being contradicted, a vision of a mythologized, dehumanized world of work in which the artist's task should be to capture its grandiosity. As one engineer points out to Wolfing—harking back to Faust and prefiguring National Socialism's "Beauty of Labor" office, "The engineer has created a new age, but the aesthete has remained behind. He cannot yet see the beauty which lies in this strength, or he doesn't want to. Here man forces the elements to obey his will. The myths of antiquity come true here. In the steel mill I feel the essence of labor. . . . The everyday disappears, and only grandeur remains" (227). When the two men walk by the new blast furnace one night, then, they stop to watch the faceless women working: "Sweating women dragged out the empty wagons and shoved the full ones in" (227). The "beasts" have been tamed and the "wildcats" molded into cogs in the machinery in a way reminiscent of the closing image in *Metropolis*. The scene of domination evokes a fantasy of forced labor in heavy industry for the service of the German nation. And the student, in his responsibility for aestheticizing the world of work with its authoritarian structures, has found his place in an organic whole, described in the novel's concluding words as the "symphony of labor" (236).

A student who becomes a miner is also the main character in Joseph Goebbels's novel *Michael: Ein deutsches Schicksal in Tagebuchblättern* (Michael: A German Destiny in Diary Pages). Goebbels wrote this novel in the mid-1920s, immediately after the apex of the work-student phenomenon, but only published it in 1929, after joining the National Socialist German Workers Party (NSDAP) in 1926.[33] With this text, Goebbels intended to create a "literary memorial" for his friend Richard Flisges, a student who had gone to work in a Bavarian mine and was killed in an accident there in 1923.[34] Written in diary form, the novel centers around the figure of Michael, a war veteran who resents the presence of France's "Negro armies" in Germany and who recalls the war as a time when "the man from the palace and the man from the miner's cottage" fought side by side in the trenches.[35] Michael becomes a student with no clear goals and quickly comes to resent his "ivory-tower" professors who emphasize "intellect" rather than "common sense" (14, 105). Searching for a meaning and a purpose in life, for a whole that he can belong to, he feels oppressed both by the self-satisfied bourgeoisie, who have no concept of sacrifice and ideals, and by all the "demoralizing tendencies" he sees as characteristic of intellectuals and urban modernity in the Weimar Republic (42). His path to becoming a miner originates in these vague discontents and out of similarly hazy desires for a connection to "life," for putting his body rather than his mind to a test. Consequently, in an anti-intellectual perspective on education that would become typical for National Socialism, Michael views developing the mind as a threat to building a strong "character" and states that it should be the task of universities to turn out "real men."[36] At the end of the semester, then, when he travels on his vacation to the seashore through the Ruhr coal-mining area, he is already predisposed to view this industrial center in a manner reminiscent of the end of Richter's novel, writing in his diary:

> Gray fog! Smoke! Noise! Shrieking! Groaning! Flames leap
> up to the sky!
> Symphony of labor!
> Grandiose work of man's hand!
> You, my brothers in the mines and factories! I greet you! (53)

Upon returning to Munich, Michael becomes increasingly dissatisfied both with his studies and with the bohemian milieu of students and artists in Schwabing. Obsessed with the desire for a "revolution of labor," he goes into long tirades against capitalists and Jews, whom he perceives as the enemies of a united German people. In tones reminiscent of Flex's Wolf Eschenlohr, he bewails the fragmentation of Germans into hostile classes in the face of enemies who are not of German "blood": "That's the miserable thing: between above and below there is a wall of arrogance, property, and education. We don't understand each other any more" (91). And in overwrought fantasies, he talks of sacrificing himself in a Christlike way for the poor people he sees marching in the streets and demanding bread. When Michael hears Hitler speak for the first time in Munich, then, the event is depicted as both a revelation and a trancelike experience of male bonding across social classes. Michael is swept away not only by Hitler's bombastic invocations of "honor," "work," and the "flag," but also by the crowd around him, made up of "workers, soldiers, officers, students." He describes this heterogeneous group as united in "brotherhood" through their identification with the speaker (102). This encounter with the führer gives Michael the psychological and ideological foundation for finally deciding to give up his university studies. Resolving to exchange the unfulfilling life of the mind for hard manual labor as a miner, he imagines that he will find in the mines the lost oneness of comradeship that he experienced earlier on the battlefield. Accordingly, he declares: "Soldiers, students, and workers will build the new Reich. I was a soldier; I am a student; I will be a worker" (119).

Michael's process of actually beginning to work in the mines is laced through with dreams of both self-sacrifice and grandiose achievements expressed in pseudo-Nietzschean language and underpinned by the two books he brings along as reading matter: the Bible and Goethe's *Faust*. He imagines that he is now going to descend into the depths to become the "lowliest among the poor," and that he will "redeem" himself and break a new path for others through his sacrificial example of hard work (122). When he travels to the Ruhr to begin working, he is depressed at first by the misery and poverty he sees. But upon going down into the mines for the first time, he throws himself with ecstatic energy into digging coal. Thinking of himself as moving from "above" to "below," Michael can hardly wait to get back into the mines every day, exclaiming somewhat later: "The mine is a demon. . . . How this work satisfies me! I am my own master!" (134). In very short order, then, Michael's first impressions of the impoverished living conditions of the miners vanish, overpowered in the narrative by descriptions of his euphoric experiences of work. His continuing rantings about his hatred of "Mammon" have nothing to do with actual economic relations between owners and workers, but are directed against those whom he sees as in control of "rootless" capital, that is, against Jews (138–39).

Michael is not depicted as a work student. He has given up his studies altogether and is working in the mines for psychological and ideological reasons rather than out of financial necessity. However, the work-student phenomenon resounds frequently in the portrayal of the relationships between Michael and the other workers. As in Richter's and Waldeyer-Hartz's novels, Michael also meets a sympathetic worker figure, here the pit foreman Matthias, who immediately addresses Michael with the familiar "du" and gives him a sense that here down below in the mines, all the men are "brothers." When Matthias sees Michael frantically digging coal on his first day in the mines, he remarks in a knowing, fatherly tone that all the students he knows share this enthusiasm at first: "That's how they all are, the young people who come to us from the universities. On the first day in the mine they work like mad. But that soon passes" (127). However, although Michael continues to work hard and even lives with a miner's family in an effort to fit in, he still realizes that the miners are hostile toward him. Matthias attempts to explain the miners' point of view to Michael: "Oh, we see so many now who come from the universities. They all work hard and do their duty down here. But most of them don't understand us miners. They look down on us. . . . That's why there's this brooding hatred between us and these guys with white hands" (142). Although the novel flattens out the variety of experiences reported in work students' autobiographies (where their dislike of hard physical labor is frequently emphasized), it also repeats the structure usually found there of blocking out all reflection on relations of production. Accordingly, Michael views the crux of the social question as lying in the separation of men who should be "blood brothers." As he says: "Blood brothers are separated by property. They speak different languages and live in ways that are foreign to each other. We have become two scraps of one people. Above and below, with a wall in between" (133).

The turning point in Michael's relationship to the miners comes when they go on strike over their subsistence wages. Still believing that Michael is a spy and strikebreaker, they beat him into unconsciousness when he tries to help a poor woman whom the miners have trampled in their frenzied mob behavior. When he awakens, Michael continues in his Christlike pose of self-sacrifice, and when he goes back into the mines everything is suddenly different. There is no mention at all of how the strike has been resolved or whether the miners have won or lost, because in the ideology being propagated here, the important thing is only that the miners now accept Michael as one of their own. "Matthias has enlightened them," thinks Michael—this is all the narrative offers by way of explaining the miners' change of heart. Finally feeling himself to be a "worker among workers," he rejoices: "They help me, I help them." The nature of this "help" is left unexplained. But in any event, Michael thinks he has found the brotherhood that he remembers from the war, and he envisions this as a model for Germany: "This is what the fatherland must become one day. Not a place where all are equals, but where all are brothers" (144). At the end of the novel, then, after Michael has been killed in a mining accident, the final passages show him being carried to his grave by miners and students. Inspired up to his last moments by the books left on his desk (the Bible and *Faust,* now augmented by *Zarathustra* and his diary), he is buried as a "worker, student, and soldier." The narrator's voice appears briefly in closing, to point specifically to Michael's death as a symbol for the future.

In this novel, where sites of contradiction and conflict in the narrative are simply ignored, shouted down with pseudo-Nietzschean pathos, or glossed over with fantasies of self-sacrifice, the effort to enter into the working world means partaking in the struggle to create the German *Volksgemeinschaft* based on "blood." Furthermore, Michael is determined to test himself in physical labor in order to find a "meaningful life." His journey thus entails a longing to escape the modern life of the intellect—

viewed here as isolating and alienating—and enter instead into a world of hard physical labor out of both individualistic motives and also a desire for "community." As is typical of much of National Socialist ideology, the final images of the novel belong more to pre-industrial times rather than to modern, technological experiences of work and production. Michael has gone to work in another mine near the Schliersee in Bavaria (where Goebbels's friend Flisges was killed), but the work is not particularly difficult for him since he is "strong and healthy." He is living with a family on a small farm, located in a landscape of unchanging, mountainous beauty. A world of stability, tradition, and rigidity is evoked here, a world where the voices of the miners which might express discordant challenges to its harmony are totally absent. Accordingly, the narrative is structured in such a way that its main concern is to show Michael both submitting himself willingly to the discipline of manual labor yet also remaining in control of its representation.[37] In the end, the representation of the miners and of their needs and desires remains solely the province of Michael and others like him who will take the same route he did from "above" to "below."

In all of these novels, it is especially striking that the characters who enter into the working world are generally not depicted as also entering into the world of poverty. In fact, this world of the poor, which most nineteenth-century social explorers had viewed as closely connected and often synonymous with the world of manual labor, actually disappears for the most part in these works by writers representative of the political right after 1918. Of course, this decision to ignore social misery was less a reflection of actual living and working conditions among the lower classes than of these authors' ideologies and goals, and more specifically, of their concepts of work. Goebbels, for example, had his Michael make a few nods toward recognizing intolerable social conditions, but as is typical of all the advocates of this point of view, these are always immediately overpowered in the narrative by three interrelated attitudes. The first is that of individualized grandiosity, which amounted to accepting the existing relations of production. After actually mentioning that workers did not make enough money to live on, for instance, Goebbels quickly shifted the focus back to the pleasure Michael takes in being self-sufficient and has him assert:

> I receive the same wages as the others. It isn't much, but it's
>   enough for one person.
> I don't use anything else. I'm standing on my own two feet.
> I'm living from the work of my hands. (134)

Second, the novel also mentions fleetingly the "poor, pale, careworn peo-ple" in the streets (91) and the urban scene of begging children, gray-faced women, prostitutes, pimps, and drunks. Yet these dark images of the city and of the "black masses" (125) serve more as a foil against which Michael can set off even more sharply his sense of his own mission and his pride in his healthy, virile body which is able to perform the most demanding physical labor. Those whose bodies are unable to function like this simply fall by the wayside in this narrative as completely negligible beings for Michael. Finally, when Michael takes note of the millions of poor people who are living "in the attic rooms of the tenements, in day laborers' barracks and transient camps full of hunger, cold, and spiritual torment," the narrative uses this perception as an occasion to voice the goal of bridging the deep chasms between social classes through "belief, struggle, and work," expressed as "breaking away from the 'I,' turning towards the 'Thou,' towards brotherhood, towards the Volk" (7). As in some of the work students' autobiographies, the idea of "brotherhood" as the foundation for the national racial community ultimately amounts to the advocacy of a brutally imposed unity across social classes in peacetime, with the ultimate goal of preparing for war against all those held to be enemies (Michael's last words on his deathbed are "work, war!") (157). And in the perspective of these novels, this unity is to be forced largely through the disciplinary effects of manual labor. Consequently, in spite of all the invocations of a spirit of brotherhood here, the basic tendency of Goebbels's novel is revealed most clearly in this diary entry of Michael's: "The people want, says the Jew. In reality it is he who wants. . . . The people don't want anything. Only to be governed decently" (57).

From their own descriptions of what it was like to be workers for a brief time, it is clear that most of the pauperized students who were compelled by financial necessity to work at unaccustomed jobs and who experienced a severe decline in social status during the Weimar period did not glorify this experience. Rather, they either tried to make the best of things in hopes of returning eventually to their accustomed positions in life, or they expressed varying degrees of resentment and hostility toward the "proles" with whom they were forced to associate. When they tried to view their experiences from positive angles, however, they tended to interpret their stints at manual labor as opportunities for overcoming class barriers, for breaking out of the "isolation" of the university and entering into "real life," for creating the kind of *Gemeinschaft* which many male students thought they had found in the war, and for strengthening the German nation in the face of inner and outer enemies. The novels by right-wing writers which center around the working student push this "nationalization of work"[38] to the extreme by omitting or glossing over all the aspects of hard physical labor that the students in fact usually found so distasteful, and by creating grandiose visions of alliances and forced unities across class boundaries in the service of the German nation. Significantly, it is the novel by the future Nazi propaganda minister that presents the most perversely "positive" view of unskilled manual labor. In the other novels discussed here, work is a testing ground for the student characters, but they all leave the realm of manual labor and return to positions as producers of ideology or aesthetics in the end. Goebbels's *Michael*, by contrast, not only gives up his studies for good, but he in no way returns to the life of the mind. Rather, Goebbels had his ex-student character die as a simple miner whose funeral brings together Germans from all social classes into the national racial community.

Labor Service for the National Community

> It remains our irrevocable decision to lead absolutely every German once in his life to manual labor, no matter who he is, whether rich or poor, whether the son of scholars or the son of factory workers.
> —Adolf Hitler, May 1, 1933[39]

FROM VOLUNTARY TO COMPULSORY LABOR SERVICE

Discussions among contemporary participants and observers about the work-student movement as one aspect of ongoing efforts to bridge the abyss between social classes were interconnected in complex ways with a much broader debate about the economic and ideological significance of instituting a national labor service in which every German would perform manual labor for a time. And although ultimately the most regressive of these ideas were put into practice, advocates of such a labor service spanned a broad range of the political spectrum before 1933, including right-wing organizations, groups of the bourgeois youth movement, adult education associations, and sectors of Social Democracy and the trade unions, with the Communist Party as the only significant opposition. As one of the many proposals for resolving the sense of a deep structural crisis in the Weimar Republic, a national labor service was viewed by its proponents as an institution for transforming society in keeping with particular pedagogical or disciplinary goals.[40] As historian Peter Dudek has explained, there were three basic reasons why various groups began to advocate a voluntary or mandatory labor service during the Weimar Republic—reasons that often overlapped.[41] The first motive was economic and viewed a labor service as a means of lessening unemployment. The second came from educators and had more of a pedagogical thrust: these groups emphasized overcoming social class distinctions and helping aimless young people find an orientation and a meaningful place in life through structured work. The third was most clearly reactionary and was often associated with members of veterans organizations who advocated mandatory labor service for men as a substitute for the military service that was no longer permitted after the Treaty of Versailles. In fact, the first calls for a mandatory labor service immediately after the war came from veterans—including some work students—who were experiencing economic deprivation and a decline in social status. Beginning in 1923 and 1924, groups from the bourgeois youth movement also began to advocate the establishment of a labor service, and from then on, the campaign expanded with the growth of the work camp movement and the appearance of countless publications that reached an audience far beyond the small number of actual participants in the work camps. In the summer of 1931, the efforts of these scattered groups became institutionalized with the creation of the Voluntary Labor Service, a national measure to decrease unemployment. Shortly after Hitler came to power, the Nazis established the Reich Labor Service, which was voluntary at first and then became compulsory for men in 1935 and for women in 1939.

The first efforts to create a labor service in which students would carry out manual labor were undertaken by sectors of the bourgeois youth movement. In 1924 about thirty of these groups—including the "Jungdeutschlandbund," the "Bund deutscher Ringpfadfinder," the "Wandervogel-deutsche Jugendschaft," the "Deutscher Hochschulring," and the "Deutsche Turnerschaft"—called for the establishment of a year of labor service. Beginning in 1925, these groups organized a number of student work camps that were planned for small numbers of participants (about fifty) and for durations of one or two weeks. As Dudek has explained, the impetus behind these early student work camps arose out of the ideology of the work-student experience with its ethos of comradeship between workers and students, out of these students' critique of the isolation of universities from practice and their belief that manual labor would balance out this one-sidedness by leading them back to the Volk, and out of their hope that the experience of the work camp would aid them in creating order out of chaos.[42] As one advocate of this early work camp movement wrote in 1932, looking back on these years:

> It was important to be forced to earn one's bread through manual labor. It was important that unfounded intellectual pretensions were controlled by the solid, taciturn criticism of the working man, whom many students were secretly proud to have made their comrade. It was important that this kind of practical learning extended across all social classes of the Volk. All of this created a new type of student, who kept his distance from university life. Based on their experiences, these students looked critically at the intellectual position of

the university within the Volk, as well as upon its scholarship and its methods. Out of this inner resistance there grew a wish for greater vitality in scholarly life than was to be found in the often haphazard, intellectualizing atmosphere and the social isolation of the universities. . . . In the moment when the work-student phenomenon became less important after the mark was stabilized, its inner significance continued to be developed in a new form. From now on, manual labor could now become a necessary component of a meaningful way of life—alongside the university—for the student groups.[43]

To be sure, the suspicions voiced here of intellectuals' distance from "reality" could certainly take a populistic, reactionary turn. However, for the most part it appears that these work camps associated with the youth movement were different from the disciplinary, militarized, authoritarian plans that the far right was developing at the same time. By contrast, these youth groups emphasized mutual responsibility and self-government in their work camps and tended to see themselves as experimenting with more cooperative ways of living.[44]

A second type of work experience that also had the aim of breaking down class barriers came out of the adult education movement and is associated mainly with Eugen Rosenstock and the Boberhaus, the largest independent residential adult education center in existence during the Weimar Republic.[45] The Boberhaus was located in Löwenberg in Silesia, an area where unemployment was high and miserable social conditions were extreme due to the partition of this region in 1921, when most of its coal, iron, zinc, and lead mines fell to Poland. Situated in the midst of this "poorhouse of the Republic," the Boberhaus—and Rosenstock as its most influential teacher—set out to develop programs that would be useful to the young workers in this area, whom they perceived as having lost their skills and their work ethic due to an economic situation beyond their control.[46] While Rosenstock was still influenced by the ideas of the work-student and youth movements to an extent, he was mainly interested in addressing young workers and in developing pedagogical measures to counteract their feelings of hopelessness and abandonment. Consequently, he conceived and carried out three "work camps for workers, farmers and farmworkers, and students" between the ages of eighteen and thirty at the Boberhaus in 1928, 1929, and 1930. These camps lasted for two or three weeks, and there were about one hundred participants in each camp. Rosenstock divided each day into periods for intellectual, artistic, and physical activity, emphasizing that shared manual labor was crucial for breaking down social differences and for creating a sense of comradeship and community. However, while these camps obviously had a certain structure and discipline, strict hierarchies of organization and command were absent there. Rather, individual autonomy and discussion of controversial topics were encouraged among their participants.[47] Rosenstock took pains to distance his ideas from those of the more militaristic, right-wing labor service advocates. Thus, while he and the student participants in these camps did conceive of their adult education program as a contribution to creating a new Volk and a new Reich, this effort at breaking down class barriers does not appear to have been aggressively nationalist or racist. It was, however, very limited in its concrete effectiveness, given the enormity of the social problems in the surrounding region.

The emphasis among these youth groups and in Rosenstock's work camps on mutual responsibility and self-government was not typical of most of the voices advocating a labor service that would break down traditional class barriers. Rather, the loudest and most extreme expressions of this vision of forced unity by work students themselves, novelists, and other contemporary commentators resonate with continuing resentments over the lost war and the abolishing of compulsory military service, anti-intellectual passions, and nationalistic, racialized thinking.[48] The most strident advocates of a national labor service viewed it primarily as a substitute for compulsory military service where values of obedience and subordination to authority could continue to be inculcated in German men of all social classes. Thus, a military leader like Admiral Tirpitz bemoaned that German youth had "gone to the dogs" since the war and that they lacked all respect for authority.[49] As a solution to this, the nationalistic veterans organization known as the "Stahlhelm" proposed as early as 1920 that a compulsory labor service should be established to counteract these tendencies.[50] In the same way, an organization like Artur Mahraun's "Jungdeutscher Orden" promoted the idea of labor service as "the social school of the nation," a phrase the NSDAP program later picked up. Furthermore, the "Artamanen Bund for Voluntary Labor Service in the Country," which was founded in 1924 and counted Heinrich Himmler and Rudolf Höss among its members, promoted the idea of German youth working in agriculture, especially in the East, in order to oust Polish workers and make room for German expansion and colonization.[51]

Similar proposals were made by students themselves who had spent time working in the fields on the Junkers' estates. In their autobiographical statements, they mentioned at times that it was highly desirable for German students to replace the seasonal Polish workers who made up a large percentage of unskilled labor on eastern estates. This "dangerous foreign element" could then be removed from Germany, they suggested, and students could develop a deeper attachment to their native soil. Along these lines, one student proposed that "It would really be a great thing if students could make Polish migrant workers superfluous and at the same time develop a relationship again to the soil and to agricultural work."[52] More generally, German industrialists and managers often supported the work-student movement, and many cooperated with student placement services in helping students find jobs in their companies. This reflected their efforts to gain control over a rebellious workforce and their hopes that students might serve as a kind of nationally oriented buffer or "dampening factor" in situations of class conflict.[53] In 1928, for example, industrialist Carl Duisberg, one of the major supporters of the "Wirtschaftshilfe der deutschen Studentenschaft" (Economic Aid Association of German Students), addressed a conference of students who had just returned to Germany from working in the United States. In a rather veiled, hazy way he spoke about the need for cooperation between superiors and workers, maintaining that in America class divisiveness was hardly known and that Germans could learn from this. "In Germany, we should also emphasize the purely human aspect more strongly," he proposed.[54] Other speakers at the conference, however, minced no words in stating what they thought these vague ideas about "humanity" really meant in the German context. They did not choose to view America primarily as a model for freedom and democracy, but rather as a model for a homogeneous leveling out of class conflicts to the ultimate benefit of capital. As one speaker put it: "German industry will really make an important advancement when superiors learn to view workers as decent men, as German men with German blood in their veins; when each of us see the Volk comrade in the other."[55]

It seems only consistent with these fantasies of unity based on the nation or on "blood" that some commentators on the work-student phenomenon began to suggest from early on that practical work should be made obligatory for all those who wanted to study and assume leading positions in Germany. Both work students themselves and other observers began to advocate a compulsory labor service as a concrete way of moving from the "work community" to the "Volk community," as one professor of economics in Dresden put it in 1924.[56] These voices emphasized the usefulness of the work experience on the one hand as a bridge between classes, and on the other hand as a method whereby students could learn to internalize the same strict discipline to which soldiers had been subjected earlier in the military. In tones often reminiscent of statements enthusiastically affirming the war experience, these advocates of a compulsory national labor service proposed that German students should prove themselves worthy of the sacrifices soldiers had made on the front by cultivating uncompromising idealism and preserving the health and purity of their bodies for the German Volk.[57] As Hans Sikorski, a member of the large veterans organization called the "Kyffhäuser-Verband," wrote in 1925: "For reconstruction we need whole people and not one-sided specialists. German students must be trained to become hardened, healthy people of strong character. They must be filled with high idealism; they must place their lives in the service of their Volk; and they must work with tenacious self-discipline at preserving their bodies and their labor power for their Volk."[58]

Admittedly, even the more extreme advocates of compulsory labor service like Sikorski seemed moved by hopes that were not entirely unegalitarian. He, and others like him, emphasized the contribution of the generation of veteran students and of all students who had gone to work to preventing the collapse of higher education after the war and to keeping university study open to many students whose parents could not afford to support them. Even in these calls from the political right for forcing students to work, there was sometimes a twisted desire to prevent education and privilege from remaining the preserve of a small, monied elite and an effort to oppose what these contemporaries called the "plutocratization" of the universities. Sikorski, however, while advocating an obligatory combination of work and study for such reasons, also provided material that foreshadowed the direction these proposals would ultimately take. For example, when the Association of German Students discussed at its convention in Marburg in 1925 whether every member should be required to work at manual labor for three months, Sikorski approvingly quoted the rationale for this proposal:

> Reconciling class conflicts is at present one of the most important tasks. . . . Experience has proven that the students who worked in agriculture, mines, and the factories did not only learn discipline, obedience, and fulfillment of duty. Rather, they also had the opportunity to get to know the worker and his world and to work in a practical, small way toward overcoming existing conflicts. And so this institution born out of necessity was good in two respects. It was a kind of substitute for the compulsory military service which had been taken away from us, and it forced the often unworldly academic to concern himself with social questions. At present, broad groups are calling for the establishment of a year of compulsory labor service for every German. But the time for this has not arrived yet.[59]

While such calls for a labor service for German men arose only after the end of World War I, the idea that German women should perform this sort of national service was older, having been debated since the late nineteenth century.[60] Most of the political tendencies in these discussions had in common the idea that women should be busied in traditionally female work such as housekeeping, agriculture, gardening, and care of children, the sick, and the wounded. Representatives of the liberal women's movement such as Helene Lange and Gertrud Bäumer hoped that women could gain more citizens' rights by assuming more duties, and they viewed a compulsory labor service for women as a contribution to peace through carrying out social work and nursing tasks.[61] Others combined a certain openness toward seeing women move into nontraditional work with the most reactionary, authoritarian attitudes about the disciplinary effects of communal labor. A good example of this tendency is the pamphlet entitled *Dienstpflicht und Dienstjahr des weiblichen Geschlechts* (Compulsory Service Year for the Female Sex, 1915), by Elisabeth Gnauck-Kühne, who had been a "female Göhre" twenty years earlier after she published her account of her short stint at factory work. Written shortly after the war began, this pamphlet predicted that Germany was sure to become the "leading military state of Europe" in its march toward inevitable victory. But while German men were proving their devotion to the national community on the battlefield, Gnauck-Kühne asserted, the paths women might take to fulfill both their "natural" duties and their duties toward the Volk were not so well delineated. Maintaining that the war situation was prompting more calls for women to complete a year of national service, she proposed that women from all social backgrounds should be compelled to serve the state in this way, going so far as to write: "Recognition of women's duty to serve the fatherland would be the crowning achievement of our Reich."[62] Here, as in most of the right-wing statements about a labor service for men, Gnauck-Kühne envisioned that such an institution would forcibly unite women across all social classes. She also suggested that women might move into traditionally male jobs, above all when men took up arms in wartime. Imagining a compulsory labor service for women, it was her hope that this militarized form of social organization could be established in Germany "without argument, as befits a people in arms. The German man could go to the battlefield with the firm assurance that everything is being taken care of at home!"[63]

Others who advocated a labor service for women did not even make this kind of nod toward busying them in nontraditional occupations. Rather, seeking to turn back the clock and gain control over what they perceived as social and familial breakdown, they hoped to convince young women to renounce more modern work and careers. These most regressive voices, which finally prevailed in 1933, sought to encourage young women to remain in traditional female spheres and even to forsake the tempting but corrupting urban world altogether for supposedly healthy, wholesome work in agriculture, above all in German settlements in the East. The militarized vocabulary used here was not as relentless as in most right-wing statements calling for a men's labor service, for after all, the goal was to keep women in their place in the family, not to subject women's traditional caregiving roles to drill and regimentation. However, these circles still placed great emphasis on the effectiveness of disciplined, common manual labor in breaking down class barriers. The following statement from *Der Frauenarbeitsdienst im Kampf um die Erneuerung Deutschlands* (Women's Labor Service in the Struggle for the Renewal of Germany, 1934) by Friedrich Hiller may stand for many by National Socialist proponents of a women's labor service: "When the daughters of the administrator and the businessman toil in the potato fields together with the daughters of the factory worker, then their shovels also plant mutual respect in their hearts."[64]

Indeed, in the plans of National Socialist ideologues, the "shovel" was to be an indispensable means of instruction in their drive toward total social mobilization and militarization. Faced as they were with skepticism from large sectors of the workforce, they set out to glorify unskilled labor while planning at the same time to intensify its use as a means of discipline. Hitler himself insisted in *Mein Kampf* (My Struggle, 1925) that he had been an "unskilled laborer" who experienced "poverty and misery" for "five years" in Vienna (an assertion biographers have disproven).[65] Filled, he maintained, with a burning desire to study the "social question," Hitler thus claimed an authentic understanding of workers' plights and an entitlement to speak for their needs: "This 'study' cannot happen from the top down. Whoever is not trapped himself in the coils of this serpent [i.e., the social question] will never get to know its poisonous bite."[66] On February 1, 1933, then, immediately upon assuming control of the government, Hitler declared the "concept of compulsory labor service" to be a fundamental element in his plans for Germany.[67] Putting the former Freikorps member and "old fighter" Konstantin Hierl in charge of organizing the Reich Labor Service, Hitler thus empowered the most regressive, anti-Semitic advocates of a compulsory labor service from the Weimar Republic. Viewing labor in what he termed an "Aryan" fashion as "honorable" service to the Volk, Hierl had already stated bluntly in his *Sinn und Gestaltung der Arbeitsdienstpflicht* (Meaning and Form of Compulsory Labor Service, 1932) that his organization would have no place for Jews with their "Old Testament" view that labor was a "curse."[68] Of course, such statements were unparalleled in their cynicism, considering the Nazis' later policy of "annihilation through work" in the concentration camps.

Now, Hitler was in a position to see that these ideas would be put into practice, and in his programmatic speech of May 1, 1933, he spoke about the necessity of breaking down barriers between "mind and hand,"

Members of the Nazi Labor Service marching on Unter den Linden in Berlin. Herbert Stetten-Erb, *Der Arbeitsdienst: Ein Bildberichtbuch* (1935).

of honoring manual labor, and of creating a labor service that would compel every "German" man to carry out such work:

> In a time when millions live among us with no understanding for the significance of manual labor, we want to make the German Volk realize through compulsory labor service that manual labor is not a shame or a dishonor. Rather, like every other activity, it brings honor to the man who carries it out faithfully and honestly. It remains our irrevocable decision to lead absolutely every German once in his life to manual labor, no matter who he is, whether rich or poor, whether the son of scholars or the son of factory workers. By experiencing this kind of work, he will be able to command more easily someday, because he has already learned how to obey. We are planning to eliminate Marxism in more than a superficial way. We are resolved to take away its preconditions. . . . Mental and manual laborers must never stand in opposition to each other.[69]

Of course, what National Socialists' claims to speak for workers' interests amounted to in practice was the immediate, brutal repression of the independent trade unions, beginning the next day, May 2, when Hitler ordered their offices to be closed and their assets confiscated. Soon afterward, compulsory labor service gradually began to be introduced. In July 1933 it became mandatory for first- through fourth-semester students, and in February 1934 it was made a requirement for university matriculation. On June 6, 1935, a compulsory six-month labor service was introduced for all young men, followed on September 4, 1939, by a similar law for young women. In particular, the decrees that required prospective university students to perform a period of manual labor were motivated by both economic considerations (plans to reduce the number of students, which had grown steadily during the Weimar Republic) and ideological goals.[70] Specifically, the language that Hitler, Hierl, Reich Minister of Education Bernhard Rust, and other National Socialist ideologues used to promote the Labor Service contained frequent references to its "educational" value for those who had never held a shovel in their soft hands.[71] Along these lines, Hitler went so far as to vow to the fifty-two thousand members of the Reich Labor Service who marched at the Nuremberg Party Congress of the NSDAP in 1934 that "One day the entire nation will go through your school."[72]

What was to be learned in this "educational institution" was clear to the propagandists. Most importantly, by forcing people from all social classes to live and perform manual labor together in closed camp communities that were for the most part isolated and primitive, class barriers and class hatred were to be broken down for the benefit of the national racial community.[73] Furthermore, the military value of comradeship was to be inculcated through the experience of the Labor Service camp. As one National Socialist participant in the Labor Service wrote in 1933: "The Labor Service is the best school for comradeship. Here everyone is only one part of the community. Here it is a matter of subordinating one's own wishes to the needs of all. Here young people get to know and respect representatives of other social groups. Here comradeship reigns between the law student and the unskilled worker. Here is the foundation for the self-evident common destiny of German Volk comrades. Their entire lives are to be ruled by the great principle underlying the new Reich: service before self. And that is comradeship."[74] Virtues such as physical fitness, participation in paramilitary drills, punctuality, orderliness, cleanliness, reliability, and love of the homeland were also held up in glowing terms as sure to result from the common experience of manual labor.[75]

These evocations of comradeship between the student and the worker often played upon the crudest anti-intellectual resentments imaginable. In tones recalling Walter Flex and some of the right-wing work-student novels and autobiographies, these propagandists held up their Labor Service as a badly needed means for curing students and other intellectuals of the bad habit of thinking and criticizing. Along these lines, for example, Hierl proclaimed: "We want to extinguish all arrogant disdain for manual and agricultural labor. We want to eradicate class arrogance and class hatred. For this reason, students should serve the Volk in a comradely work community together with young factory workers and farm hands. . . . By this means the Labor Service will become the irreplaceable school for creating a new kind of German worker and a model socialism."[76] Such a programmatic statement appears almost harmless, however, compared to others in which the propagandists could hardly contain their glee over the fact that formerly coddled weaklings were now going to be put to hard labor. Statements by Will Decker, the inspector for education and training of the Reich Labor Service, may stand for many others. In his *Wille und Werk: Ein Tatsachenbericht von der Schöpferkraft des nationalsozialistischen Arbeitsdienstes* (Will and Work: A Factual Report on the Creative Power of the National Socialist Labor Service, 1935), for example, Decker praised the "shovel" as the "schoolmaster of this generation" and pronounced construction work an "acid test for weak stay-at-homes and relativizing aesthetes, and, to tell the truth, a necessary blessing for many young people who have no idea what real work is."[77] While to be sure, many of the disciplinary goals being advocated by Decker and others had also been voiced earlier by other groups in the Weimar period, the specifically National Socialist elements here were the intensification of militarized structures, the claim to total control over the individual, and most especially, the standpoint that only those with a certain inherent, "racial" predisposition had what it took to become true comrades in labor within the national community. Consequently, in his evaluation from 1935 of the effects of the six-month Labor Service on prospective university students, one Nazi writer characterized the goal of education as carried out by the Labor Service, the schools, and the military as that of "selection and eradication."[78]

ERNST JÜNGER AND MARTIN HEIDEGGER

On the right during the final crisis years of the Weimar Republic and on into the Third Reich, proponents of a compulsory labor service were to be found not only in the ranks of the crudest political ideologues, but also in circles with intellectual pretensions as well as among holders of the loftiest positions at German universities. In this connection, the voices of Ernst Jünger and Martin Heidegger were especially prominent. For both, the idea of a compulsory labor service was central, being essential both to Jünger's abstract utopian projections and also to Heidegger's political texts from the early 1930s. Although both men tried to stylize their concepts of work and the worker and of service to the state, the nation, and the Volk as

philosophical expressions of a unified order or of unwavering Resolve—
realms they considered far above the everyday life of the masses—the
location of their writings from this period along the political spectrum may
be pinned down by focusing on their statements about labor service, and
specifically, about what it would mean for intellectuals to become workers.
In his book *Der Arbeiter* (The Worker, 1932), Jünger was concerned
with formulating the characteristics of the "Worker" as an ideal typological
model, a gestalt, and had little interest in concrete "economic questions" or
in measures to ameliorate the dismal situation of the unemployed, which he
viewed as merely secondary to his visions of a thoroughly technologized
world order.[79] However, at the end of his three-hundred-page "essay,"
Jünger picked up on the contemporary experiments with voluntary labor
service and on right-wing calls for making it compulsory. Taking this
program as his own, he concluded by attaching the highest importance
to this institution in his schemes for the future, calling it "the clearest
expression of the new relationship of the type and its forms to the state."[80]

What fascinated Jünger about plans for a compulsory labor service
was the hope so often voiced by its most authoritarian, right-wing advocates: that a compulsory military service directed toward the total mobilization of war could be replaced by the total mobilization of labor on an
even grander scale.[81] Furthermore, since Jünger imagined that this general
labor service would encompass the entire population, rather than only men
capable of bearing arms, he viewed it as the most effective means possible
of enforcing "unified discipline," of making visible "work as power"—in
short, of intensifying the "racial molding of the population" along the lines
of the ideal type. Most specifically, he gloated, "intellectuals" would be
cured of their "silly arrogance," which had led them to view manual labor
as a pitiable condition. By being forced into labor service, he proposed,
they would have to learn that "every chore, even shoveling manure out of
horse stalls, is of high standing, as long as it is not felt to be abstract labor
but is carried out within a great and meaningful order" (319). The effect
of performing manual labor, then, was to be the more complete subjection
of free-floating intellectuals, who might still be captivated by outmoded
ideas of democracy and freedom, to an unbroken chain of command and
obedience in a new world order dominated by avant-garde technology and
increasingly violent, mechanized catastrophes and chaos. Although Jünger
did not associate this "order" with any particular political movement and
maintained his elitist " 'pathos of distance' towards all parties,"[82] his emphasis here on the disciplinary effect of unskilled manual labor was a familiar
element in the plans of right-wing circles that were finally institutionalized
in the labor service of the NSDAP. It was predictable, then, that Jünger
hesitated to reissue *Der Arbeiter* after the end of the war. However, he was

finally persuaded to include it in his collected works, published in 1960, by none other than Martin Heidegger.[83]

If Jünger had been intent in his essay on spinning out grandiose, abstract, aestheticized visions with relatively little attention to their concrete political and economic consequences, Martin Heidegger set out in 1933–1934, the year of his rectorship at Freiburg University, to intervene with a heavy hand in the reorganization of the German educational system under National Socialism. And in his lectures and political speeches from that year, he attached the highest significance to the new National Socialist Labor Service, specifically, to the educational value and philosophical implications of compelling students to perform unskilled manual labor. Heidegger made a point of joining the NSDAP on May 1, 1933, the day Hitler proclaimed his intention of leading German men from all social classes to the "honorable" experience of manual labor. Immediately, the newly elected rector began to outline his concepts of the revolutionary national community and to devalue in the most decisive terms the university's claims to educational exclusivity. In a speech delivered on May 26, 1933, the day before he formally assumed the rectorship, Heidegger laid out the ideological direction he intended to promote for German students and intellectuals. This speech was a commemoration of the tenth anniversary of the death of Albert Schlageter, a former student from Freiburg University who had been shot for committing acts of sabotage against the French occupation army in the Ruhr. Portraying Schlageter to his university audience here as a heroic model and martyr, Heidegger described him in tones of pathos: "Schlageter walked these grounds as a student. But Freiburg could not hold him for long. He *was compelled* to go to the Baltic; he *was compelled* to go to Upper Silesia; he *was compelled* to go to the Ruhr."

Holding up as an ideal the student who left the university to become a Freikorps soldier and fighter, and whose "hardness of will" led him to die the "*greatest* death of all,"[84] Heidegger expanded on these ideas the next day, May 27, in his notorious inaugural lecture as rector entitled "Die Selbstbehauptung der deutschen Universität" (The Self-Assertion of the German University). Here he outlined his concept of the "three bonds" and the "three services," which he presented as equally important and valuable to German students and intellectuals. These were the bond to the *Volksgemeinschaft* through labor service, the bond to the honor and fate of the nation through military service, and the bond to the intellectual mission of the German Volk through service in knowledge.[85] Significantly, "service in knowledge" brought up the rear in this list, and in subsequent lectures and speeches delivered during the following year, Heidegger continued to expand on his hopes that in the new National Socialist university, German students would now "no longer study in the traditional way" but would become resolute fighters and workers.[86] In these political texts with titles such as "Labor Service and the University" (June 20, 1933), "The University in the New Reich" (June 30, 1933), "The German Student as Worker" (November 25, 1933), and "The Call to the Labor Service" (January 23, 1934), Heidegger emphasized repeatedly that schools and universities, with their outmoded concepts of academic freedom, could no longer claim an exclusive right to educate young Germans. Rather, he proclaimed the National Socialist Labor Service to be a "new and decisive force for education," especially in the form of "work camps," as "institutions for the direct revelation of the *Volksgemeinschaft*."[87]

In spite of his flirtations with some of the outward trappings of the youth movement (as when he delivered his inaugural lecture wearing a loose-fitting shirt and hiking shorts),[88] Heidegger took care to distance himself from the more cooperative and democratic approaches characteristic of some of the earlier work camps associated with this movement. Along these lines, he stated that "true comradeship . . . has nothing to do with the effusive exchange of psychological inhibitions by individuals who have agreed to sleep, eat, and sing under one roof."[89] Rather, speaking as rector and as Germany's most prominent philosopher, he formulated the educational goals of the Labor Service as follows:

> Such service provides the basic experience of hardness, of closeness to the soil and to the implements of labor, of the rigorous law that governs the simplest physical—and thus essential—labor in a group. Such service provides the basic experience of daily existence in a camp community, an existence strictly ordered according to the requirements of the tasks that the group has undertaken. Such service provides the basic experience of having put daily to the test, and thus clarified and reinforced, one's sense of social origin and of the responsibility that derives for the individual from the fact that all belong together in an ethnic-cultural [volkhaft] unity.[90]

In his speeches, Heidegger emphasized that by carrying out unskilled manual labor in a group and by participating in "martial sports," students would learn from the "hardness of existence" rather than from mere books and lectures.[91] Exactly what they were to learn remained undefined: the goals were to exercise inexorable resolve and will in the face of the "unknown" and to internalize the knowledge of being rooted in the Volk. Along these same lines, Heidegger also set out to attack scholarship that had become "aimless" and had lost its connection to the "whole" by having neglected "its rootedness in the Volk and its bond to the State."[92] It is easy enough here to draw a line from such statements back to those by the more idealistic right-wing work students of the early Weimar years, with their pseudo-Nietzschean dreams of learning from "life" rather than merely from dusty books, and their fantasies of breaking down class barriers through shared manual labor in the service of rebuilding the German nation.[93] Lecturing and writing in 1933 and 1934, however, Heidegger both used a more extreme vocabulary of struggle for ruthless self-assertion and domination, and also tried to raise mundane concerns of everyday existence to the loftiest and most abstract philosophical levels. And he did this in such a manner that, according to Karl Löwith, those who listened to his speeches from this period were "in doubt as to whether [they] should start reading the pre-Socratics or enlist in the SA."[94]

If Heidegger thus imagined that by performing unskilled manual labor, German students would become a "hard race" of "leaders" whereby the weak ones would lie where they fell,[95] he took another tack when addressing workers, as he did on January 22, 1934, in an address at Freiburg University to six hundred of the unemployed who had received jobs within the framework of the Labor Service program.[96] Here, Heidegger emphasized that German students, as "younger comrades" from the university, were ready to help workers acquire a firm knowledge of their place in the Volk. Attempting to speak with populistic appeal and play on any anti-intellectual resentments his audience may have had, Heidegger underscored the students' readiness to give up their formerly privileged positions for the sake of the *Volksgemeinschaft*, proclaiming that the new generation of National Socialist students

> stands ready, not as "intellectuals" ("Gschtudierten") from the class of your "betters," but as Volk comrades who have recognized their duty.
>
> They stand ready, not as the "educated" vis-à-vis a class—indeed, a "lower class"—of *uneducated* individuals, but as comrades. They are prepared to listen to your questions, your problems, your difficulties, and your doubts, to think through them with you, and, in shared effort, to bring them to a clear and decisive resolution.
>
> What, therefore, is the significance of the fact that you are assembled here in the auditorium of the University with us? This fact is a sign that a new, common will exists, the will to build a *living bridge* between the worker of the "hand" and the worker of the "head." Today the will to bridge this gap is no longer a project that is doomed to failure.[97]

In Heidegger's presentation here, "genuine" knowledge could be had by the "farmworker," the "manual laborer," and the "scholar" in their own fields of work. Thus, he could go so far as to claim that there was no need to "distinguish between the 'educated' and the 'uneducated.' " Rather, he defined "genuine knowledge" as meaning the following: "in our decisions and actions *to be up* to the task that is assigned us, whether this task be to till the soil or to fell a tree or to dig a ditch or to inquire into the laws of Nature or to illumine the fate-like force of History. Knowledge means: to be *master* of the situation into which we are placed." With the "help" of students and intellectuals, then, workers were to learn to be "clear and resolute Germans," "each in his respective class and work group," and to be content with realizing that their work was of "service to the Volk."[98]

It is most striking here that in speaking at the university to this audience of workers, who had undoubtedly been given typical Labor Service jobs of the most unskilled sort (digging ditches and shoveling manure, to draw on Heidegger's and Jünger's examples of uplifting work), Heidegger was not at all concerned with discussing questions of training and further qualification that might have enabled these workers to exercise more of their human, intellectual abilities. For this professor, the bridging of the gap between social classes was not to mean that workers would gain access to realms of learning and higher status formerly inaccessible to them, with the result that they might be able to lead fuller, more satisfying lives. Rather, contemptuous of efforts to envision paths to mere happiness, Heidegger invoked here the common, hard Resolve of intellectuals and workers faced with difficult tasks.[99] Thus, while he promoted the disciplinary value of unskilled manual labor for students who might tend to put on airs, he ultimately envisioned that they would return to the loftier realms of the mind which he had always inhabited and had no intention of leaving himself. And after having been "comrades" with workers for a short time (he avoided the more humanistic term "brothers"), these intellectuals would then proclaim the message to those down below that they should stay in their place. But this was a message that ultimately drew on the crudest, most populistic, anti-intellectual rhetoric imaginable and which thus allied itself with the most reactionary supporters of the National Socialist Labor Service.

NAZI PROPAGANDA AGAINST "CLASS ARROGANCE"

The imposing show put on by the Reich Labor Service at the Nuremberg Party Congress of the NSDAP in 1934, where fifty-two thousand of its members marched carrying their spades, dramatized the regressive notion of work being propagated here. With little concern for efficiency and productivity, masses of men from all social backgrounds were to be put to work at unskilled manual labor for a period of time before returning to their former places in the national community. In the scene of Leni Riefenstahl's film *Triumph des Willens* (Triumph of the Will, 1936), which shows these fifty-two thousand men marching and speaking in chorus before Hitler at this Party Congress, the artificial regimentation of this breaking down of class barriers comes through especially clearly. First, the lead speaker for the Labor Service calls out: "Comrade, where do you come from?" and men reply who are from all parts of Germany, and the Saarland, as well. His next question is: "Comrades, from what work do you come?" The answers resound: "From the anvil—loom—lecture hall—from the vise—from the plow." Continuing, the men vow to work for Germany "in the moors—in the marshes—in the sand" with their "hammers—axes—shovels—hoes—spades." Finally, they name the battlefields where their comrades fell in war, and swear that they will all work together, "the farmer's heir—the businessman's son—the worker's child."[100]

Strikingly, with the exception of the "lecture hall," all of the vocabulary here is drawn from pre-modern, pre-industrial forms of manual work, whether from skilled trades, unskilled labor, or rural life, and there are no allusions at all to modern industry or technology. This anti-modern, agrarian standpoint was usually able to carry the day in Nazi Party discussions and policy regarding the Labor Service during the 1930s. However, after the beginning of the war this was no longer the case. More and more women began to be placed in armaments factories rather than on farms in German settlements in the East.[101] And the men of the Labor Service were also put to work for the military, especially in anti-aircraft defense and in training recruits. In the closing phases of the war, the practical needs of a highly technologized and industrialized war effort took precedence for the most part over the ideologues' fixation on subjecting all "Germans" to pre-industrial ways of life and work. However, their goal of leveling out class differences through discipline and forced contact remained an important principle in the Labor Service.[102]

These disciplinary goals are illustrated particularly clearly in two propagandistic texts that may stand for many others by Nazi writers from the 1930s. In both of these examples, descents into the working world are reduced to their most primitive, hollow form, drained of any hints of actual receptivity to another social reality. The first, entitled *Schippen aufnehmen! Im Gleichschritt—marsch! Ein Roman vom Arbeitsdienst* (Shoulder Shovels! Forward, March! A Novel of the Labor Service, 1935), was written by Klaus Nebe, a twenty-year-old SS man from Erfurt. It may be taken as a typical example of novels by other Nazi writers that thematize the experience of unskilled, pre-industrial forms of labor.[103] Situated in a Labor Service camp, the novel describes the participants as coming from all social classes and political persuasions, ranging from unemployed workers

Lead speaker of the Nazi Labor Service in Leni Riefenstahl's *Triumph des Willens*.

to prospective university students and from Communists to Nazis. Early on, the young men talk with each other about why they joined the Labor Service. While the workers speak of unemployment and financial needs, one prospective student, called "the little doctor," explains that he and others of his social standing had different reasons:

> You worker comrades came because destiny forced you. Otherwise you would have sunk into misery. Bolshevism would have taken possession of most of you. But we came because we felt that we belonged in your midst before our studies, before our professional work. Because we knew that for the sake of the Volk community we would have to experience this camp community. An inner law commanded us to do this. And for this reason we came. And for this reason we want to work and learn with you.[104]

Impressed by these high-flown words, most of the working-class young men are ready to trust in the student's goodwill—with the exception of one named Rieß who is a Communist and, as it turns out, a saboteur. Nebe had this character voice objections that must have been in many people's minds at the time: that the Labor Service would never be able to narrow the gap between rich and poor, and that there was a great difference between having to work as a manual laborer all one's life and pretending to be a worker for a few months (13). These objections are then dismissed by the camp's commander, who urges his charges to emulate the comradely spirit of the front. In the course of the novel, almost all the young men become molded together into a unified community through their shared physical experiences of digging ditches, paramilitary training, and sports. Rieß, however, tries to build up a red cell within the camp to undermine the Labor Service. He is found out, runs away, and—in despair over his isolation—commits suicide. As a result, at the end all the other young men who might have held some Communist sympathies learn from this negative example and become committed Nazis under the leadership of their commander. The ideological direction of the novel is shown most crassly in the final ruminations of this severe, military man, who concludes that the young Communist died because of his inherent weakness: "He was broken by himself. He had to break, for this is the hard law of natural selection" (181).

As was characteristic of all such propaganda, from Goebbels's *Michael* to this SS writer's, every hint of the real relationships of power between social classes was countered with empty slogans, overwrought rhetoric, racialized attacks, and finally, threats of terror.[105] One of the clearest examples of these tactics can be found in Goebbels's campaign of 1937 against "class arrogance," in which a number of leading political and cultural officials were delegated to work for brief periods as manual laborers on a landed estate, at a shipyard, for the highway system, in a printing company, and in a tire and rubber factory.[106] This campaign may be described as Goebbels's effort to put the rantings of his *Michael* into practice, with the result that these descents into the working world were carried out in the crudest ways imaginable.[107] The most extensive account of this propaganda action is found in *Hilfsarbeiter Nr. 50 000* (Laborer No. 50,000, published in 1938), in which Reich Director of Radio Programming Eugen Hadamovsky depicted his stint as an unskilled laborer in a large tire and rubber factory in Hannover. Born in 1904, Hadamovsky was a member of the "Schwarze Reichswehr" (a Freikorps military unit) after World War I, and then spent several years abroad doing various kinds of work. In 1928 he returned to Berlin and joined the NSDAP in 1930. His career in broadcasting began the following year, when Goebbels made him the Nazis' district radio supervisor in Berlin. Immediately after Hitler took over the chancellorship, Hadamovsky organized his radio speeches so perfectly that Goebbels soon appointed him Reich Director of Radio Programming. As a ruthless careerist, he purged German radio of all elements "foreign to the Volk," with the goal of making it into what he called a "brown house of the German spirit."[108] He held his position until 1942, when Goebbels demoted him. Shortly thereafter, Hadamovsky volunteered as an officer for the eastern front and died as a tank commander there in 1944.[109]

At the beginning of his *Hilfsarbeiter Nr. 50 000,* Hadamovsky describes his process of getting a job in the Hannover factory. Simply calling up the personnel office, he told the director who he was, that he was acting on Goebbels's instructions, and that he wanted a job in the dustiest part of the factory. "I want to go into the factory as a worker," he demanded, "and I want to be hired and treated just like every other worker" (24). Rejecting the director's more than understandable offers of preferential treatment, Hadamovsky began work right away in the division of the factory where sheets of rubber were produced. Obviously, he did not plan to keep his true identity hidden. Therefore, when one worker recognized him right away, he made no effort to deny who he was, and soon the workforce of the entire factory knew he was there. Hadamovsky intended to use his entry into the working world as a way to assert that leaders and led should join together as one Volk striving for world domination. Consequently, the book says almost nothing of any substance about his actual experiences as a manual laborer. Rather, it devotes quite a bit of space to crude, violent, anti-Semitic pronouncements on international affairs (e.g., the Spanish

Civil War) and domestic policies (e.g., advocating the Nazis' involuntary sterilization program).

When Hadamovsky turned his attention to the factory itself, it was mainly to defuse possible points of criticism or to conjure up in frantic, empty phrases the supposed "togetherness" between himself and the permanent workers. With respect to the first intention, he did in fact mention occasionally the dangerous, unhealthy working conditions that prevailed in the factory. However, he always presented these as improvements over the supposedly still worse conditions before 1933. Or, he maintained casually that the workers were such tough men that they were inured to injuries such as burns and cuts. In other words, as in Goebbels's *Michael*, Hadamovsky called for a unified posture of invulnerable male strength rather than the improvement of working conditions. With respect to the "comradeship" that he claimed to have found in the factory, he put the lesson he wanted to teach into the mouth of a worker who says, in an attempt at folksy dialect: "That a guy comes into th' factory from a position like that and works with us makin' rubber—that couldn't have happened before. That'll convince everybody that you guys really mean well" (69). But the arrogant distance which in fact remained between this high Nazi official and these workers comes out unwittingly in a passage where Hadamovsky asserted most insistently that he was exactly like them after a hard day's work. Here he claimed: "I'm no different from them now. My blue work uniform is covered with dust, and my face is dirty. I've only been able to get my oil-smeared hands half-clean at the sink in the canteen" (38). The fact that his similarity is only that of outward physical appearance is so blatantly obvious that it can only be upheld in the text by a constant flood of empty slogans. Consequently, upon returning to Berlin at the end of his stint in the factory, Hadamovsky gives a closing speech to his assembled "workmates" in which he leaves them with the following message to absorb, having made it abundantly clear that any recalcitrance would be crushed with terror: "And so we all want to remain good comrades in the future. We are labor comrades in the giant work called 'Germany' which the Führer has put into operation again. And in it, he himself is the first worker, and we are all his comrades in work!" (233). In spite of all statements about overcoming "class arrogance," then, Hadamovsky ultimately upheld the old distinction between mental and manual labor. In his vocabulary, the work of the leaders was to think and command, while the led were to furnish unquestioningly the requisite labor power. In the final analysis, this Nazi journey to the working world simply disregarded all power imbalances and ideological differences between above and below, blocking out all images of workers as thinking, independent human beings.

"Those in the Darkness No One Sees": Karl Grünberg and Bertolt Brecht

For some are in the darkness
And others are in the light
And one sees those in the light
Those in the darkness no one sees.

—Bertolt Brecht[110]

It was precisely the glorification of unskilled manual labor as a means for social leveling that opponents of a national labor service criticized vehemently until their voices were suppressed in 1933. Although some sectors of Social Democracy and the trade unions were suspicious of calls for a labor service, the most sustained, significant opposition came from the Communist Party (KPD) and its youth organizations.[111] Throughout the 1920s, the KPD sought to expose plans for a labor service as covert preparations for war. Toward the end of the Weimar Republic, this party also denounced the Voluntary Labor Service as an initial step in alienating workers from their own organizations and forcing lower wages and militarization. Rejecting schemes to create what they saw as a giant "workhouse," the Communist Youth called for concrete measures to reduce unemployment, emphasizing the need for protective measures and especially for better training and qualification possibilities for workers. In short, these leftists distinguished sharply between what they termed the "capitalist compulsion to work" and the "socialist obligation to work."[112] Consequently, their concrete goal was not to subject young people to militarized manual labor, but rather to create possibilities for young workers to exercise more of their physical *and* intellectual abilities within the realities of the modern workplace. Along these same lines, for example, in 1932 the Federation of Building Trades issued the following statement, which ridiculed the idea that unskilled construction labor had any redeeming moral or pedagogical value:

> The only person who can ascribe great educational value to such work is someone who knows about it from mere hearsay. If one stands for months in the mud, rain, and snow, shoveling dirt into trucks with aching limbs, one learns to experience work *only* as an ordeal. The people who are so enthusiastic about the educational value of digging in the dirt should see how eagerly these workers long for the liberating whistle which signals quitting time. Hard, monotonous work with pick and shovel is the least suited thing for creating more enthusiasm for labor in the young worker. And it certainly has no positive effect on people who have already lost all their initiative to work.[113]

Or, as the educator Eugen Rosenstock wrote in 1931, "The German soldier of the labor service, standing at attention with his shovel, is a mindless image."[114]

During the Weimar Republic, writers on the left were generally suspicious of vague calls for class reconciliation emanating from "above" that emphasized goodwill rather than redistribution of wealth and property. A drama such as Bertolt Brecht's *Die heilige Johanna der Schlachthöfe* (Saint Joan of the Stockyards, 1932), for example, is an explicit critique of attempts to "mediate" between irreconcilable class interests. Here, the naive Johanna descends three times into the "depths" and finally betrays the workers' cause, realizing only too late the damaging consequences of her actions.[115] More specifically, writers on the left also rejected efforts to impose the leveling discipline of manual labor across social classes, and so they devoted little attention to the theme of the working student.[116] However, there is at least one novel by a Communist writer, Karl Grünberg's *Brennende Ruhr* (Burning Ruhr, 1928), in which a student who desires to enter the working world is central to the plot. Set at the time of the Kapp Putsch in 1920, this novel recounts the involvement of a student in the struggles of revolutionary workers. However, in contrast to the work students' autobiographical statements and the right-wing novels discussed above, Grünberg imagined a character from above who decides to relinquish his own privileged position after experiencing another social reality in the world below.

Born in 1891 in Berlin, Karl Grünberg was the son of a shoemaker who was a Social Democrat. In 1911 he also joined the Social Democratic Party (SPD), and during the war he fought on the eastern front, where he helped organize revolutionary soldiers' councils in 1918. In 1920 he led a workers' battalion against the forces of the Kapp Putsch in Berlin, and he joined the Communist Party in that same year. During the rest of the Weimar Republic, he was a journalist for the Communist press, helped train worker correspondents, and co-founded the League of Proletarian-Revolutionary Writers in 1928. Arrested and imprisoned in 1933 for illegal activities against the Nazis, he worked in chemistry laboratories after 1936 under constant Gestapo surveillance and as a fireman in Essen and Berlin from 1943 to 1945. Choosing the socialist East after the end of the war, he served as a district court judge in Berlin-Pankow in 1945 and then lived as a writer in the German Democratic Republic until his death in 1972.[117]

As Grünberg's novel begins, chemistry student Ernst Sukrow is traveling by train from Berlin to the Ruhr in hopes of finding a job as a mineworker. His path to this point led through officer training in the war, demotion in rank for challenging an arrogant superior, a stint in a Freikorps fighting against the Spartacists, and a failed effort to continue his studies in spite of the sudden poverty of his family. Forced by financial need to go to work, and having heard that more mineworkers are needed for rebuilding Germany's industry, Sukrow is determined to contribute to the effort of reconstruction. In the train compartment where he is riding, another passenger immediately challenges his views in a discussion about the miners' demands for a seven-hour working day. This is Ruckers, the head of the works committee at one of the mines, who points out Sukrow's ignorance of actual working conditions in the following exchange:

> "Young man, just try working at the coal face! Half naked, covered with sweat, splashed with water, lying on your stomach, half blind with coal dust, at burning hot temperatures, in the flickering lamplight! Just one day, and then you should say whether seven hours are too much or too little."
>
> "Yes indeed, I'm going to do that," Sukrow answered with a certain pride. "Of course I'm a student and not a worker by trade, but I'm not afraid of any kind of work. And it's mining that I want to experience, since there's a shortage of miners. Of course I know that it's no child's play. Last summer I helped with the harvest for four weeks. That's not easy, either, to keep going in the hot fields from four in the morning till eight in the evening. I'm telling you the truth!"[118]

Impressed by Sukrow's intentions, Ruckers takes the student home with him and offers to do what he can to help him find a job. However, as Ruckers predicts, there are no vacancies for unskilled mineworkers, and Sukrow finally has to settle for a job unloading scrap metal in a steel factory. The description here of this work reflects themes commonly found in the work-student autobiographies—Sukrow's efforts not to show any weakness, his dislike of the cramped, dirty hostel where he has to live, and his humiliating sense of being nothing but a tiny cog in an enormous machine of production. However, things soon take a turn for the better when the factory director offers him a position in the chemistry laboratory, and Sukrow is only too glad to accept.

At this point, however, Grünberg imagined a possibility for his character's development that diverges sharply from the plots of right-wing work-student novels. Looking out from the warmth of his beloved laboratory into the cold, snowy factory landscape, Sukrow cannot forget either the conversations he had with Ruckers about economic relations or the contact he had briefly with his workmates. As a result, when reports of the Kapp Putsch begin to circulate, Sukrow refuses to join the "citizens' militia" being organized by management to keep the striking workers under control. Rather, he leaves his comfortable job and returns to Ruckers and the other strikers, saying that he has learned from his experiences and that he knows he wants to be on their side now. His decision meets with approval from Ruckers's daughter, who tells him: "I like you better like this than if you wanted to dig coal for the moneybags' republic" (193). Upon Ruckers's recommendation, the other workers even make Sukrow commander of one of their battalions because of his experience leading troops during the war. However, after the armed workers are defeated and many of their leaders—including Ruckers—summarily executed, Sukrow withdraws from politics and goes back to work as a chemist. In a final conversation with one of the workers who was his comrade during the fighting, he vents his doubts that the masses can ever become enlightened enough to act in unified fashion for their own interests. His working-class counterpart, on the other hand, is not so defeatist, and expresses hope for the future in the novel's concluding passage.

In significant respects, this novel differs from those by right-wing writers that focused on working students, particularly with regard to its perspective on manual labor. Most importantly, there is no glorification here in any way of demanding physical work as a testing ground for anything like toughness, determination, will, or manliness, or as a means for breaking down class barriers in order to serve the national community. Although Sukrow intends at first to become a mineworker, he does not even succeed in entering into the mine, and the work he does perform is depicted as onerous, unhealthy, and dangerous. However, he is portrayed as receptive enough to the new experience of this different, unpleasant social reality that he is transformed, at least to a certain extent. Unlike other characters in the novel from his class of origin who brush aside their knowledge of the poverty and oppression around them, Sukrow acts on his new insights. He joins the revolutionary workers in what could be termed an authentic breaking down of class barriers—authentic because it is based on more knowledge and less self-delusion. And since his development is depicted as arising out of his experiences, it seems generally believable rather than mere ideology.

Yet considering that Sukrow is willing to lay down his life for the workers' cause, his total withdrawal from politics appears all the more sudden and unmotivated at the end. Here, after having given a rather complex portrayal of the working-class milieu, of Sukrow's hesitant development, and of the striking workers with their strengths and heroism but also with their confusion and discord, Grünberg fell back into the cliché of viewing political standpoints as determined largely by social origin. This sort of schematized thinking is the novel's major weakness, and it frequently enters into the contrasts drawn between positive proletarian figures and the opportunistic, evil forces opposing them.[119] However, in spite of these flaws, this novel is still significant for its attempt to envision an alternative to right-wing views of manual labor, which sought to blur consciousness of its unequal distribution in society as well as to promote its supposedly disciplinary effects. Here, the work-student character neither remains a strong-muscled worker for good nor returns to his privileged position with a strengthened hand over his subordinates. Rather, he is still undecided in the end as to where he stands, while other characters are continuing to work toward the kind of social change that would be necessary to reduce backbreaking manual labor so that those who perform it would have greater chances for developing their human capabilities.

After 1933, it was possible only from a position of exile for voices to be raised that cut through the ideological fog of class reconciliation promoted by the National Socialists, as Bertolt Brecht did in *Furcht und Elend des Dritten Reiches* (Fear and Misery of the Third Reich). This play was written between 1935 and 1939 and premiered in part in Paris in 1937, the same year Goebbels mounted his campaign against "class arrogance." In the incisive scene entitled "Labor Service," Brecht set out to unmask the Nazis' rhetoric about overcoming class differences in the service of the national community. He did this by uncovering the hidden class tensions and conflicts that still simmered underneath all surface appearances of uniformity and all propagandistic assertions of common interests. Accordingly, the theme of learning and knowledge is central to the scene and to the relationships among the three characters who appear in it. First, a young worker and a student appear who are shoveling dirt together in a Labor Service squad. The two have made a deal whereby the worker only breaks up a small amount of dirt for the weaker student to shovel. In return, the wealthier student gives the worker cigarettes. Next, the squad leader appears, watches the two men shoveling, and proclaims, "In his work camps the Führer wishes there to be no differences. It doesn't matter there what your papa is."[120] The student pretends to agree. But after the squad leader leaves, he accuses the worker of breaking up more dirt than he could shovel, and he threatens to find a more compliant partner to supply with cigarettes.

The secret deal that the student and the young worker strike revolves around the continued existence of class differences. In the presence of terroristic authority in the person of the squad leader, the student disavows any kind of "class arrogance." However, left to himself, he reasserts his accustomed methods of class control and domination. Thus, the figure of the student who becomes a worker here is not a hard, decisive Schlageter or Michael type, but rather a weak young man. To be sure, he has been forced into an unpleasant situation, but he is shown as dealing with it by being conniving, authoritarian, cruel, and impervious to the reality around him. Cutting through the Nazis' slogans about labor service as the "school of the nation," the young worker is depicted as understanding his situation quite well. He has no need to learn discipline through manual labor, since this is what he has already been doing all his life. On the contrary, the knowledge he desires is that of how it would feel not to be the one always kept down on the bottom, but to earn higher wages and thus, implicitly, to have more opportunities in life. Most importantly, he is not presented as a heroicized, mindless figure, but as a poor man who is conscious of his situation. That is, Brecht insisted on bringing out the linkage between the world of manual labor and the world of oppression and impoverishment—a connection that all right-wing writers and propagandists generally distorted or concealed. Lines from the concluding song that Brecht wrote for the *Dreigroschenfilm* (Three-Penny Film) in 1930 come to mind: "For some are in the darkness / And others are in the light / And one sees those in the light / Those in the darkness no one sees."[121] The young worker, and also the contemporary audience of the play, is thus left with what was the most pressing task of the day: to imagine and create working-class solidarity in the face of the darkness of fascism.

3

Social Reporters
Enter the Working World:
Three Lives, Three Journeys

Although right-wing glorifications of physical labor and terroristic efforts to employ it as a disciplinary tool gained the upper hand in Germany in 1933, writers who continued the tradition of literary reportage had undertaken very different kinds of journeys to the working world during the Weimar Republic. These writers sought to travel across class boundaries in ways that did not simply reassert old forms of domination or invent new strategies of repression, and after 1933 they were forced to undertake other journeys—this time involuntary—into the obscurity of "inner emigration" or into exile. They were determined to keep their focus on real relationships of power between social classes—that is, on the oppressive consequences of the division of labor, on constellations of disadvantage and privilege, on poverty in the world down below. But this meant that there was no place for them in the Nazis' "national racial community," which promoted the ideology of class reconciliation and suppressed brutally all challenges to it.

During the Weimar Republic, literary reportage came into its own as a socially critical genre to which writers and journalists from many points along the political spectrum turned in order to attack injustices and advance their respective causes. Indeed, as one literary historian has pointed out, it is difficult to name many authors from this period who did not write reportages at some point.[1] On the one hand, the dominant cultural trend of "New Objectivity" during the period of relative stabilization in the middle years of the Weimar period favored the explosion of reportage as a genre that promised unbiased perspectives and reliable facts.[2] However, with respect to portrayals of the world of work, such a claim to be free of any kind of political tendentiousness often fed into a fascination with technology and a glorification of the machine-world that lost sight of working people and socioeconomic class relationships.[3] On the other hand, numerous writers from the left zeroed in on precisely these sides of life in their reportages, viewing them as the defining subject matter of the genre in a manner that Egon Erwin Kisch expressed later, in 1935: "To write reportage means to make visible different ways of work and life, and in our times these are often austere, gray models."[4] In their exposés about exploitation and social injustices in Germany, their investigations of the undersides of life in the United States, and their enthusiastic reports about the transformations under way in the Soviet Union, a wide range of writers focused their attention on national and international class conflicts. These included not only well-known authors such as Ernst Toller and the writer who was most influential in establishing literary reportage as an independent genre, Egon Erwin Kisch, but also many lesser-known writers. Of these, the ones who were active in the worker-correspondents' movement often remained in obscurity, while those who participated in the League of Proletarian-Revolutionary Writers (BPRS) with its series of "Red One-Mark" reportage novels found individual places in the history of socialist literature.

For the most part, except for Kisch's earliest role-playing reportages in which he investigated the "night side" of life in the Prague area,[5] these observers of life in the social abyss did not actually set out to perform manual labor themselves as a way to gain more authentic insights or to ferret out hidden information. There certainly must have been many reasons for the lack of importance attached to actual experience in this regard—not the least of which could have been simply individual proclivities for particular methods of fact-finding. However, a more central reason was surely the fact that it was hardly the goal of any of the leftist parties and workers' organizations at this time to encourage their allies among the intelligentsia and the upper and middle classes to go "into production." Rather, their long-term goal was to reduce mindless, demeaning labor as a whole as much as possible so that workers would have more opportunities to develop all their human abilities, and to incorporate—often under tension and with sharp disagreements—the efforts of sympathizing intellectuals in their own spheres of activity to ally themselves with these struggles. On the one hand, beginning plans in the Soviet Union to distribute manual labor more equally throughout society—by compulsion if necessary—could not possibly have functioned as models in the capitalist countries. On the other, as discussed in Chapter 2, in the particular German situation, the idea of subjecting the entire population to the discipline and leveling forces of manual labor was generally looked upon as the province of right-wing ideology. Consequently, because of this political climate, there would appear to have been little cause for leftist authors to believe that they needed to enter into the working world as participants in order to write about it and expose the conflicts and injustices they found there.

Nevertheless, even during this period there were still a few writers and journalists on the left who came from the upper or middle classes and who entered into the world of manual labor and poverty themselves—for the most part, individuals with quite unusual life stories. Three such biographies provide especially vivid illustrations of the dilemmas and entanglements that such writers confronted when they became workers for a time, as well as of the paths to liberation that they envisioned both for themselves and their workmates. And perhaps not by accident, these life stories are of writers who were all émigrés in various ways for most of their lives and who were deeply involved in exploring and interpreting cultures that were to a greater or lesser extent foreign to them. Count Alexander von Stenbock-Fermor came from Livonia to the Ruhr coal mines as a right-wing work student and reported later on proletarian life as a member of the BPRS. He stayed in Germany during the Nazi period, surviving by living in obscurity. Maria Leitner fled to Germany after the failure of revolution in Hungary and then traveled through the United States, taking a variety of unskilled and low-level jobs and reporting back to the German press about the undersides of modern life in the New World. She died in exile in France sometime around 1941. And Lili Körber, who had grown up in Moscow and moved to Vienna at the end of World War I, returned to the Soviet Union to work in a factory there and write for a German reading public about the socialist transformations she witnessed. She went into exile in New York and never returned to Europe. Perhaps it was due in part to the disruption and upheavals of their own lives that these writers concentrated with such tenacity and determination on searching for signs of hope in unfamiliar places, and on shattering false evocations of social harmony in their investigation of the clashing worlds that surrounded them.

Count Alexander von Stenbock-Fermor:
My Experiences as a Miner (1928)
and *Germany from Below* (1931)

> Here is a reactionary who has descended from above into the eternally subterranean world and carried out a more meaningful expedition of discovery than that into the silent polar zones.[6]

Born in 1902 in Livonia, Count Alexander von Stenbock-Fermor belonged to a family from the Russian high aristocracy that had close ties to

German culture. Devoted to the czar, his father was a Junker and an officer, and his mother had been a lady-in-waiting at the Russian court. It was only in hushed tones that Stenbock had heard these relatives speak of the black sheep of the family, his great-uncle, the anarchist Prince Peter Kropotkin. In his autobiography, *Der rote Graf* (The Red Count, 1973), Stenbock recalled his early years on the family estate at Nitau, not far from Riga, depicting himself as a doted-upon child who—after a period of boarding school in Jena—had returned home to live the life of a spoiled, wild young aristocrat.[7] Coming from a feudalistic family that viewed the separation of the estates as the natural order of things, Stenbock had nothing in his background that would have encouraged him to make any kind of contact with the poor rural population surrounding him beyond their function as his servants. Only through some frowned-upon reading of Dickens and Kropotkin did he begin to get an inkling of other worlds outside his own secure life, but these remained distant and foreign to him.

Closely attached to the "world of his father," Stenbock fought as a teenage volunteer on the side of the White Guards from 1918 to 1920 and then fled with his family to Berlin, as did thousands of anti-Bolshevik émigrés (RG 61). In his autobiography he described his fascination with the whirl of big-city life, but also his frustration with the milieu of displaced aristocrats to which he belonged, characterizing the atmosphere among them as one of emptiness, indifference, and purposelessness ("We woke up late in the day. We ate the noon meal in our dressing-gowns. Afterwards we lay down again" [RG 139]). The turning point that was to send him in a completely unanticipated direction, however, came when he complained about his sense of uselessness and disorientation to a woman who had been his private tutor in Berlin. He recalled her suggestion to him: "How would it be if I turned everything upside down and went to the workers? She suggested I might do this temporarily, perhaps as a miner. Even a year would mean a lot. She had former pupils who had worked for a time in the mines and who had learned a good bit. And, since I had once fought against a workers' army, she asked whether it wouldn't be appealing to me to get to know this 'threatening world down below' for myself" (RG 141). Shocked at first by such an idea, but needing to earn money and having little success with the engineering studies he had begun in the meantime, Stenbock decided to set out along this path into the world of work. He soon secured a job as an unskilled mineworker, a hauler, at the Thyssen works in Hamborn and worked there from November 1922 until December 1923, when inflation was at its height.

Although this year in the mine was certainly the turning point in his life, Stenbock did not undergo a sudden, precipitous metamorphosis, but rather went through a longer, more complex transformation. For the next several years he worked in bookstores in Hamburg and for Eugen Diederichs's publishing house in Jena. His first book, *Meine Erlebnisse als Bergarbeiter* (My Experiences as a Miner), appeared in 1928,[8] and after this he began to live as an independent author, recounting his experiences in the White Guards in his next book, *Freiwilliger Stenbock* (Volunteer Stenbock, 1929). Soon afterward, encouraged by his publisher to continue his factual, documentary writing, Stenbock made plans for a series of long reportages on Germany "from below," "from the middle," and "from above" (RG 280). In 1930, having also begun to read systematically about Marxism, he set off on a trip to Germany's poorest areas, where cottage industry was still widespread, and to the Ruhr district, where he visited his former workmates. He published his observations in the reportage *Deutschland von unten: Reise durch die proletarische Provinz* (Germany from Below: Journey through the Proletarian Provinces, 1931). By that year, Stenbock was openly proclaiming his Communist sympathies and had become a member of the BPRS. As the founder and spokesman of the defense committee for Richard Scheringer, an army officer charged with high treason after joining the Communist Party, Stenbock gave more than 150 speeches in 1932 warning against the dangers of fascism. At the same time, he cultivated close ties with National Bolshevists such as Ernst Niekisch.[9] When the Nazis came to power the following year, Stenbock's *Deutschland von unten* was immediately banned. Jailed for a few months in 1933 and stripped of his German citizenship, Stenbock decided upon being set free—according to his autobiography—that he would remain in Germany in order to try to be a part of the antifascist resistance there (RG 312). Living precariously as a stateless person during the twelve years of Nazi rule, Stenbock joined the Reichsschrifttumskammer,[10] published a few short pieces of fiction and reportage, lived from a succession of odd jobs, and had contacts with various resistance groups, including Beppo Römer's "Revolutionary Workers and Soldiers." After being drafted into the Wehrmacht in January 1945, Stenbock was immediately made mayor of Neustrelitz (near Berlin) by the Soviet occupation authorities at the end of the war. He put his journalism experience to good use once more in 1949, when he compiled and edited the memoirs of Harald Poelchau, the Berlin prison minister who accompanied about a thousand opponents of the Nazi regime to their executions.[11] After a short time as mayor, Stenbock moved to West Berlin and began to write filmscripts for Deutsche Film Aktiengesellschaft (DEFA) and for West German television, which he did for many years. He died in West Berlin in 1972.

When Stenbock's *Meine Erlebnisse als Bergarbeiter* appeared, it was immediately reviewed positively by Kurt Kläber in *Die Front*, a journal with close ties to the Communist Party and the BPRS. Kläber, who had been a

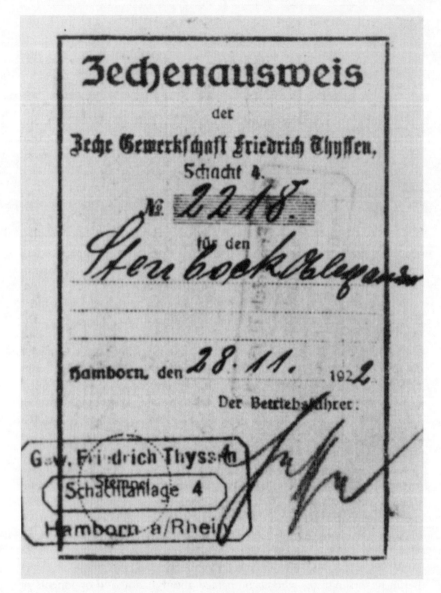

Identification card of the Thyssen firm for the miner Alexander von Stenbock-Fermor.
Alexander Graf von Stenbock-Fermor, *Der rote Graf: Autobiographie* (1973). Reprinted
with permission from Husum Druck- und Verlagsgesellschaft mbH & Co.

miner in the Ruhr area himself, began by placing Stenbock's report in the context of the work-student movement:

> In the fall of 1922 and the spring of 1923 a whole group of students arrived at our mine. They were called by the strange name of "work students." But they were there mainly because they did not have enough money to continue their studies, and mining seemed a good chance to keep their heads above water for a while. None of us was particularly happy to see them. And as it turned out, we miners weren't mistaken. They were usually in the bosses' good book; they got the cushy jobs; they were arrogant. And above all, with only a few exceptions, they became scabs when we went on strike, and they stabbed the miners in the back. But now, even though five years have passed, it turns out that one of these work students has deigned to write about his experiences with the miners. And astonishingly, his book is so vivid, exciting, straightforward, and truthful, that we can even make propaganda for it.[12]

Kläber went on to say that even though Stenbock was obviously a counterrevolutionary, he was still honest and factual enough in his observations that the book he produced irritated not only the "Baltic count's" natural allies on the right, such as the Stahlhelm, but also liberals and Social Democrats. That is, Stenbock's report about his year as a miner had turned out to be a "powerful indictment" of working and living conditions among the proletariat in the Ruhr area which—for the time being, at least—showed him as taking a political position that was very difficult to pin down.[13]

In certain ways, Stenbock's report actually fits quite well into the group of conservatively oriented, right-wing work-student texts. As in many of the work students' autobiographical statements discussed above, his beliefs in the values of his aristocratic heritage and in the traditional, organic separation of the estates seem to have been unaffected initially by his stint as a miner. Perhaps most noticeably, in reflective passages where Stenbock used metaphorical language to describe the world of manual labor that he had entered, he drew almost solely from a conservative, right-wing storehouse of images. In this vein, he characterized the working class as a whole most frequently as "soulless" and "dull"—describing these people almost as a class of subhumans, with no higher strivings. Furthermore, he depicted the overpowering, awesome industrial landscape he entered as a region of fascination and terror where, to his mind, workers could have no hopes for becoming anything but unthinking appendages of machines. A passage such as the following, for example, which gives his first impression of the mines, recalls the visual depiction of the workers' city far below the earth in *Metropolis:* "Day and night the cranks ram into humming generators; the flywheels and armatures rotate; the cylinders rumble; the immense mine cages roar down into limitless depths where they draw up coal from the dark night. Day and night men are hammering, shoveling, hacking, pulling, shoving, laboring deep underground. Without end! Only *one* God could rule here—the machine. . . . Whoever was born and spent his life here could become nothing but a slave of labor, a machine!" (ME 8).

In addition, whenever Stenbock indicated his intellectual interests at the time, these seemed quite predictable for someone of his background. Like Goebbels's Michael, who spends his time reading the Bible, *Faust,* and *Zarathustra* to balance out his hard physical labor, Stenbock wrote quite unselfconsciously about reading Spengler and Nietzsche at night in the hostel after a hard day's work in the mines and about rushing to see a performance of Goethe's *Urfaust* after completing his first shift. In his text, his interest in high culture serves mainly to support his claim to an elevated position in society, in contrast to his lowlier workmates.

Yet unlike many of those whose experiences of diminished social status made them more susceptible to right-wing ideology, Stenbock's exposure to the world of manual labor was the catalyst that led him to break away from his origins. His "experiences as a miner" hint at different processes of consciousness, a different kind of receptivity to this unaccustomed situation, and a different attitude toward physical labor than those that appear most often in the work students' statements compiled by the right-wing editors Johann Hermann Mitgau and Paul Rohrbach. Therefore, even though this book does not record the entire process of his transformation, it is still a valuable counterexample to the excursions into the working world by those who remained on the right. Ultimately, both the conservative work students' stories and other contemporary right-wing perceptions of the working world never moved beyond fantasizing about outright domination and subjugation. By contrast, the effects of Stenbock's reactionary theses and regressive images are undermined and countered to a large extent within his own report by the much longer sections where he turned his attention to the working world he actually experienced. Desiring, he wrote, to function in an "unprejudiced," "objective" way, like a "camera,"[14] he produced a text in which both unaccustomed experiences as well as points of view other than his own are allowed to emerge in ways that are not immediately dismissed or given ideologically negative labels. This achievement—surely the reason why a journal such as *Die Front* reviewed his book so positively—comes through most clearly in Stenbock's depiction of manual labor in the mine, in his characterization of the other miners, and in his report on a strike and a lockout that he went through together with his workmates.

With respect to Stenbock's depiction of the actual work he did in the mine, the most striking contrast to right-wing portrayals of such manual labor is that here—aside from stating occasionally his determination not to give up—there is absolutely no metaphorical heightening or he-man-like glorification of the experience of demanding physical work. On the contrary, in his descriptions of going down into the mine, of walking and crawling long distances through dark tunnels to get to his assigned jobs, and of shoveling debris and digging coal, Stenbock repeatedly emphasized the difficulties and dangers that he and the other miners constantly had to face. Highlighting his feelings of vulnerability and fear, he wrote about the ever-present threat of being injured or killed, describing accidents and deaths that were often due to lax safety precautions and regulations. The work itself held nothing romantic for him. Rather, like the other miners, he was glad when his shift was over and when he could recover from the tedious, backbreaking labor. In this regard, his text is similar to those shorter statements by other work students who simply wanted to do their job, make the best of an unpleasant situation, and leave this unpleasant world when their time was up.

In the sections of his reportage about his workmates, however, Stenbock let a unique kind of interaction shine through. Making no secret of his background, he was soon nicknamed the "White Guard" and the "Little Count" by the miners and was drawn immediately into debates with them over politics and economics (RG 161). The direct tone of these interchanges was struck right away on Stenbock's first day in the mine, when he reported the following conversation with Franz, a workmate who was showing him the ropes:

> "You must be from the university?" "Yes, I was a student."
> "Then this must leave a bitter taste in your mouth. We had another guy like you, a Baltic baron, a student, but he didn't last long."—"I'm from the Baltic, too."—"Another baron?"—"Yeah, sort of: a count!" Franz scratched his head: "Hell! Hell! You people are one hell of a riff-raff! Were you kicked out, too?"—"Yeah, our estate was expropriated and we had to flee."—"You got what you deserved, you damned dogs. You always drained the people dry, and so they threw you out!" (ME, 27–28)

The two men went on to argue over the legitimacy of private property, finding no points of agreement, and this was to be the pattern for most of the interactions Stenbock portrayed between himself and the left-leaning miners. Nevertheless, he always made a point of noting that he got along well with most of his workmates. He characterized his relationship with them as one of mutual respect based on the forthright expression of differences, which also contrasts with any kind of right-wing insistence on militaristic comradeship based on conformity.

Soon after beginning work, Stenbock had a dispute with the miners over whether a dictatorship of the proletariat was possible or desirable. Unable to contain himself, he had blurted out his own opinion: "I tell you, the dictatorship of a reactionary general like Ludendorff is ten times better than the rule of the proletariat, or of the street, which is the same thing!" (ME 71). Shocked by his own foolhardiness, he expected to be beaten up. However, the most vocal Communist, a miner named Heinrich, immediately turned the confrontation in an unexpected direction, saying to the assembled miners that they should learn a lesson from Stenbock's willingness to stand up for his beliefs. After this clash, Stenbock often spent time with Heinrich and was even invited by the miner to discussion evenings in his home, a "real Communist household" where a small, ideologically diverse group of workers gathered monthly (ME 103). In long passages recounting their debates, Stenbock presented his own convictions as one of several voices, frequently letting it show that he had no remedies for the political, social, and economic problems that were life-and-death matters for these workers. For Stenbock, the irreconcilable standpoints he heard here exposed separate worlds demarcated by unbridgeable gaps: "It seemed to me as if I had come from another planet and was confronted by people from an unknown, incomprehensible, utterly alien world" (ME 128). However, he did not respond in a manner typical of more dyed-in-the-wool reactionaries, who generally went on to demonize the efforts of workers attempting to act in their own interests through trade unions or leftist parties. Rather, he was flexible enough to let himself be impressed by the fact that these politically active workers were not only thinking of their more narrow personal interests, but also of working toward greater goals. In this vein, he described his feelings toward Heinrich, whom he later recalled as his "friend and teacher" (RG 469): "I felt a strong affection for this man, who was ready to make every sacrifice for his ideals—he dreamed of a communist world" (ME 72).

In contrast to the right-wing texts discussed in Chapter 2, this story of a sojourner in the world of work gave a completely different picture of the author's workmates. Rather than remarking pejoratively about trade unions and employing crudely negative stereotypes of Bolsheviks, Stenbock presented the politically active, leftist miners most positively, as the workers who were striving for a better life and who possessed a certain breadth of political and intellectual vision. Also in contrast to right-wing approaches, he did not attach any kind of importance to finding "father figures" among the workers to whom he could subordinate himself. And furthermore, he in no way held up workers who were betraying their class interests as figures worthy of emulation. Rather, he presented a panorama of this world below the earth's surface that brought out the variety in the miners' political standpoints—from the most committed Communists to those who were basically indifferent and only wanted to be left alone. Finally, Stenbock presented these differing attitudes toward politics as alternative strategies for dealing with the miners' real economic situation, which was at its most desperate in the year he worked in the mine. That is, he did not block out from his report the experiences of poverty and deprivation that were so central to the politics he discussed. From his own experience of living in a hostel for single workers, to his visits to his workmates' households, to his descriptions of street scenes in the area, Stenbock registered the misery of people living on the brink who were surviving only by performing the most difficult, arduous labor. And his willingness to see these things counteracted the tendencies he surely had from his conservative upbringing to view the solution to these grave problems as lying solely in individual effort and strength of will.

Stenbock's response to the conditions he encountered among the Ruhr miners comes through most clearly in the sections of his report about a strike and a lockout that occurred during his year in Hamborn. In the first instance, the miners began a strike in the summer of 1923 over the issue of higher wages. When Heinrich asks Stenbock what his position would be in this confrontation with the employers, he replies: " 'In this instance I'm entirely on your side. I know this strike is justified, and I won't work either, even if the chance were offered to me. Since you'll starve on these wages and can't get an agreement for higher ones, you have to help yourselves!' Heinrich shook my hand" (ME 87). After little more than a week, however, hunger had forced many of the miners to go back to work, and so the strike was called off—to the dismay of some of the more politically active miners who had been determined to hold out. In the second instance where the former member of the White Guards was forced to choose sides, the mine owners announced later in the year that the seven-hour workday—one of the miners' few gains immediately after the war—would be revoked, and that the eight-hour day would be reintroduced along with higher production quotas. When the miners refused to accept these changes in their working conditions, management responded by locking them out. Stenbock went through this period of forced unemployment with the other miners, a time he described as his most difficult experience of the year. With hardly any money and little food available, single men like Stenbock were badly enough off, but the full brunt of the hard times was borne by men with families. The men held out for six weeks this time, but hunger again forced them back into the mines, under the new conditions that had been announced earlier: the eight-hour day, higher production quotas, and lower wages. Stenbock described his reaction upon returning to work: "It was more than enough, and it already wore us out to work seven hours in the mine, in the hot air and coal dust. Every minute longer was too much of a strain. The additional hour that we had to work now was almost as hard as the other seven put together! I could understand completely why the miners insisted so tenaciously on their seven-hour shift!" (ME 195–96). Unlike his workmates, however, who had no alternative, Stenbock's year in the mine was over soon afterward, and with great relief tempered only slightly by regret, he was able to escape the realm of backbreaking labor for good.

Stenbock's ideological position during his year in the mines can be characterized as one of attempting to hold on to his conservative worldview while cultivating an attitude of "objectivity" and behaving in a decent and respectful way toward the miners who seemed to him to be from "another planet." Along these lines, he described the goal of his report in its preface as "to depict truthfully some brief scenes from this strange world which most people know so little about. My only goal is to tell the absolute truth. . . . If I should be successful at increasing understanding for the miners whose lives consist of hard labor and gloomy misery, I will have achieved what I intended with this book. For after all, it is only lack of understanding which separates human beings from each other" (ME 5). Stenbock was still attached to the belief in class reconciliation through goodwill and largesse coming down from above, though many of his experiences had pointed to the unlikelihood of such a process. However, unlike other conservatively oriented work students who turned their backs on the world below upon returning to their accustomed environment, Stenbock had received an indelible impression from his experiences in the world of work. In the next few years, while working in bookstores and for publishing houses and while writing his autobiographical report,[15] he "developed towards the left," as he put it (RG 224). He began to read Marxism systematically, met writers such as Ernst Toller and Arnold Zweig, and joined the BPRS.

By 1930, in the midst of deepening economic crisis, Stenbock set off to travel back into the world of work and to produce a different kind of text: this time not an autobiographical report, but a social reportage illustrated with shocking photographs of the most miserable living and working conditions he could find. In the preface to this book, *Deutschland von unten: Reise durch die proletarische Provinz* (1931), Stenbock drew on his own life experience to illustrate some of the ways in which perceptions of social reality were often colored by ideological presuppositions. He stated that in the journey he had just undertaken, the Germany he had seen was not that of lovely landscapes or high culture, but rather a world of extreme deprivation, hunger, and exploitation.[16] The focus of this reportage was characterized by Axel Eggebrecht in a newspaper review: "Within the proletariat there is a half-forgotten, more oppressed and unfortunate group in the provinces, the dregs who are living in pure hell. And it is from their perspective, that of the lowest of the low, that this book sees Germany."[17] In what Eggebrecht termed this "travel guide" through the most impoverished areas of Germany, Stenbock reported primarily on two groups. These were workers outside the large industrial centers, such as those in lumbering, rafting, and cottage industry, whose occupations were gradually being displaced and made obsolete; and Stenbock's former workmates in the Ruhr mines, whom he went back to visit. Through his acquaintance Siegfried Kracauer, Stenbock had contacted trade union representatives who guided him through unfamiliar areas, taking him into workplaces and homes (RG 284). From lumberjacks in Franconia, to weavers still sitting at their hand looms in Lower Silesia, to toymakers and miners in the Erzgebirge, to glassblowers, Christmas ornament makers, embroiderers, and basketmakers in Thuringia, Stenbock met workers everywhere who were living in the most abject circumstances. And, accumulating examples of increasing "misery, bitterness, and desperation," he no longer retreated from these impressions as he had in his first book to philosophize about supposedly natural, given class hierarchies (DVU 7). Rather, he took pains to bring out some of the causes of this social and economic misery—namely, foreign competition, industrial modernization, and economic rationalization, which were all integral to what he now termed the "inhuman capitalist system" with its exclusive emphasis on profit (DVU 96). Consequently, Stenbock's reportage showed the politically active and organized workers who were trying to change these conditions in the best light, as a glimmer of hope among the rest, who seemed for the most part to be isolated, passive, dull, and worn down by their circumstances.

In the concluding stage of his journey, Stenbock returned to Hamborn to visit his former workmates for the first time since he left them in 1923. Enthusiastically welcoming him, they told one story after another about their deteriorating situation, complaining of speedups, arbitrary regulations, and increasingly unsafe conditions. In this section of his reportage, however, Stenbock concentrated less on depicting proletarian life and more on recounting his own development and transformation. Discovering that his workmates had read his book about them with approval, he attended a political meeting during his visit where his old friend Heinrich asked him to relate his story and explain where he now stood. Thinking to himself,

"These people are your allies, your comrades, your brothers" (DVU 111), Stenbock described to the gathering of workers how his year in the mine had shocked him into rethinking his old beliefs. He announced that as an activist writer and journalist he was firmly on their side, among all those who were striving for justice (DVU 117). Fittingly, then, the final images in the reportage are not of isolated, remote areas, but of organized workers' demonstrations and resistance in Berlin, the great center of class struggle (DVU 159).

To be sure, Stenbock's choice to devote so much attention to groups of cottage workers who were practically unorganizable leads to a disjuncture in the text between the misery the reportage uncovered and the strategy for change that it suggested. However, in those politically explosive times, the book's rather unmediated ideology was not what mattered to its numerous reviewers. Rather, they zeroed in on Stenbock's uncovering of worlds that were often invisible, along with his blunt statement that the times were ripe for changing a social order that was increasingly incapable of providing for its members' basic needs (DVU 8). And they praised or condemned the book according to their attitudes toward such fundamental social transformation. In other words, Stenbock's development as a journalist and political activist in the years between the two texts discussed here can be characterized as a move from a stance of uncommitted "objectivity" typical of many writers during the middle phase of the Weimar Republic to the left-wing partisanship of social reportage that pushed its readers to take a stand.

Consequently, when Stenbock wrote of having a sense of "brotherhood" with those groups he met who were "on the bottom" in the closing years of the Weimar Republic, this connection differed in fundamental ways from right-wing evocations of "comradeship" within the national racial community. First, seen from the perspective of the formerly privileged outsider entering the working world, he had no tendencies at all to glorify mindless manual labor as an escape from the isolated world of the intellect and thus to uphold its supposedly populistic, disciplinary value. Rather, he emphasized the terrible ways in which this kind of work stunted human lives, and he showed his own dislike of it in a direct, authentic manner. Second, rather than upholding an ideal of militaristic comradeship that supported the most oppressive, unchanging class domination, Stenbock presented those workers most positively who were not totally beaten down by their circumstances, but who were intellectually alive and trying to take active steps to improve their situation. Of course, the directions they pursued grew out of life experiences that were different from his own. But unlike right-wing ideologues, he did not respond by immediately defaming political positions and strategies that challenged his initial convictions. In a nutshell, his experiences as a miner did not lead him to produce a novel like Goebbels's *Michael*, which blotted out the connection between the worlds of manual labor and oppressive poverty in favor of a grandiose, self-centered insistence on creating the national racial community. Rather, his last piece of writing in the final years of the Weimar Republic was a social reportage that emphasized class contradictions from the point of view of a critical writer who hoped to ally himself with the struggles of those on the bottom rungs of society's ladder. It is safe to assume that other work students developed similar sympathies from their experiences, though their stories have hardly been recorded. Furthermore, a related idea of community, which emphasized the effort to work toward common goals of liberation while recognizing and dealing openly with differences, surely existed in embryonic form in the work camps associated with the youth movement in the years when Stenbock was writing.[18] And in the broadest sense, Stenbock's development can be understood as symptomatic of the path taken by many writers sympathetic to social change who tried in the most various ways to associate themselves with working-class political movements during the Weimar Republic. Yet these advocates of emancipatory coalitions were not the voices that prevailed in 1933.

Maria Leitner: *A Woman*
Travels through the World (1932)

> We go to the factory together. Quick, the lunchbox. Then we leave. We are living in the slums. Our alley looks as if it were drunk, it winds over the hill so crookedly. It's endless. . . . Here live Spaniards, Germans, Hungarians, Creoles, Italians, Bohemians.
> —Maria Leitner[19]

While Stenbock was fighting in the White Guards toward the end of World War I, Maria Leitner was already on the opposing side, as a young Communist deeply involved in the struggle for a Hungarian Soviet Republic. Leitner was born on January 19, 1892, into a German-speaking, Jewish family in Varaždin (then part of Austro-Hungary, today in Croatia).[20] Her father was a small businessman who sold construction materials, and she had two brothers, Maximilian, an archaeologist who died in 1942 in the Soviet Union, and Johann, who died in 1925 in the United States. Her family moved to Budapest in 1896. Between 1910 and 1913 she studied abroad, apparently concentrating on art history and Sanskrit. From 1913 on she was a journalist in Budapest, and she was also a correspondent during World War I for left-radical newspapers in Stockholm. Toward the end of the war she became a co-founder of the Communist Youth League of Hungary and a member of the Communist Party of Hungary. After the fall of the Hungarian Soviet Republic in 1919, she and her brothers fled to Vienna, where she wrote for the publishing house of the Youth International. A group photograph in Willi Münzenberg's autobiography, *Die dritte Front* (The Third Front, 1931), shows Leitner seated among other youth delegates to the Second Congress of the Communist International in Moscow in 1920.[21] From 1921 to 1924 she lived in Berlin, where she put together her collection and translation of *Tibetanische Märchen* (Tibetan Fairy Tales, 1923), and in 1924 she returned to Vienna. Her brother Johann had gone to the United States in 1922 to edit the Hungarian-language newspaper *Új elöre* (New Forward), and she must have arrived in New York around the time of his death in 1925. For the next five years she traveled widely in North and South America and in the Caribbean, with even a brief trip to South Africa around 1928, writing numerous reportages commissioned by the Ullstein publishing house in Berlin. In these articles, Leitner combined journalism, autobiography, and travelogue to report on the lives of working people in the areas she visited. Furthermore, she actually entered into the working world as a participant observer in most of her travels through the United States, taking unskilled positions as a domestic, white-collar, or blue-collar worker where she could be hired immediately—positions that would have been typical for many women at this time. Her reportages about these experiences appeared both in Germany (in the popular Ullstein magazine *Uhu* [The Owl] and also in the left-wing and Communist press) and in the German-language workers' press in the United States (*New Yorker Volkszeitung*). *Eine Frau reist durch die Welt* (A Woman Travels through the World), published in 1932, is her collection of many of these articles.

Late in 1930 Leitner returned to Germany and became a member of the BPRS. In that year she published her documentary novel *Hotel Amerika,* which, based on her own experiences, portrays one day in the life of a laundry worker in a New York luxury hotel. In this novel, the main character learns not to wait for a rich man to marry her and rescue her from her grim life, but rather to join together with her co-workers to struggle for their own interests. The book was on the first list of works banned by the Nazis after Hitler came to power in 1933. And so in the spring of that year, Leitner went first into hiding, then finally to Paris, where she lived from 1934 until April 1940. Apparently, she had false papers—perhaps a U.S. passport—that enabled her to go back into Germany without being recognized, and she undertook several illegal trips there which she reported on in the exile press, including *Das Wort* and the *Pariser Tageszeitung*. These articles concentrate primarily on two topics: preparations for rearmament and war, and everyday life in the Third Reich. So, for example, Leitner reported on the manufacture of

Youth delegates at the Second Congress of the Communist International, Moscow, 1920.
Maria Leitner is sitting second from left, delegate of the Communist Youth of Hungary.
Willi Münzenberg is sitting sixth from left. Willi Münzenberg, *Die dritte Front* (1931).

poisonous chemicals at an IG-Farben/Höchst factory on the Main River,
including her own conversations with workers. Furthermore, in reportages
such as "Dorfschule im Dritten Reich" (The Village School in the Third
Reich) and "Porträts dreier Erbhofbauern" (Portraits of Three Farmers
with Inheritance Rights), she investigated the consequences of Nazi rule in
areas of daily life outside the workplace.[22] Along with these shorter pieces,
Leitner also published her novel *Elisabeth, ein Hitlermädchen* (Elisabeth,
a Hitler Girl) in the *Pariser Tageszeitung* in 1937. This work focuses on
women's lives, specifically, the Women's Labor Service in the Third Reich.[23]

Living in exile in France, however, Leitner was barely able to make
enough money from her writing to survive. On April 16, 1940, she wrote
in a letter to New York: "I've been sick almost all the time for the past
six months. It started with a bad case of flu, and in an unheated garret,
without enough to eat, it's hard to get your health back, especially when—
on top of everything else—world history makes itself felt in our so modest
private lives. But in spite of everything, or maybe because of everything,
I've been working a lot."[24] In May 1940, when French internments of
foreign (particularly German) émigrés were in full swing, Leitner was sent
to Gurs, the French internment camp in the foothills of the Pyrenees.
Conditions were notoriously bad in this camp, which, at the time Leitner
was there, held up to twenty thousand refugees from the Spanish Civil
War, foreign women and children, and Jewish deportees from southern
Germany. In her novel *Stadt ohne Männer* (City without Men, 1945),

Gertrud Isolani recalled this station of exile: "When the word 'Gurs' is mentioned, memories awaken of gnawing hunger, dirt, vermin, epidemics, and lurking death."[25] After two months in Gurs, Leitner managed to escape, fleeing first to Toulouse and then to Marseilles, where she was seen in the spring of 1941 for the last time by several exiled German writers, among them Anna Seghers and Alexander Abusch.[26] The last documents of her life are from this time: letters to the American Guild for Cultural Freedom which show that Leitner, like so many other exiles from Nazi Germany, was trying desperately and without success to secure a visa to the United States. Her situation as a lesser-known writer with no dependable source of income was one of the most extreme, and in these letters she spoke of her isolation, lack of money, and physical collapse.[27] It seems likely that she died of illness and hunger in Marseilles.

Leitner's collection of reportage pieces, *Eine Frau reist durch die Welt,* documents a unique journey to the working world by a woman who was an émigré for almost all of her adult life, who stayed constantly on the move after her first flight into exile. In the first place, her focus on working and living conditions among those at the bottom of the social abyss in North and South America situated her book as one among a growing number of social reportages published during the late Weimar Republic which took an increasingly critical view of the United States. In contrast to those European travelers who had expressed mainly fascination with the new and modern in the "land of opportunity," an alternative view of the underside of this world was emerging in reportages such as Egon Erwin Kisch's *Paradies Amerika* (Paradise America, 1929), Alfons Goldschmidt's *Die dritte Eroberung Amerikas* (The Third Conquest of America, 1929), Arthur Holitscher's *Wiedersehen mit Amerika: Die Verwandlung der U.S.A.* (Reunion with America: The Transformation of the U.S.A., 1930), and Ernst Toller's *Quer durch* (Straight Through, 1930). Counterposing their perspectives against more positive images of "America" as a land where social pacification and harmony supposedly prevailed, these writers concentrated on bringing to light the tensions and struggles they encountered there, particularly with regard to social injustices. Furthermore, Leitner's perspectives as a radical woman journalist who was "traveling through the world" opened up new possibilities for this kind of socially critical reportage with regard both to the kinds of work she chose to focus on and also to the images of solidarity she presented to the reader.[28]

Leitner's itinerary as set down in *Eine Frau reist durch die Welt* is difficult to reconstruct precisely, but it seems likely that she arrived in New York in 1925 and spent about the next five years traveling down the East Coast of the United States, through the southern states to Florida. She then traveled to British and French Guiana, Curaçao, Venezuela, Puerto

Rico,[29] Haiti, and Trinidad before returning to Europe. The uniqueness of her undertaking lies both in this amazing itinerary itself as well as in her interests and perspective, her combination of travelogue and socially critical journalism. Unfolding a panorama of the "other America" during the years immediately preceding and following the world economic crisis, Leitner's entire project can be described as an exercise in seeing, in uncovering socioeconomic, gender-based, and racial tensions underneath the glittering surface impressions that greeted foreign travelers. An editorial comment from 1925 in the Ullstein illustrated magazine *Uhu* back in Berlin introduced Leitner's reportages to its readership: "We have sent our correspondent Miss Maria Leitner to America with the difficult and courageous task of going to work herself. By doing this, she will investigate how those who have had enough of Europe can find gainful employment there."[30] Even though her articles were commissioned, however, it appears that Leitner also needed to work while she was abroad in order to have enough money to live on. Accordingly, in her reportages on the United States, Leitner wrote as a participant observer of the working world, focusing on three main areas that would have been accessible to immigrant women depending to some extent on their language skills: factory work, domestic positions, and white-collar jobs. Moving along rapidly from one workplace to the next, Leitner took jobs as an unskilled worker in a Hershey candy factory in Pennsylvania, in textile mills in Pennsylvania and in the South, and in cigar factories in Massachusetts and Tampa; as a maid in hotels in New York, Richmond, and Charleston as well as for a number of individual families along the way; and as a clothing saleswoman in New York, a waitress in Pennsylvania and Tampa, and a busgirl in a New York automat restaurant.

In contrast to a writer such as Stenbock, who initially had little knowledge about class relations and was opposed to workers' organizing efforts, Leitner set out from the beginning to interpret the working world she entered by focusing on socioeconomic conflicts. That is, her starting point was a position of solidarity with those she was choosing to observe. In this regard she was similar to a politically engaged journalist such as Max Winter, who had written his investigative reportages for the Austrian Social Democratic press with the goal of contributing both factual material and emotional élan to the organized workers' movement. However, Leitner's focus on the work typically performed by women, as well as her interest in the situation of different racial and ethnic groups in the New World, also had the effect of creating a more complex, less clear-cut vision of the social changes that would be needed for members of all these groups to be able to lead fuller, less restricted lives. Accordingly, her depictions of both her own experiences on the job as well as the lives of the working people she met relate a multi-layered, multi-directional journey through the working world from a perspective that was certainly shaped by her earlier experience of political upheavals in Europe.

Through recounting her searches for work, her periodic unemployment, and the wide variety of jobs she held as she traveled southwards, Leitner presented in condensed form the story of a woman attempting to support herself in the New World. Her descriptions of her own reactions to these many workplaces as well as her characterizations of her co-workers highlight the constant tension between situations of dependency and different forms of self-assertion. First of all, the kinds of jobs that Leitner had frequently required her to work alone, or at least in a more solitary way than was the case with factory work. For example, in her reportage about her first job as a cleaning woman in the "biggest hotel in the world,"[31] the Hotel Pennsylvania in New York City, she expressed feelings of disorientation and frustration arising out of the isolating, numbing work. These are juxtaposed with sharp, sometimes ironic insights into the structure of the social microcosm of the hotel, as well as with undeniable attraction to the whirl of big-city life "in the shadow of the skyscrapers" (5). Leitner also noted her resentment over having to work so hard in order for wealthy people to enjoy themselves in the hotel. In such a situation, it seemed to her that the only possibility for rebellion was to try to work as slowly as possible:

> The hotel guests watch me work. Probably they are thinking: she's really not trying very hard. And the women: I wouldn't like to have that pearl as a housekeeper. Because I don't rush. I set the tempo for myself: very slowly, and follow it most conscientiously. I have half a mind to splash a few people "accidentally" when I go by with a bucket full of dirty water. That actually happened once, although I didn't do it intentionally. Oh, the patent-leather shoes, and the furious eyes, and to top it off, I couldn't keep from laughing. (15)

Leitner's description of the jobs she held as a maid and a waitress bring out similar attempts to resist demeaning, unpleasant conditions through individual self-assertion. However, her vignettes of her female co-workers also stress the fact that those who were less mobile than she and more dependent on steady wages would have had to stifle such urges for rebellion. It was not in her reportages about what she actually experienced in these kinds of workplaces, then, but rather in her novel *Hotel Amerika* where she imagined that one day these workers, too, would organize around their common interests.

Leitner's reportages about her stints in factories continued to focus on situations of dependency and possibilities for resistance by uncovering underlying class relations that were often not obvious at first glance and also by devoting attention to the dynamics among her co-workers. For example, in her account of working for the General Cigar Company in Northampton, Massachusetts, she showed how this business sought to thwart union organizing. Rather than consolidating its operations, the company spread its many branches throughout the United States to make communication— and strikes—among workers more difficult. Also, it showed a preference for small-town locations where women typically had few or no alternative job possibilities and were willing as a result to work longer hours for lower wages (92). Furthermore, Leitner always brought out the extremely heterogeneous makeup of the workforces she joined. This situation was typical for this cigar factory and for much of U.S. industry, and it always hindered efforts to organize around common interests. Along these lines, she described her co-workers as "women of all ages, old peasant women, Slovaks, Hungarians, Austrians from the Burgenland in their traditional costumes, with scarves and long, full skirts, and carefully made-up young girls in low-cut dresses" (85).

In such a working situation, it appeared that individual acts of solidarity were the maximum possibility for resistance at the time. So, for example, on her first day in the factory, when she was assigned to a machine that stripped the tobacco leaves from their stems, Leitner found that it was the other women, rather than the foreman, who warned her about the dangers of injuring her hands and who helped her to hide the tobacco she had ruined by her clumsy operation of the machine. Leitner noted similar instances of cooperation among workers faced with difficult conditions at many of the other jobs she took. By doing this, she intended to counter the widespread opinion in Europe that America was a paradise for satisfied workers. Although most of her own experience in the United States appears to have been in factories like this one where workers were not yet unionized, she was still able to draw on her own observations to recount organizing efforts in a few cases. These include her reportages entitled "Als Weberin in einer Seidenfabrik" (As a Weaver in a Silk Factory), on Bethlehem, Pennsylvania; and " 'Weißer Abschaum': Aus dem amerikanischen Arbeiterparadies" ("White Trash": From the American Workers' Paradise), on strikes in textile factories in North Carolina and Tennessee.[32]

With both an openness to registering new experiences and a marked ability to place herself into the background, Leitner often reported conversations with her co-workers or with others she met in hotels, homes, restaurants, and factories. These exchanges document widely varying reactions to different working and living situations. On the one hand, many of her vignettes bring out the relative fixedness of these circumstances. This stability, however, was often only superficial, being pervaded frequently with resignation to unchanging constraints or desperation over being entrapped in diminished lives. Thus, the stories Leitner recounted included those of women who seemed basically satisfied with their work, or who looked forward to pleasures in their leisure time. But also, she told of women such as the hotel maids whose work was so exhausting that they hardly did anything else but sleep, or the cigarmakers who had to keep constantly at their piecework. In such sections of Leitner's reportages, the work performed by these women appears mainly as an oppressive necessity which—due to the prevailing class relations—often drained all their physical and mental resources.

On the other hand, through Leitner's own journey and her sketches of the women she met along the way, a dramatic picture also emerges of working women of many nationalities on the move. The reportages entitled "Was ich an Amerikas Milliardärs-Küste sah" (What I Saw on America's Gold Coast) is her most striking account of this mobile female workforce. Having heard that Florida was the "promised land of America," Leitner decided to try her luck in Tampa, a city with a particularly attractive reputation. Once there, she found a job in one of the large cigar factories, but she soon discovered that her wages were hardly enough to live on. Meeting an acquaintance one day who was on her way to work at the exclusive resort of Palm Beach, she then decided to leave the factory and go along. However, after two weeks of waiting on demanding, petty guests in a large hotel restaurant, she decided to quit in order to explore the richer and poorer neighborhoods of Palm Beach. Finally, needing money again, Leitner and her traveling companion searched out an employment agency, where it seemed to her that the paths of people from all social levels and nationalities were crossing: "A group of young girls was there who had quit their jobs as hotel maids in Bermuda. A Swabian woman had just arrived from Chicago" (109). Leitner went on to take her last job in Florida, working as kitchen help for a wealthy family, before setting off for the Caribbean. In such sections of her reportages, then, her own experiences flow seamlessly into images of women "traveling through the world" in search of work and a better life, images that hint at enormous reserves of will, energy, and longing in the working world she entered.

Along with her focus on women, Leitner was particularly interested in reporting on the lives of African Americans—with respect to both working situations and the effects of segregation—which adds to the uniqueness of her travel account.[33] Her depictions of individuals as well as life in African American communities are sometimes tinged with exoticism and predictable stereotypes, but more often they show an effort to make connections, along with a sense of outrage over the discrimination and prejudice she witnessed. Leitner presented racial oppression in the South as the most regressive side of American life, a world that foreign travelers frequently did not register. In one instance, she told about meeting a female African American student from Howard University who was studying to become a foreign-language teacher, but who had to comply with the Jim Crow laws as soon as she returned to the South. In other examples, she wrote about her African American coworkers in hotels and kitchens, including a young man in Charleston who took her to dances and who dreamed of leaving the South for Boston or New York, "where the Negro is a human being, too" (134). And at a number of points, in reports about chain gangs and lynchings, she focused sharply on the terroristic system that kept the descendants of slaves on the bottom, the lowest of the low in a society divided along the lines of race and class.

This determination to get at the hidden underpinnings of wealth and privilege continues just as intensely in Leitner's reportages about the Caribbean and South America. On this part of her journey she did not work, but neither was she an uninvolved tourist. Always looking for situations that brought out the real, material conflicts and contradictions of the societies she was observing, she sought out information about the lives of workers and even of prisoners there. In these sections, her portrayals of working people and of related struggles against domination tend in three directions: a fascination with individual adventure, depictions of the worst sides of colonialism, and briefly flashing images of liberation. First, Leitner's journey was a daring undertaking in itself, traveling as she did with nothing but a "small suitcase" (142) to the penal colonies of French Guiana, to the diamond and gold mining areas of British Guiana, to the oil fields of Curaçao and mainland Venezuela, and to Trinidad and Haiti. Whether reporting on her amazement at forests filled with exotic plants and wildlife, or introducing a variety of colorful characters, such as a pilot who had become a gold prospector, Leitner created a panorama of European adventurers heading into unfamiliar, only partially explored areas of the New World. In this respect, her collection of reportages reflects pervasive tendencies in central Europe after the disorientations caused by World War I and unsuccessful revolutions to set off in a wild variety of directions in search of intense "authenticity"—whether by going on the road, going back to nature, or dropping out altogether.[34] It is easy to imagine that Leitner's own experiences with the failure of revolution in Hungary fed into a desire to escape stagnation by staying on the move through a series of unusual challenges and risks.

However, even in this stage of her travels, Leitner was not seeking the excitement of adventure primarily for its own sake. Rather, she was determined to investigate the living and working conditions of those on the absolute bottom in these geographical areas, and this path led her into precarious and dangerous situations. Consequently, with this goal always in mind, she focused above all on two things: the extremely heterogeneous racial and ethnic makeup of the populations she encountered, and the inhumane, exploitative working conditions created by unrestrained capitalism and colonialism with their penal systems. She continued to sketch the courses of individual lives moving across borders, such as a woman from Poland who had immigrated to New York, gone along with a friend to Venezuela, and ended up as a prostitute in the mining areas of British Guiana. Or, in a reportage entitled "Industrie im Urwald" (Industry in the Jungle), she described the diversity of her fellow ship passengers, who were heading to the bauxite mines in the Guianas: "It's a strange group of people who have come together here. Bush Negroes, Indians, Javanese, people from India, whites, all mixed together. There are also people from Arabia, China, and Japan, so that almost all the races of the world are represented on our primitive little ship. It's a fantastic Noah's Ark, which is journeying into the jungle."[35]

After noting that all the third-class passengers on her ship were looking for work, Leitner concentrated on depicting the penal colonies in French Guiana, the "land of terror" where prisoners had no escape from hard labor. Upon landing in Saint Laurent, her first impressions were ones of shock at the gangs of dirty, malnourished, ill prisoners working in the streets and on the docks. Setting out to enter more deeply into this nightmare, she walked through the town's streets, where guards prevented her from seeing the prison guillotine. She then traveled on to another prison compound deep in the forest where conditions were even worse than in town. Here, she talked to prisoners about their crimes (which ranged from murder and robbery to military and political offenses), the length of their sentences, and the terms of their imprisonment, which forced them to clear the forest for development with only the most primitive tools and the sparsest rations. Having promised some of the men to take letters back to their families, Leitner left Saint Laurent with this final impression of the inhumane system of punitive labor there: "Convicts return home from working in the jungle, but in what a condition. Those who can't go on any more are lying in a cart drawn by the prisoners who can still stand up. Pale bodies are thrown together and on top of each other as if they were objects. They're just barely alive, already half dead" (76). During her stay, Leitner discovered that many of these prisoners had no alternative but to stay in Guiana after serving their sentences, due to lack of money for the return trip to Europe. And governmental policy apparently favored this state of affairs, since the former prisoners were forced to keep on working for a living and thus developing France's colonial resources. Leitner's portrayals of Venezuela, Trinidad, and Puerto Rico bring out similar hardships and abuses, exploring the darkness of exploitation in the social depths in ways that are analogous to Stenbock's view of Germany "from below."

In most of these reportages, Leitner concentrated on the most extreme situations of inescapable dependency, which always entailed the most difficult manual labor and often approached demeaning servitude. However, it was also in this part of the world that Leitner discovered evidence of a successful struggle for liberation, in Haiti, which she called the "island of Negro republics" (161). Meeting on her ship a Haitian man who was returning from studying in France, she quoted him as voicing pride in the fact that the "Negroes" had thrown out the French and created their own republic. And after landing on the island and observing street life in Port-au-Prince under occupation by U.S. marines, Leitner contrasted the demeanor of "American Negroes" with that of Haitians: "Here, they are the masters, in spite of the occupation. And the Americans complain, too, that they can't cure them of their impudence. Impudence? Yes, they dare to revolt against being slaves" (170). This positive image of liberation, however, appeared to be compromised by the inroads of American capital that had disinherited the island's small farmers and created a new rural proletariat on large, modernized sugar plantations. In the words of a Caribbean writer whom Leitner cited: "The newly emerging workers' question is putting pressure on the conquerors, too. Whether copper-colored, black, or white, this question is the same everywhere" (172). Leitner clearly agreed with this insistence on the primacy of class relations for struggles against domination. However, the images she created of women at work and on the move as well as of racial and ethnic tensions and conflicts all evoke a more expansive view of the working world than that found in texts that left such matters aside. That is, her reportages about traveling through the working world brought larger areas of human activity into view, which in turn functioned against advocating any kind of overly simplistic, monocausal strategy for resistance and potential liberation.

After publishing this account of her "journey through the world," Leitner was able to live in Germany for only a short time before she had to flee into exile again. And this time, she was escaping from a regime that was bent on using compulsory manual labor as a force to paper over class conflicts and forcibly establish a "national racial community." Through her illegal trips back into Germany while she was living in Paris, Leitner stayed in touch with everyday life in the Third Reich. In her last novel, *Elisabeth, ein Hitlermädchen: Roman der deutschen Jugend* (Elisabeth, a Hitler Girl: A Novel of German Youth), published in the *Pariser Tageszeitung* in 1937, she depicted the experience of young women in the Nazi Labor Service.[36] If Bertolt Brecht had pointed out the continued existence of class-based domination in his scene about the Labor Service from *Furcht und Elend des Dritten Reiches,* Leitner focused in her novel more on the racial biology of National Socialism in order to cut through ideological notions about forced reconciliation of differences.

Spanning a narrative time of one year beginning in 1933, this novel centers around the figure of Elisabeth, a young department store clerk who is a committed member of the Nazi League of German Girls (BDM) and who falls in love with a young SA man named Erwin. The novel begins with Elisabeth's impressions of the celebrations on May 1, 1933, when Hitler vowed to lead every "German" to manual labor, and which Elisabeth experiences as an uplifting expression of common national will and goals. Shortly afterward, it is announced that the single salesgirls at her store are expected to "volunteer" for Labor Service camps. Elisabeth, however, is pregnant, which would preclude her going along to the camp. But she is also afraid to marry, since this would only be looked upon as an attempt to shirk her duty to the nation. After some delay, she decides to have an abortion, which Leitner portrays in an unusually factual, graphic way in the chapter entitled "Das Reich der Ungeborenen" (The Realm of the Unborn).

After this harrowing experience, which already exposes contradictions between Elisabeth's desires for her own happiness and the demands of the state, the scene shifts to the Labor Service camp. Here, young women from all class backgrounds have been brought together to live rigidly organized lives under the control of a tyrannical squad leader, a woman who is a ruthlessly committed Nazi. In her portrayal of camp life, Leitner did not concentrate on the experience of work. Rather, she focused on the conflicts between the girls' own needs and desires, as rooted in their physical, mental, and emotional integrity, and the requirements of a brutal system. Specifically, she introduced the character of a girl who has been sterilized under the Nazi eugenics laws in a state institution for wayward children and whose story frightens the other girls deeply. Finally, fearing the same fate and having discovered that the squad leader is collecting information about their health and family backgrounds, the girls rebel and burn all these records, only to be punished and sent away to work on distant farms. Elisabeth, however, who is taken to be a leader of the revolt, is expelled from the BDM and rejected by Erwin as no longer worthy of participating in the national community. In the end, she is left to wonder if she will ever find a secure place and sense of belonging again.

Leitner's effort in this novel to take up the theme of involuntary sterilization and to imagine the effects of the awareness of this policy on a group of young women is—to my knowledge—unique in German exile literature. In spite of some aesthetic weaknesses, then, as one critic has noted, this novel presents insights unusual for its time into how women's lived experience (and real fear of physical mutilation) could have worked against forcible efforts to establish a "community" centered around manual labor where those whose bodies were judged to be "foreign" or "racially inferior" were to be excluded or annihilated.[37] Viewed from this perspective, Leitner's novel of exile, which looks back into the abysses of Nazi Germany, is a complement to her earlier journey away from Europe into the depths of the New World. Through her own experiences and her observations of others at work, she had created pictures of social conflicts which—while emphasizing the centrality of economic dependency—also validated resistance to other forms of oppressive conditions based on gender and race. In her novel about the Nazi Labor Service, she sought to expose the hollowness and artificiality of notions about "community" that ignored women's individual needs for the sake of authoritarian, racist goals. At many points in her writing, then, Leitner was able to bring out connections between worlds of labor and other areas of life in ways that gave a sense of the full range of potentialities all these working people possessed—potentialities that could hardly be realized, however, without profound, liberating social change.

Lili Körber: *A Woman Experiences Red Everyday Life: A Diary-Novel from the Putilov Factory* (1932)

> And so it became clear that there was only one way for me to really get to know them: to become one of them by working in a factory. Of course, I thought immediately of the Putilov factory, whose workers had made a name for themselves in the first revolution of 1905.
>
> —Lili Körber[38]

Although Lili Körber was not a member of the aristocracy like Count Stenbock-Fermor, she also grew up before the Russian Revolution in a milieu where there was little contact with the poorer sectors of the native population. Born in Moscow in 1897, Körber was the daughter of a Polish woman and a well-to-do Austrian businessman, and she grew up in secure, protected surroundings, first being tutored at home and then attending a high school with Russian girls her own age.[39] At the beginning of World War I, however, her father was expelled from Russia as an enemy alien, and the family returned to Vienna. Körber studied literature in Geneva, where she joined the Union des Etudiantes pour la Paix et les Droits de la Femme, and in 1923 she completed her doctorate in Frankfurt with a dissertation on Franz Werfel's poetry. Going back to Vienna, Körber soon began to write for the *Arbeiter-Zeitung* edited by Max Winter, the central party newspaper of the Austrian Social Democrats.

Book jacket for Lili Körber's *Eine Frau erlebt den roten Alltag* (1932) by John Heartfield.
Copyright (c) 1999 Artists Rights Society (ARS), New York/VG Bild-Kunst, Bonn.

She also worked in a local party library and was apparently affiliated with the BPRS. In 1930 these contacts led to an invitation from the Moscow State Publishing House to travel to the Soviet Union with a delegation of writers, including Anna Seghers, Johannes R. Becher, and others. During this trip, Körber—who was fluent in Russian—decided that she would stay in the Soviet Union for a longer period and go to work in a Leningrad factory in order to find out through firsthand contact with workers how well the new socialist system was functioning. Her "diary-novel" based on her experiences as an unskilled metalworker in the Putilov tractor factory, *Eine Frau erlebt den roten Alltag,* appeared in Berlin in November 1932 and was an immediate success.

In January 1933, on a trip back to Vienna from lecturing about the Soviet Union in Amsterdam, Körber stopped in Berlin, where she observed Hitler's rise to power. She depicted the beginning of the Nazi reign of terror in her next novel, *Ein Jüdin erlebt das neue Deutschland* (A Jewish Woman Experiences the New Germany, 1934), which was immediately banned in Austria under the pretext that it contained blasphemous passages.[40] By then, her reportage about the Soviet Union had also been banned in Germany, and she was cut off from her reading public. Upon receiving the Japanese translation of her reportage in 1935, then, Körber decided spontaneously to take a trip through the Soviet Union to Japan and China. But this trip was only the prelude to permanent exile. Returning to Vienna in 1936 and publishing two books based on her experiences in the Far East, Körber's situation as an active Social Democratic writer became more and more precarious. A few days after the Anschluss, in March 1938, she left Austria, fleeing through Switzerland to Paris, where her husband joined her a few months later. She did not pause with her writing, and her next novel, *Eine Österreicherin erlebt den Anschluss* (An Austrian Woman Experiences the Anschluss) was serialized in the Zürich *Volksrecht* beginning already in April 1938. But her career as an engaged writer, which she had pursued with dedication for over a decade, was brought to an end by the hardships of exile. During the three years she and her husband spent in France, most of their time was taken up by the struggle to earn money and to secure the visas that would allow them to flee the approaching Nazi danger. Finally, they left Europe and arrived in New York in June 1941. Körber managed to publish one more novel, *Ein Amerikaner in Rußland* (An American in Russia), which was serialized in the New York *Neue Volkszeitung* in 1942–1943, but then her writing stopped. The hurdles of language and culture were not to be overcome for a writer of this generation living in permanent exile. Körber worked as a nurse in New York for many years, and she died there in 1982.

Körber's *Eine Frau erlebt den roten Alltag* is one among a large number of literary reportages about the Soviet Union written—mostly by men—during the period of the Weimar Republic.[41] After the Russian Revolution, interest was keen in the capitalist countries in the experiments with building a new kind of society to the east, in the efforts to leap over what had seemed to be unavoidable stages of historical development, in attempts to modernize what were often almost medieval conditions. Accordingly, authors and journalists set out to observe the lives of workers and farmers in the new world of socialism and to report their findings in books that were read avidly and often translated into many other languages. To name only the best-known, these include Ernst Glaeser, Alfred Kurella, and F. C. Weiskopf's *Staat ohne Arbeitslose* (State with Full Employment, 1931), Arthur Holitscher's *Drei Monate in Sowjet-Rußland* (Three Months in Soviet Russia, 1921) and *Stromab die Hungerwolga* (Downstream on the Volga of Hunger, 1922), Egon Erwin Kisch's *Zaren, Popen, Bolschewiken* (Czars, Priests, Bolsheviks, 1927) and *Asien gründlich verändert* (Asia Transformed, 1932), Berta Lask's *Kollektivdorf und Sowjetgut* (Collectivized Village and Soviet Estate, 1932), Ludwig Renn's *Rußlandfahrten* (Russian Travels, 1932), Ernst Toller's *Quer durch* (Straight Through, 1930), and F. C. Weiskopf's *Zukunft im Rohbau* (Building the Future, 1931). With respect to their depictions of the world of manual labor— whether in factories or in agriculture—most of these writers, including Körber, were full of sympathy for the socialist experiment. Therefore, they generally approached their subject from a radically different point of departure than that taken by left-leaning writers of social reportages about the condition of the working classes in the West, in which a sharply critical perspective on the negative effects of capitalism usually dominated. And in turn, the effort to take a more positive, affirmative approach to the genre of reportage, which had historically had the function of exposing and critiquing social wrongs, meant that these writers all faced unfamiliar and complex aesthetic problems.[42]

Körber's book is a particularly good illustration of both the new possibilities and the inherent difficulties in reporting with solidarity, yet critically, about the world of manual labor under socialism which she entered as a participant for a time—to my knowledge, the only one of the many German-speaking travelers to the Soviet Union who did so and published a book about her experiences.[43] In her portrayal here of her journey to the Soviet working world, there are three main aspects that stand out: the view of manual labor as only one aspect of everyday life, the changing attitude of the narrator toward her job as an unskilled worker, and the focus on gender roles and matters of special importance to women. As the title of the book indicates, Körber intended to give a broad picture of "everyday life" in the Soviet Union from a woman's perspective. Furthermore, although the book is a reportage based on her own experiences and investigations, the genre designation of "diary-novel" indicates an element of fiction. The persona of the narrator is not meant to be equated seamlessly with Körber herself.

Covering a period of two months, Körber's reportage begins with her first day on the job in the Putilov tractor factory and ends with her trip back to Berlin.[44] As one of the oldest and largest factories in the Soviet Union, the Putilov plant had turned out cannons and locomotives in the nineteenth century and arms during World War I. After the chaos of revolution and civil war, the plant was rebuilt, and the first tractor rolled off its assembly line in 1924. By the time Körber came to Leningrad, during the period of the first Five-Year Plan when the collectivization of agriculture was going into full swing, the Putilov factory was producing thirty-two thousand tractors per year. The photographs of farm life in the Soviet Union in Glaeser, Kurella, and Weiskopf's *Staat ohne Arbeitslose* give a vivid impression of the significance of tractors and other machines in the project of modernizing traditional agricultural practices. Counterposed to pictures of the handmade wooden plows still in use are the images of these implements being cast away and burned when the new tractors arrived for the collective farms—images that highlight the reduction of exhausting manual labor brought about by mechanization.[45] Clearly, then, Körber entered into a factory whose production was particularly crucial for constructing a modern socialist economy. Her depiction of the microcosm of the tractor plant aimed toward bringing out both the promise and overwhelming difficulties in this giant project.

With respect to the work process itself, it is striking how little space Körber devoted to describing her actual time on the job as an unskilled metalworker whose task was to bore holes into tractor parts. Beyond several remarks about the work being monotonous and tiring and about her almost Chaplinesque clumsiness, she did not concentrate extensively on her own experience of manual labor. Furthermore, the book does not dwell on workplace conditions in general, although Körber did point out the recurring problems with disorganization, sloppiness, disrepair and breakdowns of equipment, and lack of materials—problems that frequently slowed down production or even brought it to a halt. There are several possible reasons for this approach, which have to do with the intended audience of the book and also with the transformation of socioeconomic conditions in the Soviet Union. First, in contrast to many of the journeys to the working world discussed previously, Körber's project was not to enter into a dark, unknown world of manual labor and interpret it to readers from the upper classes who were unfamiliar with the social depths. Rather, she set out to give German-speaking readers a broader-ranging panorama of life among working people in the Soviet Union based on her own experiences and contacts with them in many areas of life, including, but not limited to, work. Furthermore, her point of departure was also different from that of social explorers such as the Christian Socialist Göhre and the middle-class feminist Wettstein-Adelt, who had also devoted a large amount of attention to aspects of lower-class life outside the workplace. These earlier travelers had believed that the inhabitants of the social abyss needed to be improved and raised up to their own standards of bourgeois morality. Körber, by contrast, reported positively on some of the ways in which workers themselves were attempting to transform not only factory and farm conditions, but also some of the oldest, most deeply rooted morals, customs, and habits of everyday life.

This reportage is constructed in such a way that the narrator herself—though always sympathetic to the new world she enters—is depicted as moving from a more individualistic standpoint to a stronger sense of connection with the other women workers and also to a deeper understanding of the crucial importance of their factory jobs. This psychological transformation of the narrator, which is the most unconvincing and awkwardly expressed part of Körber's "diary-novel," revolves around her initial romantic interest in an American engineer who is working in the factory. He is there as an indispensable foreign expert for the adventure and good pay, but he has no interest at all in the wider social and political dimensions of the socialist project. In her first days in the factory, the narrator misses work to spend time with this engineer. It is only when she is taken to task by some of her co-workers that she realizes the problems with this kind of behavior, namely, that she has created tensions between herself and the other women, and that every worker is needed in the production process. Subsequently, the narrator sees less of the engineer and works more conscientiously, mending her relationships with her co-workers and stating abruptly, with rather implausible exaggeration: "Only in the factory do I find myself again. Here everything has a meaning. Here one can realize the dream of one's childhood and build a world, not one made of snow or sand, but a real world."[46]

Approaching the project of constructing a new kind of world with what she describes as less "individualism," a newfound sense of "maturity" (218), and a closer identification with the world of work, the narrator encounters situations where her responses indicate that she has little understanding of the repressive sides of the Soviet system. On the one hand, she makes light of procedures for compulsory self-criticism and ideological purging (44), of the obsession with hunting for spies and saboteurs (145), and of arrests by the State Security Police (224), speaking in these passages with a flippant tone that belies the seriousness of these issues.

On the other hand, in her effort to become "one" with the most class-conscious members of the world she has entered, she swings at points to the opposite pole, that of extreme dogmatism. For instance, upon hearing that an inspector who lied about missing work was not fired because she was irreplaceable in the factory, the narrator complains: "We have to agree on what we want: a viable, profitable workplace or a new world" (223). She rejects uncompromisingly the argument that improved production is more important than absolutely pure socialist morality. In such passages, where the narrator tends either to brush serious issues aside or to advocate a rigid ideological position, her authentic voice disappears from the text. That is, in describing her own effort to enter into the world of the revolutionary workers' movement, she either retires too far into the background or, by contrast, asserts too strongly her "likeness" with her new comrades. The effect of this strand in the narrative is to diminish the cogency of Körber's effort to develop a tenable position for an intellectual such as herself within contemporary struggles for social justice.

In general, however, this reportage on everyday life in the Soviet Union is at its best in its sections that do not attempt to be argumentative or reflective but report more straightforwardly on workers' attitudes, activities, and institutions. As a writer with a special interest in the development of new possibilities for cultural expression, Körber turned her attention frequently to evolving structures of life among working people that augmented and broke through the old cycle of long working hours, truncated family and leisure time, and preoccupation with the naked struggle for existence. Accordingly, she reported on the thriving scene of workers' amateur art, theater, and music clubs, on an art school for workers' children, on trips organized through the workplace to historical and cultural sites such as Peterhof on the Bay of Finland, and on the new opportunities for university study being created for young people from working and farm families. In one instance, Körber recounted the visit of a Pioneer youth group to her factory where a boy invited her to speak to his organization and informed her that even young people his age were performing an important task in the Putilov works by teaching illiterate workers how to read (63). Within the reportage as a whole, the effect of these passages is to create a much less dismal picture of the life of these factory workers than in any of the journeys to the working world discussed so far. There is a sense here of the concrete achievements and ongoing transformations in everyday life that were enabling workers to develop more of their human capacities, in contrast to the situation in capitalist countries, where such possibilities still had to be projected as demands and hopes for an indeterminate future.

By no means, however, does Körber's reportage summon up the figures of muscular, single-minded heroes of socialist labor and upright, inhibited, morally flawless comrades who people the most stereotypical, politically and aesthetically unconvincing texts of socialist realism.[47] Rather, her sketches of her co-workers, particularly of the other women, depict them as human beings with strengths and weaknesses, trying with varying degrees of success to negotiate satisfying, fulfilling paths through the upheavals of their lives. In the sections of the reportage on the workplace, which focus for the most part on the mentality of the workers and their interactions with each other both informally and in organized ways, the reader always senses the tension between the old and the new. For example, upon entering the factory on her first day at work, the narrator is surprised that it is the women workers, rather than someone from the administration, who show her around, and she is impressed by their proud sense of ownership (13). Throughout her stay in the factory, she notes her co-workers' belief in the importance of responsibility, initiative, and conscientiousness for the production process. However, she also encounters other workers who, quite understandably, do not identify nearly so closely with the new economic system. These include a pharmacist's daughter who is working in the factory in order to improve her chances of being admitted to the university (97) and an illiterate farm woman who—set in her old ways—has no use for the new tractors and works at a maddeningly slow pace (89). To an extent, the reportage is structured around such juxtapositions between figures with a more "backward" consciousness and ones who are more "progressive," reflecting the conviction that regressiveness could be overcome and that it would be possible to put hopes for social transformation into practice. Yet a more complex picture also emerges through the narrator's accounts of conversations and events outside the workplace—for example, in the hostel for women workers where she lived. Here, for all the women, no matter what their ideology, daily dramas revolved around difficulties with men; frustrating efforts to create relationships that would make room for work, family life, and individual development; dissatisfactions with communal childcare; and the normal quarrels among people forced to live together in such close quarters. Throughout Körber's reportage, then, the narration reflects the unresolved political tension between the need for didacticism and hopes for creating conditions where greater autonomy and opportunities for self-development would one day be possible.

In trying to find ways to make connections with little-known worlds and even to renounce the worlds from which they came, to find lasting rather than temporary brotherhood, writers such as Stenbock, Leitner, and Körber were seeking the goal which August Bebel had expressed much earlier with such great hope: "not to live like proletarians, but to abolish the proletarian way of life of the great majority of people."[48] In the best parts of their writing, they recounted empathetic journeys into the working world. They showed talent both for putting their own positions into the background (in their insightful reporting about what they saw and experienced) and at the same time for remembering them (in not trying to speak as if their positions were identical with those of the working people they were observing). That is, these three life stories demonstrate three related ways of decentering original positions based on relative privilege in favor of substantial engagement with the world of work. But there was no place for such utopian dreams and such complex optics in the world that was forcibly created in Germany in 1933.[49] And when writers began to enter the working world again in both German states after the war's immense destruction, they were often hardly aware of the efforts of their forerunners—so thoroughly had the traces of these earlier journeys been erased.

4

From Insider to Outsider: Journeys to the Working World in the German Democratic Republic

With labor emancipated, every man becomes a working man, and productive labor ceases to be a class attribute.

—Karl Marx[1]

I am no longer certain that communism is the destiny of humanity, as my father told me, quoting an Indian philosopher, when I was eight years old. But communism remains a dream of humanity which one generation after the next will work to fulfill until the end of our world.

—Heiner Müller[2]

Deferred Dreams of Overcoming the Division of Labor

In the German Democratic Republic, writers' journeys to the working world were interwoven in new ways with workers' tortuously winding paths to social and intellectual advancement—paths shaped and controlled by the Socialist Unity Party (SED), which ruled in the workers' name.[3] During the entire forty years of this state's existence, GDR authors registered the complexity of these shifting social constellations and allegiances. However, the years from the late 1950s into the 1960s, when writers were officially urged to make connections with the worlds of industrial and farm workers within the framework of the Bitterfeld Program, marked the most intense period of such contacts. As literary historian Peter Zimmermann has stated, in spite of the party's restrictions, this experience deserves to be remembered as unique in the history of German literature. As an alternative to the division between elitist and mass culture in the Federal Republic, high-quality literature was to be created that was closely tied to the lives of the majority of the population, the workers and farmers.[4] Writers were to go into the sphere of production, and workers themselves were to be encouraged to write, all this with the goal of gradually lessening the separation between "art and life."

By thus seeking to contribute to breaking down the division between mental and manual labor, the Bitterfeld Program continued a long socialist tradition that held up democratic, egalitarian goals of supportive community and self-development. Karl Marx himself had declared that in the future classless society, when the privileges attached to private ownership of the means of production would be abolished, when stupefying, routine manual labor would be reduced to a minimum, and when all would have unrestricted access to the education necessary for developing their abilities, labor would take on a creative aspect. It would no longer be a burden, but rather a source of unalienated fulfillment, "not only a means of life but life's prime want."[5] In its most positive manifestations, socialism always hoped to broaden opportunity for the working majority by providing for basic necessities and opening up previously inaccessible paths for their lives. However, in the "proletarian tragedy" of our century, this grand vision of liberation was of course far from realized in the authoritarian, insular forms that "really existing" socialism took.[6] Thus, due to fears and resistances from within as well as to outside pressures and threats, the "Workers' and Peasants' State" of the GDR was not able to sustain the emancipatory alternatives in work and life that might have held the loyalties of more of the people whom it purported to represent.[7] For on the one hand, many of those in power settled for stability, promoting an overly harmonious view of the community of interests in which antagonistic class divisions were said to have been overcome. In turn, these petrified structures were challenged periodically by voices arising from the "base" as well as by initiatives in many spheres of life that always threatened to spin out of control. And this tension was never resolved.

The specific ways in which the SED promoted, controlled, or discouraged contacts between writers and other intellectuals and the working world over the years in the GDR should be taken as one aspect of much broader efforts in this country to reshape traditional divisions between mental and manual labor, educational privilege and deficiency, and work and leisure. That is, it was not only in the cultural sphere that those who had traditionally occupied more elite positions were to be steered into having more direct contact with the world of material production. Rather, at the same time when the Bitterfeld Program was proclaimed in 1959, the system of polytechnical education was also being established. It sought to break down old class barriers by requiring all school pupils to work for a certain time in factories or on farms as part of the curriculum. Furthermore, also in the late 1950s, the first "Brigades of Socialist Labor" were created, formalizing and anchoring firmly the system of "socialist competition." This method of workplace organization aimed not only at increasing production, but also at integrating the workplace more closely with other areas of life, encouraging workers' continuing education, and promoting cooperation between workers and the intelligentsia.

In these three broad areas of education, the workplace, and cultural politics, according to official ideology, observing and experiencing the world of material production and striving to improve its more negative aspects were to have two main effects (which in practice often collided): the expanding of individual opportunities based on a firmer grounding in collective "reality," and the training of these same individuals along very specific lines of "socialist morality."[8] As narratives of these shifting relations between "above" and "below," of the tensions between liberation and subordination, GDR literary journeys to the working world always center around the conflicts between acceptance and rejection of the educational and ideological goals associated with the work experience. And in fact, these narratives often focus specifically on themes related to the school and university milieu or to the brigade structure of the workplace. Consequently, before turning to a discussion of particular texts, it is useful as background to examine briefly both the kinds of contact between social strata which polytechnical education and the system of socialist competition intended to promote, as well as some of the grave problems and inadequacies in these areas which have become objects of open discussion only since 1989. Before that date, it was mainly in works of literature that critical voices could be raised to a limited public—voices that problematized existing social relations and kept alive more emancipatory visions of a transformation— or at least a sharing—of power.

Since the late 1950s, everyone who went through the GDR school system had the experience of entering into the working world for a time.[9] The system of polytechnical education established there for all pupils in 1958–1959 was influenced significantly by older pedagogical theories of "work education." These theories held that the performance of manual labor was an invaluable tool in inculcating virtues of respectability such as diligence, conscientiousness, punctuality, orderliness, cleanliness, and self-denial.[10] Beyond this, however, referring to the writings of Marx and Engels on using education to develop flexible, versatile individuals and leaning heavily on Soviet models, GDR educators and political leaders set out to promote much grander goals of "socialist education" in which contact with the world of manual labor was to play a central part.[11] Through close interaction with workers and farmers under the guidance of teachers and party activists, young people were to strengthen their convictions about

Dr. Gerhard Neubert

Arbeiter als Erzieher der Pioniere und Schüler

Book cover for Gerhard Neubert's *Arbeiter als Erzieher der Pioniere und Schüler* (Workers as Educators of Young Pioneers and School Pupils). (1963).

Book cover for Jürgen Polzin's *Sozialistische Arbeitserziehung auf dem Lande* (Socialist Worker Education in the Country).(1962).

the crucial importance of material production, develop solidarity with the working class and its party, and deepen their commitment to the struggle for socialism.[12]

Accordingly, the system of polytechnical education as it was set up in the GDR encompassed two central fields: practical experience and ideological objectives. In the first place, schools stressed the industrial aspects of many subjects being taught, and pedagogues developed new areas of instruction geared toward the working world. These included "Introduction to Socialist Production," "Productive Labor," and for young people in grades seven through twelve, the weekly period of work in a factory or on a collective farm.[13] In contrast to older conservative or right-wing efforts to discipline unruly or all too independent young people by subjecting them to regimented manual labor, it must be said that at least the theory of polytechnical education in the GDR contained an intellectual component.[14] Pupils were to gain a firmer grounding in technical subjects, and brigades of workers and farmers were assigned to the school classes that worked with them to instruct the young people in their practical knowledge.[15] All this was done, as one GDR educator stated, with the aim of overcoming the "chasm between the school and life, that is, the antagonism between intellectual, scholarly activity and physical, practical activity."[16]

Today, the lack of extensive, reliable sources about how GDR citizens actually experienced these contacts with the world of material production makes it difficult to draw differentiated conclusions about this pedagogical experiment, and a broad oral history project focusing on these topics would be invaluable.[17] Lacking this kind of information, what can be said at present is that while many pupils doubtlessly learned something of value through their contacts with the workplace, in practice this aspect of the educational system fell far short of its goals. Above all, because of increased mechanization on the one hand and the shortfall in available employees on the other, young people were often put to work at routine tasks or at unskilled agricultural work that filled in gaps in the labor force but which held little or no educational value. Such unsolved problems were an object of ongoing internal discussion among party members and educators in the GDR,[18] and after 1989 they often surfaced in frank criticisms of the system of polytechnical education. Writing in 1994, for example, historian Jürgen Kuczynski described what he termed the "shock of practice" in the following anecdote:

> So-called polytechnical education was really a monotechnical education which nobody liked, neither the factories nor the teachers nor the pupils. Many years ago, when my youngest son entered the grade in school where polytechnical educa-

tion began, he came to his mother after the fourth day of instruction and asked her: "What's the point of all this? I had to stamp the firm's name on rubber balls again for the whole time today!" His mother gave him the right explanation: "Well, you must have learned one thing. You must have learned what boring, tedious jobs a lot of our workers still have to do so that you can go to school and then perhaps to the university."[19]

According to Kuczynski, because technology was still underdeveloped, polytechnical education could not possibly be successful in overcoming the division of labor. No matter how often monotonous, stifling work was proclaimed to be socially useful, no one could feel inner identification with such alienated labor, which was still pervasive under socialism.[20] Similarly, theater director Freya Klier, who was expatriated from the GDR in 1988, pointed out in her *Lüg Vaterland: Erziehung in der DDR* (Lies of the Fatherland: Education in the GDR, 1990) that pupils were frequently assigned to jobs according to economic necessity rather than educational value. Interestingly, however, even this sharp critic of the GDR did not voice a totally negative view of the temporary work experience: "To say it clearly: It did not harm any of us. Stripped of all ideological trappings, these constant side-trips into the 'world of work' accomplished at least one thing. They taught us to respect the work of other people, even the most primitive work. Every graduate of the GDR school system probably retains something of this attitude of respect—even those who remember their stint at the workplace with horror."[21] Such a statement indicates the ongoing presence of at least some degree of identification with the worlds of "workers and farmers" among large sectors of the East German population. This mentality is different from that in the West, and it will probably continue to be a noticeable social and political factor in Germany for some time to come.

Corresponding to the extensive political measures in the realms of culture and education to bring together "art and life" and "school and life" was the emphasis on "socialist competition" at the workplace. Under the slogan "Work, Learn, and Live in a Socialist Manner," the system of work in socialist collectives was expanded and consolidated in 1958–1959. The goals here were to improve and increase production, further workers' education, encourage social and cultural contacts among brigade members outside the workplace, and foster cooperation between intellectuals and production workers, especially with regard to utilizing new and complex science and technology.[22] The brigades that became the general form of workplace organization throughout the GDR were therefore not only work collectives with economic objectives, but also served ideological and cultural functions.[23] Central here was the idea that while routine, monotonous manual labor was economically necessary, its worst effects should be counteracted as much as possible by technological improvements and by encouraging workers to take the initiative and advance themselves—to be sure, in strictly controlled ways. And most generally, the experience of collective solidarity rooted in the workplace yet extending beyond it was intended to have ideological, educational effects on all levels of society. By breaking down the old barriers between "above" and "below," each GDR citizen was to strive toward developing a new kind of "socialist personality" characterized by intellectual and practical versatility, a high level of socialist consciousness and morality, and an optimistic outlook.[24]

The great disjunctures between such goals and the continuing division of labor in the workplace, between priorities set by the party and individual desires and interests, were always a central theme in much GDR literature that focused on the working world. The most probing of these texts, such as the dramas of Heiner Müller, Volker Braun, and the early Peter Hacks, always insisted on bringing out the complexity of these relationships between above and below as well as the unfulfilled hopes for overcoming traditional privileges. Accordingly, these writers frequently depicted workers' resistance to their own advancement, or conversely, workers' desires for greater advancement than was allowed to them. Furthermore, their texts constantly revolved around the interactions of intellectuals and functionaries with the world of manual labor—interactions that ranged from encouraging emancipatory developments to preventing them by stupidity, bureaucracy, or blatant force. In the last years of the GDR, little remained but negative evocations of exhaustion, entrapment, and bitterness. One of the most penetrating expressions of this historical moment was Heiner Müller's 1988 production of his first "brigade play," *Der Lohndrücker* (The Wage Shark, 1957), at the Deutsches Theater in East Berlin. The final scene captured the multiple, refracted layers of oppression and longing within the collective project in the GDR of building alliances at the workplace across the old fault lines of social classes. Three times, Party Secretary Schorn's stranglehold around the worker Balke's neck glided into a tired embrace as Schorn shouted out: "Who asked me if I can work with you?"[25] Schorn's gesture and cry stood both as a requiem for the struggles within "really existing" socialism to overcome the division of labor and also as an unfulfilled wish for a true community of equals in work and life.

When GDR writers depicted journeys to the working world in their fiction or reportage, then, their efforts to bring together "art and life" were one important facet of the extensive efforts to transform relations between "above" and "below." In their texts, the central political issue they confronted was how the experience of manual labor and the workplace was meant to shape and mold those members of socialist society who were previously unacquainted with the lives of workers and farmers. And the central aesthetic problem for them was how to portray individual responses that were often at odds with the intended effects of these unaccustomed situations. In contrast to writers of earlier times, GDR writers were encouraged in certain ways to enter into the working world by the ruling party, which claimed to represent working-class interests. Therefore, the voluntary and forced elements of their journeys, as well as the tensions between domination and marginalization in their relationships to workers, took on new configurations. To recall earlier journeys to the working world discussed here, while Göhre and his imitators had set out to learn about the unfamiliar world of manual labor, they viewed workers as objects to be educated, improved, and shaped according to the observers' plans and wishes. They held workers' own consciousness and desires to be either threatening or negligible and believed that the social question could be solved by reforming the existing capitalist system. Weimar work students, propelled into the working world against their will, tried to make the best of an unwanted situation, often speaking in exalted terms of contributing to the nation and the Volk or of "following" for a time before returning to their foreordained positions as "leaders." In specifically volkish and National Socialist calls for creating the "national community" of all "Germans" as a closed front against those defined as outsiders, forced subjection to physical labor was intended to bond together the nation in a unified cause with work as the lowest common denominator. Here, an intense anti-intellectualism fed into a glorification of the virtues this kind of work was supposed to inculcate: submission to authority, group cohesion, strength and virility, militarized precision. Finally, left-wing social reporters who entered into the working world during the first half of the century did so with the goal of enlightening their reading public about intolerable conditions and also about workers' own efforts to better their situation—that is, they were writing from an oppositional perspective.

In contrast to all these approaches, GDR journeys to the working world were rooted in a desire to participate in the socialist state's project of building up a society qualitatively different from that of the past. These writers wanted to help dismantle older hierarchies of privilege and create new opportunities for the working majority to develop all their human faculties. It is the frequent willingness of these authors to form alliances with the working world in ways that did not have an anti-intellectual thrust which distinguishes their texts from many earlier ones and generates the special complexity of these texts. In their efforts not to write solely from a standpoint of opposition, these writers were constantly negotiating the tension between resistance and authoritarian structures in their aesthetics as well as in their politics.

Broadly speaking, GDR journeys to the working world can be characterized as moving from a certain acceptance of the "education through work" deemed necessary for "arriving" in the socialist community to an increasing skepticism about this process and disillusionment with this entire project. Until 1990, GDR writers continued to create such texts, producing works that were at times anachronistic, reflecting efforts to hold on to ideological lessons once learned well, and at times more insightful about the dead ends and immobility in "really existing" socialism. That is, while these narratives may express both undercurrents of resistance to unwished-for marginalization as well as continuing assertions of power and control over voices that might arise from the depths, they also continue to provide glimpses of the desire for creating a community of equals. Looking back at these texts today, they seem infused by an almost impenetrable tangle of motives: the genuine effort to renounce privilege and the acceptance of force and compulsion; an attempt to seize hope and an underlying sense of fear; guilt over the crimes of the immediate German past and grounding in the great historical promise of socialism; and in the later texts, resignation, despair, and anger over lost hopes, yet sometimes also an ongoing, if problematized, assertion of solidarity with those who were still "down below."

Frozen Images and Moving Pictures: GDR Writers Arrive in the Working World

THE BITTERFELD PATH INTO THE WORKING WORLD

Writers, go to the base![26]

On April 24, 1959, SED party officials, writers, and workers met in the Palace of Culture of the Electrochemical Combine in Bitterfeld to call for overcoming the separation between "art and life," between writers and the people.[27] From Walter Ulbricht, general secretary of the SED, to Erwin Strittmatter, the head of the Writers' Union, to miner Sepp Zach, participants urged workers to "reach for the pen" and exhorted writers to cast away worn-out bourgeois concerns in favor of joining the process of socialist construction and producing its new literary classics.[28] Workers were to "storm the heights of culture," and writers were to "go to the base"—all this with the implicit goal of creating the "new socialist man" whose "community" would no longer be marred by the division between "head" and "hands."[29] In this manner, the speakers at the Bitterfeld Conference sought to point the way—both artistically and ideologically—to those authors who had as yet shown little inclination to focus on the transformations taking place in factories and agriculture as material for their literary works.

Yet since the founding of the GDR, there had always been some writers who made their way to production sites with or without the party's guidance, writers who had attempted to cultivate and give literary form to alliances with industrial and farm workers. Thus, when Walter Ulbricht and Alfred Kurella, the head of the Politbüro's Commission on Culture, called for writers to go to the "base" in order to ground their depictions of contemporary life in the GDR in the new reality, they were not so much proposing a new direction as seeking to channel and control tendencies that were already present. For they feared that these tendencies would always have the potential of catapulting in dangerously anti-centralist directions.[30] Decidedly anti-bureaucratic perspectives, for example, had already come to the fore in a number of early GDR novels such as Karl Mundstock's *Helle Nächte* (Bright Nights, 1952).[31] Here, two Free German Youth functionaries give up their posts, "deserting to the base" to become workers at the construction site of the "Eisenhüttenkombinat Ost" (Ironworks Combine East). By doing this, they hope to bridge "the abyss which shouldn't exist, but which is there,"[32] that is, the abyss between planning and controlling authorities and those still in subordinate positions. Consequently, they encourage their fellow workers not only to increase their efficiency and output, but also to press for their own interests and resist ill-conceived, arbitrary regulations and plans handed down from above.

If such early industrial novels generally presented more or less forced, overly harmonious resolutions to clashes between above and below, such evasions of conflict were not characteristic of the dialectical theater of Bertolt Brecht's successors which soon began to emerge. Rather, dramatists Heiner Müller, Volker Braun, Peter Hacks, Helmut Baierl, and Hartmut Lange sought in varying degrees to energize and activate their audiences through their portrayals of unresolved conflicts in contemporary GDR reality.[33] And, developing their perspectives out of their own observations and experiences of industrial production and farm life, these dramatists were apparently not influenced significantly by the pronouncements of the Bitterfeld Conference.[34] In his autobiography *Krieg ohne Schlacht* (War without Battle, 1994), for example, Heiner Müller recalled his early connections to the working world, which he had drawn upon for his first major play, *Der Lohndrücker*: "My knowledge about the workers' milieu, about the beginnings of GDR industry, came from my time in Frankenberg, where I had scraped rust off lathes. And it wasn't difficult for me to describe workers. I knew how they talked. That was the world where I had grown up."[35] Müller went on to describe his trip with his wife and collaborator Inge to the construction site of the lignite combine called "Schwarze Pumpe" (Black Pump), where they interviewed workers and lived in their barracks for two or three weeks. Impressions from this visit provided the material for Müller's next "brigade drama," *Die Korrektur* (The Correction), which was written in the winter of 1958 as a radio play, also before the Bitterfeld Conference.[36] Looking back in 1994, then, at the calls for intensifying contact between writers and workers at the conference of 1959, Müller stated in typically cynical, yet incisive fashion: "This Bitterfeld Program called 'Reach for the pen, mate' was quite sensible, but it turned into a parody. Domestication instead of class emancipation. Also, a temporary employment opportunity for unsuccessful writers. The heights of culture had to be leveled so that they could be stormed."[37]

What, then, did the calls that were heard at Bitterfeld for writers to "go to the base" actually mean? While a few speakers, such as Willi Bredel, stated explicitly that writers needed to work for one or two years in factories in order to comprehend this world adequately,[38] most did not urge writers to perform manual labor themselves for a time. That is, there was no emphasis on trying to establish a "community" through the lowest common denominator of shared, hard physical work. Rather, for the most part the conference statements remained rather general and somewhat flexible about what it was supposed to mean for writers and other intellectuals to go out and experience "life." Writers were to "adapt their own lives to the life of the people" (Kurella); they were to "participate in socialist construction" (Ulbricht); they were to find a "second home in a factory or on a collective farm" (Strittmatter). In turn, workers were to improve their educational and cultural niveau.[39] The emphasis on production was connected to the economic campaign of "socialist competition" that was just getting under way in earnest with the goal of surpassing the Federal Republic's standard of living. Accordingly, what these calls meant most specifically was that writers were to develop close connections to the newly formed Brigades of Socialist Labor in order to observe and depict the creation of the "new socialist man" that was being promoted there. (After all, the Bitterfeld Conference had been sponsored by two Brigades of Socialist Labor from the Electrochemical Combine, "Nikolai Mamai" and "Unity.") Speakers referred to writers who had recently established relationships with brigades or taken up residence at construction sites.[40] There they were engaged in giving readings, advising Circles of Writing Workers, contributing to factory and village newspapers, writing local histories, and participating in other cultural activities.[41]

In the next few years after the Bitterfeld Conference, many new literary works both elaborated earlier tendencies and focused more intensely on contemporary life in the GDR, based on writers' own observations of industrial and rural work. And their central theme was almost always the problematic alliances between above and below, among party functionaries, the intelligentsia (whether engineers, technicians, writers, or other artists), and workers and farmers. Within and among all these levels, these works depicted tensions and clashes between activity and passivity, commitment and rejection, identification with common goals and individual self-assertion. In particular, the problem of alliances, of building the "socialist community," appears as if under a magnifying glass in a specific group of texts depicting the experience of unaccustomed manual labor. These works are either reportages about the author's own experiences or fictionalized portrayals based on the author's observations of brigades and various workplaces. They all revolve around the process through which GDR writers set out to displace themselves somehow, to relinquish accustomed positions of privilege through allying themselves with those who had traditionally been on the bottom, but who were now supposed to ascend. These works demonstrate both the continuation of old patterns of hierarchical thinking and what might have been new possibilities for potentially more liberating alliances, though these were thwarted in the long run. The Bitterfeld Conference did not dictate one single acceptable approach to journeying into the working world. However, Ulbricht specifically mentioned one writer as demonstrating in exemplary fashion the "path for writers to take in the new age."[42] This was a writer who, in her speech at the conference, had recounted what she learned from going down into a coal mine and trying out a miner's work for herself.

Regina Hastedt

If you want to be like them, you must work like they do.
—Regina Hastedt (1959)[43]

Writer Regina Hastedt and coal miner Sepp Zach spoke together at the Bitterfeld Conference—she to describe her almost completed book *Die Tage mit Sepp Zach* (Days with Sepp Zach, 1959), and he to testify to the importance of creating literature about the lives of those like himself who had previously been excluded from full participation in the higher realms of culture. Born in 1921, Hastedt was a press photographer in Chemnitz after 1945 and the author of a number of novels and short stories.[44] In her book, which Ulbricht praised as a model for other writers to emulate, she portrayed a writer's journey to the unfamiliar working world of this miner and active SED member. The narrator, who is shown as having dwelled too long on the past traumas of war and the uncertainties of the present, is rather unenthusiastic about her project at first and intends to write only a brief reportage. However, she is drawn ever further into the miners' lives and actually works for about two weeks shoveling coal in order to contribute to fulfilling the plan's quota in a crisis situation.

In this text, "going to the base" entails the effort to connect writing and life, the search for security and a sense of belonging, and the narrator's actual experience of the most demanding manual labor. By "going into production," the narrator sets out to learn and write about workers' biographies, whereas their task, in turn, is to help her overcome her previous bourgeois attachments and attain the proper class standpoint. And the text leaves no doubt about what this standpoint is to be: unreserved identification with what the narrator terms the "mother Party" (53) and the "fathers in the mines" (82), the strong, disciplined, class-conscious workers. For Hastedt's narrator, participating in the unfamiliar world of manual labor means negating all subjective interests. She learns to take pleasure in giving up her individuality and merging with the irresistible historical force that the miners represent. Above all, in her brief stint of actually working as the only woman among the miners, she undergoes a nearly religious, awkwardly portrayed revelation about the ideological power behind the miners' unified strength:

> I looked up [from Sepp] along the coal-face, where one miner after the next stood. And seeing him and his comrades, I recognized at this moment the face of his class. They were all alike: proud and certain of victory. For they always had reserves everywhere. In the offices of the factory directors, the Party, the bookkeepers. . . . They would laugh and enjoy this hard work. . . . Now we were united. . . . With an indescribable feeling, the last remnant of my ego dissolved. Now I flowed into this powerful stream without looking back. (162–63, ellipses in original)

Here, the narrator's depiction of her relationship to the miners is both infantilized and sexualized in a stereotypical way. For on the surface, she appears to give up all claims to the validity of her own life story. At such points, Hastedt's text reproduces conventional gender stereotypes found in earlier proletarian literature which have the effect of promoting a conformist, authoritarian model of personal and social relationships.[45]

Yet paradoxically, through these frozen images of her narrator renouncing egotism and becoming united with class-conscious miners hard at work, Hastedt asserted the authority of the writer, here the producer of ideology, over them.[46] Her workers are basically all alike, filled with assurance, obsessed with performance, naively cheerful, and folksy—anything but multidimensional human beings.[47] This flattened, one-sided perspective allowed no room for the portrayal of differences or conflicts. Therefore, Hastedt could only depict the unaccustomed experience of manual labor fleetingly, as a means to an inevitably heroic end rather than a site of ongoing struggles. That is, while this was the kind of journey to the working world that produced harmonized images useful to the party's cultural programs and power politics, it was a dead end as far as opening dialogue between writers and workers on an equal level was concerned. If one speaker at the Second Bitterfeld Conference in 1964 had later declared that "the path to Bitterfeld is not a stroll into a socialist garden arbor,"[48] Hastedt's book from 1959 belied such pronouncements by promoting what was essentially a socialist idyll grounded on acceptance of patriarchal authority.

Unexpected Trajectories

> Through working hard, it was our task to transform
> bitterness, resignation, aimless rebellion, and the feeling
> of our own complicity into assurance and conviction.
> —Christa Wolf (1959)[49]

If conformist texts such as Hastedt's were blessed with official sanction, other depictions of journeys to the working world in the immediate aftermath of the Bitterfeld Conference gave more complex pictures of the process of forming alliances with workers while still maintaining a clear identification with the socialist state.[50] Such works always brought out—often unintentionally—the difficulties in moving out of the spotlight and into the margins, in taking those outside the traditional boundaries of the educationally privileged upper and middle classes seriously as equal partners in cultural exchange and debate as well as in political action.[51] Looking back today, after the events of 1989–1990—which, following a short period of utopian euphoria, starkly revealed the distance between many GDR intellectuals and the "people"—the shortcomings of these earlier GDR narratives are perhaps even more apparent.[52] This is especially true for the tendencies in most of these texts to present an overly romanticized view of the world of manual labor which both ignores most of its unpleasant aspects and also rarely allows the diverse voices of workers themselves to emerge and to be taken seriously. And as the other, equally problematic and stereotypical side of this coin, these works also frequently hold up the generalized experience of manual labor as a necessary and even welcome disciplinary tool for bringing flighty, rebellious, pleasure-seeking individuals into line under controlling authorities.

However, what is also striking upon rereading these texts today are the ways in which these writers made demands upon themselves to enter into and try to depict worlds that were strange, faraway, and almost impenetrable to them at times. Not from the working class themselves, these authors belonged to the generation that was old enough to have experienced war and fascism in childhood and youth. Accordingly, they were often more immediately concerned with the traumas of the past and their own personal transformations than with the project of building up alliances with groups who were now supposed to constitute the new ruling classes. Nevertheless, these journeys to the working world were also grounded in experiences of present realities, in efforts to set aside privilege for the sake of common goals. Two novels and two reportages from these years provide exemplary illustrations of these problems: Adolf Endler's *Weg in die Wische* (Journey into the Wische, 1960), Brigitte Reimann's *Ankunft im Alltag* (Arrival in Everyday Life, 1961), Christa Wolf's *Der geteilte Himmel* (Divided Heaven, 1963), and Franz Fühmann's *Kabelkran und Blauer Peter* (Cable Crane and Blue Peter, 1962). While Endler began writing his collection of several short texts already in 1958, the calls at Bitterfeld for writers to "go to the base" clearly sent the other three authors on trajectories into the unfamiliar working world which they might not otherwise have chosen. Reimann, born in 1933, had been a teacher in the 1950s and spent time in 1960 developing close connections with a brigade in "Schwarze Pumpe," the lignite combine in Hoyerswerda.[53] Wolf, born in 1929, was working as an editor for the Mitteldeutscher Verlag in Halle in 1959 when she set out to observe a brigade in a factory that produced railroad cars and to participate as an adviser in "circles of writing workers."[54] And Fühmann, born in 1922 and once a committed Nazi soldier who had been "reeducated" in Soviet prisoner-of-war camps, worked in 1959 as an unskilled laborer with a brigade in the Warnow shipyards close to Rostock.[55]

Adolf Endler

Born in 1930 into a middle-class family in Düsseldorf, Adolf Endler worked for various newspapers and magazines in the Federal Republic in the early 1950s and moved permanently to the GDR in 1955.[56] He is best known for his later poetry and as the co-editor of the controversial anthology *In diesem besseren Land* (In This Better Country, 1966), which sparked the "poetry debate."[57] Endler's first published text, *Weg in die Wische,* recounts his experiences working with a Free German Youth (FDJ) brigade for two weeks in 1959, after he had studied from 1955 to 1957 at the Johannes R. Becher Institute for Literature in Leipzig. The "Wische" was a swampy area around the Elbe River close to Magdeburg that the FDJ had chosen as the site for a huge project early in 1958. Brigades of young people were to take turns working there for several weeks at a time, digging drainage ditches and creating a productive agricultural area. According to Endler, about four thousand FDJ members participated in these brigades

Free German Youth members digging drainage ditches. Adolf Endler, *Weg in die Wische* (1960).

in 1958 and five thousand in 1959. In describing his own path to this point, Endler expressed both astonishment and relief at the turn his life had taken: "It was really strange to imagine that I was going to be one of them, considering my past."[58] Recalling the "wasted" years he had spent in the West, he juxtaposed them to his new sense of performing a useful task together with others. At the same time, he took pains to assure his readers that by leaving East Berlin for a rural area, he was not searching for an idyllic escape but rather hoping to encounter new challenges: "Although it looks that way, don't think that it was an escape like that of Rimbaud's to Ethiopia and the life of a poor shopkeeper, of Thoreau's to Walden Pond, or of Wiechert's to the 'simple life' " (12).

However, if Endler denied that his journey to the Wische had anything in common with retreating to a simpler life, his depiction of the unaccustomed manual labor he performed there was still imbued with a decidedly romanticized view of the world he had entered, a world that did in fact appear somewhat exotic to him. He admitted that the work of shoveling ditches through the heavy, clinging mud was terribly difficult. Yet he generally played down this experience in comparison to the satisfaction of being part of something much larger than himself, as in this passage: "The work made everybody groan. We all wanted to throw down our spades immediately and run away. Why had we let ourselves in for something like this in the first place? This question alternated with the feeling of pride at holding out and seeing the ditch grow longer" (23). Seeing that his own brigade would not complete the project in the short time allotted, Endler also realized that other brigades would follow and continue what they had begun. In this narrative, then, the experience of work functions as an expression of hope and assurance for the future of the "socialist community" in which all members carry out their assigned tasks. Here, the pressure of collective goals and strict moral standards brings lazy brigade members into line, to accept being trained as disciplined socialists. Furthermore, the young people's tenacity is shown as gradually winning over the eccentric farmers in the area who—set in their old-fashioned ways—are skeptical initially about the entire modernization project.

After his two weeks with the brigade, Endler decided to move to the Wische area and settle in a village where there would be a great deal of work for him. There, he attempted to stay in contact with the "base" through activities such as writing poetry for the brigade newspaper and heavy-handed agitprop pieces, including one entitled "Wische—Bauplatz der Jugend: Agitpropgedicht für acht Sprecher" (Wische—Construction Site of Youth: Agitprop Poem for Eight Speakers, 51–69). In Endler's effort to sustain a positive identification with the socialist project, the dominant tone is one of youthful enthusiasm for working together with others in a somewhat exoticized world. The dry language of the Five-Year Plan had stated that the Wische was to become the first unified area of socialist production close to Magdeburg. But according to Endler, the young socialists who came there to work soon declared the Wische to be a synonym for the "new ground" that was being broken in the spirit of "revolutionary romanticism" (77). Following the model of the Soviet subbotniks and the Komsomol youth organization,[59] the FDJ held up the Wische as the model for other large-scale youth projects in the GDR (98).[60] Concluding the diary section of his book in 1959, Endler apotheosized the goals being formulated and put into motion at the time in the worlds of work and of literature: "Construction sites of the Free German Youth, socialist brigades, Bitterfeld Conference with the 'Writing Workers,' Rostock Parliament of Youth. 1959, the year when the GDR is celebrating its tenth anniversary, I call it the 'Year of Youth' " (113).

Brigitte Reimann and Christa Wolf

The literary texts from this period in the GDR that revolve around fictional or autobiographical experiences with unaccustomed manual labor should be viewed against this background of widespread participation—partly coerced, partly voluntary—in the social projects that Endler mentioned, with the addition to his list of the system of polytechnical education. As discussed above, according to this pedagogical approach taken over from the Soviet Union, pupils were to gain an understanding of factory and agricultural production through working in state-owned enterprises for a few hours each week while in school. Furthermore, high-school graduates were pushed to spend a "practical year" working before going on to higher education, and university students were required to spend at least one summer (the "student summer") at a job in production. The young people were to be instructed by workers and farmers themselves, under the theory that through this process, walls of educational and class privilege would fall, progress would be made in overcoming the distinction between mental and manual labor, and—it must be added—shortfalls in production would be made up by using young people to augment an insufficient workforce.

Two of the most widely discussed GDR novels from the early 1960s, Brigitte Reimann's *Ankunft im Alltag* and Christa Wolf's *Der geteilte Himmel,* draw on this effort to connect "learning and life" by focusing on prospective students' journeys to the working world. Reimann's novel traces the stories of three high-school graduates—Nikolaus, Curt, and Recha—who spend their "practical year" working in the lignite combine "Schwarze Pumpe" before beginning their university studies. In the early Weimar Republic, these three young people would have been called "work students," but their reasons for entering the working world and their reactions to unfamiliar manual labor bear little similarity to those of their earlier counterparts. The first, Nikolaus, is from a working-class family and wants to be a painter. He is spending a year in the factory at the insistence of his mother, who wants him to remember his origins and the source of his opportunity to study.[61] As the solid, stable, somewhat awkward but thoughtful one of the three, Nikolaus has the least difficulty integrating himself into the working world and finally being accepted by the workers as one of their own. Reimann portrays this process of identification through both the physical appearance and the inner perspective of her characters. In Nikolaus's case, the narrator describes his transformation as follows after several weeks of working in the factory: "When Nikolaus came stamping into the canteen now, in his rubber boots, with his wind-reddened face and rough, chapped hands, he was no longer any different from the other workers. And no one would have suspected that he was a high-school graduate and a guest" (195). The only thing that makes Nikolaus stand out—his huge, floppy hat inherited from his father's years in the "Wandervogel" youth movement—is nothing more than a harmless idiosyncrasy.[62] It symbolizes his artistic interests, which, however, are not shown as clashing in any way with the working world he has entered.

The second student is both the polar opposite of Nikolaus and his rival for Recha's affections. Curt has agreed most unwillingly to spend a year in the factory rather than two years in the army, which his father—a longtime Communist and now director of a state-owned textile factory—would have preferred for his son. A lazy show-off who tries to impress others with his money and to avoid work at every opportunity, Curt bears only outward similarity to the other workers until the very end of the novel. Here, the narrator describes his remorseful mood: "Today, for the first time, he heard [the "International"] sung in a factory hall by workers whom he resembled outwardly, with his blue, oil-spattered mechanic's uniform and his grimy hands. And he saw how the older ones removed their caps and held them in their hands. . . . They struck up the second verse, and Curt moved his lips, but he didn't sing. He had never felt so insignificant and pitiful as in this moment" (263). Although Reimann did not go so far as to show exactly how Curt finally accounts to his brigade for his errors, the narrative leaves no doubt that the irresistible power of working-class solidarity transforms him. He will no longer be a jaded individualist. Rather, he will be a young man willing to accept being educated and trained in both the standards of required workplace behavior and the expected political values and perspectives.

Two other figures in the novel have more complex life stories, as they have always had to confront hierarchical preconceptions that classified individuals as having more or less "value" for "communities" established by force. The first of these is Recha, the "half-Jewish" student whose mother was murdered in the Holocaust. Having grown up in an orphanage in the GDR, Recha has decided to work for a year out of a desire to be "independent," to become "less fearful," and to be like everyone else, rather than to be pitied constantly as a "victim of fascism" (18). Like Nikolaus, she also identifies strongly with the process of socialist construction. However, as a young woman, her integration into the world of work is shown as proceeding in a different, less direct manner. Stereotypically, she is not subjected to the same strict discipline as the men, and she appears more as a decoration than an essential part of production. Furthermore, although the narrative is pervaded by a sense of the romanticism of creating the new, it is Recha with whom this youthfully naive enthusiasm is most closely associated, as in the following passage: "Today the baggy uniform didn't bother her. She was even proud of it, in a kind of romantic way, and she was proud of her black, rough hands. At least outwardly, her uniform and her hands made her just like the others in the brigade. And perhaps this was just what she wished for—to be like them and to belong to them—although she had avoided everyone until today" (104). At this point, Recha dares to speak up for the first time at a brigade meeting in defense of a young worker named Erwin who constantly causes disruptions because of his sloppiness and unreliability. The source of these habits, however, is a most troubled background: Erwin's parents died in the war; he failed in school and was finally placed in an institution for juvenile delinquents; and his ability to work is greatly lessened by a vision impairment.

Reimann structured her narrative so that these two characters, Recha and Erwin, who are both searching for a sense of belonging, do in fact find a place they can call their own among supportive co-workers in the combine. Here, in fundamental contrast to invocations of the "national racial community" before 1945, two outsiders who formerly would have been violently and brutally excluded are portrayed as being potentially valuable participants in the workplace. However, their feeling of being at home there is only to be had for the price of "normalization," for the disavowal or overcoming of the things that make them "different." No further explicit mention is made of Recha's Jewishness (which is circumscribed by the coded references to her exotic "Egyptian eyes"). And Erwin's vision impairment is to be surgically corrected, not only to improve the quality of his life, but also to enable him to perform work of full value to his brigade.

In this early GDR novel, the three young students all experience varying degrees of uncertainty, mistrust, sadness, and fear at the beginning. Indeed, the narration often seems deepest and most authentic in such passages, which generally have to do with experiences and memories related to the war. These negative emotions are countered with hopes for finding more satisfying connections with others and are finally resolved through the students' acceptance of being educated and molded by the workplace experience. That is, imbuing its protagonists with the wish to escape from isolation,[63] the novel expresses unmediated hopes for more unity and brotherhood, which lead to gaps and false harmonies in the narrative. For the two male students, becoming a part of the working world entails proving their strength, repressing weakness and moody reluctance, and falling into line under controlling authorities, although there is still some room for intellectual interests and harmless personal tastes. For Recha, the working world becomes more of an emotional identification point. Focusing mainly on the students' development, the novel devotes relatively little attention to the workers whom the students meet in the "Schwarze Pumpe." They remain mostly in the background, appearing mainly as somewhat eccentric characters or as benevolently paternal authorities, but certainly not as the students' equals. Yet on the other hand, the desires expressed in this novel to break the chains of tradition and of individual biography, to reach out for broader and more useful connections with others, remain moving expressions of early hopes in the GDR for liberation which Reimann linked with the muted accomplishments of everyday life.[64]

Like the characters in Reimann's novel, the protagonist Rita in Christa Wolf's *Der geteilte Himmel* encounters the unfamiliar world of factory work in a way that is central to the narrative and crucial for her ultimate development. Using extended flashbacks and overlapping time levels, the narrator recalls the initial impetus behind Rita's decision to enter the working world for a short period of time. Having finished school and settled down to a job in an insurance office, the seventeen-year-old Rita feels trapped in an unsatisfying, boring, isolated existence. The course of her life changes, however, when a party official appears in her village to recruit new teachers and convinces her both to begin university study and also to work in a factory beforehand, declaring that every teacher now needs to have this experience.[65] Rita joins a brigade in a factory that manufactures railroad cars, and a new world of struggle and precarious achievement unfolds for her. In contrast to the portrayal of Rita's office job, her stint in the factory is depicted in positive terms that make no mention of the monotonous, strenuous, or stultifying aspects of unskilled manual labor. She soon becomes comfortable there and takes pleasure in her small but essential role in producing the vitally necessary railroad cars. Above all, she meets the worker Rolf Meternagel, who becomes her mentor, teaches her how to use tools, clues her in on the relationships and tensions among the brigade members, and gives her an unforgettable example of tenacious commitment to socialist ethics and goals.

Later, after a difficult first year at the university, where Rita is exposed to hypocrisy and egotism, she decides to return to the "solid" world of the factory during vacation. It is at this point that her fiancé, Manfred—older than her and no longer able to believe in greater goals due to his disillusioning wartime experience in the Hitler Youth—leaves for West Berlin. In turn, Rita chooses against love and for commitment to socialism, to what the narrator terms "the harder, more rigorous life" (181). This decision is motivated in two ways. First, Rita's attachment to the world of production has become too strong to give up. The narrator states: "Yesterday evening, an hour before midnight, she was the last person from the second shift to come out of the gate of the factory hall. As she usually did, she looked around again and counted the railroad cars awaiting the first shift for final assembly. She couldn't part from the dull gray, heavy, enormous things" (163). And second, as the narrator explains, her moral commitment to the collective values represented by Meternagel is not something she can cast away for the sake of mere individual happiness: "Sometimes she herself had thought: Meternagel is ruining himself for nothing. He's bitten off more than he can chew. But it was just because of this that she couldn't bring herself to leave him in the lurch" (175). Speaking at the Second Bitterfeld Conference in 1964, the head editor of the Mitteldeutscher Verlag," Heinz Sachs, validated this psychological portrayal as a reflection of new social relations in the GDR, stating approvingly: "The decision of Rita in Christa Wolf's *Der geteilte Himmel* is unthinkable without the concrete, new circumstances which have been created here in the GDR. What would her decision have been before she worked in the railroad car factory?"[66] This text is less concerned, then, with depicting manual labor and those who perform it in a differentiated way than with presenting emotional experiences gained in the sphere of material production as the decisive forces that steer Rita's development from naïveté to "maturity," which mold and train the prospective teacher. In the end, Rita's assurance and conviction are held up as exemplary, and the novel's sense of distance from the complex realities of the working world infuses the narrative with an attitude of gentle arrogance toward all those whose consciousness, self-control, and self-denial have not yet attained similarly high levels.

In the short prose piece entitled "Dienstag, der 27. September 1960" (Tuesday, September 27, 1960), written while Wolf was having regular contact with the brigade and writing the first drafts of *Der geteilte Himmel*, her difficulties in penetrating beneath the surface of the unfamiliar world of factory work come out rather clearly and consciously. For example, after one particularly tense brigade meeting complicated by hidden rivalries, she described her reaction as follows: "I go home quickly, excited, with agitated thoughts. I hear once again what they say, and also what they don't say, what they don't even give away with their eyes. Whoever would be successful at fathoming this almost impenetrable tangle of motives and counter-motives, actions and counter-actions. . . . To make large the lives of people who appear condemned to small steps. . . ."[67] Indeed, as one literary historian has pointed out, it seems from this text that Wolf's strongest impression from visiting and observing the factory was the huge gap between this world and her own life.[68] And in turn, this perception clashed with her conviction that it was the duty of writers like herself to speak for those who had previously been condemned to living diminished lives. Consequently, she went on to voice her beginning doubts about the entire process of trying to take over "arbitrary experiences" as material for a novel, rather than for a more superficial reportage, musing, "We come to the role of experience for writing and to the responsibility one has for the *content* of his experience. Is one really free to have experiences which are perhaps desirable from a social standpoint but for which one is not suited because of one's origin and character structure? Of course one can get to know many things, but can one really *experience* them?"[69] Wolf answered her own questions in her novel by creating Rita as a character who participates in factory production for only a short time. And she replied to these questions in her subsequent writing by not depicting the world of workers again.

Franz Fühmann

In contrast to most other GDR writers, whose journeys into the working world were limited to rather brief experiments or to periods required in connection with university study, Franz Fühmann not only heeded the call of Bitterfeld in the late 1950s but also continued with grim determination to try various types of manual labor for twenty years.[70] Having served as an official for the National-Democratic Party (NDPD) since 1949, Fühmann resigned from his position in 1959 in order to devote full time to writing. In 1959 and 1960 he worked at the Warnow shipyards, where he collected material for the reportage *Kabelkran und Blauer Peter,* and in 1961 he completed a training course as a welder. During the rest of the decade he worked occasionally in various locations, including a construction site in Guben, a collective farm in Wustrau, and a factory in Teltow. In 1974 he visited a copper mine close to Mansfeld for the first time, and for the next five years—fascinated by this hidden world below the surface of the earth and calling it his "primal experience"—he went into various mines, working for short periods and belonging to a miners' brigade until 1979.

Literally until the end of his life in 1984, Fühmann struggled with finding adequate literary form for these experiences; his unfinished manuscripts dealing with this material were published posthumously in a book entitled *Im Berg* (In the Mountain, 1991). From his early reportage filled with optimism to his last fragmentary texts, which he himself called the "report of a failure,"[71] Fühmann repeatedly attempted to overcome his guilt-laden political past by entering into the working world, and to make this experience fruitful for his writing. His ultimate sense of failure should be taken as the story of a writer who was intent on bridging the gaps between above and below and who was thwarted by psychological, cultural, and political forces much larger than himself.

Fühmann's two texts *Kabelkran und Blauer Peter* and *Im Berg* recount his efforts to enter into the world of manual labor, which he viewed as the realm of the absolute "other" in contrast to his own class background as the son of a pharmacist. In the earlier reportage, he described the first venture of his narrator ("Franz") into the working world as tentative and full of anxiety. Franz goes through a process of overcoming inner resistance before he actually makes the decision to go to work and to write about this experience. At first, he merely plans to visit Rostock and the surrounding area. However, an old friend who is now an economic functionary proposes that Franz should write a reportage about the shipyards—a project he is quite reluctant to undertake. Franz professes his ignorance about the world of industrial work:

> The world of big industry was alien and remote to me. In my childhood, the factories seemed as gloomy as dungeons; workers didn't go to high school like I did. . . . I felt a great urge to write about our new life, but I knew this life only very imperfectly. Its innermost realms were alien to me. And I felt apprehensive and fearful of this iron world with its incomprehensible machines and its threatening rushing and roaring. I stared through the fog towards the shipyard, and the shipyard lay invisible in the looming grayness.[72]

In spite of all these doubts, however, Franz allows his friend to guide him on a tour through the shipyards. His first reactions to the giant production site are a jumbled swirl of confusion, uncertainty, and even fear, juxtaposed with more comforting or fascinating impressions. On the one hand, as a visitor from "above," Franz selects from the storehouse of "gruesome images" that the upper classes had often used to depict the lower, working classes since the nineteenth century.[73] Accordingly, he describes this unfamiliar world as chaotic, incomprehensible, threatening, disorienting, and even wild and junglelike. On the other hand, also desiring to praise what he discovers there from the standpoint of his commitment to socialist ideology, he reaches for appropriately positive images, as well.

Some of these are basically idyllic and function to defuse this world's threatening aspects, while others originate in the timeless realms of fairy tale and myth and have the effect of elevating and heroicizing the working world beyond human proportions.

In Franz's first impressions of the shipyard, the workers themselves remain strangely absent and invisible. Rather than expressing curiosity about the individuals who are building the ships, Franz immediately aestheticizes the work process to which he is being exposed. So, for example, when told about how sheet metal is cut into parts for the ships, he immediately thinks of the fairy tale about a little tailor who could cut and sew gold and silver. And in an emblematic image that appears at several crucial points in the text, he sees the flame of a welder working high up on a ship's mast, shining out of what he describes as the realm of the sagas of old (66). At first, his sense of displacement in this unfamiliar world prevails over his longing to be a part of it, and he decides not to follow the path that is beckoning him: "I thought about the worker who had stood on the tip of the mast, and I was envious of him. I was envious of everyone who went in and out of the shipyard. I felt myself excluded; I wanted to leave" (24–25). However, the turning point comes when he attends a ship-launching on what he intends to be his last day in Warnow, a day full of sights that overpower his doubts and resistance. The workers themselves, the shipbuilders who are his potential workmates, appear like a closed, fascinating phalanx to him: "The shipbuilders stood motionless. Their faces could not be recognized. They stood chest to chest, leaning on the rail" (27). And they are only the most alluring part of the swirling crowd surrounding the ship. Caught up in what seems to be a dreamlike, "powerful and beautiful" image of togetherness (30), Franz decides impulsively to stay and work at the shipyard—that is, to enter into this "community."

Once Franz is assigned to a brigade, his reactions to the actual work and to the workers he gets to know alternate between submissive expressions of his inferiority and hymnic praise—two sides of the coin for this outsider who wants to identify positively with this new world. At the beginning, he particularly emphasizes his timidity, clumsiness, and nervous fear of being conspicuous and not fitting in with the others, presenting himself as the "helpless clown."[74] This worry about not being able to conform is a new psychological element in the historical tradition of journeys to the working world, as it was hardly ever voiced earlier by reformers who were certain that they knew what was best for the working classes, by work students entering out of economic necessity into a world they viewed negatively or with indifference, by those on the right who simply asserted the forced unity between social classes, or by leftists whose main goal was exposure of social wrongs. In a GDR text from this period such as Fühmann's, the narrator is becoming a worker for a time primarily out of a desire to submit to being educated and formed himself through experiencing the world of manual labor. Consequently, his frequently expressed fears of not behaving correctly, of being "different" from the other men, articulate his apprehensions about his own inadequacies, which could have the terrible effect of causing him to drop out of the community he so strongly desires. Characterized by the absence of serious conflicts, this community is made up of brigade workers who appear as basically a good bunch of men—competent, reliable, and kind, for the most part. And, following the Bitterfeld Program, Franz's own contribution to this world is to encourage one highly motivated worker who has advanced from laborer to engineering student to "reach for the pen" and write about his life—a harmonious depiction of the relations between the intellectual and the "base."

As far as the actual work on the ships goes, Franz occasionally describes it as monotonous and strenuous. However, he concentrates primarily on his efforts to "be a man" and work as hard as everyone else, which finally give him the deepest satisfaction and sense of belonging. Accordingly, even a night spent drilling holes into sheet metal does not seem boring or dull to him, but rather provides him with a pleasurable sense that he is doing what is expected and being rewarded for this with aesthetic pleasure, as in the following passage: "A beautiful job, beautiful on the quiet ship in the night, which was growing. I felt my arms and hands slowly becoming heavy, as if they were being filled with a heavy flood. And the work ran peacefully down the hours, like a stream crosses through its delta, without whirlpools and rapids" (64–65). The nature of this aesthetic experience, however, goes far beyond that of individual perception, as Franz continues to describe his feelings at the end of his shift: "I felt a kind of freedom that I had never felt before. I was at the shipyard; my wish was fulfilled; my time at the office desk lay behind me; a new phase of my life had begun; and the shipyard belonged to me; and the ships and the smoke and the night. The welding flame shone. Its violet ran over the silver, and the night lay mild over the shipyard, like a saga over a darkly murmuring place" (66). The flame of the faceless welder appears here again as an image intended to elevate the process Franz is undergoing and the world he wants to join from the realm of everyday struggle and toil into the sphere of myth.

By becoming a worker for a time with a brigade in this nationalized enterprise, then, Franz undergoes a process that both lowers and elevates him. He begins as the naive, unknowing intellectual who willingly submits to being educated and formed by activities and people formerly "beneath" him. By accepting their tutelage and also by conforming to ideological expectations, he then becomes a temporary member of both the male world of strong comrades and also—more grandiosely—the world of mythological heroes. Because of his fascination with such static, timeless images, the narrator is able to conclude with the illusion that, through his experience as a worker, he has actually penetrated the "fog" that hid the shipyards from him initially, stating at the end in biblical tones: "Over [the reality of the shipyard] there lay a veil. But now this veil was pushed aside and I looked into the face of my country and saw that it was beautiful. It was beautiful in a human way, not in an unearthly way—a worker's face, not a madonna's smile. . . . The veil was pushed back; I saw the face, and it was beautiful. Good eyes, a high forehead, free speech, and no misleading features" (131).

In such passages, this text and others like it from the socialist cultural tradition hover dangerously close to right-wing visions of *Gemeinschaft* that repeatedly employ images of changeless manual labor and of virile, aestheticized physical strength, images that insist on the "beauty of labor" and admit of no latitude for human variety and difference.[75] And—tragically for those who sought to give their expressions of commitment to socialism a firmer grounding in reality—this perspective was often encouraged by official cultural pronouncements in the GDR at the time, which preferred images of relative unity and harmony over unsettling exposés.[76] On the other hand and just as importantly, in a text such as Fühmann's the narrator's fascination with making himself fit into the world of manual labor is also relativized by his refusal to adopt a heavily anti-intellectual perspective with respect to his fellow workers. Rather, in accordance with long socialist traditions, he envisions a future in which, through technological advances and rational, nonbureaucratic planning, there would be little need for stupefying drudgery.[77] Having already encountered workers at the shipyards who are taking advantage of new possibilities for advancement, he looks forward to a day when the majority are not condemned to live diminished lives, and when those like himself from more privileged backgrounds have overcome their blind spots. But in yet another entanglement, the final image with which Fühmann's narrator approvingly describes the process of transformation going on at the shipyards is one of control: "It seems to me as though a wildly luxuriant jungle is going to be transformed here into a well-tended garden with lawns and flower beds and arbors" (127). Here, the chaos to be overcome is not only that of the irrational capitalist mode of production, which paid no heed to the human needs of workers—although this is certainly one thing that Fühmann meant. Rather, it is just as much the disorderliness long associated with those on the bottom, who may not feel themselves to be represented at all by the ideology being propagated from above in their name. In this vision, the anarchy of production is to be brought under control through rationality and planning, and the potentially challenging and threatening voices from below are to be dampened by the writer who will speak for them in his basically affirmative "hymns" (127). And in any event, in this dream of transforming the "jungle" of production into a weedless socialist garden, it is the sojourner in the working world who still occupies the center, while those who were his workmates for a time remain in their place on the margins.

In preparation for the Second Bitterfeld Conference in 1964, the GDR Ministry of Culture asked a large group of writers and other intellectuals to evaluate the Bitterfeld Program. Fühmann's response was a long open letter expressing his skepticism about the call for writers to go into production and explaining why he had decided not to expand his reportage into the industrial novel that many had expected from him. Here, he asserted that it was impossible for a writer of his age and background to gain the necessary insight into the working world that was so foreign to him simply through short periods of participating in it:

> For there are two areas . . . which I will not be able to master no matter how hard I try: first, the vast land of memory . . . which every literary work must have in order not to remain superficial; and second, the vast realm of universal human feelings also lies "beyond me." These can only be developed in a believable way in literature if they are shown in their individuality which has been shaped by specific social forces. But I do not know this individuality, and, coming "from outside," I have too little access to it. It's enough for a political debate but not for an artistic depiction. For example, if someone knows that he is going to do the same work for the same wages for his entire life, what does he find satisfying or oppressive about this work? What does he find stimulating? Where does he find joy and suffering? How, in what images, does the work appear in his thoughts and feelings? And so forth. I do not know, and I have no feeling for these things. And even though the worker is my friend, he doesn't talk about them . . . because one has the answer in one's flesh and blood, and not in one's mouth.[78]

The themes that would remain central to his writing, Fühmann went on to say, were not those from the working world that he had compelled himself to visit, but those more integrally tied to his own subjective experiences—

that is, the life stories of people from "petty-bourgeois backgrounds" under fascism and after the war. Similarly, in her 1960 essay Christa Wolf had already voiced doubts about the ultimate consequences for literary creativity of the experience of participating in the working world for a time. She expressed these doubts even more explicitly in a 1978 interview:

> In one of my earlier books there are characters who are workers. Today I believe that the complexity of certain milieus, of certain ways of thinking and feeling, can only be described by people who are at home in these milieus, who, for example, were or are workers themselves. I need to know about their lives and their problems for *every* literary work—whether it is "about" them or not. And I hope that every book which takes up important contemporary problems is also relevant to them.[79]

Statements such as these by Fühmann and Wolf mark a shift from perspectives focused on class to more decentered optics that emphasized the writer's positionality or identity and which were often sensitively attuned to the hollowness of ritualized invocations of an all too easily proclaimed socialist "community."[80]

However, in these statements there also resonates the profound tragedy of failed efforts under socialism to bridge the chasms between social classes, between restricted and relatively more privileged lives. By stating that only workers themselves could give adequate literary form to their own worlds, authors such as Fühmann and Wolf were expressing both their genuine sense of their own limitations as well as their intent (doubtlessly tinged with relief) to pursue writing as a means of more subjective self-reflection. For although official cultural politics had encouraged the depiction of everyday life on the one hand, it was also obvious that writers would constantly be subjected to censorship and disciplinary measures whenever they went too far in their portrayals of the working world—that is, if they dared to lay bare sharp conflicts too reminiscent of those under capitalism between the SED and the workers in whose name it ruled. In 1966, for example, Wilhelm Girnus had voiced the party's deep suspicion of points of view that gave too much weight to the perspectives of the workers "down below" at the expense of those in control "above." In a discussion about Heiner Müller's censored play *Der Bau,* he stated his position in the journal *Sinn und Form* (Meaning and Form):

> How does the writer actually come to understand the processes which go on in a factory? To understand these processes both from below as well as from the perspective of

those who are in charge? If he looks around in the factory, he generally experiences these processes only through the eyes of the workers, at best. . . . But is that sufficient? Can one really comprehend these processes without also seeing them through the eyes of those at the top, who coordinate everything and give the impulses?[81]

Under such pressures, then, which meshed partially with their own inclinations as intellectuals who were generally not from the working class themselves, most of the GDR writers who had journeyed into the working world during the Bitterfeld period turned their attention to topics that were either less obviously connected with contemporary GDR life or which reflected more closely their own life experiences. As one literary historian has summarized, "The state's attempt to liberate literature from being reserved for the well-educated, to connect it closely to the working world, and to turn it into a means of propaganda for economic planning or for the reflection and self-depiction of proletarian interests, was broken off and quietly laid to rest."[82] Of course, the themes that many of these writers took up often continued to be highly controversial and politically explosive. To name only two of their most significant areas of concern, the numerous GDR literary works that focus on the continuities and ruptures of German history and on women's lives constitute an enduring aesthetic legacy that challenged entrenched power structures and interpretative frameworks. However, after the mid-1960s the world of workers and farmers was no longer a significant element of this legacy, having largely vanished from literature in this socialist state.

THE ROAD NOT TAKEN TO BITTERFELD: VOLKER BRAUN'S "THE MUD"

> On the day before I departed, I had burned the pictures in the wash-house stove—the pictures in which I was unable to capture the country. . . . I knew: this age, which makes unimagined things possible, needs another kind of art than canvases, than paper. It was through work, with many and for many, that I could become something, could develop. But what had I done here? Did I finally see the project which the new age called for? My life, which I wanted to begin, what should it be like? It was passing . . .
> —Volker Braun, "Der Schlamm" (The Mud, 1959)[83]

In his open letter from 1964, Franz Fühmann had confined his doubts about the possibility of giving adequate literary portrayals of the working world to writers from his own generation who had grown up having little contact with this milieu. Referring approvingly to the GDR's system of polytechnical education, which required all school pupils and university students to spend a certain amount of time in industrial or agricultural production, he maintained that this sense of being an outsider in the working world was already ceasing to be a significant problem for writers of the younger generation.[84] What a statement like this represented, however, was not so much a useful insight into differing experiences of social reality, but rather the commonplace assertion that young people could undergo change more easily and unproblematically than their elders.[85] A text such as Volker Braun's "Der Schlamm," written in 1959 when the author was twenty years old, runs counter to this wish for easily achieved community by demonstrating that the way from "above" into the working world was by no means smooth or self-evident for younger writers in the GDR, either. In this, his impressive first work, which was only published in 1972 as the first of four "reports"[86] in *Das ungezwungene Leben Kasts* (The Casual Life of Kast), Braun wrote about a journey to the working world that intertwined the prevalent tendency to romanticize and elevate the unfamiliar world of manual labor with a frank depiction of its still primitive, backward character. To a greater extent than in the works by Reimann, Wolf, and Fühmann discussed here, this text is a complex reflection on the hopes and deformations woven through the early project of socialist construction in the working world.

Although "Der Schlamm" is a fictional text that is not purely autobiographical, it clearly "shows parallels to the author's own experiences" in the world of manual labor that he had entered already before the proclamation of the Bitterfeld Program—experiences he shared with many others of his generation.[87] Braun had finished high school in 1957 and completed a customary "practical year" before university study by working for a print shop in 1957–1958. Bureaucratic difficulties forced him to postpone matriculation for two more years, and during this time he worked on construction sites in the lignite combine "Schwarze Pumpe" in Hoyerswerda and as a machinist in Burghammer, an open-pit mine.[88] Literary historian Wolfgang Emmerich has characterized this crucial early period in Braun's development: "In these years, so to speak, he followed his own individual 'Bitterfeld Path.' He experienced the division between manual and mental labor, that is, the vertical division of labor, as a continuing problem in 'actually existing socialism.' And, until today, this remains a theme in his literary works which he has pursued tenaciously."[89] The interrelationships, separations, and conflicts between mental and manual labor, the place of education and qualification in this constellation, and the accompanying impressions of standstill and motion are in fact all central to Braun's first text. As "Der Schlamm" begins, the young protagonist, Hans Kast, is traveling to Hoyerswerda, "the largest construction site on the continent," to get a job as an unskilled worker. His feelings of emptiness and detachment from his surroundings are reminiscent of Büchner's "Lenz." As the reader discovers later, Kast has left school after an altercation with the principal, and the path to university study is no longer open to him. Exasperated by the "hypocrisy" surrounding him, he had been overheard complaining about how the teachers only wanted to hear "lip-service" for four years, and furthermore, how the newspapers did not trust the population "with the full truth." All this, to his manner of thinking, blocked the urgent, imperative process of "construction" taken in the broadest sense (22). Consequently, his descent to the world below—that is, his journey to the construction site—comes about because of his expulsion from the world of learning above. In other words, Kast is not consciously searching out contact at first with workers and their world for the sake of "participating in building up socialism"[90]—although to be sure, his dissatisfaction with school indicates that he is a young man seeking depth and authenticity in some form.

Once on the job at the construction site, where his main task is to shovel mud from ditches meant for concrete pipes, Kast experiences for the first time both heavy manual labor and also contact with the motley assortment of men working there—from the so-called "gold-diggers" to relatively passive types to more committed activists.[91] Called "the student" by the other workers in his brigade, he feels his distance from them keenly. At first, he tries to compensate for this separateness by voicing an overly positive, romanticized view of the lives of those with "calloused hands"—a perception narrated ironically, which the workers themselves laugh at and which hardly narrows the gap between them and Kast (11). At certain points, however, the narrative also holds up Kast's work as giving him the positive experience of creating something useful together with others, as in the following passage:

> I had never had such a relationship to the things around
> me. Earlier I had lived in the fantasies which I experienced
> on paper. But now a great, full landscape flowed around me
> which was being moved by our hands, slowly, but without
> stopping; always with the same images, but forming itself
> into something else which I already saw behind the mud.
> This strange feeling—it was like standing in a river of earth,
> concrete, wood, moving everything with my two arms, while
> running, and surrounded by the seasons, which I thought
> could be changed, used, and restructured just like the coun-
> try. (31–32)

At such moments, Kast derives his temporary strength and energy from a sense of being at one with the course of history,[92] of being involved in the hopeful project of building up something qualitatively different out of the "mud," the metaphor for all the ruins of the past.[93]

However, this text is by no means a flat, one-sided glorification of either the supposed "beauties" of communal manual labor (with the fatal associations of the "shovels")[94] or the stereotypically positive moral qualities that protagonists often develop in more conformist GDR literature through experiencing the workplace. Rather, along with its more hopeful elements, Braun's narrative portrays starkly both the continuing primitiveness of this kind of backbreaking toil and the ongoing disagreements and discord among the workers at the construction site, sustaining a tone that is more one of questioning and searching than of didacticism and assurance. Accordingly, while Kast does find intimations of a new sense of belonging and purpose through participating in the construction project, the text by no means shows him as being "trained" through manual labor in any kind of authoritarian sense. In this respect, he differs fundamentally from the male high-school graduates in Reimann's novel and from Fühmann's narrator, who are shown as being integrated into the working world through disciplining their bodies and giving up their individuality. By contrast, Kast voices "disappointment" with the weeks and months of constant, monotonous shoveling, says that he had imagined the construction of socialism to be "different" from this, and poses the unanswered question: "How long can one live this way?" (21–24). He finds no support from his former schoolmates, who—enjoying their secure prospects of university study—laugh at his working in the social depths, at the "antediluvian" enterprise in the "taiga," and mock him as a "martyr, a hero of labor" (26). Furthermore, Kast's life outside the workplace—that is, his relationships with women—is in such turmoil and disorder that there is also no question here, either, of partnership and community having been found and realized.

The portrayal of the other workers at the construction site also highlights the differences among them, rather than evoking any kind of false image of community based on a too-easily-won acceptance of socialist morality and values. When Kast is punched in the face by a worker who cannot stand the sight of his Free German Youth shirt, the narrative lets this action stand for itself, without passing judgment in favor of the naive Kast or against the worker reacting out of his different life experience. Or, while some of the brigade members are working hard, making sacrifices, and learning more for the sake of building up socialism, and others are lazy and resistant to taking advantage of new opportunities, the narrative does not preach the virtues of the former at the expense of the latter. Kast (and by implication, the young Volker Braun) clearly sees hard work and advancement through education and further qualification as holding hope for the future, the hope for expanding the life possibilities of those who had previously been "nothing" and could now be "everything."[95] And of course, this insistence on the potential of those who have often been written off throughout history as mere "work animals" is a defining moment in this kind of socialist journey into the working world. Here, there is a vision not only of going down, but even more so of the possibility of rising up from below. Yet at the same time, the probing, sometimes melancholy tone of the narrative means that it does not propound facile solutions to old, pervasive fears of breaking the chains of tradition for the sake of an uncertain future. When the workers at the construction site finally agree—reluctantly and almost as an afterthought—to compete for the title "Brigade of Socialist Labor" (meaning that they will attempt to work more efficiently, educate themselves further, and support each other outside the workplace), the reader has already seen so much of their often justified skepticism toward plans coming down from above that the outcome seems quite uncertain. And as far as Kast himself goes, he still has reason to complain bitterly about his failure to find meaning and goals for his life, saying at one point:

> We own everything, but everything still happens so slowly, sluggishly, from the bottom, out of the mud! How long will it be like this? Everything we do is dictated by scarcity; everything still happens according to bare necessity. And we behave like that, too. As if enchained by the conditions we encounter and break apart with tiny files. We still treat many things as if we don't own them: life, too. With some things we are stingy; others we hide; still others we trade and barter. (38)

Associating himself here with the workers by using the pronoun "we," Kast can only voice the unfulfilled utopian vision of being able to produce one day out of a situation of abundance rather than scarcity—an "unimaginable" process of acting and creating where "production" would become "art," that is, where the painful experience of the division of labor would be made obsolete (39). For the present, Kast can only participate through his work and his life in the "motion" of building up the country with which he identifies, in spite of everything. However, he is still always conscious of both his painful separateness from the methods and the end result of what is being created, as well as his deep need—still unsatisfied—for his own happiness.

Perhaps the most significant difference between Braun's journey to the working world and those of Reimann, Wolf, and Fühmann is that his text does not focus on the education, training, improvement, or discipline of its protagonist through contact with the world of manual labor. Consequently, while "Der Schlamm" still tells a story about moving temporarily from above to below, there is not the same stress placed here on achieving a relatively finished, commendable level of development through renouncing individual, subjective needs and desires. The character Hans Kast contrasts with Reimann's male characters and Fühmann's narrator, who discipline their bodies in order to integrate themselves into the hard, unforgiving production process. He also contrasts with the female characters of Reimann and Wolf, who discipline their feelings in the process of finding emotional identification points and moral models to follow in the working world. Kast expresses both less fear and anxiety about being able to fit into the working world, and also—the other side of the coin—less forced optimism about the outcome of his journey. Furthermore, taken as a whole, the tone of Braun's narrative is far removed from both the more self-satisfied sense of possessing superior consciousness in Reimann's and Wolf's novels, as well as from the distasteful, studied foolishness of Fühmann's narrator. On the contrary, Braun's Kast—though he also wants to live a meaningful and satisfying life—is not shown as trying to accomplish this by becoming "like" the other workers, whatever this might mean.

The point is not that Braun necessarily knew more about the world of work than the other authors, but rather that his text is based on a more complex aesthetic that does not deny difference by gliding into evocations of false harmonies. Kast speaks with his own voice throughout the narrative, but he is also not shown as being in possession of the whole truth. Rather, there is also more of a sense that the workers around him have their own voices, too. These are not necessarily the same as his or as those of the controlling forces from above who are trying to speak in the workers' names but not always acting in their interests. In other words, the "socialist community" does not appear here as a stable, polished image with relatively clear divisions between right and wrong, but as an always unfinished creation out of an ongoing, living process of interaction and struggle. Here, the truly utopian element is the intimation that those who have previously led diminished lives might speak and act for themselves in ways that could at least carry equal weight with those of this community's other members. Yet this relativizing of authority by employing a more complex optic always encountered more suspicion than receptivity from those in control in the landscape of GDR cultural politics. By the time Braun's text was published in 1972, it appeared almost as an anomaly, as a story about a receding era when proletarian interests had been more central themes in the literature of this socialist state. In this regard, it can stand as an example of the road not taken to Bitterfeld.

Journeys to the Abysses of Socialism

RELEASED ON PROBATION into factory work. But what kind of thinking
is it to view this as a punishment?
—Volker Braun (1975)[96]

After the mid-1960s, the relatively few journeys to the working
world by GDR writers appeared more as isolated texts or as truncated
comments on intolerable situations than as responses to a general cultural
program. The earlier GDR journeys "down" into the working world had
always been coupled with the hope of raising workers "up" in many ways.
However, the more critical, negative tone of the later texts reflected a
situation of consolidation and even stagnation, of diminishing hopes for
overcoming the division of labor and perhaps, too, a diminishing interest
in this social goal. To a much greater extent than in the previous texts
discussed here, these authors now focused as sharply as they could on the
divisions that still existed in their society. In doing this, they reutilized older
paths into the working world at times, but their texts always resonated with
expressions of bemusement, irony, or tragedy over the jarring disjunctures
between lived experiences and ideals of the socialist community. And
because of their focus on the gaps between the working world and official
claims about its empowerment in the socialist state, a number of these texts
by GDR writers could only be published in the Federal Republic.

Generally speaking, these "journeys to the abysses" of socialism took
four major directions: first, a grim, almost anachronistic effort to continue
earlier ventures at hard physical labor with its disciplinary and authoritarian
overtones, which gives way to deep disillusionment, exemplified by Franz
Fühmann's *Im Berg* (1991); second, utilization of the genre of social
reportage in a more critical, less affirmative way, as in Landolf Scherzer's
Fänger und Gefangene (Catchers and the Caught, GDR/1983); third,
portrayals of the working world as the realm of outsiders or dropouts, as in
Ulrich Plenzdorf's *Die neuen Leiden des jungen W.* (The New Sorrows of
Young W., GDR/1973) or even more strongly in Jurek Becker's *Schlaflose
Tage* (Sleepless Days, FRG/1978); and fourth, allusions to the practice of
using manual labor as a means of demotion or punishment, of sentencing
offenders to work "in production."

Only published posthumously in 1991, Franz Fühmann's fragmentary text entitled "Im Berg: Bericht eines Scheiterns" (In the Mountain:
Report of a Failure) chronicles the author's obsessive efforts between
1974 and 1979 to establish contact with brigades of mineworkers, to
experience mining for himself, and to make this journey to the depths
productive for his writing.[97] Still longing for this type of connection with
the working world, Fühmann initially planned that the title of his final large

Book jacket for Franz Fühmann's *Im Berg* (1991). Fühmann's helmet is marked with a "B" for "visitor." Reprinted with permission from Hinstorff Verlag GmbH.

creative project would be "Schriftsteller und Arbeiter: Platz der Literatur im Arbeiterstaat" (Writers and Workers: The Place of Literature in the Workers' State). His ultimately unsuccessful efforts to realize this undertaking left him with a deep sense of failure at the end of his life. And as one literary historian has noted, this personal crisis was closely connected to the precarious situation of socialism in the final decade before the collapse of the GDR.[98]

In a manner reminiscent of his earlier "Open Letter" from 1964, Fühmann reasserted in this unfinished text the inaccessibility of large parts of the working-class experience to someone of his petty-bourgeois origins, but he went further here in his self-criticism. Stating that for him, "the worker" had always represented "the Other," Fühmann expressed his discomfort with two tendencies in his own development. The first of these was his inclination to exoticize the "low life" of the working world as the site of adventure and untamed desires, which he described as follows: "My schoolmates longed to go to the prairies or the South Seas, or to follow Karl May into the wilds of Kurdistan. But I longed for the gray factories which I saw from my room. They were the world of the Others, the other world" (31). According to Fühmann, this fascination with the working world as an alternative to middle-class respectability had drawn him to Nazism, to the nationalist party that had claimed to be a "socialist workers' party." As the antithesis to the form that this longing for the working world took in his younger years, Fühmann then recounted how the "Worker" had seemed to provide a way out of the "dead end of his life" after he had made a conscious decision for the GDR and for socialism. At this point, the world of manual labor appeared to be the tempting alternative to his life as a writer surrounded by "dusty books." He recalled somewhat ironically his impatience to leave his desk behind: "Hardly had I finished taking stock of my life when I began making pilgrimages again into factories: to construction sites, to steel and machine-tool factories, and, yes indeed, even to a chocolate factory!" (31).

Now, however, Fühmann sought to reject his earlier acceptance of officially prescribed paths into the working world, stating that he wanted something different: to combine his individual, subjective perspective somehow with a view from "below": "Not like before, when I was really an object but had the delusion of acting as a subject.—That was what happened to me at the shipyard. I took a path there which was prescribed to me by others, but which I took to be my own freely chosen path. And it was like this everywhere else, right from the start, at construction sites, in machine-tool factories" (43). When Fühmann first went down into a mine in 1974, having asked for a tour as remuneration for giving a reading, he was looking for a more autonomous, self-directed experience in this workplace. Hoping that this would be his "place of truth," he asked himself: "Where, if not in a mine, would I be so close to workers and so much a part of their world, even as a visitor? . . . Would I be able to explain there, down below, the thing which was becoming more and more unclear to me: what it was that I was writing?" (33). Not wanting to be accompanied constantly by a guide, he insisted on working as an unskilled member of a brigade. However, party and union officials made his contacts with the mine increasingly difficult and then impossible after he signed the petition against Wolf Biermann's expatriation from the GDR in 1976 and resigned from the Writers' Union in 1977. In 1979 his connections with the mining brigades broke off for good.

These outward obstacles, however, were not the only stumbling blocks in the way of Fühmann's efforts to create a less forced, more authentic literary expression of his contacts with the working world. Rather, a careful reading of "Im Berg" shows that in spite of his almost desperate attempts, he was generally not able to get beyond the two tendencies he had criticized in his earlier views of the workers as the "Other": the desire for the world of manual labor as an exoticized site where non-intellectual drives could be acted out; and—the other side of the coin—the desire to subject himself to manual labor as a site of discipline. All this continued to result in a sentimentalizing and mythologizing of the "Worker." At many points, then, "Im Berg" continues in the same kind of forced, overly naive tone that Fühmann adopted in his first reportage, *Kabelkran und Blauer Peter.* This tone arose out of the fact that he was entering into the working world more out of guilt over his own Nazi past and determination to put correct ideological convictions into practice than out of more positively grounded connections to workers themselves. On one level, Fühmann saw through these problems, stating that he realized his writing about the working world often turned into a guilty devaluation of the writer as a "parasitic" intellectual in favor of a kind of "obsequious admiration" of those who performed manual labor (98). Yet having defined himself as a writer whose sense of artistic validation came from a conviction that he was fulfilling useful functions for the socialist state, he was not able to cast aside so easily these ingrained ways of thinking.

Consequently, in spite of the fact that Fühmann continued longer than any other GDR writer to try to follow the path prescribed at Bitterfeld, these later texts revolve much more around his relationships with hierarchies and his difficulties with writing than around the working world he entered. In 1983, the year before his death, he described his "mine" project in a letter: "The mine as my 'place' in two ways: first, my landscape, and second, the place where I can think about my work. I depict how a disturbing factor enters into my work. I want to serve the Party, and in theory everything is correct, but in practice it doesn't work out" (151). The most striking things about such a statement are its high degree of self-absorption and its focus on serving the party. What is missing here is a focus on Fühmann's co-workers, the miners themselves. Fühmann had tried to make himself into a "servant" and accept the party of the working class as his "master"[99] by forcing himself to enter into the working world. But this effort to extinguish his own voice also entailed consigning the voices of his fellow workers to the periphery. The real tragedy of his bitter sense of failure is that despite all his insights, he was ultimately unable to create a narrative that relativized his own position as the visitor from above in the working world he entered.

In contrast to a writer such as Fühmann, who intended to train and discipline himself by entering into the working world, journalist Landolf Scherzer set about his journey in a much more matter-of-fact way that built to a greater extent on the traditions of oppositional social reportage. As a result, his portrayal of this unfamiliar realm did not focus on himself as the naive, bumbling outsider. Rather, he gave a more differentiated picture of his workmates and of the multiple layers of social divisions and conflicts that he encountered. Born in 1941, Scherzer was the author of numerous reportages and the head of the Section for Literary Journalism in the GDR Writers' Union. In 1978 he spent three months working on a large GDR fishing trawler in the North Atlantic. Five years later he was finally able to publish his reportage about this stint as an unskilled production worker, entitled *Fänger und Gefangene: 2386 Stunden vor Labrador und anderswo* (Catchers and the Caught: 2386 Hours off Labrador and Elsewhere).[100] In contrast to most reportages from the early years of the GDR, which tended to force their factual material into a preconceived ideological framework,[101] Scherzer's account of his journey into the working world can stand as an example for a number of later reportages and collections of interviews that were significantly more open and critical.[102]

According to the afterword to the second edition, Scherzer's reportage was quite popular when it first appeared in 1983, even among some of the workers it described—which has certainly not always been the case with such texts (277). This appeal to a relatively broad reading public was due to two factors: the depiction of the unusual milieu of adventure on the high seas, and the realistic characterization of the workers and their environment, which generally did not avoid bringing out unsolved problems and less than perfect aspects of their lives. Structured as a montage, the text alternates between descriptions of daily life on board the trawler, centering around catching, killing, and packing masses of fish; historical and scientific passages that stress the ecological impact and brutal methods of such technologized factory fishing; and reports of conversations among the workers, which range from anecdotes to more substantial discussions. The picture of the working world that emerges here—not least through Scherzer's own reactions to his long, unpleasant hours filleting and packing fish—is far removed from what he termed the "cheerful, proud, optimistic" images shown in the state's publicity about the fish combine. Rather, although the reportage gives positive examples of dedication, reliability, and intelligence among the workers, the overwhelming impression here is one of men who are "caught." They have no alternative but to perform the most difficult manual labor for long periods of time, in a situation made worse by backward technology, arrogant superiors, and arbitrary regulations. In contrast to the experiences of a writer such as Fühmann, Scherzer's journey was by no means to an elevated, let alone mythologized world. Rather, it was to a world still separate enough from the realms of power that those who inhabited it seemed to have little hope of escaping the most stunting, damaging effects of the prevailing division of labor.

By insisting consistently on the distance between entrenched power structures and workers' realities, Scherzer located his writing squarely within the tradition of critical social reportage that had always sought to change perceptions and encourage transformative actions. However, the absence of an alternative public sphere in the GDR where such contradictions could be debated and worked through in practice blocked the possibilities for such texts to have operative functions—a limitation Scherzer was well aware of. Asked during the 1980s what he thought of Günter Wallraff's method of undercover reporting in the Federal Republic (which had gone hand in hand with workers' activism there, at least for a time), he replied that this was not possible under the different social conditions in the GDR. And he added tactically that it was also not desirable, even though it was interesting and important (282). Consequently, in spite of its critical thrust, such a reportage served less as an impetus for positive change than as a vent for the frustration and dissatisfaction arising from the world below, whose inhabitants often seemed indifferent or hostile toward the ruling powers who were speaking in their name.[103]

In sharp contrast to earlier journeys to the social abysses of capitalism, where the worlds of workers and poor usually coincided, the living standard for the vast majority of people had been raised high enough in the GDR that writers' portrayals of the lower social strata hardly emphasized poverty and squalor. However, there are a number of texts that depict another kind of abyss within socialism: those showing the sphere of manual labor as the realm of outsiders, dropouts, and—standing in most jarring contradiction to earlier hopes—of the powerless.[104] As in previous GDR journeys to the working world by writers such as Endler, Reimann, and Wolf, these works often center around young people trying to find their place within socialist society in the contexts of the educational system and the workplace. Here, however, the persisting divisions between above and below result in deep skepticism toward pressures to perform, and finally, the perception that forced contact with the working world had been reduced to nothing more than a method of discipline or even punishment.

Ulrich Plenzdorf's popular and controversial novel *Die neuen Leiden des jungen W.* (GDR/1973), for example, revolves around the protagonist Edgar's attitude toward work, raising uncomfortable questions about the possibilities open to such young people in the GDR while maintaining—perhaps for tactical reasons—an ambivalent belief that solutions could and would be found.[105] Edgar's initial dissatisfaction with his training as an apprentice arises out of the fact that his supervisor insists on teaching old-fashioned, monotonous methods of working with metal rather than making use of more efficient, modern technology. Running away from home because of his disgust with this work experience, Edgar then lives for a time as a dropout in an old garden house in Berlin. When he runs out of money, however, he wants to return to work and heads for the nearest construction site, recalling the saying "Wer nichts will und wer nichts kann, geht zum Bau oder zur Bahn" (Whoever wants nothing and has no skills, works in construction or for the railroad).[106] Once there, he joins a brigade of painters headed by Zaremba, an old Communist who still believes in hard work and socialist ideology but who—rather than being inhibited and moralistic—is also simply a "cool guy" with his wild tattoos and blue jeans. Although the text still hints at the alienating aspects of unskilled manual labor, Edgar basically settles down under Zaremba's influence. However, his deep desire for creative expression leads to tragedy in the end when he is killed by an electrical explosion while trying to invent a better type of paint sprayer. With regard to the sphere of performance, the main conflict that Plenzdorf depicted here was the social and political priority attached to orderly, steady work—no matter how unfulfilling—at the cost of other satisfying sides of life.

Plenzdorf's story of a young man's encounter with the world of work still contained a figure like the old Communist worker Zaremba, who, by his living example, encouraged his brigade members to keep trying to find a meaningful place in the world of work and performance. A text such as Jurek Becker's *Schlaflose Tage* (FRG/1978) presents a much bleaker picture of the unbridgeable divisions between the sphere of workers and that of official ideology, here represented by the schools and the educational system. At the beginning of this novel, the teacher Karl Simrock feels a pain in his chest one day while in the classroom. Fear that his days are numbered causes him to resolve to eliminate routine and complacency from his life, to live authentically, and above all, to be more honest and forthright with his pupils. Simrock realizes, however, that putting such moral standards into practice may very well lead to his dismissal. Accordingly, he decides to take a trial run at working in a factory during summer vacation—partly, as he says, out of a desire to make connections with people whom he knows little about, but also because he is sure that manual labor will be his only alternative if he is fired.[107] Once he announces his plans, he feels equally uncomfortable with the reaction of his supervisors, who praise him for wanting to go to the "base," and with that of his girlfriend, who thinks he is acting merely on a whim and tries to joke: "Just like other people go on safari to Africa, he wants to go into the factory" (78).

The descriptions of Simrock's search for a job highlight how un-informed this teacher is about difficult, unpleasant manual labor. This sphere is so separate from his own that the gatekeeper at the bread factory where he finally applies thinks he has been sentenced to work there while on probation. Going to his job on the first day, early in the morning, Simrock—wearing his oldest clothes—notices how different the people on the streetcar look compared to those he usually sees. He anxiously hopes that he fits in: "Like some of them did, he opened his newspaper and hoped that he looked like a worker behind it" (86). For four weeks, he delivers bread together with a man named Boris, a good-natured worker who is completely disillusioned with politics. Although Simrock knows he is performing a necessary task, he soon learns that there is nothing enjoyable about this kind of monotonous work. That is, he experiences the contradiction between the realities of alienated labor and ideological pronouncements about such work as enriching and inspiring.

After this first stint in the working world, Simrock returns to teach-ing and begins to put his new convictions into practice. Upon asking probing and embarrassing questions in front of his pupils to a recruiting officer of the National People's Army, Simrock is in fact dismissed from his position, and he searches out Boris and the bread truck again. Although the school authorities finally offer to reinstate him if he apologizes, thinking that a dismissed teacher is a potential troublemaker, Simrock refuses to admit any wrongdoing and remains down below with Boris in the working world, far removed from the realm of education and ideology above. In the critical, pessimistic view of this novel, there no longer seems to be any possible bridge between above and below. Here, the teacher enters into the working world in order to try to find closer connections with reality. However, what he finds stands in jarring contradiction to the official ideology that he is supposed to teach in the classroom. His subsequent efforts to encourage honesty and forthrightness in his pupils by setting an example lead to his final expulsion from the world above. For Simrock, his final descent into the working world leaves him trapped in a realm of the powerless, where apolitical refusal seems to be the only alternative to opportunism and conformism.

At a level even below that of the outsiders in Plenzdorf's and Becker's novels, the sphere of manual labor appears fleetingly in its most reduced form in works by several GDR authors as nothing but a sphere of hated punishment for unacceptable actions and ideological deviations. Earlier GDR literature had frequently portrayed demotions of offenders from higher positions to work in material production. But more conformist writers had presented this as a necessary, unproblematic political measure, and even less conformist ones who pointed out its unjust aspects had generally balanced it off against what they held to be the greater good of a society developing in a positive direction.[108] It goes without saying that works which hinted at fundamental flaws and contradictions in this practice as an aspect of the criminal justice system hardly appeared in the GDR.[109] Yet a significant number of the writers, artists, musicians, and others who had been involved in some way in protest activities there, especially against the Warsaw Pact's invasion of Czechoslovakia in 1968, and who had then been forced to leave the GDR and settle in the Federal Republic, had had the experience of being sentenced to work as punishment.[110] Two brief biographies may stand for many among the GDR intellectuals who were expatriated or who left the GDR more "voluntarily" between 1961 and 1989.

Singer-songwriter Bettina Wegner was born in 1947 to Communist parents who moved to East Berlin in 1949. From 1966 to 1968 she attended acting school there, and in 1968 she was arrested for distributing leaflets protesting the invasion of Czechoslovakia. Sentenced to sixteen months' probation, she was sent "into production" in a Treptow factory. Afterwards, she continued her singing career with constant difficulties, signed the protest statement against Wolf Biermann's expatriation in 1976, and finally left the GDR in 1983.[111] Writer Thomas Brasch, born in 1945 in England to Communist, German Jewish parents, grew up in East Berlin after his family returned in 1946. As the son of a high-ranking SED functionary, Brasch had been sent as a ten-year-old boy to the Cadet School of the National People's Army (NVA) in Naumburg. Later, his first difficulties with the authorities began when he refused to enlist in the NVA. After finishing high school in 1963, Brasch worked for a year as a typesetter, a mechanic, and an unskilled laborer digging drainage ditches. In 1964 he began to study journalism in Leipzig but was expelled the following year for "disparaging GDR leaders" in public. For a while he supported himself with various unskilled jobs, and then began to study again in 1966, this time at the Film Academy in Potsdam-Babelsberg. In 1968 he was expelled again after distributing leaflets protesting the Prague invasion and was sentenced to twenty-seven months in prison. The following year this sentence was changed to "probation in production," and Brasch was sent to a job as a metalworker in Berlin. In the early 1970s he continued to write, and shortly after signing the petition in support of Biermann in 1976 he left for West Berlin.[112]

Brasch's short fictional text *Vor den Vätern sterben die Söhne* (The Sons Die before the Fathers, FRG/1977) captures the feelings of entrapment, alienation, and anger among many of the younger generation in the GDR whose experiences were similar to his. Here the student protagonist, Robert, who has been expelled from the university because of "ridiculing leading GDR statesmen," goes to work digging drainage ditches.[113] Meeting others there whose lives are portrayed as sad and crude, he begins to think of suicide and can only imagine the factory job that will probably be his lot as an unbearable existence. Accordingly, he confides in desperation to one worker who is his friend: "I wouldn't be able to stand it, . . . to get up every day at four, have two weeks of vacation and maybe four weeks of sick leave. I would go to the dogs" (33). Alienated from a political system unable to integrate the life experiences of many of his generation, Robert tries to escape being subjected to the disciplinary, punishing aspects of manual labor by fleeing to the West. He is shot and killed in the attempt.

In his short fictional work "Unvollendete Geschichte" (Unfinished Story, GDR/1975), Volker Braun also portrayed poignantly and incisively an atmosphere of stagnation, mistrust, and dissimulation. Now, the hopes that even a critical writer such as himself had connected earlier to entering into the working world, to breaking down old social divisions, appeared only as fleeting dreams with hardly any imaginable relevance to practice any longer. Here, the young trainee Karin loses her position with a newspaper because party functionaries, including her father, wrongly believe that her boyfriend is thinking about fleeing to the West. Told that she must now complete a period of "probation in production," she sets out to find a job after her naive trust in the moral legitimacy of her society has been destroyed. The narrator depicts her encounter with the working world:

> She went through the city, which roared with industry, a powerful, moving, sooty landscape. She had always been attracted by the flow of people changing shifts in front of the factory gates. And the violent, monotonous, fatalistic aspect of this suction had repelled her (or she only felt spontaneously the enormous masses of humanity pumping in and out, with an uncertain sensation of pleasure). Now any kind of job was fine with her, and she went in everywhere, into all kinds of factories and stores. She just wanted to have

WORK. Work was half of life. As we work today and so forth.
Work together, plan together, and I don't know what all.[114]

Such an image of the working world no longer contains any socialist visions that workers might rise up and that walls between above and below might be broken down. Rather, this picture recalls the industrial landscape of a much earlier time. It is an almost expressionistic, fatalistic evocation of masses of the powerless, of people at the mercy of their fate. Here, the slogans of participating fully in social and political life through work have become meaningless and empty. And the workplace appears as only a site of subjugation and discipline. It is the polar opposite of a scene in one of Karin's dreams, where a woman worker passes judgment on powerful leaders and the vision of a democratic socialism characterized by equality, openness, and participation appears to Karin for a fleeting instant, only to fade away. In this text by Braun from 1975, unlike those by Becker and Brasch that were published in the late 1970s in the West, this dream still flashes in painful contrast to the fears that both the "story" told here and the "history" it is part of may come to a dead end in indifference and apathy brought about by fatally flawed policies from above. What a distance from the earlier calls for writers to "go into production" with the grand design of connecting art and life. Here, only "probation in production" remains. And all the failing hopes of socialism resonate in Karin's question: "But what kind of thinking is it to view this as a punishment?" (66).

"I Still Belonged to Them":
Volker Braun and the "People of Hoywoy"

Hoyerswerda, where is that? The darkest world . . .
—Volker Braun (1992)[115]

After German reunification in 1990, reflections on what was once called the "social question" and thus on different levels and kinds of work have been absent for the most part in new literary texts.[116] On the one hand, many GDR writers of the older generation who formerly hoped to break down the class barriers between mental and manual labor seem to have worked through these parts of their biographies long ago, put them to rest with sadness, resignation, or relief, and moved on. And on the other hand, it appears that a much younger East German writer such as Thomas Brussig depicts reminders of the social question as nothing but oppressive or ridiculous injunctions not to be such a rabid consumer, as he did in his novel *Helden wie wir* (Heroes Like Us, 1995). In some few instances where writers reflect on intellectuals' distance from the worlds of those who perform work of the lowest status, the emotions expressed range from perplexity to frustration and grief over having lost a common, hopeful project. Brigitte Burmeister's novel *Unter dem Namen Norma* (Known by the Name of Norma, 1994), for example, contains a key passage where the narrator observes two workers in a bar whose GDR clientele is being displaced rapidly by West Germans.[117] In an effort to imagine how the transition to capitalism is affecting them, the narrator tries to draw on her memories from her "year in the factory" long ago in the GDR, between school and university study. However, she finds that such a bridge to the workers' world in the past was much too tenuous to enable her to imagine their thoughts and feelings in the present.

Another depiction of such broken connections after reunification appears in the brief essay by Volker Braun entitled "Die Leute von Hoywoy II" (The People of Hoywoy II, 1992).[118] "Hoywoy" is Hoyerswerda, the paradigmatic site of socialist construction in the 1950s and early 1960s, the site of the journeys of many GDR writers into this world of work (such as Inge and Heiner Müller, Brigitte Reimann, and Volker Braun himself), and most recently, the site of racist attacks against asylum seekers in 1991.[119] The title of Braun's text refers back to his earlier short essay "Die Leute von Hoywoy," written in 1971.[120] Here, Braun had already reflected on the mood of stagnation in the GDR and the resulting chasm that he felt had opened up between himself and his former workmates at the lignite combine "Schwarze Pumpe." Accordingly, he presented himself as the intellectual who could no longer find a way into their world. In "Hoywoy II," Braun highlighted even more strongly his sense of distance between himself and the city's inhabitants. In this text, he is not even physically present in their city, but rather is watching events there unfold on television: "It was thirty years after the small excavations in the hole of middle Germany which had cost me my youth. On the television screen I saw that once famous city where we had dwelled, now in horrible confusion." The labors of Braun's past have diminished from the great excavations he described in "Der Schlamm" to "small" ones. And even these now seem to have been all in vain as he watches the mob, people similar to his former workmates, using the "tools we once worked with as weapons" while shouting racist epithets. He tries to decipher the faces he is observing, to see if he can still recognize any features of the construction workers "to whom I had once belonged." But now he can only discern the hate-filled visages of young men who are being applauded by smug adults.

Deeply disturbed by this sight, Braun then reflects on the underlying reasons for this outbreak of racist violence, this descent into darkness.[121] First, in his view, are the prevalent personality traits of weakness, suspicion, and cowardice.[122] However, these do not appear to him as merely the individual failings of the "people of Hoywoy," but even more so as rooted in the flaws of their provincial country, with its pervasive restrictions on expansiveness. Here, Braun presents the "darkness" of Hoyerswerda as arising out of the banality of everyday life as it was shaped by the party and state, out of narrow-mindedness, rigidity, ignorance, and fear of difference. Finally, however, Braun also reflects on what had happened to these people most recently, since reunification: "Something had befallen the former builders, the famous people." Namely, after they had lost even their "uncertain property," their jobs, and their "security," the message had been driven home to them that the efforts of their lives had been worthless, that they were contemptible creatures.[123] That is, while this text censures the "people of Hoywoy" as racist perpetrators, it also shows them as victims of forces beyond their control—victims who then release their fear and insecurity by scapegoating and attacking those weaker than themselves.

Braun's relationship to these inhabitants of the world he had once been a part of, then, is one of horror, disgust, and distance, on the one hand—and on the other, still one of pained empathy and solidarity. That is, he refuses to write off these people either as inherently brutal or as mere dupes of a dictatorial system. Rather, he also insists that their actions arise out of fears that the upheavals they are presently experiencing will not bring about the liberation that they have been promised. Consequently, when he turns off his television, he does not simply banish the images of the workers' ghosts from his past and the "miserable creatures" of the present. He portrays them as hovering in the darkness of his room, repeating the old miners' greeting "Glück auf" (Good luck) and the still unanswered question arising out of the defining experience of their lives: "Who owns the world?"

Braun lets this question stand unanswered, implying that for this GDR writer at this historical moment, the only tenable position is to refuse to speak in the name of the people he is observing. This reluctance to claim a privileged narrative voice with respect to the working world is also illustrated in another recent story by Braun entitled *Die vier Werkzeugmacher* (The Four Toolmakers, 1996), which traces the upheavals in the lives of GDR skilled workers after reunification. It concludes with this pronouncement: "This history/story has no intention, and as far as the people are concerned, they must express their own intentions."[124] That is, Braun's wish for solidarity—now almost only a memory—does not become the material any longer for a literary text grounded in the search for practical and emotional connections with the working world. Rather, he replies to his former workmates in the darkness of Hoyerswerda with his moral refusal to deny shared biography, asserting defiantly that in spite of everything, "I still belonged to them."[125]

5
"I Was One of Them":
On the Bottom in the Federal Republic

Social Partners in Economic Reconstruction

Mensch, sei schlau,
Bleib' im Überbau!
(Man, be smart,
stay in the superstructure!)
—West German student slogan of the 1950s

Immediately after the end of World War II, in all four zones of occupied Germany, voices were raised across the political spectrum—from Communists to Social Democrats to liberal Christian Democrats—that called for the creation of a "truly social society" without exploitation as the most pressing lesson to be learned from the entwinement of the largest German business interests with National Socialism.[1] These proponents of a new beginning generally advocated policies falling between the capitalism of the Western allies and what they saw as the "totalitarianism" of the dictatorial Soviet Union. To their way of thinking, freedom and security could be guaranteed for the majority of Germans only through a combination of nationalizing important industries and preserving individual rights in a democratic fashion. However, such calls for socializing the economy did not last for long in the three zones that were to become the Federal Republic. For after 1947, when the cold war geared up in earnest, this part of Germany was drawn ever more tightly into the Western sphere of influence. Simultaneously, by means of the currency reform of 1948 and other economic measures, the most influential conservative political leaders hoped to defuse the tensions of social inequality by creating "prosperity for all" rather than by making fundamental changes in economic structures. With the restoration of the capitalist free market economy in the Federal Republic, then, a course was set which, for the next fifteen years, dismissed any efforts to call attention to the structural causes of socioeconomic inequalities as either Communist-inspired or hopelessly behind the times.

The pervasiveness of the ideology of social consensus, along with the understandable preoccupation of the majority of the population with recovering from the war's devastation, meant that the world of manual labor hardly figured any longer in the public sphere of political action as a locus of fundamental resistance to unsatisfactory conditions. Furthermore, there seemed to be little awareness remaining in the cultural arena of prewar progressive traditions that had been associated with the struggles of those close to the bottom of society. As a result, it was only in the early 1960s, when this ideological consensus began to face more serious challenges, that a small number of outsiders began to journey once again into the working world. Whether in the form of journalist Günter Wallraff's reportages or the essays and novels associated with the end phase of the student movement, these efforts to renounce privilege for a time attracted significant public attention only relatively late and relatively briefly in the Federal Republic. In order to visualize the more or less isolated position of these writers in the midst of West German affluence, as well as the controversies that sometimes swirled around their texts, it is helpful to cast a brief glance back at two relevant aspects of West German society as it developed up to the early 1960s: first, the makeup and mentality of the student body; and second, the ideology of "social partnership."

Immediately after the end of the war, the material situation of German students resembled that of Weimar students in the period of inflation in certain important ways. On the whole, however, their responses to impoverishment and want necessarily developed along quite different lines. The first classes of postwar students who began studying at newly opened universities in the fall of 1945, as well as those for some time afterward, faced food and housing shortages and often were unable to count on their parents for support. These students, often veterans in their mid-twenties who had also belonged to the Nazi Labor Service, frequently had to work at any jobs available in order to survive. Yet the total discrediting of the racist nationalism that had led to the Holocaust and to the war's unprecedented destruction precluded any overt calls for continuing to "nationalize" the experience of work. Rather, most students seem to have dealt with the exigencies of their situation by withdrawing from political involvement and simply trying to get through the years of hardship as best as they could.[2] This approach soon began to pay off after the founding of the two German states in 1949 and the even more explosive growth of the West German economy in the "miracle" years of the 1950s. Thus, already by 1952 only about 15 percent of West German students had to work in order to finance all or part of their education. By 1962–1963 this portion had been reduced to about 10 percent, and of these, more were able to confine their jobs to vacation periods rather than having to work during the semester.[3] Furthermore, employment, personal income, and the standard of living had increased so much in the course of the 1950s that about 45 percent of students could rely totally on their parents for support, while others were able to depend on the Honnef financial aid program that had been established in 1955. Increasingly well-to-do, these students had little need to work at all, let alone to subject themselves to exhausting, distasteful manual labor or to seek out contact with those still on the lowest rungs of society's ladder.

The restoration of the capitalist market economy and the consolidation of its traditionally powerful groups went hand in hand, of course, with the perpetuation of traditional privileges of access to higher education. In contrast to the German Democratic Republic, where it was a priority from the beginning to break the property-owning classes' monopoly on most aspects of the educational system and to enforce a system of equal access to higher education for the children of workers and farmers, no such goals of educational restructuring were high on the agenda in the Federal Republic.[4] Consequently, the number of students from working-class backgrounds stagnated on a minimal level, making up 3.7 percent of the student body in 1949–1950 and 6.0 percent in 1962–1963. Similarly, only about 5 percent of West German students were from rural areas in the mid-1950s, a figure that decreased to 3.6 percent in the early 1960s.[5] These groups were so small that even if they had wanted to integrate their life experiences into their intellectual pursuits—which is not at all to be taken for granted—their voices would not have been strong enough to have a significant impact on the academy. Consequently, in the early 1960s the separation remained quite extreme between the worlds of those with access to higher education and the careers and power it promised, and those who continued to work with their hands in a rapidly evolving economy, who were also often the poorest groups of West German society.

While these trends toward separation were becoming more fixed, however, the ideology of "social partnership" between all socioeconomic levels of West German society was becoming more and more pervasive. This was due to the huge economic growth and increasing availability of consumer goods that came about during the 1950s largely as a result of the policies put into effect by Ludwig Erhard, who was named the first minister of economics in 1949 and who later came to be known as the "father of the socialist market economy." Influenced by neoliberal thinking, Erhard succeeded in countering immediate postwar endorsements of economic planning and nationalizing of key industries by both the Social Democrats (SPD) and the Christian Democrats (CDU). Instead, he convinced Chancellor Konrad Adenauer that economic and social stability could be achieved by restoring the free market and combining it with social programs designed to cushion its most detrimental effects. On the one hand, the restorative nature of these policies was clear: leading industrialists who had supported Nazism suffered few consequences, former owners recovered their large factories, and tendencies toward concentration of wealth intensified.[6] On the other hand, after the years of war and hardship, the prospect of economic security, full employment, and a rapidly rising standard of living enjoyed understandably widespread popular support, all the more so as Erhard's promises gradually became reality over the course of the 1950s. The statistics are well known that document the steadily rising percentages of West Germans who became able to afford household appliances, automobiles, a wider variety of food, fashionable clothing, and vacation trips during this period. And at the same time, because of increasing modernization and mechanization, those who were still performing purely manual labor in a society increasingly oriented toward the service sector often benefited from fewer working hours, better working conditions, higher wages, and more leisure time than ever before.[7]

Erhard's efforts to create "prosperity for all" seemed to have been so successful at establishing a broad acceptance of his economic policies that the Social Democrats finally threw in their Marxist towel. In its Godesberg Program of 1959, the SPD disavowed what seemed to be outmoded ideas of class struggle in favor of also hitching its political future to developing the social market economy. At this point, then, the most influential figures in the political arena seemed to agree that the affluent society was now arriving. And in such a new world based on the perpetual creation of new consumerist desires, the most successful ideological model seemed to be that of the classless society where all would have ample opportunities to spend money. The belief here was that disparities between rich and poor, between the property-owning classes and the "proletariat," would become increasingly insignificant in the face of a constantly expanding middle class characterized by access to a relatively large discretionary income. As early as 1952, for example, a middle-of-the-road sociologist such as Helmut Schelsky had simply dismissed the concept of class as no longer applicable to the West German situation. In this respect, he spoke for many West German sociologists and economists of the time who viewed their own society as "classless," as having overcome the need for "ideology," or simply as "non-totalitarian."[8] And this point of view was to become so widely accepted that in 1965, the year that marked both the climax and the beginning of the end of the economic miracle, Ludwig Erhard—now chancellor—could declare at a party convention of the Christian Democrats: "We have realized the modern, classless society."[9]

But even in the face of these undeniable economic accomplishments and this overriding social consensus, there were always those who called attention to the socioeconomic structures that favored some and disadvantaged others, and to the social and psychic abysses that persisted beneath the glittering surface of reconstructed West Germany. By the early 1960s, political, social, and economic conditions had evolved in such ways that some of these voices began to be no longer so easily ignored but to gain a wider hearing.[10] Yet the entrenchment of the ideology of social partnership meant that those who challenged it met with vitriolic responses often out of all proportion to their actual proposals for reforms.[11] One of the most controversial examples of such an effort to expose the structures of social class in the Federal Republic was dramatist Rolf Hochhuth's essay "Der Klassenkampf ist nicht zu Ende" (The Class Struggle Is Not Over), which was published in 1965, the same year Erhard proclaimed the realization of a "classless society" in the Federal Republic while running for reelection as chancellor. In this piece, Hochhuth analyzed social conditions in the Federal Republic that demonstrated the continuing existence of class-based privileges and economic injustices.[12] As concrete examples, he cited instances of miserable slum housing conditions that he contrasted with the wealth accumulated by a tiny number of entrepreneurs; he noted the extremely vulnerable situation of foreign workers; and he called attention to the ways in which the Springer newspaper empire blocked wide public debate. Above all, he noted that while 76 percent of West German citizens owned no substantial property, about twenty-five hundred wealthy individuals controlled much of the economy and exerted vastly disproportionate influence over the government. As in his dramas, however, Hochhuth presented these disparities as primarily a moral problem rather than a political one. He appealed to the goodwill of those who desired limited reforms as solutions to the social inequalities he had uncovered rather than advocating any more far-reaching steps.

Yet in the atmosphere of the Federal Republic at this time, the architects of the restoration and the economic miracle were not accustomed to hearing even such mild proposals for social change raised by citizens as prominent as Hochhuth, whose essay was one example of the many calls for a political "alternative" issued in the early 1960s by West Germany's best-known writers, including Günter Grass, Heinrich Böll, Martin Walser, and Hans Magnus Enzensberger. Not able to disprove the facts of social and economic inequality that Hochhuth had cited, conservative circles took the approach of questioning his qualifications to speak out at all on these matters. The controversy culminated on July 9, 1965, when Chancellor Erhard himself gave a hateful speech attacking writers such as Hochhuth as "philistines and incompetents," as "self-important little pip-squeaks" who had no idea what they were talking about.[13] Hochhuth was defended by the Social Democratic candidate for chancellor, Willy Brandt, as well as by other writers and intellectuals. However, Erhard's strategy seems to have been successful in diverting attention from the substance of Hochhuth's essay: the inequality between the well-to-do and the less well-to-do, not to mention those who still remained poor, in West German society. After the fall election Erhard remained chancellor, and the disparities between above and below still seemed to be far removed from the center of public debate.

Günter Wallraff's Journeys to the Abysses of the Economic Miracle

> Right across from the "prominent castle tower" lies another "center-piece of the cityscape," which the guidebook does not mention. Giant factory complexes cover a huge expanse, hidden behind low houses. Three times every day and night they suck in human masses, only to spit them out again at the end of the shift. There are far more than two thousand men every day and night, and I am one of them.
>
> —Günter Wallraff (1966)[14]

Writing in 1963 from the depths of Adenauer and Erhard's CDU state, leftist theologian Helmut Gollwitzer introduced a collection of reports entitled *Die Welt des Arbeiters: Junge Pfarrer berichten aus der Fabrik* (The World of the Worker: Young Ministers Report from the Factory) with the following observation about how earlier journeys to the working world had been forgotten or brushed aside in the reconstruction years of the Federal Republic:

> To a not inconsiderable extent, members of today's generation of middle-class men and of the clergy have labored as work students or as prisoners of war in factories and mines. But the time they spent there was obviously too brief to have made a lasting impression on them. They have forgotten or repressed their observations and experiences, or in any case not analyzed them thoroughly. Sixty years after Paul Göhre's report, forty years after Count Stenbock-Fermor's experiences as a miner, after decades of reporting with modern survey methods, after proletarians' memoirs and workers' literature, this other world is still an unknown world. Reports from it always seem new and disconcerting,

disillusioning. . . . These reports seem like big news, in part, because as a Russian proverb says, the well-fed man cannot understand the hungry one. But people also do not want to see what is being reported here. For the ideology of social partnership is so much more reassuring, and it seduces people into thinking that what is really only the music of the future has already been realized in the present.[15]

In tones that recalled Arnold Zweig's warning from 1927 about the distance of much of German literature from everyday working-class reality, Gollwitzer reiterated here the topos that the world below was still an unknown world to many of those "above." And as a new explanation for this blindness, he introduced the pervasive willingness to view West German society through the rose-colored glasses of the ideology of social partnership. Gollwitzer's observation is substantiated by looking back at those works of West German literature that actually did revolve around the world of work in the period from 1945 until the early 1960s. As literary historian Krystyna Nowak has shown, a considerable number of writers turned their attention to this topic then. However, almost without exception they merely extended the tradition of "petit-bourgeois workers' literature" that stretched back into the late nineteenth century.[16] Consequently, they continued to glorify the "universal" creative force of labor and to propagate conciliatory visions of community in which concepts such as "class struggle" or "capitalism" hardly played a role any longer. These authors, many of whom had already published during the Weimar Republic and the Third Reich, simply went on writing about order and comradeship at the workplace, industrious workers and factory owners, and joy in work. In short, they took up the slogans of the "social welfare state" and of "prosperity for all" as if tailor-made for them.

It appeared, then, in the face of this overwhelming ideological consensus, that memory had vanished of both earlier proletarian culture originating from the "base" as well as earlier efforts by oppositional writers and journalists to ally themselves with workers in ways aiming toward social change. The extinguishing of these traditions meant that those individuals who set out beginning in the early 1960s in the Federal Republic to journey into the working world did so with hardly any knowledge that they were carrying on a century-old undertaking. Rather, they had to rediscover for themselves some of the methods that their predecessors had used and change these to suit their own situations. Or, they had to strike out from new positions altogether as they became increasingly aware of the falseness of consensus in the country that had brought about the Holocaust. Two main approaches to entering into the working world developed in the

Federal Republic. The first, taken above all by journalist Günter Wallraff, recuperated the tradition of oppositional social reportage going back to Max Winter in Austria and developed by many others during the Weimar Republic—without, however, being closely allied to Social Democratic or Communist cultural politics. The second was the path taken by a number of radical students in the declining years of the student movement around 1970. Unlike Weimar work students, who were propelled into the working world by financial necessity, or students and other young people in the GDR whose participation in the working world was organized by the Socialist Unity Party with the goal of integrating them into the socialist state, these West German students hoped for a short time to become the avant-garde of a reborn proletarian revolution.

In 1963, the same year Gollwitzer commented on how earlier journeys to the working world had been forgotten, Günter Wallraff began his project of working temporarily in various factories and reporting on conditions there as well as on the lives of his fellow workers. First published in 1964 in the trade union newspaper *Metall*,[17] these reportages of Wallraff's were brought together in 1966 in his first book, *"Wir brauchen Dich": Als Arbeiter in deutschen Industriebetrieben* ("We Need You": As a Worker in German Industrial Firms), which was later reissued until the title *Industriereportagen* (Reportages from Industry, 1970). In the five long, substantial pieces collected here, Wallraff recounted his experiences at some of the most high-profile companies in the Federal Republic: as a worker on an assembly line at the Ford factory in Cologne, as an unskilled metalworker being paid according to piecework at a Siemens plant, and as an unskilled metalworker at the shipyards of Blohm and Voss and in the Thyssen and Benteler steel mills.[18] Wallraff later described his approach: "Actually I just wanted to experience for myself what was really behind all the talk about the 'economic miracle,' 'social partnership,' and other such nice-sounding ideas."[19] And what he found was so shattering that his early reportages became one of the most resounding early signals of the emergence of the broad movement in the 1960s that sought to question the ideology of "social partnership" and to create relevant links in all manner of spheres between intellectual activities and radical social practice. Consequently, because of this embeddedness in a larger social movement, and due to Wallraff's attention-getting skills at infiltration and exposé, these reports were quite widely read. Furthermore, they provoked a great deal of debate—not to mention lawsuits—in which the journalist usually came out on top and so attracted even more publicity. The Wallraff phenomenon was noteworthy enough that a sociologist such as Oskar Negt declared him to be "the most politically effective writer of workers' literature, and the one workers read the most in postwar West Germany." At the time, Negt viewed Wallraff's reportages as an important contribution to creating an "alternative public sphere."[20]

Born in Cologne in 1942, Wallraff finished an apprenticeship as a bookstore clerk and served briefly in the army in 1963 before being discharged for "psychological" reasons which in fact stemmed from his pacifist convictions. Needing to earn money and having already begun to write, Wallraff decided to "start from below" and follow in the footsteps of his father, who had been a worker at the Ford assembly plant in Cologne.[21] Entering into the factory for the first time, Wallraff immediately settled on the technique that he continued to use throughout his career as a journalist. He became a participant observer in order to expose hidden wrongs and create public debate—or, as he described it himself, he "deceived in order not to be deceived."[22] In his first reportages, Wallraff presented his experiences in the sites of the working world where he sojourned as excursions into areas where nineteenth-century conditions still prevailed in the midst of the affluent Federal Republic, which claimed to be so modern and new. Yet in contrast to the journeys to the depths of the working world that were being written at roughly the same time in the GDR, he could not draw upon any kind of ideology of self-sacrifice for the sake of realizing the greater mission of socialism, or of relinquishing his bourgeois ego to place himself under the tutelage of workers and party leaders more knowledgeable than himself.

Rather, in each of the working situations he entered, Wallraff depicted a similar experience of utter victimization, which reflected both the kind of unskilled manual labor he was performing and his perceptions of his role and his fellow workers. Thus, in the Ford reportage he characterized his work painting cars as unbearably boring, empty, and disempowering, noting, "After three hours I'm nothing but part of the assembly line myself."[23] In "Auf der Werft" (At the Shipyard), Wallraff described himself and his fellow workers as completely beaten down by the tasks they had to perform, picturing them as follows after a hard day's work: "Their faces are rigidly expressionless, showing neither irritation, nor impatience, nor joy, nor hope" (53). In "Im Akkord" (Piecework), Wallraff stressed the monotony and low pay of his job as an unskilled metalworker for Siemens and also the alienation of never being told what final products would result from his work. And in the longest reportage of this collection, "Sinter zwo—im Stahlwerk" (Sinter Two—In the Steel Mill), which recounts his job sweeping and shoveling grit and dust at the Thyssen steel mill, all of these negative experiences coalesced. Here he portrayed the backward conditions prevailing for the workers who had not yet been replaced by mechanization, who still moved through the "dark, forbidding" factory landscape in dead-end jobs that required only physical strength and stifled all human capacities for thought and creativity.

Wallraff's depiction of his response to these conditions as well as that of the other workers whom he met evidences a timeless quality of victimization in which wage laborers seem completely at the mercy of their superiors—foremen, personnel managers, the industrialists themselves.[24] The following description, for example, of workers on their way to the steel mill early in the morning reads like an only slightly updated version of naturalist depictions of the social abyss that were current in Paul Göhre's time:

> 5:30 A.M., a ghostly procession is moving through the city streets. Milky and yellowish car headlights hardly penetrate the gray, gloomy, soupy drizzle. Lines of bicycles, swaying, bent shapes leaning into the gusty wind, and pedestrians with turned-up collars, their hands buried in the pockets of pants or jackets, worn-out briefcases or just a bag with sandwiches tucked under their arms. Old men, careworn, shuffling along with strangely fast steps, as if they had been wound up, men whose last shift is not far off. And young ones with long strides who sometimes break into a run, their shoulders hunched up, their faces already seeming old. Over the street an orange-colored light which dyes the hedge-leaves blue, the people's faces blackish and their lips violet, the negatives of a badly lit color film.
>
> In the factory there is no morning, no noon, and no evening. Here it is always night. A neon-lit night, which is never followed by day. (92–93)

In this world of perpetual darkness and subordination, workers appear to have no control at all over factory conditions—either because of the nature of the work itself or because their superiors have everything firmly in hand. Thus, Wallraff described those doing piecework as "robots" whose faces were "motionless and gray" (78). With few exceptions, he emphasized the workers' inability to communicate with each other, as well as their lack of knowledge about their legal rights, declaring, for example: "Any resistance is pointless. The factory noise carries you away with it" (101). Furthermore, Wallraff maintained that these workers hardly tried to balance out such exploitation with more satisfying leisure-time pursuits. In general, then, he gave quite a hopeless picture of the lives of these men, showing them as stunted beings who were not interested in politics, hobbies, friendships, or self-improvement and who, in short, lived only "in order to work" (124).

In a similar manner, Wallraff acted out his role by emphasizing his passivity and the lack of possibilities for resistance which he wanted to show as inherent in his situation. Accordingly, in one instance where a supervising engineer selected him to perform a particularly dangerous repair job in the steel mill, he portrayed himself as forced to accept endangering his life for the sake of keeping his job: "There is no point in protesting. It would be considered refusal to work, and the penalty for this is dismissal if you haven't been here for three months. Otherwise you could try to fight it with the help of the works committee. But in this case, the factory would not even have to justify firing you" (120–121). What emerges here, then, in Wallraff's understanding of himself in his role as a worker among other workers is a basically fatalistic view of the absence of possibilities for resisting unshakable authorities.

It is the undeniable achievement of Wallraff's reportages about his journeys into the working world to have helped put the "social question" and issues of class and class consciousness back on the agenda of public debate in the Federal Republic, and to have done so in a form based on his personal experience, a form that could not be easily dismissed or glossed over. The effect of these reportages is shown by the reactions of both workers themselves and the leading business circles who felt attacked by Wallraff's exposés. First of all, in spite of the fatalistic tone of these reportages, it has often been noted that Wallraff's texts were more widely read by workers themselves than any other similar literature by West German writers on the working world,[25] and that workers frequently agreed with Wallraff's presentations of the facts and helped him gain access to more information. In this manner, they showed that they often felt he was really speaking for them and representing their interests. Also, in contrast to the strong sense within the reportages themselves that workers had little possibility or even desire to act, there were numerous instances in the spheres of literary distribution and political action where Wallraff did make common cause with workers who were attempting to improve their own lives. For example, in a piece entitled "Wie die Arbeiter reagieren, wenn einer ihnen nützlich ist" (How the Workers React When Someone Is Useful to Them, 1970), Wallraff noted that after his first reportage on the Ford assembly plant appeared, workers came to him while he was still on the job and praised him for speaking out about conditions there.[26] By publishing his reportages in union newspapers, participating in union organizing campaigns, and supporting workers' grievances and strikes, Wallraff integrated his reportages into workers' ongoing efforts to change unacceptable conditions.[27] And in the cultural sphere, he played a decisive role in founding the "Werkkreis Literatur der Arbeitswelt" (Workshop for Literature of the Working World) in 1970, which created opportunities for workers themselves to write and publish before dwindling away during the more conservative 1980s.

Further evidence that Wallraff's exposés were touching on real sore points in West German society emerged in the defensive, vindictive reactions of those who felt themselves and their business practices attacked in his texts. Thus, in a concerted effort to prevent him from continuing to infiltrate what they saw as their private sphere of power, the "Employers' Warning Service" circulated his description and photograph to factories throughout the country.[28] Companies that Wallraff had reported on frequently brought lawsuits against him for the alleged damages he had caused them. Unable to rebut the content of his findings, the plaintiffs almost always focused on his "despicable method" of infiltration, and Wallraff usually won these lawsuits.[29] Furthermore, in an article entitled "Einige Erfahrungen mit den Schwierigkeiten beim Veröffentlichen der Wirklichkeit hinter Fabrikmauern" (Some Experiences with the Difficulties of Publishing about the Reality behind Factory Walls, 1971), Wallraff also pointed out how business interests often threatened to withdraw lucrative advertising from newspapers and magazines that dared to publish texts focusing on class conflicts.[30] By this time, Wallraff asserted that the leftist journal *Konkret*, which hardly relied at all on advertising from industry, was almost the only place where he could still publish his reportages about the working world.[31]

All of these reactions to Wallraff's reportages, whether from "below" or from "above," testify to their effectiveness, for a short period of time, as operative texts in the best sense—as documentary literature that helped open up new areas of consciousness and public debate. Because of the favorable social situation of the 1960s, then, Wallraff was able to ally himself in ways aiming toward social change with the workers whose world he had entered into briefly. Looking back at his journeys into the West German working world today, after thirty years have passed, it is important to recognize and remember these successes, especially now that what was earlier called the "social question" has been pushed more to the margins of public debate. However, it is equally important in looking back at these reportages, which now seem quite dated in many respects, to try to understand the sources of their shortcomings. Sociologist Oskar Negt, for example, put his finger on a crucial reason for Wallraff's success in forging alliances, namely, his efforts to approach his fellow workers as equals and to avoid both didactic, patronizing, "avant-gardist" attitudes as well as any tendencies toward a false heroicizing of the realm of physical labor.[32]

Negt's assessment was correct as far as it went, but it overlooked the fact that the strength of Wallraff's approach was also linked to a significant weakness. To be sure, Wallraff did not conceive of himself as representing any kind of organized political avant-garde of the working class—he was much too individualistic for that.[33] Yet his posture of individual suffering—or, to put it differently, of trying to present himself as nothing but "one of the workers" he was becoming for a time—caused his reportages to revolve more around his role-playing persona and less around his fellow workers as human beings with their own potential strategies for resistance. And this in turn meant that his basic tactic of expressing moral outrage over unacceptable conditions often proceeded more from his own perceptions—as a writer coming from outside—of what was necessary, rather than from workers' own experiences and assessments of their situation and needs. Wallraff's own statements about his method bring these limitations into sharper focus. In 1970 he described his understanding of himself as a worker for the time being as follows:

> For me it was a temporary thing. And a critic once re-proached me very correctly by saying that I was never in the situation of people who had to work under these conditions for their whole lives, who are totally powerless, and who know when they are thirty years old that nothing is going to change in their lives.
>
> For the social truth of my reports it's a minus that I was just an intruder who could drop everything and take off at any time, and who was not tied down forever like the other workers. But on the other hand, the advantage was that I didn't accept the things I discovered. I denounced the abuses and called them by their names. I didn't have to worry about losing my job. I could make trouble, resist, get excited without having to fear the consequences. . . . [The workers] often fool and cheat themselves by acting as if their working conditions are all right, or as if noth-ing can be done. . . . That's why there are relatively few attempts to protest. And that's also why they are ready to swallow everything. Of course, as someone who was only working temporarily, I didn't have to subject myself to this self-regulation.[34]

Even more pointedly, Wallraff described the effect of his Ford reportage on his fellow workers there: "There were conversations and interactions among them which of course end abruptly when the one who opened his mouth and protested is either punished by being transferred or fired, or changes jobs voluntarily."[35] According to this view, political activity seems to arise only at the instigation of the brave individual (from outside) who is willing to suffer and protest. In other words, there is hardly any sense that long-term strategies for resistance and change might possibly build on workers' own experiences and understanding. Most fundamentally, Wallraff's approach was to express moral indignation from a position of superior consciousness; that is, to assume a position of individualistic "opposition" within late capitalist society where no effective connections to any organized left-wing workers' movement seemed possible anymore.[36]

"We Are *Not* the Base; We *Need* a Base": West German Students Enter the Factories

Thilo and Hansen have done the only logical thing. They have inter-
rupted their studies and are in the factory now. Fish swimming in the
water of the proletariat—the vanguard of their theory.
—Roland Lang (1975)[37]

Wallraff's successes, however limited, with attracting a readership among workers, allying himself with their organizing activities, and calling public attention to social wrongs distinguish him from most of the West German students who—in the waning period of the student movement around 1969–1970—decided to leave their studies behind and enter into the world of factory work.[38] In the preceding few years, these students had gone through an anti-authoritarian phase of rebellion against their parents (a generation filled with former Nazis and their supporters), the university (with its fossilized structures), and the state (in which, from 1966 to 1969, the years of the "Grand Coalition" between the CDU/CSU and the SPD, real opposition began to seem possible to these students only in an "extra-parliamentary" form). In this early phase, these students raised demands that either had to do with overcoming the deficits they felt so keenly in their own lives, or which—in solidarity with student protests around the globe—arose as a response to international anti-imperialist struggles, especially the Vietnam War. Almost entirely the children of parents who had become well-to-do in the course of the "economic miracle," yet beginning to register the emptiness of consumerist values, these students had not yet discovered the less privileged worlds that lay directly beneath them in their own society.[39]

For some, however, this was soon to change after the student Benno Ohnesorg was shot by a policeman during a demonstration protesting the visit of the Shah of Iran to West Berlin on June 2, 1967, and even more so after the attempted assassination of charismatic student leader Rudi Dutschke, also in West Berlin, on April 11, 1968. This latter event, especially, spurred on the search for new organizing strategies. Large numbers of students had immediately attacked the headquarters of the Springer press in West Berlin, believing that the inflammatory articles aimed against them in its widely read *Bildzeitung* had incited the attack on Dutschke.

Subsequently, these students felt the entire weight of the riot police come down on them and the hostility of much of the public directed against them. Therefore, some began to think that they had to reach out beyond their own social group to more of those whose interests were not being represented adequately by the state, the established political parties, and such media manipulation if they were ever going to challenge effectively the power held by those above. As one student who had participated in the actions against the Springer headquarters later wrote: "The reaction of the state apparatus and the city was so sweeping that it became clear from one day to the next: we are *not* the base; we *need* a base."[40]

These students' newfound interest in the "base," another stage in their ongoing efforts to break out of isolation, kindled their sudden responsiveness to Günter Wallraff's reportages on the working world. Already in 1967, students from the "Sozialistischer deutscher Studentenbund" (SDS) had demonstrated outside the yearly meeting of writers who belonged to the prestigious "Group 47," demanding that they come down off their aesthetic pedestals and award their literary prize to Wallraff.[41] Looking back at this tumultuous period twenty years later, in 1987, writer and former student activist Peter Schneider evaluated Wallraff's importance for these students: "After twenty years of Wallraff's reportages people might smile today at this writer-worker's pathos of enlightenment. But at the beginning of the 1970s, high-school pupils and university students read his reports about the assembly line like revelations of a distant world which they had previously known nothing about."[42] A socially engaged journalist such as Wallraff, then, appeared to be pointing the way to students who had had their fill of "value-free" scholarship.

One path into the distant world of the "base" was that taken by the students who left their seminar papers and lecture halls behind to go to work in factories for a short time. These students wanted to make common cause with workers, but not at all in the sense of the volkish nationalism advocated by right-wing work students in the 1920s,[43] and also not along the lines of the "socialist community" being propounded in the GDR. Rather, allied with workers who were to rediscover their class consciousness under the students' tutelage, they aimed at overthrowing the state, which they saw as disguising the actual power of privileged elites under the cloak of a hypocritical, false consensus. As Uwe Timm had his student protagonist Ullrich in the novel *Heißer Sommer* (Hot Summer, 1974) declare agitatedly to working-class bystanders in front of the Springer headquarters after Dutschke was shot: "But workers and students are all in the same boat." The challenge that one woman laughingly throws down to him, "Then come work in the fish cannery with us, kid," pointed the way to this fictional character that a number of students actually took in reality.[44]

In entering into what they defined as the working world, these students acted out what can only be described as a romanticized view of the proletariat—a view which, no matter how hard they tried to break away from their family backgrounds and classes of origin—seemed to be defined more by a retrograde view of the past than by productive ways of transforming the lived present. Their image of the workers they were joining was shaped mainly by the theory and the proletarian novels of the 1920s that they had read. Accordingly, they organized themselves into left-sectarian Trotskyist or Maoist "red cells," "base groups," or small parties known as "K-groups," envisioning these as the political avant-garde. As such, they believed they could infuse their fellow workers with class consciousness in a Leninist fashion and become the leaders of a revived proletarian liberation movement. But when the "real" workers did not welcome their political proselytizing, but rather met them with skepticism, hostility, or simple indifference, these students were soon forced to admit the shortcomings of their outmoded ideas about political organizing and class structures, which were for the most part out of touch with the realities of these workers' lives.

Quite a few novels or autobiographical reports written by partici- pants in the student movement during the 1970s touch at least in passing on these attempts at political organizing and the obstacles these students ran up against, including Christian Geissler's *Das Brot mit der Feile* (The Bread with the File, 1973), Gerd Fuchs's *Beringer und die lange Wut* (Beringer and the Long Rage, 1973), Peter Schneider's *Lenz* (1973), Timm's *Heißer Sommer,* Roland Lang's *Ein Hai in der Suppe oder das Glück des Philipp Ronge* (A Shark in the Soup or the Happiness of Philipp Ronge, 1975), Michael (Bommi) Baumann's *Wie alles anfing* (How It All Began, 1976), Peter Mosler's *Was wir wollten, was wir wurden* (What We Wanted, What We Became, 1977), the K-group documentation *Wir warn die stärkste der Parteien* (We Were the Strongest Party of All, 1977), and a number of essays by Michael Schneider.[45] Among these texts that reflect on the journeys students took into the world of manual labor, their images of this world beforehand, the ways workers reacted to them once they were there, and their eventual reasons for leaving again, the most extensive and vivid examples are those by the brothers Peter and Michael Schneider. Already in 1970, Peter Schneider published an impressively self-reflective reportage entitled "Die Frauen bei Bosch" (The Women at Bosch), which also provides an illuminating contrast to Wallraff's depiction of the relation- ship between himself and his fellow workers.[46] Along with other student activists, Schneider had decided in 1969 to go to work for a time in a factory in order to gain practical acquaintance with the world of the "base" that he had been studying with his friends in Marxist reading groups. He chose a branch of the Bosch company in Wilmersdorf in West Berlin that employed about 140 mostly female workers and produced electrical equipment for automobiles. Assigned as an unskilled worker to take care of odd jobs such as cleaning and transporting material, Schneider was able to move through the factory and talk to the women on the assembly line.

Schneider did not focus so much on his own reactions to the work as on analyzing the relations of production that he observed. Also, he reflected on the relationship between himself and the other workers, that is, on whether his pre-formed theories dovetailed with the reality he experienced. Consequently, he discussed in some detail the effects on these workers of the flight of capital to low-wage countries and the difficult working conditions created by the enforcement of rigid time-motion studies along the assembly line. All of this, Schneider noted, only served to confirm his theoretical knowledge. However, more interestingly, he also saw that the workers reacted quite differently to their situation than he had expected:

> On the other hand, I noticed that these contradictions in the workers' experiences had an entirely different significance than I had imagined. . . . In reality, [these contradictions] are balanced out with a system of jokes, secret boycotts, and spontaneous outbursts of anger which are difficult to describe. They are also balanced out with conversations about clothes, the weather, and family matters; with all kinds of contortions and grimaces; with practical jokes and masquerades; with a strange good-naturedness and leisureliness. And concepts such as compensation or apathy only capture the negative side of these things. . . . In my opinion, it is necessary to study and get to know these spontaneous forms of proletarian resistance in order to be able to agitate effectively. (60)

In contrast to Wallraff, Schneider did not present the workers he met as beaten down and passive. Instead, rather than simply dismissing certain forms of activity as "pre-political," he highlighted examples of workers' self-assertion throughout his reportage. These included things such as making noise and singing together, taking breaks in the bathroom to smoke, read, talk, joke, and complain (all forbidden on the factory floor), refusing to apologize to supervisors or to follow their directions, figuring out how to make products faster but with hidden defects so as to meet the piecework quota, brushing off the sexual advances of superiors, and petitioning for foreign workers to have the same kind of bus transportation to work that the German women had. In this unaccustomed situation, Schneider actually felt that the women often confronted their bosses much more combatively than he himself dared to do, noting: "It struck me that I was much more inhibited around the foreman than most of the women were" (76). Consequently, the experience of this new world contradicted his initial conception of himself as representing the political avant-garde:

> These and other experiences made it seem rather ridiculous to me to behave like an agitator from the start. It would take several months to get to know the factory and the needs of the women. Also, the workers distrust newcomers who divulge nothing but their altruism and their enthusiasm for the working class. . . . Since they experience assembly line work as a punishment, they wonder what a student is up to who voluntarily submits to such a punishment. (74–75)

Schneider validated these women's assessments of their reality as different from his own in important respects. Consequently, he emphasized here how understandable it was that workers who were dependent on a wage might not want to take the risks of moving in new political directions without being fairly sure of the concrete advantages to be gained.

A little later, Schneider integrated what he had learned from his stint in the factory into his widely read short novel entitled *Lenz* (1973), in which a working-class character questions the radical students' temporary attachment to his world:

> But how long will you stay here? Your enthusiasm for our cause—where does it come from? You don't have the same problems we do, because you don't have to do the same work. As long as we're following your ideas, everything's fine. But what's going to happen when it doesn't help us any more to follow your ideas, when we have to disappoint you? When we're happy about a success that you think is too insignificant? We know our interests because we have to defend them every day. But your interests—do we know them? Do you know them?[47]

By having his protagonist finally separate himself from the working world in favor of a rediscovered insistence on personal needs, Schneider seemed to suggest now that the only authentic answer to these questions was for the students to return entirely to the worlds they came from. In this paradigmatic text of the so-called "New Subjectivity," the gaps between social classes, originating out of different interests, seemed as unbridgeable as ever in the end.

Like his brother, Michael Schneider was also one among the West Berlin students who, desiring to overcome their political isolation, went to work in a factory in the summer of 1969 with the goal of building up political "groups at the base." In two long articles entitled "Gegen den linken Dogmatismus, eine Alterskrankheit des Kommunismus" (Against Left-Wing Dogmatism, a Geriatric Disorder of Communism, 1971) and "Peter Schneider: Von der Alten Radikalität zur Neuen Sensibilität" (Peter Schneider: From Old Radicalism to New Sensitivity, 1974),[48] Schneider gave a political and literary analysis of these students' sudden descent into the world below and their ensuing flight away from it, which was generally just as abrupt. Schneider had gone to work as a mechanical inspector in a Siemens plant in West Berlin, and his assessment of the relationship between himself as the student outsider and the workers he met was quite similar to that described by his brother in "Die Frauen bei Bosch." In his first two months in the factory, Michael Schneider recalled, he was so fixated on his Leninist mission of transforming the workers' consciousness that he had no interest in getting to know them as human beings with problems and desires of their own. And, as Schneider described it self-critically, the workers had no patience for his attempts at political missionizing:

> I was always trying to make the young workers, in particular, see the light. Because from the perspective of "pure theory," they were committing one political sin after another. But this meant that some of them soon stopped asking me any political questions at all. They were simply annoyed that the student "always knew best." Yes, and sometimes they told me quite clearly that I was really not "one of them." I was just a "worker for the time being" who would leave the factory again after a few months. . . . It was not the fact that I talked so much about their oppression and exploitation which made them reject me. Rather, it was the fact that, as a "Sunday worker," I could claim the privilege of talking about these things.[49]

It was only after he "let his Leninist mask fall," then, showing himself as a person with his own hopes and problems and also recognizing that his fellow workers resisted their subordinate positions in all kinds of ways, that he began to feel accepted in the factory.

Schneider analyzed this experience, which he saw as typical for the students who chose this path, by focusing on the suddenness of the transformation they underwent from the anti-authoritarian to the organized phase of their movement. He viewed the extreme rigidity of the students' proletkultist approach as rooted in their unacknowledged guilt over class privilege. In his critique from 1974 of his brother's story *Lenz,* Schneider gave the clearest statement of this perspective. Recalling that Rudi Dutschke had once said that everything moved much too fast after June 2, 1967, Schneider zeroed in on these students' discovery of the world of capital and labor: "Many heretofore obedient sons of the middle classes developed with frightening speed into the avant-garde of a class whose existence they had hardly known about before. If they had only talked about themselves for twenty years, now they only talked about the 'proletariat.' . . . An enormous self-denial was the result."[50] On the one hand, Michael Schneider took his brother's story to be an accurate portrayal of the mood among students who were disillusioned with their efforts to "break from their past." They recalled to him Brecht's Saint Joan of the stockyards by setting off on their "journey into the depths"— that is, into the factories—where, in a kind of martyrdom, they willingly took on the hardest and most unskilled work. Of course, this sort of voluntary self-victimization could not last very long. However, Schneider also criticized the students whom the story's protagonist represented for abandoning their interest so quickly in the working world they had entered, describing his brother's zigzag course as follows: "Peter Schneider once broke rigorously with his bourgeois fathers. Now, four years later, he is breaking just as rigorously with their wayward sons, that is, with his own comrades. And because he is so furious, the baby is being thrown out with the bathwater again."[51] The baby that was being thrown out here with the bathwater of dogmatic theory was the effort to renounce positions of privilege and forge useful, egalitarian connections with those closer to the bottom of society.

However, as Michael Schneider had already noted in 1971, these students were generally drawing on outdated theoretical concepts and had little to offer in the way of practical strategies for change. Consequently, it was only so much the worse that when workers actually did come to the political groups organized by the students, they rarely went away with any new ideas that might have helped them understand their situation better, let alone transform it. Rather, they encountered arrogant leftist pedants, for the most part, instead of partners who were willing to take their experiences and insights seriously. As Schneider stated: "A dialectic between teaching and learning, a dialectical relationship between leftist intellectuals and leftist workers, seldom or never materialized in our political groups. But it would be emancipatory for both sides."[52] In general, then, when these students realized how difficult it would be to combine their political theories with effective organizing, their response was to leave the world of the "base"—peopled as it was by workers who were hardly inclined to endanger their relative prosperity anyway. For some students, represented by Timm's protagonist who returns to his studies with the goal of becoming an elementary school teacher in a working-class district, the path in life that seemed to preserve the most hope for social change was that of the "long march through the institutions." Many others, however, were represented by Peter Schneider's Lenz, who leaves the factory and buys a train ticket for Italy—that classic escape route for frustrated northern Europeans. For these students, the next way station was that of an extreme individualism which now rejected or simply was not interested any longer in efforts to bridge those societal gaps that were created by economic structures.

In the final analysis, no matter how stubbornly these students sought to create new modes of resistance to the authorities they so disliked, the ways in which they journeyed into the working world show that they were in fact shaped by the hierarchical thinking of their pasts, in ways that they became aware of only through painful, frustrating experience. To be sure, the comforts they had enjoyed as a result of West German prosperity had probably immunized them against any tendencies to heroicize brute manual labor. Thus, although these texts are all by men, they do not contain any of the nationalistic paeans to the strong, muscular, dimwitted workers who stand their ground in earlier right-wing and Nazi texts, or any of the indications of taking pleasure in difficult physical labor that are so prevalent in GDR texts about constructing socialism. For these students, going into the working world did not mean finding jobs where they experienced manual labor in itself in a positive way or in which they took virile pleasure in communal physical effort. In this sense, forms of masculinity that were so characteristic of many earlier journeys into the working world had been made passé by the development of the West German economy.

By contrast, however, these students' journeys entailed another kind of masculine response to voluntary victimization that was based more on thought than on experience. Feeling betrayed by the generation of their (Nazi) parents, these students had sought to break out of the isolation brought on by rigid socialization and repression of emotions, especially those of pain, guilt, and emptiness. Almost all of the documentations, autobiographies, and novels that touch on the early phase of the student movement register the joyful euphoria in breaking down constricting barriers, in suddenly speaking and acting publicly, together with other young people, in ways that were formerly taboo. Yet after this phase of relative openness, the students' journeys into the working world re-created structures of psychic repression in many respects, or reacted against them in ways that prevented productive energies from being applied to the tasks at hand. In the process these students underwent, they denied the validity and importance of many of the perceptions and issues that had given their movement its élan during the anti-authoritarian phase, rejecting these as the concerns of "petit-bourgeois" intellectuals. They then accepted the industrial working class as the only possible revolutionary subject in a manner that applied outmoded Leninist concepts from the 1920s to contemporary reality. However, as the theoretical avant-garde, they still asserted their control over the path the revolutionary movement was to take. On the one hand, then, the rigidity and arrogance these students manifested were holdovers from the authoritarian family and social structures that had so stunted their spontaneity. On the other hand, their desire to take up a position as victims, to become unskilled workers for a time, represented the opposite extreme of their desire to be pure in their theory, to reject any taint of complicity in oppression, to be absolute in their resistance.[53]

In an essay written in 1983, feminist scholar Christina Thürmer-Rohr analyzed incisively the gendered bias of this way of entering into the working world:

> For a few years I had tormented myself with trying to follow the specious arguments of male intellectuals. They maintained that our concrete experiences as non-proletarians led us away from social reality rather than bringing us closer to it. We were supposed to accomplish the psychic and intellectual acrobatic act of thinking and acting from the class standpoint of the proletariat. But that didn't work. In any case, a "proletarian practice," as the only possible way of breaking through the limits on our knowledge, was not our practice and could not become such a thing no matter how good our intentions were. Marxist epistemology did not show women how to comprehend their social and personal experience. Our mistaken ideas about the conditions for "real" knowledge prevented us from being able to recognize reality in our own scandalous and shameful experiences.[54]

For those who had gone through this phase of the student movement, then, and turned toward the new social movements—feminism, gay liberation, ecology, peace—in the mid-1970s, their deemphasis on the politics of social class grew directly out of their knowledge of their oppression and their needs for liberation. For others, however, their disillusionment with their brief sojourn in the working world sent them on a course back into inwardness and concern with self whose political, emancipatory dimensions were not so evident.

Book cover for Günter Wallraff's *Ganz unten* (1985).

A Turkish Worker Like Me:
Günter Wallraff's *Lowest of the Low* (1985)
and the Politics of German Minstrelsy

I was able to feel identical with myself again in this new role, and therefore I can definitely say "I" again today. In this book I say "I" again by drawing near to this Turkish foreign worker named Ali whom I played. This is why I always wrote "I(Ali)," which is rather clumsy to read. Here, the "I" must be read as my first name, and the "Ali" as my last name. I was always both.

—Günter Wallraff, 1985[55]

Most of the students who journeyed into the working world around 1970 saw themselves as attempting to be the political avant-garde of industrial factory workers, whom they viewed as the potential revolutionary subject of history. Consequently, they did not link their political project with entering into the social abysses that had been so central for many of those who had taken this path before. Furthermore, with the narrowing of focus to the *German* working class, they also often lost sight of the transnational dimensions of class conflicts that had been so important to them shortly beforehand in their protests against the Vietnam War and calls for solidarity with the Third World. Günter Wallraff, however, not sharing their inflexible political perspective, preserved a much broader sense for the "dark" sides of the Federal Republic in his investigative reporting. In particular, he did not let the fact that West German workers were relatively well off deter him from continuing his efforts to bring social wrongs to light. On the contrary, this state of affairs seems to have spurred him on to venture down into even lower depths, to investigate the lives of those who had hardly profited from West German prosperity. In an interview conducted in 1974, for example, Wallraff referred critically to the new trend toward "subjectivity" in West German literature and predicted that his commitment to resisting this tendency might eventually lead to his marginalization: "Within the trend towards nostalgia which is becoming so fashionable now in literature, I will be a voice which always returns to the problems of the 'majority,' the people who are not able to afford this nostalgia. . . . This may mean that I will be marginalized with respect to the bourgeois cultural context."[56] In his collection of *Dreizehn unerwünschte Reportagen* (Thirteen Unwelcome Reportages, 1969), which he had published next after *Wir brauchen Dich* and which recall earlier traditions of social reportage, Wallraff had already recounted his brief stints posing as a homeless man in a Hamburg shelter, an alcoholic who commits himself voluntarily to a mental hospital, and an unemployed metalworker unsuccessfully looking for a new job in Dortmund. However,

Workmates. Wallraff is at the far right. Günter Wallraff, *Ganz unten* (1985).

along with such concerns, Wallraff also did not lose interest in the working world that had been his central focus at the beginning of his journalistic career. Rather, realizing that the makeup of the workforce had changed fundamentally in the Federal Republic, he set out to investigate the lives of those who were increasingly performing the dirtiest and most difficult work there—that is, the foreign workers who had been coming to the country in greater and greater numbers since the late 1950s.

In his first reportage on this subject, entitled " 'Gastarbeiter' oder der gewöhnliche Kapitalismus" ("Foreign Workers" or Ordinary Capitalism, 1972),[57] Wallraff concentrated mainly on denouncing the Springer press's chauvinistic articles about these foreigners and on exposing the squalor of their living conditions in company housing, rather than focusing on their experiences at the workplace. However, this short piece was only a trial run at what was to become his longest and most spectacular journey into the working world. This was his project of disguising himself to live for two years as an unskilled Turkish foreign worker, which he reported on in the phenomenal best-seller *Ganz unten* (Lowest of the Low, 1985). But by continuing to use his method of hidden participant observation to investigate this group of foreign workers, Wallraff was not only crossing the barriers of social class, but also the demarcation lines of ethnicity, which introduced a whole new set of problems and dynamics. By simply assuming that a "German" could "become" a "Turk" in order to uncover truths about this minority group, Wallraff unintentionally exposed hidden and not-so-hidden preconceptions about ethnicity and race, as well as about privileges of representing the "non-German" within Germany. In this respect, his book recalls a much earlier project in the United States, John Howard Griffin's *Black Like Me* (1961), which recounted this white writer's journey through the segregated South disguised as a black man.[58] And if Griffin's odyssey as a "White Negro"[59] can be located squarely within the long tradition of blackface performance in the United States, Wallraff's transformation into a "German in Turkface" unwittingly transposed characteristics of U.S. minstrelsy into the German arena.[60]

Although African Americans had long been writing and speaking about the outrages of segregation that Griffin exposed in his book, *Black Like Me* was published at a point in the early stages of the civil rights movement when much of white America had not yet been moved to register the demands of those who were the targets of Jim Crow racism. However, the experiences of Griffin, a "first-class citizen" who set out to explore the "night side of American life" by darkening his skin and traveling through the South, were extreme enough in their moral appeal that his book became an instant best-seller.[61] It provoked white liberal readers to examine their consciences, and it even met with tactical approval from many black readers, who viewed Griffin's project as just one more means of bringing these facts before the public, in spite of their irritation about his naïveté.[62]

Unlike Wallraff, Griffin was not concerned with questions of social class but solely with issues of race, and so it is in this sense that his book fits into another tradition of crossing boundaries in the United States, that of "white men literally assuming a 'black' self." From the enormously popular blackface minstrels of the nineteenth century, to Griffin with his "earnest anti-segregationist politics," to contemporary popular culture, a tradition of "racial mimicry" has reemerged over and over again.[63] This phenomenon, of course, divulges little about the lives of African Americans, but quite a lot about the perceptions and fantasies of the whites—mostly men—who desired to become "brothers for the time being" with black men, as one famous nineteenth-century minstrel put it.[64] In Griffin's case, as was also true for the early minstrels, his journey was "less into a black world than into a 'black' part of himself," and his interest was much less in what blacks thought of him than in how whites would treat him.[65] Thus, his preconceptions of what "blackness" was clearly shaped what he became and what he experienced. On the one hand, the text abounds with scenarios of victimization and despair; on the other, it is obsessively fixated on the sexuality of black men in a manner typical of the white racial unconscious in the United States. Griffin's solution to what he experienced as a destabilizing, threatening breach of forbidden boundaries between black and white was to withdraw into the politics of liberal whiteness, which was based mainly on existentialist appeals to individual goodwill.[66] Yet this approach represented only the opposite extreme of the fascination with the bohemian, "low" sides of life that have so often been coded as "black" in U.S. popular culture.

When Günter Wallraff set out in *Ganz unten* to explore the "night" sides of life in the Federal Republic, he chose to play the roles of both a manual laborer and a member of another ethnic group. That is, he was still focusing on questions of work and social class, which overlapped here with issues of ethnicity. Or to put it another way, just as he had wanted from the beginning to uncover the abysses of the "economic miracle," here he also aimed at exposing the xenophobia and racism that he saw as pervading West German society. And this necessarily meant, in the context of German history, that he was setting out to make a statement about continuities between the Nazi past and the present-day Federal Republic. These two concerns shaped the persona that he assumed for two years and named "I(Ali)." In the preface to his book, Wallraff noted with astonishment how easy it was for him to "pass in reverse" as a Turk: simply by wearing dark contact lenses and a dark hairpiece, speaking broken German, and concocting a story about having spoken Greek rather than Turkish as a child in order to avoid the language issue.

There were two basic components in Wallraff's conception of his role. First, by seemingly trading his German identity for an identity as a Turkish foreign worker, he imagined himself claiming a position as a social outsider, a victim. Second, however, and equally important, he presented "I(Ali)" as not only passive, but also as actively provoking his German environment to show itself at its worst. He did this by taking on the role of a humorously naive innocent—a kind of updated "happy primitive."[67] As Wallraff maintained regarding this characteristic of the "I(Ali)" figure: "My pretended foolishness made me more clever. It revealed to me the narrow-mindedness and icy coldness of a society which takes itself to be so intelligent, superior, definitive, and just. I was the fool to whom people tell the undisguised truth."[68] Or even more bluntly: "The advantage of this role was that I could ask the kind of questions I can't ask as a journalist or a writer. By pretending to be stupid, and by masquerading as a fool who was not to be taken seriously, I could allow myself to ask everything again, to call everything into question again. I was in the situation of really being able to ask questions like a child, and that was a splendid feeling."[69] To be sure, with overtones of his earlier investigative ventures, Wallraff claimed to be aware of the artificiality of his role: "Of course I wasn't really a Turk. But you have to disguise yourself in order to unmask society. You have to deceive and dissemble in order to find out the truth" (12). Yet as he developed the role throughout his project, this initial assertion appears to be fundamentally a statement of false modesty. For over the course of time, he also claimed to become increasingly identical with his role in an unproblematized way that was similar to Griffin's transformation.[70] That is, what Wallraff uncovered often had much less to do with the worlds of Turkish workers than with his own preconceptions of their lives and with facets of his own personality suddenly given free rein by his no longer having to act like a "German."[71]

Taking on this role for a period of two years, Wallraff concentrated on three main areas of investigation and exposé: prejudice within religious and political organizations, exploitative labor practices, and pervasive racism and xenophobia. The first of these, while symptomatic of broader social attitudes, clearly had the least to do with concerns of foreign workers and instead reflected Wallraff's own dislikes and resentments. For example, the naive, almost childishly silly "I(Ali)" requests at one point to be baptized, declaring that he prefers Jesus to Mohammed, and then seeks to join the Baghwan community, proclaiming: "We Turk always much alone, rather live together in commune with German and other" (75). And both times he is turned away: by xenophobic Catholic priests as well as by followers of the New Age guru.

The second area of focus recalls most obviously Wallraff's earlier reporting: his experiences with seeking out the lowest-paid, dirtiest, most dangerous work he could find, above all in the shady world of subcontracted jobs often performed by illegal aliens along with German workers who were especially down and out. To enter into this hidden world at first, Wallraff simply placed an ad in several newspapers that read as follows: "Foreigner, strong, wants work, any kind, will take hardest and dirtiest, will take low pay. If interested call 348 458" (11). After trying out his role in a few short-term jobs, he moved on to McDonald's and to a stint as a human subject testing medications for a pharmaceutical firm. The greatest part of his investigation, however, was devoted to exposing the terrible, often illegal and even life-threatening conditions allowed by firms who subcontracted labor to heavy industry. Specifically, Wallraff was hired by a subcontractor he called "Adler" who supplied workers to the Thyssen steel mill in Duisburg. First, Wallraff worked at difficult and dangerous cleaning and maintenance tasks in the mill itself, and then he talked his way into a position as Adler's chauffeur. Having gained Adler's trust to an extent, Wallraff finally created a scenario to test how far his profit-oriented thinking and his contempt for the value of human life went. And as it turned out, Adler actually would have been willing to send Turkish workers to repair a supposedly damaged nuclear reactor, even though he knew that they would have received a harmful dose of radiation. In these sections, as in Wallraff's earliest reportages, the images of workers—whether German or foreign— are, on the one hand, those of victims who are at the mercy of arbitrary regulations and heartless superiors. However, the actions of the "I(Ali)" figure also evidence another dimension, as in the following passage where he promises to defend Adler in his role as chauffeur: "In what follows Ali plays the role of a somewhat clumsy, overeager person who is ready to sacrifice himself for his master, no matter what. 'I have karate learned, Turkish special karate, called Sisu. Whoever wants to kill Adler must kill Ali. I Adler's man' " (166). Here, the victim "I(Ali)" takes on a more active role, but in minstrelsy's form of subaltern humor and self-deprecation.

The third main area of investigation in *Ganz unten* is the racism and xenophobia that Wallraff presented here as permeating all levels of West German society, including the working world, and as demonstrating direct continuities with the Nazi past. From Catholic priests and conservative politicians who seem nostalgic for the days of "Aryan supremacy," to hostile German workers who turn anti-Semitic jokes into anti-Turkish ones aimed against "I(Ali)," to businessmen such as Adler who recall the Nazis' labor policies approvingly and are quite ready to send their subcontracted workers into life-threatening situations, Wallraff uncovered a swamp of unbroken fascist structures of mentality, untouched sediments from the past.[72] So, for example, "I(Ali)" imagines that his feelings of being an outcast in the midst of a Christian Social Union gathering in darkest Bavaria mirror those that a gypsy might have felt in a Nazi beer hall rally. Or, realizing that Adler was quite prepared to endanger Turkish workers' lives, he reflects that Eichmann, too, never saw the mountains of corpses but "only" organized the transports to the death camps.

This tactic of drawing simple parallels between the persecution of

Jews and other groups in the Third Reich and the situation of foreign workers in contemporary West Germany was already evident in Wallraff's first reportage on foreign workers from 1972. There he had highlighted similarities between Nazi racist vocabulary and that used by the Springer press in reporting on foreign workers. Furthermore, he had also emphasized the absolutely dependent status of these new ethnic minorities in the Federal Republic. At this stage in the 1970s and 1980s, when critical writers such as Wallraff first began to turn their attention toward the situation of foreign workers in the Federal Republic, this emphasis on continuities with the Nazi period seems to have been fairly common. Thus, for example, journalist Gerhard Kromschröder, who described himself as having written the "overture" to Wallraff's "opera," briefly took on the role of a Turkish street-sweeper, publishing a piece entitled "Als ich ein Türke war" (When I Was a Turk) in the magazine *Stern* in 1983, and he also included a role as a Sikh asylum-seeker in his collection of reportages entitled *Ich war einer von ihnen* (I Was One of Them, 1987).[73] In both Kromschröder's and Wallraff's accounts of their temporary metamorphoses, the Germans who briefly take on other ethnicities seem to move into the position of Jews in the Third Reich, and little of significance seems to have changed in Germany over the past forty years.

Of course, foreign workers in the Federal Republic have been a particularly vulnerable group lacking many legal protections, and it is a journalistic achievement of these reporters to have exposed tenacious fascist mentalities with the goal of educating their readers. Yet upon viewing these reportages as part of the tradition of journeys into the working world, it also seems curious that there is such exclusive emphasis here on presenting foreign workers as victims, given the context of the Federal Republic as a democracy that supposedly offers possibilities for individual choices and initiatives. After all, thinking back to the first such journey into the darkness of Imperial Germany, even Paul Göhre did not only report on the misery and exploitation he encountered in his three months in the workshop. Rather, he also saw that workers were organizing on their own behalf, and realized, as the young Max Weber wrote in defense of Göhre's book, that they had no need or desire for "charity" or "forbearance" from those above, but rather for a larger share in the earth's wealth.[74] Yet Göhre was writing at a point when Social Democracy seemed to hold out the greatest hopes that those who were "nothing" could one day become "everything." Wallraff, however, set out on his journey into the social abyss one hundred years later, in a situation where no viable left-wing workers' movement existed anymore in the Federal Republic. And furthermore, he was writing in a situation where any serious political effort to take a stand on issues of ethnicity and race necessarily had to recall the crimes of the Holocaust.

Book cover for Gerhard Kromschröder's *Als ich ein Türke war* (1983).

Gerhard Kromschröder in his role as a Turkish street-sweeper in Frankfurt. *Als ich ein Türke war* (1983).

These factors shaped the portrayal of the foreign worker as victim in *Ganz unten* in three ways. First, as in Wallraff's earliest reportages about German workers, there is hardly any significance attached here to joint action and organizing by workers themselves as a way to remedy abuses. Rather, reflecting the prevalent values of his society, Wallraff chose to take a more individualistic, existential approach, that of moral appeal as the path to social change. "I don't depend on groups at all," he said of himself as early as 1970. "I do what is humanly possible."[75] Second, and more particular to these portrayals of ethnicity, in pieces such as *Ganz unten*, "Als ich ein Türke war," and *Ich war einer von ihnen,* Wallraff and Kromschröder were not writing only about the position of ethnic minority groups in the contemporary Federal Republic. Rather, the unspoken reference here is to the Holocaust and to the Germans in the past who did not identify with "them." By simply asserting in these reportages that the continuities were obvious between fascism and the Federal Republic, between Nazi anti-Semitism and present-day xenophobia, these reporters were able to claim for themselves a position of delayed antifascist resistance.[76] Yet because of this constant oblique reference back to a traumatic past, these projects failed to do justice to the complexity of the present, in which transnational migrants themselves were increasingly voicing their own wishes and demands within the Federal Republic and elsewhere. Finally, Wallraff and Kromschröder claimed the position of the victim in an effort to escape any kind of identification with the role of "perpetrator" and its unbearably heavy historical burden of guilt. But the only kind of resistance they could imagine emanating from this role was that of minstrelsy: the tricks, slyness, and humor of the solitary outsider who has not yet reached either the civilized level of rationality or the threatening level of power politics. The strange nonsynchronicity of this perspective is indicative of how unaccustomed even these socially critical German writers were to relinquishing their position at the center and registering the heterogeneous voices arising from the new ethnic minorities in their midst.[77] At any rate, by identifying so seamlessly with the position of the Turkish worker as "victim," Wallraff and Kromschröder absolved both themselves and their well-meaning readers from any sense of guilt or of complicity in xenophobia and racism.

Such a perspective actually facilitated a reception of *Ganz unten* that generally passed over the issue of ethnic and racial prejudice altogether, or merely remained limited to moralistic calls for tolerance. In the first place, most press analyses of the unexpected, enormous success of Wallraff's book—the lines in front of bookstores, the three million readers, the thousands who attended speeches by Wallraff and his Turkish collaborators[78]—placed this publishing phenomenon into the contexts of Wallraff's own notoriety ("Wallraff was there again!") and also the tradition of adventurous journeys into the social abyss. Accordingly, journalists termed him a "James Bond of the little people," a "Zorro of late capitalism,"[79] or a "postmodern Robin Hood"[80] who had utilized the role of a "Turk" in order to create a suspenseful account of a journey to the depths of the "capitalist system"[81]— thus extending the line of writers such as Sue, Hugo, Zola, and Sinclair into the present.[82] Second, both in the mainstream press and in various court cases brought against Wallraff over the book's allegations, the main focus was not on racism and xenophobia, but on the abuses he exposed in the shady world of subcontractors' firms. In this respect, Wallraff's journey into the working world had a positive effect that his ethnic mimicry did not, in that his exposés spurred on local and state authorities to investigate exploitative practices and institute tighter regulations in some instances.[83] Similarly, the left-wing press also hardly focused on the plight of foreigners as presented in the book. This sector of the media, however, bogged down in controversy over the accusations of Hermann Gremliza, editor of the magazine *Konkret*, that Wallraff had not written the entire book himself but rather had used material from Gremliza and others without giving them proper credit.[84] On the whole, then, the path of "I(Ali)" through West German social abysses did not stimulate any broad effort to confront questions of racism and xenophobia in the heated discussions that swirled around the book for two years or so after its publication.

It fell to critics who were more on the margins of public debate in the Federal Republic to point out that in *Ganz unten* "Günter Wallraff misused the role of the victim in order to expose the role of the perpetrator."[85] The most extensive discussion about the ethnocentric assumptions underlying Wallraff's role as "I(Ali)" was carried out from 1986 to 1988 in *Die Brücke* (The Bridge), a magazine devoted to furthering the rights of ethnic minorities in the Federal Republic. Here, Turkish as well as some German commentators on Wallraff's book posed the question, "Are there nothing but dreadful things 'down below'?"[86] They criticized both Wallraff and much of the public reaction to the book as evidencing mainly the "mentality of the 'white man' who wants to be a guardian and a protector. But this is also a form of ethnocentrism."[87] Accordingly, these writers took issue with Wallraff's too facile parallels between the contemporary situation and the Nazi past and also with the naive, childish persona of "I(Ali)." They declared these features to be evidence of a fundamentally pessimistic attitude that was not at all a threat to the "ruling classes" and which made no place for hope, resistance, or change.[88]

In this vein, several of the Turkish workers and others who had collaborated with Wallraff on the "Ganz unten" project emphasized their rejection of the idea that foreign workers were mere objects for German social work.[89] They asserted emphatically that "the immigrants are not objects

Left: Günter Wallraff on the bottom. *Right:* Günter Wallraff on the top. *Die Brücke* 37 (June–July 1987): 36.

Erdogan Karayel, *Ganz in der Fremde. Karikaturen.* (In a Foreign Land. Caricatures.) *Die Brücke* 38 (August–September 1987): 40.

for pity. What we want is equal rights."[90] By this they meant concrete actions undertaken by the immigrants and their supporters in their own interests, ranging from equal participation in projects against xenophobia and racism, to efforts to improve their legal and residence status, to advocating a liberalization of voting and naturalization laws in the Federal Republic.[91] With their emphasis here on rational and unified political action, these writers turned the focus away from representations of the foreign worker primarily as an object of German perceptions and actions, that is, from what they termed the "melancholy, Oriental masochism" of "I(Ali)."[92] Rather than this, the articles and debates over *Ganz unten* in *Die Brücke* bring out the multiplicity of voices among the new ethnic minorities insisting on equal rights, and the differing opinions among these groups as to how or whether they wished to interact with their German environment. Viewed in this light, then, despite his good intentions, Wallraff's project in *Ganz unten* appears as part of the Orientalist tradition. He was able to assume the role of living and writing as a "Turk" in order to inform his liberal German readers (and corroborate many of their preconceptions). But "Turks" could hardly participate fully in "German" society and had to make an enormous effort even to refuse the solicitous interest of Germans in favor of self-expression.[93] Of course, the Orientalism of this entire approach is nowhere more evident than in Wallraff's statements that he "was" Ali, or in the title of Kromschröder's article, "Als ich ein Türke war." Here, as in Griffin's *Black Like Me*, these writers claim the privilege of speaking in the place of those whose lives they supposedly shared, of nullifying the differences they set out to investigate.

From his earliest reportages up through *Ganz unten*, Wallraff set out to journey into the social abysses of the increasingly wealthy Federal Republic, into the darkest realms of the working world and of social outcasts. His accomplishment for a time was to reach a wide reading audience, to establish himself as a public voice with a certain moral authority, and, especially during the hopeful years of the student movement, to challenge political and cultural perspectives that sought to paper over serious social contradictions. Unlike some of the radical students who gave up their political commitments after becoming disillusioned with factory workers' revolutionary potential, Wallraff preserved a much broader sense for the multitude of ways in which those at the bottom levels of society were marginalized and trapped in dead-end jobs, and he kept on using his skills of exposé to bring these issues before his wide reading public. It was these substantial achievements that led a number of prominent writers, including Günter Grass, Max von der Grün, Peter Rühmkorf, Heiner Müller, and Peter Schneider, to declare their support for Wallraff in the controversies around *Ganz unten* and to protest against what they termed the overblown charges of plagiarism and the "smear campaign" directed against this "uncomfortable" author.[94] As some of these writers pointed out, the frequent pettiness of the attacks on Wallraff from formerly progressive quarters reflected how these critics, too, were going along with the conservative flow of the 1980s and losing interest in the questions of social stratification that had always been so central to Wallraff's journalism.

On the other hand, however, neither Wallraff nor his supporters ever came to grips satisfactorily with the justified objections to his stance of speaking as if he really were identical with his role. They never tried to work through the implications of his failure to represent the "Turkish objects" of his investigations in their differences from his own ideas about them.[95]

It was the effect of the controversies around *Ganz unten* to silence Wallraff, who has not published another major reportage since then.[96] As far as the tradition of journeys to the working world and the social abyss goes, this is a loss, unfortunately brought on to a significant extent by Wallraff's blind spots in his last large project. For in his first roles as a "German" worker, Wallraff had taken the approach of being a "participant observer" where he preserved at least a certain amount of respectful distance between himself and the working world he entered. By this means, he created a space where his journalistic endeavors could complement and support workers' own organizing efforts. However, in *Ganz unten* he described himself as an "observing participant."[97] This meant that he provoked many of the encounters he reported on—almost in the manner of a performance artist—while hardly reflecting at all on how or whether these exposés could be of use to the foreign workers who were already engaged in their own educational and political initiatives. In other words, when the distance between social classes became compounded by issues of ethnicity due to the changing makeup of the workforce, Wallraff's preconceptions prevented him from entering into an unknown world—a world in which voices like those of his critics in *Die Brücke* would have challenged his privilege of speaking for them, from an unquestioned, stable center.

Conclusion

Since 1990, with the accession of the German Democratic Republic to the Federal Republic, the tradition of German journeys to the working world appears to have ended, at least for the time being. Consequently, it was almost a curiosity that the National Organization of Employers in the Metal Processing Industries sponsored a conference on the "working world in contemporary German literature" at the German Academy for Language and Literature in 1991. Here, participants raised questions reminiscent of the early 1960s as to why the workplace rarely appeared in recent literary texts.[1] Other speakers hoped to use this conference as one more forum to drown out any remaining vestiges of opposition to their visions for the future of Germany. For example, the president of the sponsoring employers' organization, Werner Stumpfe, maintained that it was impossible to "generalize" about the working world and criticized the earlier tendency of leftist writers to "demonize" the world of industry. The more liberal speakers, by contrast, described the literature of the working world from the 1960s and 1970s—in which Günter Wallraff's journeys had been so central—as "repressed and forgotten" in reunified Germany. In the midst of this overwhelmingly conservative conference, they called rather helplessly for writers to renounce their privileged positions, develop a new realism, and renew their interest in making visible the hidden worlds of both the working poor and the unemployed.

While it is true that German writers are hardly creating literary texts today that reflect on disparities between fulfilling and unfulfilling work, or between wealth and poverty, this is not only a matter of intellectual arrogance or simple disinterest. Rather, both East and West German writers who tried earlier to create emancipatory coalitions by journeying to the working world arrived at definite impasses. And these impasses had to do with the ways in which the structure and distribution of work itself

249

are changing fundamentally. The literary tradition discussed in this book, which focused on work in the manufacturing sector or on unskilled manual labor, was linked with the centrality of industrial production as a site of mass employment. Since the late nineteenth century, writers and others who journeyed into this kind of working world did so because they perceived its clashes with their own worlds as embodying the most important explosion points of social conflict. And as we have seen, they viewed the challenging voices arising from below as either a threat they wanted to control or a promise of liberation they wanted to join. But for quite a few years now, the number of workers in industrial production has been shrinking due to the migration of many companies to developing countries and to widespread use of the latest automation and computer technology. Therefore, because of the ongoing decline of the manufacturing base in countries with advanced economies, a smaller percentage of the workforce than ever before is engaged in producing goods there. At the same time, more and more employees in the service sector are being displaced through information technology, and the number of temporary workers is growing steadily. Even in developing countries, which are manufacturing ever larger proportions of the world's goods, the use of the new technologies also portends mass displacement and unemployment of production workers in the long run. A study published by the International Metalworkers Federation in Geneva, for example, forecasts that "within thirty years, as little as two percent of the world's current labor force will be needed to produce all the goods necessary for total demand."[2] In view of these developments, the ways in which older journeys to the world of manual labor tapped into society's most pressing class-based conflicts seem increasingly to be a closed chapter.

Yet the dilemmas which the travelers to the world of industrial work and manual labor faced are, if anything, even more urgent today, in view of the overwhelming disorientation, social fragmentation, and heartlessness that now surround us. While the elimination of traditional forms of work and, indeed, the devaluation of "work" itself as a source of stability and identity are worldwide tendencies in our era of globalization, the added factor of reunification makes these structural changes particularly unsettling in Germany. As in other countries with advanced economies, work is becoming less important in Germany for creating wealth. Thus, by 1997 wages and salaries there accounted for only 40 percent of the population's disposable income, while about 60 percent came from profits, stocks, and other assets.[3] This trend means that not only the economic gap, but also the social and cultural rupture between those above and those below, is becoming more extreme.

During the 1990s there was a greater willingness than ever before in postwar German history to accept and even promote the collapse of the "social consensus" and to write off relatively large numbers of people—often those still performing manual labor in an increasingly high-tech society—as inessential and marginal.[4] As one political commentator observed in 1994, "everyone feels that the gap between the poor and the rich has become frighteningly large in Germany," but the leading politicians have "forgotten how to talk about the social question."[5] These developments have been particularly drastic in the new Federal States, where modernization of older, dilapidated industries has entailed introducing the most up-to-date technology. As a result, fewer workers than ever before produce a much higher output—for example, in the new chemical factories in Bitterfeld. These structural changes are borne out by official statistics. Thus, in 1997, 9.9 percent of West Germans and 19.4 percent of East Germans were registered as unemployed (though actual numbers are likely higher), and about five million Germans were partially or totally dependent on welfare, more than twice as many as in 1980.[6] Yet while it seemed as though the "social question" had returned with a vengeance, the costs associated with reunification as well as the forces of the capitalist world market lent more credence to those who argued for cutting benefits, weakening the "social net," and steering a harder course directed against the weakest members of German society.[7] Accordingly, author Walter Jens remarked in 1998 that "today Ludwig Erhard would be considered a leftist" in view of the headlines now proclaiming that both the unemployment rate and the stock market are going up in Germany.[8]

The most recent texts discussed here by both East and West German writers express a sense that the explosion points of social tensions are shifting along these lines, while remaining uncertain of the directions to take in creating emancipatory coalitions with those below. Accordingly, these writers no longer concentrate on the industrial working world, but on other groups in today's social abyss. Volker Braun portrayed the "people of Hoywoy" not as his productive former workmates, with whom he had once felt allied in creating something new. Rather, he viewed them from a distance as a chaotic mass of people who were unemployed and displaced due to political and economic developments. And even Braun's "four toolmakers," who were once highly skilled factory workers, now appear as either demoted at their workplace or unemployed. Similarly, Günter Wallraff did not focus in his last project on the world of industry, where workers had long since developed organized ways of representing their own interests. Rather, he concentrated on more vulnerable and exploited groups. He entered into the worlds of foreign workers, reflecting the globalization of the labor force; and of temporary workers, reflecting prevalent corporate moves toward "outsourcing" which have undermined traditional forms of workplace organizing. And by doing this, Wallraff illuminated some of the most significant ways in which conflicts between above and below are changing. However, his insensitivity to the dimension of ethnicity defeated many of his emancipatory intentions when the foreign workers to whom he had journeyed began speaking back in ways he did not expect. In cases such as these, writers who formerly journeyed into the working world are expressing in their texts (and in the case of Wallraff, with his long silence) a greater sense of distance between themselves and the social abyss as it is presently configured. The positive feature of this development may be that some writers are more aware of the problematic aspects of trying to "speak for others" if these "others" are not accepted as equal partners in dialogue.[9] The negative feature is that because it is so difficult to imagine what mass organizing forms these marginalized groups will develop to further their own interests, it is also difficult to imagine how to create new kinds of effective coalitions. At the moment, the result seems to be a situation of political standstill.

The history of journeys to the working world is sobering in that it often seems to be a history of repetitions and dead ends, to have less to do with those on the bottom than with these travelers' projections of their own needs and desires onto them. However, this history also contains a more hopeful element, showing as it does that efforts to bridge gaps, make connections, and renounce positions of privilege never ended altogether but were always revived again after periods of darkness and amnesia. The texts in the past which hinted at more emancipatory visions of community and coalition were those where the sojourners in the working world let the voices of workers and others in the social abyss shine through, where their efforts to give up privilege coincided with social movements arising from below. At the moment, those writers who might still be concerned with these problems seem to have a greater consciousness of the difficulties involved in crossing these divides. But the present socioeconomic situation and the epochal upheavals in the structure of work leave them unsure about how to reconceive such a common project. Perhaps future journeys to the social depths that tap most deeply into the explosion points of existing conflicts will enter into the worlds of those who are working at computer terminals, those who are working only intermittently, or those who have no work at all. In any event, the cultural history of journeys to the working world shows that the human project of giving literary form to efforts at breaking down social inequities will resurface in the future in ways yet to be imagined.

Notes

Introduction

1. Raymond Williams, *The English Novel from Dickens to Lawrence* (London: Chatto and Windus, 1970), 17.
2. "Die Reichen reicher, die Armen ärmer—und warum in Deutschland Arbeit immer weniger einbringt," *Der Spiegel,* September 29, 1997. This and all further translations from German are my own unless otherwise noted.
3. See also the article "Wohlstand für wenige," *Die Zeit,* October 31, 1997, 8–9, for statistics that document this trend.
4. See Joan Campbell, *Joy in Work, German Work: The National Debate, 1800–1945* (Princeton: Princeton University Press, 1989); and Frank Trommler, "Die Nationalisierung der Arbeit," in Reinhold Grimm and Jost Hermand, eds., *Arbeit als Thema in der deutschen Literatur vom Mittelalter bis zur Gegenwart* (Königstein: Athenäum, 1979), 102–5.
5. Georg Herwegh, "Bundeslied für den Allgemeinen Deutschen Arbeiterverein," in his *Werke in einem Band* (Berlin: Aufbau, 1967), 232–33.
6. See Bodo Rollka, *Die Reise ins Souterrain: Notizen zur Strategie des aufklärerischen Erfolgs: Eugène Sues "Geheimnisse von Paris" und Günter Wallraffs "Ganz unten"* (Berlin: Arsenal, 1987).
7. Arnold Zweig, "Bericht aus dem Unbekannten," *Der Klassenkampf,* October 1, 1927, 26–27.
8. Of course, Zweig had just accomplished this himself in his novel *Der Streit um den Sergeanten Grischa,* which appeared in 1927, also, at the same time as this review.
9. See James Clifford and George E. Marcus, eds., *Writing Culture: The Poetics and Politics of Ethnography* (Berkeley: University of California Press, 1986); and Linda Alcoff, "The Problem of Speaking for Others," *Cultural Critique,* no. 20 (Winter 1991–1992): 5–32.
10. Charles Decker et al., *What's Left? Radical Politics in the Post-Communist Era* (Amherst: University of Massachusetts Press, 1995), 151.

Chapter 1

1. See Peter Keating, ed., *Into Unknown England: Selections from the Social Explorers* (Manchester: Manchester University Press, 1976); Deborah E. Nord, "The Social Explorer as Anthropologist: Victorian Travelers among the Urban Poor," in *Visions of the Modern City*, ed. William Sharpe and Leonard Wallock (New York: Columbia University Press, 1983), 118–30; Deborah E. Nord, *Walking the Victorian Streets: Women, Representation, and the City* (Ithaca: Cornell University Press, 1995), especially the section on female social investigation; Gail C. Low, *White Skins/Black Masks: Representation and Colonialism* (New York: Routledge, 1996); and Klaus Bergmann, *Schwarze Reportagen: Aus dem Leben der untersten Schichten vor 1914* (Reinbek: Rowohlt, 1984).

2. Of course, this list could be extended almost indefinitely. One additional U.S. example is Michael Harrington's *The Other America* (New York: Macmillan, 1962), which was an important impetus behind the "war on poverty" of the 1960s and deserves to be remembered today, now that the "war on the poor" is so prevalent. See also Harrington's *The Vast Majority: A Journey to the World's Poor* (New York: Simon and Schuster, 1977).

3. For a collection of texts about these groups in Germany before 1914, see Bergmann, *Schwarze Reportagen*.

4. See Klaus Bergmann, "Spaziergänge in die Tiefen der Gesellschaft," in *Neue Horizonte: Eine Reise durch die Reisen*, ed. Klaus Bergmann and Solveig Ockenfuß (Reinbek: Rowohlt, 1984), 219.

5. See Bodo Rollka, *Die Reise ins Souterrain: Notizen zur Strategie des aufklärerischen Erfolgs: Eugène Sues "Geheimnisse von Paris" und Günter Wallraffs "Ganz unten"* (Berlin: Arsenal, 1987), 60; Helga Grubitzsch, *Materialien zur Kritik des Feuilleton-Romans "Die Geheimnisse von Paris" von Eugène Sue* (Wiesbaden: Athenaion, 1977); and Karl Marx and Friedrich Engels, "Weltgang und Verklärung der 'kritischen Kritik,' oder 'die kritische Kritik' als Rudolph, Fürst von Geroldstein," in *Marxismus und Literatur*, ed. Fritz J. Raddatz (Reinbek: Rowohlt, 1969), 1:98–143.

6. Eugène Sue, *Les Mystères de Paris* (Verviers: Marabout, 1962), 1:9.

7. See Patrick Brantlinger, "Victorians and Africans: The Genealogy of the Myth of the Dark Continent," in *"Race," Writing and Difference*, ed. Henry Louis Gates, Jr. (Chicago: University of Chicago Press, 1986), 185–223, for a discussion of the intertwining missions of imperialism abroad and domestic suppression of the working classes and the poor.

8. Jost Hermand, "Der verdrängte Naturalismus," in his *Der Schein des schönen Lebens* (Frankfurt: Athenäum, 1972), 26.

9. Klaus-Michael Bogdal, *Schaurige Bilder: Der Arbeiter im Blick des Bürgers am Beispiel des Naturalismus* (Frankfurt: Syndikat, 1978), 57ff.

10. See ibid.

11. Karl Böttcher, *Sünden unsrer Zeit: Soziale Sittenbilder* (1888), quoted in ibid., 58.

12. Bogdal, *Schaurige Bilder*, 58. This point also forms the core of the Social Democratic critique of naturalism. See Norbert Rothe, ed., *Naturalismus-Debatte, 1891–1896* (Berlin: Akademie, 1986).

13. See the case studies reprinted in Bergmann, *Schwarze Reportagen,* as well as Bergmann's afterword, entitled "Zur Entstehung der Sozialreportage," for further examples of this kind of social work.

14. See ibid., 72.

15. Of course, the most famous such advocate of moral uplift was the founder of the Salvation Army, William Booth, who expounded on his plans in his book *In Darkest England and the Ways Out* (1890). See the discussion of this book and similar ones in Keating, *Into Unknown England.*

16. See Jost Hermand, *Old Dreams of a New Reich: Volkish Utopias and National Socialism* (Bloomington: Indiana University Press, 1992), 52–61.

17. See Michael Geisler, *Die literarische Reportage in Deutschland* (Königstein/ Ts.: Scriptor, 1982), 230ff.

18. See ibid., 227; and Georg Weerth, *Vergessene Texte* (Cologne: Leske, 1975), 1:262.

19. See Weerth, "Das Blumenfest der englischen Arbeiter," in Weerth, *Vergessene Texte,* 1:266–75.

20. Friedrich Engels, *The Condition of the Working-Class in England* (Moscow: Progress, 1973), 9.

21. For a twentieth-century example that also emphasizes the geographical separation between classes, see Michael Harrington's *The Other America.*

22. Engels, *Condition of the Working-Class,* 66.

23. Ibid., 84–85.

24. Geisler, *Die literarische Reportage,* 238ff.

25. Anthony Oberschall, *Empirical Social Research in Germany, 1848–1914* (Paris: Mouton, 1965), 137.

26. The German original reads:

> Das Buch schlug ein; es ward verschlungen und ging sogar von
> Hand zu Hand,
> Denn anders hat das doch geklungen, als was im Wochenblättchen
> stand.
> Man war verblüfft; nicht abzuweisen war ja, woran man nie gedacht,
> Der Vorwurf, daß Entdeckungsreisen man jetzt im eignen Volke
> macht.
> Ihr kennt die Schwarzen, die sich weiden am grellen Glanz des
> Tropenlichts—
> Vom eignen Volk und seinen Leiden, von seinem Leben wißt ihr
> nichts!

> Rudolf Lavant, *Gedichte,* ed. H. Uhlig (Berlin: Akademie, 1965), 51–52. Lavant's poem was first published in *Der wahre Jakob,* no. 132 (1891).

27. See Thomas Nipperdey, *Deutsche Geschichte, 1866–1918* (Munich: Beck, 1992), 1:292ff.

28. Ibid., 317–18.

29. On the relationship of Social Democracy to bourgeois culture, see in particular Georg Fülberth, *Proletarische Partei und bürgerliche Literatur* (Neuwied: Luchterhand, 1972); and Peter Brückner and Gabriele Ricke, "Über die ästhetische Erziehung des Menschen in der Arbeiterbewegung," in *Das*

Unvermögen der Realität, ed. Peter Brückner et al. (Berlin: Wagenbach, 1974), 37–68.

30. During the years of the Anti-Socialist Laws, Social Democratic meetings, publications, organizations, demonstrations, and festivals had been forbidden. Prison sentences handed down to Social Democrats had totaled over one thousand years. About one thousand of the most active leaders had been banned from the towns where they resided, and other leaders had emigrated or gone into permanent exile abroad.

31. Martin Wenck, *Friedrich Naumann: Ein Lebensbild* (Berlin: Verlag der "Hilfe," 1920), 45–46.

32. This is quoted in the commentary to the new edition of Paul Göhre, *Drei Monate Fabrikarbeiter und Handwerksbursche: Eine praktische Studie,* ed. Joachim Brenning and Christian Gremmels (Gütersloh: Mohn, 1978), 128. The quote comes from a letter Göhre wrote to the minister Martin Rade on June 9, 1890, shortly before beginning his journey.

33. Wenck, *Friedrich Naumann,* 46.

34. Richard T. Ely, preface to Paul Göhre, *Three Months in a Workshop,* trans. A. B. Carr (New York: Scribner, 1895), viii. The "conservative newspaper" referred to here is *Die Kreuzzeitung.*

35. This biographical information is given in Arthur Bonus, "Paul Göhre," *Die Gesellschaft* 15 (1899): 21.

36. These letters are summarized in Joachim Brenning, "Christentum und Sozialdemokratie. Paul Göhre: Fabrikarbeiter—Pfarrer—Sozialdemokrat. Eine sozialethisch-historische Untersuchung" (Diss., Marburg, 1980), 3.

37. In addition, it appears that a sensationalistic piece of undercover reporting by Rudolf Martin on the various anarchist groups in London may have also given Göhre the idea to infiltrate another milieu, that of the working world. See ibid., 23, on Rudolf Martin, *Der Anarchismus und seine Träger: Enthüllungen aus dem Lager der Anarchisten* (Berlin: Neufeld und Mehring, 1887).

38. Göhre's book was first published in serialized form in the journal *Christliche Welt,* edited by Martin Rade.

39. Paul Göhre, *Drei Monate Fabrikarbeiter und Handwerksbursche: Eine praktische Studie* (Leipzig: Grunow, 1891), 1–2. Further page references to this book will be given in the body of the text.

40. The factory is identified in Brenning, "Christentum und Sozialdemokratie," 5.

41. Quoted in ibid., 6.

42. See ibid. and Brenning and Gremmels's edition of Göhre's book for extremely detailed summaries of these controversies.

43. See Brenning and Gremmels's edition of Göhre's book, 153.

44. Quoted in Brenning, "Christentum und Sozialdemokratie," 64.

45. See ibid., 53ff.

46. Konrad Jarausch, *Students, Society, and Politics in Imperial Germany: The Rise of Academic Illiberalism* (Princeton: Princeton University Press, 1982), 361. Also see Paul Göhre, *Die evangelisch-soziale Bewegung* (Leipzig: Grunow, 1896), 137.

47. Hermand, *Old Dreams of a New Reich,* 61 and 293. Apparently Heinrich Himmler saw the National-Social Union as the beginning of the National

Socialist movement, as explained here on p. 293. See also Gerhard Taddey, ed., *Lexikon der deutschen Geschichte* (Stuttgart: Kröner, 1983), 864.

48. Hermann Cremer, "Die Predigtaufgabe unserer Kirche gegenüber der Sozialdemokratie," *Christliche Welt*, November 3, 1892, col. 1036.

49. Max Weber, "Zur Rechtfertigung Göhres," *Christliche Welt*,(1892), cols. 1104–9. Martin Rade's statement appears in the same issue in cols. 1109–11.

50. Ibid., col. 1105.

51. Ibid., col. 1106,

52. Ibid.

53. Ibid., col. 1107.

54. See note 41 above for one statement by a worker about Göhre's book.

55. Max Schippel, "Drei Monate Fabrikarbeiter," *Die Neue Zeit* 9 (1890–1891), in two parts, 468–75 and 499–506. On Schippel, see Stanley Pierson, *Marxist Intellectuals and the Working-Class Mentality in Germany, 1887–1912* (Cambridge: Harvard University Press, 1993), 12ff. Pierson's book is a thought-provoking analysis of the relationship between intellectuals and the working-class movement during the period in question, and it also treats Göhre in this context.

56. Göhre, *Evangelisch-soziale Bewegung*, especially 102ff.; and Paul Göhre, "Meine Trennung von den Nationalsozialen," *Die Zukunft* 29 (1899): 282.

57. Paul Göhre, *Wie ein Pfarrer Sozialdemokrat wurde* (Berlin: Vlg. der Expedition der Buchhandlung Vorwärts, 1900). This pamphlet was distributed in approximately 500,000 copies and translated into several languages.

58. In the 1970s, interest in Göhre reawakened briefly among some literary historians who rediscovered these texts and showed how Göhre's national and religious orientation influenced his editing and censoring of this material. Göhre's prefaces and the role he played in publishing these autobiographies are discussed in detail in Jost Hermand, "Carl Fischer: 'Denkwürdigkeiten und Erinnerungen eines Arbeiters,'" in his *Unbequeme Literatur* (Heidelberg: Stiehm, 1971), 87–107. The other autobiographies that Göhre edited were Moritz Bromme, *Lebensgeschichte eines modernen Fabrikarbeiters* (Leipzig: Diederichs, 1905); Wenzel Holek, *Lebensgang eines deutsch-tschechischen Handarbeiters* (Jena: Diederichs, 1909); and Franz Rehbein, *Das Leben eines Landarbeiters* (Jena: Diederichs, 1911).

59. See the correspondence between Diederichs, Fischer, and Göhre in *Eugen Diederichs: Selbstzeugnisse und Briefe von Zeitgenossen* (Düsseldorf: Eugen Diederichs Vlg., 1967), 135–38.

60. Hermand, "Carl Fischer," 91.

61. See Pierson, *Marxist Intellectuals,* 133, on Göhre's insistence that Marxism did not have to be understood as a worldview.

62. See ibid., 131–32, 160.

63. Bonus, "Paul Göhre," 24.

64. One example of a naturalist novel that refers explicitly to Göhre is Wolfgang Kirchbach's *Das Leben auf der Walze* (Berlin: Verein der Bücherfreunde, 1892). In this novel, economist Hans Landmann sets out to descend even deeper than Göhre and study the exotic milieu of journeymen, vagabonds, beggars, and thieves in hopes of snagging a professorship after publishing his

revelations (25). Kirchbach portrayed the milieu of the lower classes here as a source of comic background, colorful characters, and sensationalistic crimes à la Sue.

65. Minna Wettstein-Adelt, *Dreieinhalb Monate Fabrik-Arbeiterin: Eine practische Studie* (Berlin: J. Leiser, 1893), 1. Further page references to this book will be given in the body of the text.

66. See Nord, "The Social Explorer as Anthropologist"; and Nord, *Walking the Victorian Streets* on women social workers among the poor.

67. Theodor Wangemann, "Aus meinem Wandertagebuch," *Die Arbeiter-Kolonie* 10 (1893): 257–80, 321–23, 353–62; and 11 (1894): 5–15, 33–38, 65–69.

68. Brenning and Gremmels's edition of Göhre's *Drei Monate* discusses the Church's reaction to Wangemann and the inquiry among the regional churches, 135ff.

69. Quoted in ibid., 135–36.

70. Quoted in ibid., 137.

71. Elisabeth Gnauck, "Lieder einer freiwilligen Arbeiterin," *Die Hilfe*, January 20, 1895, 5; and "Erinnerungen einer freiwilligen Arbeiterin," *Die Hilfe*, February 17, 1895, 3ff., and February 24, 1895, 2–4. The debate about these texts appeared in *Die Hilfe* in 1895 in the following issues: March 17, 3ff.; March 31, 4ff.; April 7, 3ff.; April 14, 5; and April 21, 2ff. This journal was edited by Friedrich Naumann and included Göhre and Max Weber among its contributors.

72. Gnauck, "Erinnerungen," *Die Hilfe*, February 10, 1895, 4.

73. Gnauck, "Erinnerungen," *Die Hilfe*, February 17, 1895, 4.

74. See note 71 for the sources of this debate. See also Elisabeth Gnauck-Kühne, "Die Lage der Arbeiterinnen in der Berliner Papierwaren-Industrie," in *Schmollers Jahrbuch* NF, 20, no. 2 (1896): 25–93.

75. "Evangelische Arbeitervereine und 'Hilfe' im preußischen Landtag," *Die Hilfe*, March 17, 1895, 4.

76. Ibid.

77. Brantlinger, "Victorians and Africans," 185.

78. See Nord, "The Social Explorer as Anthropologist."

79. Booth wrote in *In Darkest England and the Ways Out:* "As there is a darkest Africa is there not also a darkest England? Civilisation, which can breed its own barbarians, does it not also breed its own pygmies? May we not find a parallel at our own doors, and discover within a stone's throw of our cathedrals and palaces similar horrors to those which Stanley has found existing in the great Equatorial forest?" Quoted in Keating, *Into Unknown England*, 145.

80. Thus, some commentators drew analogies between journeys such as Göhre's and the Orientalistic fantasies of Europeans traveling in disguise to penetrate the mysteries of Islam. For example, in an article about Göhre written for the journal *Die Gesellschaft*, Arthur Bonus recalled the "romantic" aspect of Göhre's "adventure" as follows: "There are those who might disguise themselves, learn foreign languages, and carefully study foreign customs in order to penetrate unrecognized into the Moslem sanctuaries and report what they are like. Similarly, Göhre also set out here to find out about the sanctuaries, about the deepest, most characteristic, holiest convictions of this

interesting, strange world of the future." Bonus, "Paul Göhre," 15. See also Jost Hermand, *Stilkunst um 1900* (Berlin: Akadmie, 1967), 150–51, who describes Bonus as the "house philosopher" of the Diederichs publishing house, which led in publishing neoromantic works.

81. Quoted in Schippel, "Drei Monate Fabrikarbeiter," 506.

82. This was also the point of view expressed by Social Democrat Max Schippel in his review of Göhre's book (ibid.).

83. For example, one of the spokesmen for German work students in the Weimar Republic, Paul Rohrbach, described "Negroes" as "Untermenschen" (subhumans) in his *Der deutsche Gedanke in der Welt* (1912) and in his other writings about colonialism. On Rohrbach, see Hermand, *Stilkunst um 1900*, 35–38.

84. Göhre's volkish leanings are shown by, among other things, his membership in the National-Social Union.

85. Max Winter, "Bei den Sklaven der 'Alpinen': Eine Nacht im Schwechater Werk," in *Arbeitswelt um 1900: Texte zur Alltagsgeschichte von Max Winter,* ed. Stefan Riesenfellner (Vienna: Europaverlag, 1988), 50.

86. For biographical material on Winter see Riesenfellner, *Arbeitswelt um 1900;* Stefan Riesenfellner, *Der Sozialreporter: Max Winter im alten Österreich* (Vienna: Vlg. für Gesellschaftskritik, 1987); and Max Winter, *Das schwarze Wienerherz: Sozialreportagen aus dem frühen 20. Jahrhundert,* ed. Helmut Strutzmann (Vienna: Österreichischer Bundesvlg., 1982).

87. Strutzmann, introduction to *Das schwarze Wienerherz,* 16.

88. This biographical sketch is based largely on ibid., 7 and 23ff.

89. According to Riesenfellner, *Arbeitswelt um 1900,* iii, Winter almost certainly was familiar with Friedrich Engels's *Lage der arbeitenden Klassen in England* through Victor Adler.

90. These three reportages are reprinted in Friedrich G. Kurbisch, ed., *Der Arbeitsmann, er stirbt, verdirbt, wann steht er auf? Sozialreportagen 1880 bis 1918* (Berlin: Dietz Nachf., 1982), 40–53.

91. Winter, "Bei den Sklaven der 'Alpinen' " and "Wien I: In Diensten des Herrn von Wittek," both in Riesenfellner, *Arbeitswelt um 1900,* 49–78 and 127–42; and Winter, "Kanalstrotter," in his *Im dunkelsten Wien* (Vienna: Wiener Vlg., 1904), 1–30.

92. Winter, "Ein Tag Lagerhausarbeiter," in Riesenfellner, *Arbeitswelt um 1900,* 12–29; Winter, "Vor und in der Wärmestube," in Kurbisch, *Der Arbeitsmann,* 81–90; Winter, "Eine Nacht im Asyl für Obdachlose," in Strutzmann, *Das schwarze Wienerherz,* 45–59; Winter, "Eine Nacht Polizeihäftling," in ibid., 72–85.

93. Winter, "Ein Tag Lagerhausarbeiter," 15.

94. Ibid.

95. Ibid., 17–18.

96. Winter, *Im dunkelsten Wien,* 4.

97. Max Winter, "Wiener Heimarbeiterinnen," in Riesenfellner, *Arbeitswelt um 1900,* 198.

98. See note 92 for the bibliographical information about this reportage.

99. On Winter's method as related to oral history, see Riesenfellner, *Arbeitswelt um 1900,* iv.

100. Winter, "Eine Nacht im Asyl für Obdachlose," 55.
101. Max Winter, "Hotel Ringofen," in Strutzmann, *Das schwarze Wienerherz,* 60–74. Winter reported on a similar expedition with other homeless people in his reportage "Im Hotel 'zur Teppichklopferei,' " in his *Im dunkelsten Wien,* 56–81.
102. Winter, "Hotel Ringofen," 71–72.
103. The extent of Winter's beliefs in progress and improvement is highlighted in his novel *Die lebende Mumie: Ein Blick auf das Jahr 2025* (Berlin: E. Laubsche Verlagsbuchhandlung, 1929), in which he imagined a utopian future. In the United States of Europe, all property has been socialized, children are well treated, and eugenic marriage laws contribute to the improvement and beauty of the human race.
104. Hermand, *Old Dreams of a New Reich,* 41ff.
105. See Frank Trommler, "Die Nationalisierung der Arbeit," in *Arbeit als Thema in der deutschen Literatur vom Mittelalter bis zur Gegenwart,* ed. Reinhold Grimm and Jost Hermand (Königstein: Athenäum, 1979), 102–25.
106. Hermand, *Old Dreams of a New Reich,* 52.
107. Ibid.
108. See Hermand, *Stilkunst um 1900,* 67ff.; and George Mosse, *The Crisis of German Ideology: Intellectual Origins of the Third Reich* (New York: Schocken, 1981).
109. Jakob Kneip, "Ein deutsches Testament," in Werkleute auf Haus Nyland, *Das brennende Volk: Kriegsgabe der Werkleute auf Haus Nyland* (Jena: Diederichs, 1916), 29. See Trommler, "Nationalisierung der Arbeit," 15, on how the "Werkleute auf Haus Nyland" arrogantly neglected the social question.
110. Hermand, *Stilkunst um 1900,* 412.
111. Walter Flex, *Wolf Eschenlohr,* in his *Gesammelte Werke,* ed. Konrad Flex (Munich: Beck, n.d.), 185–257. Further page references to this novel will be given in the body of the text.
112. See Jarausch, *Students, Society, and Politics,* 362, on these courses for workers which German students sometimes offered.
113. On Flex's lack of interest in social reform issues, see Raimund Neuss, *Anmerkungen zu Walter Flex: Die "Ideen von 1914" in der deutschen Literatur: Ein Fallbeispiel* (Schernfeld: SH-Vlg., 1992). See also the chapter entitled "Männerkörper und Weißer Terror" in Klaus Theweleit, *Männerphantasien* (Frankfurt: Stroemfeld/Roter Stern, 1978), vol. 2: 165–398.
114. An entirely different way of depicting the war experience and the experience of physical labor is given by Arnold Zweig in *Erziehung vor Verdun* (1935). Here, Zweig depicted the soldier Bertin as learning to renounce naive nationalism in favor of pacifism after his experiences with digging trenches, seeing corruption in the military, and encountering soldiers who were Social Democrats.

Chapter 2

1. J. Hermann Mitgau, ed., *Erlebnisse und Erfahrungen Heidelberger Werkstudenten: Eine Sammlung von Berichten* (Heidelberg: Hörning, 1925), 18. Further references to this book appear in the text as M.
2. Paul Rohrbach, *The German Work-Student* (Dresden: Wirtschaftshilfe der

deutschen Studentenschaft, 1924), 73. Further references to this book appear in the text as R.

3. Michael H. Kater, "The Work Student: A Socio-Economic Phenomenon of Early Weimar Germany," *Journal of Contemporary History* 10, no. 1 (1975): 93.

4. See ibid., 72–75.

5. See ibid., 87–88.

6. Konrad Jarausch, *Deutsche Studenten, 1800–1970* (Frankfurt: Suhrkamp, 1984), 144.

7. This statistic is cited in ibid.

8. See Mitgau's other writings, including *Studentische Demokratie*, 2nd ed. (Heidelberg: J. Hörning, 1927), which advocates volkish tendencies of the youth movement such as a longing for wholeness and the organic; and also his *Das deutsche Alltagsleben im zeitgenössischen Bild (Für den Sippenforscher)* (Görlitz: Starke, 1937).

9. Among Rohrbach's many publications, the following give the clearest idea of his nationalistic, imperialistic, and racist views: *Der deutsche Gedanke in der Welt* (Düsseldorf: Langewiesche, 1912); *Der Tag des Untermenschen*, 2nd ed. (Berlin: Safari-Verlag, 1929); *Abriß des Deutschtums im Ausland und in den deutschen Kolonien* (Leipzig: Kohlhammer, 1938); *Afrika: Beiträge zu einer praktischen Kolonialkunde* (Berlin: Weiner, 1943). For the larger context of Rohrbach's writings, see Jost Hermand, *Stilkunst um 1900* (Berlin: Akademie, 1967), 35–38.

10. See Mitgau, *Erlebnisse und Erfahrungen*, 10–11, who states that these are the two main themes running through the autobiographical statements he collected.

11. See Kater, "The Work Student," 77; and Linda Alcoff, "The Problem of Speaking for Others," *Cultural Critique*, no. 20 (Winter 1991–1992): 5–32.

12. J. Hermann Mitgau, "Studium und Nebenerwerb" (3 Vorträge, gehalten Juni 1923 in Gießen). 1. Vortrag: "Der Werkstudent. Entwicklung und Möglichkeiten," in *Deutsche akademische Rundschau*, (January 1, 1925), 8.

13. Quoted in Hans Gehrig, *Wirtschaftsnot und Selbsthilfe der deutschen Studentenschaft* (Berlin: de Gruyter, 1924), 22.

14. For a general discussion of these fears of pauperization, see Georg Schreiber, *Die Not der deutschen Wissenschaft und der geistigen Arbeiter: Geschehnisse und Gedanken zur Kulturpolitik des Deutschen Reiches* (Leipzig: Quelle und Meyer, 1923). These fears are frequently reflected in the literature of the Weimar Republic, especially in the "Angestelltenroman," of which Hans Fallada's *Kleiner Mann, was nun?* (1932) is an especially well-known example.

15. See in this connection Frank Trommler, "Die Nationalisierung der Arbeit," in *Arbeit als Thema in der deutschen Literatur vom Mittelalter bis zur Gegenwart*, ed. Reinhold Grimm and Jost Hermand (Königstein: Athenäum, 1979), 102–25.

16. See Rohrbach, *The German Work-Student*, 47; and Erich Brautlacht, *Der Spiegel der Gerechtigkeit: Ein Richterbuch* (Munich: Piper, 1942).

17. See Rohrbach, *The German Work-Student*, 48; and also the discussion of Joseph Goebbels's *Michael* below, where similar rhetoric is used.

18. Quoted in Gehrig, *Wirtschaftsnot und Selbsthilfe*, 83–84.
19. For another view of the Kapp Putsch, see the discussion below of Karl Grünberg's novel *Brennende Ruhr* and its work-student character.
20. Quoted in Gehrig, *Wirtschaftsnot und Selbsthilfe*, 91.
21. For example, "mediators" between high and low appear in dramas such as Georg Kaiser's *Gas* (1918) and *Gas II* (1920) and Ernst Toller's *Masse Mensch* (1920) and *Die Maschinenstürmer* (1922).
22. Gottfried Benn, "Der neue Staat und die Intellektuellen," in *Literatur unterm Hakenkreuz*, ed. Erich Loewy (Frankfurt: Europäische Verlagsanstalt, 1966), 53.
23. Siegfried Kracauer, *From Caligari to Hitler: A Psychological History of the German Film* (Princeton: Princeton University Press, 1947), 164. Referring here to Goebbels's speech at the Nuremberg Party Congress of 1934.
24. See Andreas Huyssen, "The Vamp and the Machine: Technology and Sexuality in Fritz Lang's 'Metropolis,' " *New German Critique*, no. 24–25 (Fall/Winter 1981/1982): 221–37; Roger Dadoun, " 'Metropolis': Mother—City—'Mittler'—Hitler," *Camera Obscura* 15 (Fall 1986): 137–63; R. L. Rutsky, "The Mediation of Technology and Gender: 'Metropolis,' Nazism, Modernism," *New German Critique*, no. 60 (Fall 1993): 3–33.
25. Thea von Harbou, *Metropolis* (Norfolk, Va.: Donning, 1988). Further page references will be indicated in the text (translator's name is not given). As Rutsky explains (see note 24), "Lang claimed that the idea for 'Metropolis' originated while viewing the New York skyline during his 1924 trip to the United States. His wife, Thea von Harbou, then wrote a novel based on this idea, which the two adapted into a scenario" (4). The film was then cut drastically for its American release, with the result that the original version was destroyed. Missing subplots and motivations can sometimes be found in von Harbou's accompanying novel.
26. Von Harbou's novel introduces another twist here by having Georgi, the worker whom Freder replaced at the Paternoster, jump in front of Freder just as another worker tries to stab him to death. Giving his life to save Freder, Georgi dies with the words "brothers—murderers" on his lips (108).
27. Huyssen in "The Vamp and the Machine" is mistaken in this connection by emphasizing that Maria is inactive and desexualized at the end. She appears with Frederson and Freder; she and Freder kiss passionately, indicating that nothing will keep them apart in the future; and she urges Freder to bring Fredersen and Grot together.
28. Hans Richter, *Hochofen I: Ein oberschlesischer Roman* (Leipzig: Keil, 1923), 173.
29. Hugo von Waldeyer-Hartz, *Werkstudent und Burschenband: Roman aus dem deutschen Studentenleben der Nachkriegszeit* (Leipzig: Koehler, 1924). Further page references will be indicated in the body of the text.
30. See also Paul Höcker's novel *Die sieben Stufen* (Berlin: Scherl, 1930), in which a female student of economics supports herself by working as a housemaid and exhorts her fellow household employees to accept their station in life with dignity and patience.

31. Felix Riemkasten, *Stehkragenproletarier* (Leipzig: Gerstenberg, 1920), 13. Further page references will be indicated in the body of the text.

32. Richter, *Hochofen I,* 67–68. Further page references will be indicated in the body of the text. Richter's other works include *Der Hüttenkönig* (1924), *Die unter Tage* (1939), *Hier spricht Südost!* (1936), and *Buntes Afrika* (1939).

33. See Jost Hermand, *Old Dreams of a New Reich: Volkish Utopias and National Socialism* (Bloomington: Indiana University Press, 1992), 106, for a useful discussion of Goebbels's *Michael.*

34. See Ralf G. Reuth, *Goebbels* (Munich: Piper, 1990), 64ff.

35. Joseph Goebbels, *Michael: Ein deutsches Schicksal in Tagebuchblättern,* 6th ed. (Munich: F. Eher Nachf., 1935), 109. Further page references will be indicated in the body of the text.

36. Goebbels, *Michael,* 14, 50. On this Nazi view of education, see Jost Hermand, *Als Pimpf in Polen: Die erweiterte Kinderlandverschickung, 1940–1945* (Frankfurt: Fischer, 1993).

37. On the National Socialist concept of work as it relates to *Michael,* see Klaus Theweleit, *Männerphantasien* (Frankfurt: Roter Stern, 1977), 2:268ff.

38. See Trommler, "Die Nationalisierung der Arbeit."

39. Adolf Hitler, *Reden und Proklamationen, 1932–1945,* ed. Max Domarus (Munich: Süddeutscher Verlag, 1965), vol. 1, pt. 1:262.

40. Peter Dudek, *Erziehung durch Arbeit: Arbeitslagerbewegung und Freiwilliger Arbeitsdienst, 1920–1935* (Opladen: Westdeutscher Verlag, 1988), 11–14. In this section on the background to the National Socialist Labor Service, I am largely following Dudek.

41. Ibid., 57ff.

42. Ibid., 121–22.

43. Georg Keil, *Vormarsch der Arbeitslagerbewegung* (1932), quoted in ibid., 121.

44. See Dudek, *Erziehung durch Arbeit,* 118ff.; and Wolfgang Benz, "Vom freiwilligen Arbeitsdienst zur Arbeitsdienstpflicht," *Vierteljahreshefte für Zeitgeschichte,* no. 16 (1968): 321.

45. On the Boberhaus, see Dudek, *Erziehung durch Arbeit,* 128ff.

46. See ibid., 134. The work-student autobiographies and novels about the work-student experience refer frequently to Upper Silesia. See also the discussion in Chapter 3 below of Alexander von Stenbock-Fermor's *Deutschland von unten,* which contains sections on this area.

47. See Dudek, *Erziehung durch Arbeit,* 136, 150–54. Several members of the resistance group known as the "Kreisauer Kreis" had connections to the Löwenberg work camps, including Helmuth James von Moltke. Harald Poelchau, who was a prison minister in Berlin during the Nazi period and spoke with many resistance members before their executions, and who was a member of the "Kreisauer Kreis" himself, described this group as follows in his memoirs: "The Kreisauer Kreis was not limited to diplomats. It also included economists, administrators, ministers, and trade unionists. It grew up from the workers' and students' camps in Löwenberg in Silesia, and was in close contact with the trade unions. The socialists included Carl Mierendorff, Theo Haubach, and Adolf Reichwein." See Harald Poelchau, *Die letzten Stun-*

den: Erinnerungen eines Gefängnispfarrers aufgezeichnet von Graf Alexander Stenbock-Fermor (Berlin: Volk und Welt, 1949), 103. On Stenbock-Fermor, see Chapter 3 below.

48. On the Labor Service, see Benz, "Vom freiwilligen Arbeitsdienst zur Arbeitsdienstpflicht," and Henning Köhler, *Arbeitsdienst in Deutschland* (Berlin: Duncker und Humblot, 1967). See also in this context Maria Kahle's *Akkordarbeiterin: Aus meinem Tagebuch* (Gladbach-Rheydt: Volksvereins-Vlg., n.d. [1929]). In this report on working in several factories, the Catholic, volkish writer Kahle bemoaned the passing of traditional peasant life with its ties to the land and God and called for a renewal of "Volk consciousness" as the only possible solution to the "social question."

49. Cited in Köhler, *Arbeitsdienst in Deutschland*, 18.

50. Benz, "Vom freiwilligen Arbeitsdienst zur Arbeitsdienstpflicht," 317.

51. See ibid., 328. See also Monika Harand, *Die Aussteiger als Einsteiger: Zivilisationsflüchtige Romanhelden in der völkischen Literatur (1931–1944)* (Stuttgart: Heinz, 1988), for a discussion of a number of novels with a protagonist who flees the urban life to go back to nature as a farmer, often in German settlements in the East.

52. Mitgau, *Erlebnisse und Erfahrungen*, 78.

53. Kater, "The Work Student," 84–85.

54. Wirtschaftshilfe der deutschen Studentenschaft, ed., *Deutsche Werkstudenten in Amerika* (Berlin: De Gruyter, 1928), 23. For an earlier example of an account by a German student who came to the United States to work, see Alfred Kolb, *Als Arbeiter in Amerika: Unter deutsch-amerikanischen Großstadtproletariern* (Berlin: Karl Siegismund, 1904). Similar perspectives on the absence of class divisiveness in America are found in two more accounts by work students in the United States: Wolfgang Ernst Langewiesche-Brandt, *Das amerikanische Abenteuer: Deutscher Werkstudent in USA* (Stuttgart: J. Engelhorns Nachf., 1933); and Ernst Stolper, *Werkstudent im wilden Westen: Aus dem Tagebuch eines jungen Deutschen* (Leipzig: List, 1933).

55. Wirtschaftshilfe der deutschen Studentenschaft, ed., *Deutsche Werkstudenten in Amerika*, 22–23.

56. Gehrig, *Wirtschaftsnot und Selbsthilfe*, 95.

57. Compare the following reference to Walter Flex's *Wolf Eschenlohr* in ibid., 84: "In spite of hostile attacks, students have offered courses for workers for decades, and they are continuing to do this even in their dire economic straits. These courses offered possibilities for personal contact, human understanding, and bridging the gaps between students and workers. (Many students desired this, like the fraternity student Wolf Eschenlohr in the last work of Walter Flex, who died in the war.) Such possibilities may be realized even better by work students. This increase in social understanding is one of the most significant side effects of the work student experience, which takes place in workshops *outside* the universities."

58. Hans Sikorski, *Studentische Selbsthilfe: Ein Blick in studentisches Leben der Gegenwart mit Bildern aus der Marburger Arbeit* (Marburg: Vlg. des kunstgeschichtlichen Seminars, 1923), 39.

59. Ibid., 33.

60. See Stefan Bajohr, "Weiblicher Arbeitsdienst im 'Dritten Reich,'" *Vierteljahreshefte für Zeitgeschichte* 28, no. 3 (1980): 332.

61. See ibid., 333; and Dudek, *Erziehung durch Arbeit*, 54.

62. Elisabeth Gnauck-Kühne, *Dienstpflicht und Dienstjahr des weiblichen Geschlechts* (Tübingen: Mohr, 1915), 20.

63. Ibid., 33.

64. Quoted in Bajohr, "Weiblicher Arbeitsdienst," 343.

65. Werner Maser, ed., *Adolf Hitler· "Mein Kampf": Geschichte, Auszüge, Kommentare* (Esslingen: Bechtle, 1981), 121ff.

66. Adolf Hitler, *Mein Kampf* (Munich: Zentralverlag der NSDAP, 1943 = 795–99th ed.), 1:23 (first published 1925).

67. See Köhler, *Arbeitsdienst in Deutschland*, 257; and Benz, "Vom freiwilligen Arbeitsdienst zur Arbeitsdienstpflicht," 332.

68. Quoted in Dudek, *Erziehung durch Arbeit*, 69–70.

69. Hitler, *Reden und Proklamationen*, vol. 1, pt. 1:262.

70. Jarausch, *Deutsche Studenten*, 170.

71. On Bernhard Rust and the Labor Service, see Benz, "Vom freiwilligen Arbeitsdienst zur Arbeitsdienstpflicht," 344. These fantasies of punishing "soft" intellectuals appear frequently in Nazi propaganda and rhetoric. An especially crude example is Wilhelm Krug's poem "Der Werkstudent," which appeared in the Nazi satirical journal *Die Brennessel*, September 6, 1933, 423. Before the student went to work he appeared like this: "So he moved quietly through the changing times, / And his hands were women's hands / And soft and white like fresh snow." And afterward: "Now we see the student building roads. / Now he moves paving stones over the land. / And his hands are like men's hands— / So beautiful. And hard as wood. And brown."

72. Quoted in Will Decker, *Wille und Werk: Ein Tatsachenbericht von der Schöpferkraft des nationalsozialistischen Arbeitsdienstes* (Munich: F. Bruckmann, 1935), 140. Decker gives here the entire text spoken by the Labor Service representatives at the Nuremberg Party Congress of 1934, as it is used in Leni Riefenstahl's film *Triumph des Willens*.

73. See Dudek, *Erziehung durch Arbeit*, 232ff. For one of the innumerable contemporary examples, see Karl Heinrich (Rektor in Falkensee), *Deutsches Arbeitertum* (Vol. 6 of *Der nationalpolitische Unterricht: Ein Handbuch für den Lehrer*) (Frankfurt: Diesterweg, 1935), especially p. 32 on the goals of the Labor Service: "Two of the most important educational tasks of the Labor Service are to abolish class hatred and transform the concept of work. Furthermore, the Labor Service will promote the spirit of comradeship and require young people to be punctual, orderly, clean, and reliable. And when big-city people are put into the midst of nature . . . they will learn to love their homeland and to understand German soil."

74. Jesco von Puttkamer, *Deutschlands Arbeitsdienst* (1933), quoted in Dudek, *Erziehung durch Arbeit*, 235.

75. See Heinrich, *Deutsches Arbeitertum*, 32; and, as another example, Friedrich W. Heinz, *Kameraden der Arbeit: Deutsche Arbeitslager: Stand, Aufgabe und Zukunft* (Berlin: Frundsberg, 1933), especially the section on students and the Labor Service, which states: "A year of work at the beginning of

their studies will give students the great communal experience of work, comradeship, service, and connection to the Volk" (140).

76. Hierl quoted in Wolfgang Eggerstorfer, *Schönheit und Adel der Arbeit: Arbeitsliteratur im Dritten Reich* (New York: Lang, 1988), 30.

77. Decker, *Wille und Werk,* 42.

78. Paul Seipp, "Formung und Auslese im Reichsarbeitsdienst" (Diss., Gießen, 1934), quoted in Dudek, *Erziehung durch Arbeit,* 250.

79. Jost Hermand, "Explosions in the Swamp: Jünger's *Worker* (1932)," in *The Technological Imagination,* ed. Teresa de Lauretis (Madison, Wis.: Coda, 1980), 125.

80. Ernst Jünger, *Der Arbeiter: Herrschaft und Gestalt,* in his *Werke* (Stuttgart: Klett, 1960), 6:319. Further page references will be indicated in the body of the text.

81. Jünger, *Der Arbeiter,* 317. See also Harro Segeberg, "Regressive Modernisierung: Kriegserlebnis und Moderne-Kritik in Ernst Jüngers Frühwerk," in *Vom Wert der Arbeit: Zur literarischen Konstitution des Wertkomplexes "Arbeit" in der deutschen Literatur 1770–1930,* ed. Harro Segeberg (Tübingen: Niemeyer, 1991), 372.

82. Hermand, "Explosions in the Swamp," 130.

83. Ibid.

84. Martin Heidegger, "Schlageter," *New German Critique,* no. 45 (Fall 1988): 96–97, emphases in original.

85. Heidegger's inaugural lecture is quoted in Victor Farías, *Heidegger und der Nationalsozialismus* (Frankfurt: Fischer, 1989), 159ff.

86. Quoted in ibid., 207.

87. Martin Heidegger, "Labor Service and the University," *New German Critique,* no. 45 (Fall 1988): 98.

88. Rüdiger Safranski, *Ein Meister aus Deutschland: Heidegger und seine Zeit* (Munich: Hanser, 1994), 293.

89. Martin Heidegger, "The Call to the Labor Service," *New German Critique,* no. 45 (Fall 1988): 109.

90. Ibid., 108–9.

91. Heidegger, "Labor Service and the University," 98; and Martin Heidegger, "The University in the New Reich," *New German Critique,* no. 45 (Fall 1988): 100.

92. Heidegger, "The University in the New Reich," 101.

93. Safranski, *Ein Meister aus Deutschland,* takes such statements by Heidegger and right-wing students of that time as an occasion to draw a polemical comparison with the student movement generation of 1968. His efforts to defame this later generation lose sight of the fact that these students did not view their actions as a contribution to building the national racial community, but rather as an "Extra-Parliamentary Opposition." They sought to uncover the class tensions and conflicts that still existed underneath the overwhelming ideology of social consensus. See below, Chapter 5.

94. Karl Löwith, "The Political Implications of Heidegger's Existentialism," *New German Critique,* no. 45 (Fall 1988): 125.

95. Heidegger, "The University in the New Reich," 101.
96. Martin Heidegger, "National Socialist Education," *New German Critique,* no. 45 (Fall 1988): 110–14.
97. Ibid., 112, emphasis in original.
98. Ibid., 112–13, emphasis in original.
99. Löwith, "Political Implications," 127.
100. Quoted in Decker, *Wille und Werk,* 138–40.
101. Bajohr, "Weiblicher Arbeitsdienst," 355–57. For a large collection of statements by women squad leaders in Labor Service camps, see *Chronik des weiblichen Arbeitsdienstes in Ostpreußen* (Burgdorf: Much, 1983).
102. Dudek, *Erziehung durch Arbeit,* 245 and 250, discusses the difficulty in determining the actual effect the Labor Service had on its participants. Whereas its male and female squad leaders have continued to meet up to the present and to hold up the Labor Service as an institution of timeless relevance, it is much more difficult to determine the reactions of those conscripted into it.
103. Eggerstorfer, *Schönheit und Adel der Arbeit,* discusses a number of other novels that thematize the Labor Service.
104. Klaus Hermann Nebe, *Schippen aufnehmen! Im Gleichschritt—marsch! Ein Roman vom Arbeitsdienst* (Berlin: Westermann, 1934), 12. Further page references will be indicated in the body of the text.
105. See Timothy W. Mason, *Social Policy in the Third Reich* (Providence: Berg, 1993), 153ff., for a discussion of Nazi propaganda techniques.
106. Eugen Hadamovsky, *Hilfsarbeiter Nr. 50 000* (Munich: Zentralverlag der NSDAP, 1938), 12, gives this information. Further page references will be indicated in the body of the text. Mason, *Social Policy,* 154, mentions this text and Goebbels's campaign against "class arrogance."
107. Goebbels's *Michael* continued to be reissued in various forms, for example, in an abridged version as *Michaels Weg zum Volke* (Frankfurt: Diesterweg, 1941). See also Joseph Goebbels, *Der geistige Arbeiter im Schicksalskampf des Reiches: Rede vor der Heidelberger Universität am Freitag, dem 9. Juli 1943* (Munich: Zentralverlag der NSDAP, n.d. [1943]).
108. Quoted in Christian Zentner and Friedemann Bedürftig, *Das große Lexikon des Dritten Reiches* (Munich: Südwest, 1985), 234.
109. Biographical information about Hadamovsky is taken from ibid. and from Ludwig Peters, *Volkslexikon Drittes Reich* (Tübingen: Grabert, 1994), 304.
110. Bertolt Brecht, "Und so kommt zum guten Ende," in his *Gedichte 4/Große kommentierte Berliner und Frankfurter Ausgabe* (Berlin/Frankfurt: Aufbau/ Suhrkamp, 1993), 14:102.
111. Dudek, *Erziehung durch Arbeit,* 14.
112. See ibid., 75, 92, and 214.
113. Quoted in ibid., 223.
114. Quoted in ibid., 152–53.
115. See Hans Peter Herrmann, "Wirklichkeit und Ideologie: Brechts 'Heilige Johanna der Schlachthöfe' als Lehrstück bürgerlicher Praxis im Klassenkampf," in *Brechts "Heilige Johanna der Schlachthöfe,"* ed. Jan Knopf (Frankfurt: Suhrkamp/ST Materialien, 1986), 306–33.

116. See, for example, the statement in Erik Reger's novel *Union der festen Hand* (Kronberg: Scriptor, 1976; reprint of 1931 edition), 323, which characterizes the work-student phenomenon as "nothing but a nice episode."

117. Biographical information on Grünberg here is drawn from Simone Barck et al., eds., *Lexikon sozialistischer Literatur* (Stuttgart: Metzler, 1994), 182–83.

118. Karl Grünberg, *Brennende Ruhr: Roman aus der Zeit des Kapp-Putsches* (Berlin: Aufbau, 1959), 23. Further page references will be indicated in the body of the text.

119. This use of stereotypes comes through particularly clearly in the portrayal of the female characters in the novel: the virginal, angelic Mary (Ruckers's daughter) on the one hand, and the vampiristic, reactionary Gisela on the other.

120. Bertolt Brecht, *Furcht und Elend des Dritten Reiches* (Frankfurt: Suhrkamp, 1979), 80–81.

121. Brecht, "Und so kommt zum guten Ende."

Chapter 3

1. Michael Geisler, *Die literarische Reportage in Deutschland: Möglichkeiten und Grenzen eines operativen Genres* (Königstein/Ts.: Scriptor, 1982), 278.

2. For a critique of the approach many writers took to reportage during the era of the "New Objectivity," see ibid., 47ff.

3. See Helmut Lethen, *Neue Sachlichkeit, 1924–1929: Studien zur Literatur des "Weißen Sozialismus"* (Stuttgart: Metzler, 1968).

4. Quoted in Friedrich G. Kürbisch, ed., *Dieses Land schläft einen unruhigen Schlaf: Sozialreportagen, 1918–1945* (Bonn: Dietz, 1981), 14.

5. These reportages can be found in Egon Erwin Kisch, *Aus Prager Gassen und Nächten. Prager Kinder. Die Abenteuer in Prag* (Berlin: Aufbau, 1987), vol. 2, pt. 2 of his *Gesammelte Werke*. They include reportages with titles strongly reminiscent of those by Max Winter: "Eine Nacht im Asyl für Obdachlose" [A Night in the Homeless Shelter] (51–60), "Volksküchen," [Soup Kitchens] (118–23), "Die Verhaftung" [The Arrest] (138–43), "In der Wärmestube" [In the Shelter] (195–203), "Weihnachten im Gerichtsgefängnis" [Christmas in Prison] (245–50), "Als Hopfenpflücker ins Saazer Land" [As a Hops Picker in the Saaz Countryside] (433–55).

6. Review of *Meine Erlebnisse als Bergarbeiter* by Oskar Fontana in *Das Tagebuch* (Berlin), quoted in Alexander von Stenbock-Fermor, *Der rote Graf: Autobiographie* (Berlin: Verlag der Nation, 1973), 264.

7. Stenbock, *Der rote Graf,* 13ff. Further page references are indicated in the body of the text by RG.

8. Alexander von Stenbock-Fermor, *Mein Erlebnisse als Bergarbeiter* (Stuttgart: J. Engelhorns Nachf., 1929). This book actually appeared in 1928. Further page references are indicated in the body of the text by ME. The English translation, *My Experiences as a Miner* (London: Putnam, 1930), was done by Frances, Countess of Warwick.

9. Simone Barck et al., eds., *Lexikon sozialistischer Literatur* (Stuttgart: Metzler, 1994), 454.

10. In his autobiography, *Der rote Graf,* Stenbock maintained that publisher Ernst Rowohlt urged him to join the Reichsschrifttumsskammer as a camouflage for his efforts to establish contacts with resistance groups. While this may be true, I have found no independent sources that confirm this (RG 368).

11. Harald Poelchau, *Die letzten Stunden: Erinnerungen eines Gefängnispfarrers, aufgezeichnet von Graf Alexander Stenbock-Fermor* (Berlin: Volk und Welt, 1949). This book was an important source for Peter Weiss's novel *Die Ästhetik des Widerstands* (1975–1981), in which the figure of Poelchau appears in vol. 3.

12. Kurt Kläber, "Ein Graf als Bergmann," *Die Front* 1, no. 3 (1928): 27.

13. Ibid., 30.

14. Stenbock, *Der rote Graf,* 160ff. For a critique of such metaphors of photography in reportage, see Geisler, *Die literarische Reportage,* 62–88.

15. In *Der rote Graf,* Stenbock mentions that he traveled around Germany giving readings from his book on his experiences as a miner, and that it was translated into English and Czech (264 and 274).

16. Alexander von Stenbock-Fermor, *Deutschland von unten: Reise durch die proletarische Provinz* (Stuttgart: J. Engelhorns Nachf., 1931), 7. Further page references are indicated in the body of the text by DVU.

17. This review by Eggebrecht is reprinted in the new edition of Stenbock's *Deutschland von unten* (Frankfurt: Bucher, 1980), 158; along with a number of other reviews of the book.

18. On the work camps associated with the Youth Movement, see Chapter 2.

19. Maria Leitner, "Als Weberin in einer Seidenfabrik," in *Elisabeth, ein Hitlermädchen: Erzählende Prosa, Reportagen, und Berichte,* ed. Helga Schwarz (Berlin: Aufbau, 1985), 93.

20. Maria Leitner's biography has been difficult to reconstruct in great detail. My summary here is based on Gisela Brinker-Gabler, *Lexikon deutschsprachiger Schriftstellerinnen, 1800–1945* (Munich: dtv, 1986); Wolfgang Emmerich, "Maria Leitner," in *Neue deutsche Biographie* (1985), 14:171–72; Hartmut Kahn, "Nachwort," in Maria Leitner, *Eine Frau reist durch die Welt* (Berlin: Dietz, 1986), 197–205; Helga W. Schwarz, "Nachwort," in Leitner, *Elisabeth,* 469–89; Eva-Maria Siegel, *Jugend, Frauen, Drittes Reich: Autorinnen im Exil, 1933–1945* (Pfaffenweiler: Centaurus, 1993), 81–109; and the entry on Maria Leitner in Walther Killy, ed., *Literaturlexikon* (Munich: Bertelsmann, 1991), 7:218.

21. Willi Münzenberg, *Die dritte Front: Autobiographische Aufzeichnungen* (Berlin: LitPol, 1978 reprint of 1931 edition), photograph facing p. 254.

22. For all of these reportages and the bibliographical information about their original publication, see Schwarz, ed., *Elisabeth.*

23. This novel was reprinted for the first time in ibid.

24. Quoted by Schwarz in ibid., 486.

25. Quoted in Klaus-Peter Schmid, "Gefangen in der zweiten Heimat. Internierungslager noch immer ein großes deutsch-französisches Tabu," *Die Zeit,* May 25, 1990, 47. Many of the best-known German exiles in France were interned at some point in these camps, including Lion Feuchtwanger, Theodor Wolff, Rudolf Hilferding, Rudolf Breitscheid, Gustav Regler, Max Ernst, Alfred Kan-

torowicz, Lotte Eisner, Walter Benjamin, Walter Janka, Walter Hasenclever, Golo Mann, Bruno Frei, and Wilhelm Reich, to name only a few.

26. Helga Schwarz, "Maria Leitner—eine Verschollene des Exils?" *Exilforschung* 5 (1987): 132–33. Anna Seghers captured the atmosphere among exiles in Marseilles in her novel *Transit* (1948).

27. Schwarz, "Maria Leitner," 132–33.

28. Leitner's book is an important document for the international history of radical women journalists, as well as, in the broadest sense, an unusual example from the tradition of travel literature by women. In their anthology *Writing Red: An Anthology of American Women Writers, 1830–1940* (New York: Feminist Press, 1987), Charlotte Nekola and Paula Rabinowitz have collected fascinating examples of U.S. women journalists who set out on trips as unusual and adventurous as Leitner's. On the tradition of women's travel literature in Germany, see especially Annegret Pelz, *Reisen durch die eigene Fremde: Reiseliteratur von Frauen als autogeographische Schriften* (Köln: Böhlau, 1993).

29. Leitner's reportage "Puerto Rico, die schöne Tropeninsel—eine arme Kolonie des reichen Amerika" is not included in *Eine Frau reist durch die Welt*, but it is reprinted in Schwarz, ed., *Elisabeth*, 120–23.

30. Quoted in Schwarz, ed., *Elisabeth*, 473.

31. Maria Leitner, *Eine Frau reist durch die Welt* (Berlin: Agis, 1932), 7. Further page references are given in the body of the text. It is not clear whether Leitner's co-workers ever knew about her identity as a journalist.

32. These reportages are both reprinted in Schwarz, ed., *Elisabeth*.

33. See the discussion of Leitner in Sara Markham, *Workers, Women, and Afro-Americans: Images of the U.S. in German Travel Literature from 1923 to 1933* (New York: Lang, 1986).

34. See Klaus Bergmann, "Die Revolution ist vorbei. Auf zu anderen Ufern. Über Abhautendenzen in den 20er Jahren," in *Abhauen: Flucht ins Glück*, ed. Klaus Bergmann et al. (Reinbek: Rowohlt, 1981), 111–39.

35. Maria Leitner, "Industrie im Urwald," in Schwarz, ed., *Elisabeth*, 129.

36. This novel is reprinted in ibid.

37. See Siegel, *Jugend, Frauen, Drittes Reich*, 22 and 93.

38. Quoted by Viktoria Hertling in her article "Abschied von Europa: Zu Lili Körbers Exil in Paris, Lyon, und New York," *Germanic Review* 62, no. 3 (1987): 119.

39. My biographical information on Körber is taken from ibid. and also from Viktoria Hertling, "Literarische Reportagen über die Sowjetunion in der Zeit der Weimarer Republik" (Diss., University of Wisconsin, 1980); and Viktoria Hertling, "Nachwort," in Lili Körber, *Eine Österreicherin erlebt den Anschluß* (Vienna: Brandstatter, 1988), 151–57.

40. This novel was reprinted until the title *Die Ehe der Ruth Gompertz* (Mannheim: Persona, 1984). Its main character is a Jewish actress who experiences the Nazis' rise to power and who finally commits suicide out of despair over these political developments. Although most of Körber's writing was highly autobiographical, she herself was not Jewish, according to Viktoria Hertling, who interviewed Körber at length.

41. On reportages about the Soviet Union, see Hertling, *Literarische Reportagen,* which was published as *Quer durch* (Königstein/Ts.: Forum Academicum, 1982), and the bibliography contained there.

42. See Geisler, *Die literarische Reportage,* 264ff., on Egon Erwin Kisch, and 294ff. on the difficulties of writing "affirmative" reportage in the GDR.

43. See also Berta Lask, "Als Hilfsarbeiterin in der Moskauer Textilfabrik," in *Smoking braucht man nicht* (Berlin: Aufbau, 1975), 132–35. This short reportage, which was originally published in 1928, is the only other one I know by a German writer that shows the writer participating in manual labor in the Soviet Union. See also John Scott, *Behind the Urals: An American Worker in Russia's City of Steel* (Bloomington: Indiana University Press, 1989 reissue of 1942 ed.), which is on Magnitogorsk.

44. According to Hertling, Körber probably worked for somewhat longer than two months and condensed her experiences when she wrote the book after returning to Vienna; *Literarische Reportagen,* 234.

45. Ernst Glaeser, Alfred Kurella, and F. C. Weiskopf, *Staat ohne Arbeitslose* (Berlin: Kiepenheuer, 1931), 102–3. The importance of tractors in modernizing agriculture is also a significant theme in early GDR literature. Arrogant remarks by some literary critics about "Traktoren-Romantik" miss the point, failing to consider the labor-saving capacities of such machines.

46. Lili Körber, *Eine Frau erlebt den roten Alltag: Ein Tagebuch-Roman aus den Putilowwerken* (Berlin: Rowohlt, 1932), 51. Further page references are given in the body of the text.

47. See Michael Rohrwasser, *Saubere Mädel, Starke Genossen: Proletarische Massenliteratur?* (Frankfurt: Roter Stern, 1975).

48. August Bebel, *Die Frau und der Sozialismus,* 25th ed. (Stuttgart: Dietz, 1895), 339.

49. Of course, many of those who fled into exile during the Nazi period had to take all kinds of jobs in order to survive, and these often included various kinds of manual labor. See, for example, the autobiography of Egon Schwarz, *Keine Zeit für Eichendorff: Chronik unfreiwilliger Wanderjahre* (Frankfurt: Büchergilde Gutenberg, 1992), in which the author recounts his childhood in Vienna, years in exile in Bolivia with his parents, and path to university study in the United States. As a young man in Bolivia, Schwarz worked at various unskilled jobs in a textile factory and on construction sites, and as an employee for a large tin mine, which he termed his central experience of exile. He viewed his experience of these sorts of jobs as having had a permanently radicalizing effect on him, as in the following statement about the textile factory where he worked: "My thoughts and feelings were tremendously radicalized by seeing the contrast between the prosperity of the factory's owners and managers and the misery and submissiveness of the workers. I saw how the owners exploited the workers' labor power and kept them in ignorance" (174).

Chapter 4

1. Karl Marx, *Der Bürgerkrieg in Frankreich,* in Karl Marx and Friedrich Engels, *Werke* (Berlin: Dietz, 1964), 17:342.

2. Heiner Müller, "Das Liebesleben der Hyänen," in *Was von den Träumen blieb:*

Eine Bilanz der sozialistischen Utopie, ed. Thomas Grimm (Berlin: Siedler, 1993), 8.

3. See Paul Michael Lützeler, "Von der Arbeiterschaft zur Intelligenz: Zur Darstellung sozialer Mobilität im Roman der DDR," in *Literatur und Literaturtheorie in der DDR,* ed. Peter U. Hohendahl and Patricia Herminghouse (Frankfurt: Suhrkamp, 1976), 241–81.

4. Peter Zimmermann, *Industrieliteratur der DDR: Vom Helden der Arbeit zum Planer und Leiter* (Stuttgart: Metzler, 1984), 27.

5. Karl Marx, *Critique of the Gotha Program,* in *The Marx-Engels Reader,* ed. Robert C. Tucker, 2nd ed. (New York: Norton, 1978), 531. See also the relevant articles, especially on "Arbeit" and "Arbeitsteilung," in *Historisch-kritisches Wörterbuch des Marxismus,* ed. Wolfgang F. Haug (Berlin: Argument, 1994).

6. I take the term "proletarian tragedy" from Heiner Müller's comments on his play *Wolokolamsker Chaussee* in his *Shakespeare Factory 2* (Berlin: Rotbuch, 1989), 259. This play focuses heavily on class shifts and allegiances, especially in the third part. See also Rudolf Bahro, *The Alternative in Eastern Europe* (London: Verso, 1981), originally published in 1977, which critiques "really existing" socialism for having perpetuated the division of labor and calls for the creation of a "developed communist society" where individuals would be "equally and simultaneously present at all levels of subjective interest" (440).

7. The disjuncture between the hopes of intellectuals and the perspectives of many other GDR citizens often came starkly to the fore in 1989 and 1990. See, for example, the statements by GDR and FRG writers collected in "Germany 1989–1990: A Dossier," *New German Critique,* no. 52 (Winter 1991): 31–108. See also Karl Deiritz and Hannes Krauss, eds., *Der deutsch-deutsche Literaturstreit* (Hamburg: Luchterhand, 1991).

8. See, for example, Walter Ulbricht's "Zehn Gebote der sozialistischen Moral," which he proclaimed in 1958. These are quoted in the entry on "Moral, Sozialistische," in *DDR Handbuch,* ed. Bundesministerium für innerdeutsche Beziehungen (Cologne: Verlag Wissenschaft und Politik, 1985), 2:918.

9. See especially the section on "Bildung und Arbeitswelt" in Oskar Anweiler et al., eds., *Bildungspolitik in Deutschland 1945–1990: Ein historisch-vergleichender Quellenband* (Bonn: Bundeszentrale für politische Bildung, 1992), 311ff. Some of the most useful sources on the GDR educational system that include discussions of efforts to integrate the working world into instruction include Heinz Frankiewicz et al. eds., *Kleine pädagogische Enzyklopädie* (Berlin: VEB Deutscher Verlag der Wissenschaften, 1961); Helmut Klein, *Polytechnische Bildung und Erziehung in der DDR* (Reinbek: Rowohlt, 1962); Karl-Heinz Heinemann, *Arbeit und Technik in der Erziehung: Studium zum polytechnischen Unterricht in der DDR* (Cologne: Pahl-Rugenstein, 1973); Helmut Klein, *Bildung in der DDR: Grundlagen, Entwicklungen, Probleme* (Reinbek: Rowohlt, 1974); and Sterling Fishman and Lothar Martin, *Estranged Twins: Education and Society in the Two Germanys* (New York: Praeger, 1987).

10. For a brief discussion of earlier concepts of "work education" see Chapter 2 above, which makes use of the discussion in Peter Dudek, *Erziehung*

durch Arbeit: Arbeitslagerbewegung und Freiwilliger Arbeitsdienst, 1920–1935 (Opladen: Westdeutscher Verlag, 1988). See also Fishman and Martin, *Estranged Twins,* 81ff.

11. For the relevant references to Marx and Engels that were constantly quoted by GDR educators and which were always cited as the source of the Soviet Union's concept of "polytechnical education," see Klein, *Polytechnische Bildung,* 118ff.; and Heinemann, *Arbeit und Technik,* 41ff. See also the discussion in Günter Wettstädt, *Bürgerliche Bildungskonzeption und "Arbeitswelt": Auseinandersetzung mit bildungspolitschen Auffassungen in der BRD zur Verbindung von Schule, Arbeit und Wirtschaft* (Berlin: Volk und Wissen, 1979), 24ff.

12. Fishman and Martin, *Estranged Twins,* 81, quoting GDR sources.

13. For an outstanding discussion of educational discrimination against the lower classes throughout history, see Robert Alt, *Das Bildungsmonopol* (Berlin: Akademie, 1978). For discussions of the actual instruction in subjects geared toward the working world see Fishman and Martin, *Estranged Twins,* 80; and for GDR perspectives on this see Jürgen Polzin, *Sozialistische Arbeitserziehung auf dem Lande* (Berlin: Volk und Wissen, 1962); Gerhard Neubert, *Arbeiter als Erzieher der Pioniere und Schüler* (Berlin: Volk und Wissen, 1963); and Jürgen Polzin, *Kommunistische Arbeitserziehung* (Berlin: Volk und Wissen, 1979).

14. Of course, this insistence on integrating intellectual aspects into manual labor constitutes the great difference between socialist and right-wing approaches to overcoming the division of labor. See the discussion in Chapter 2 above, particularly of Martin Heidegger and Ernst Jünger.

15. On the system of "Patenbrigaden," see Hartmut Vogt et al., *Schule und Betrieb in der DDR* (Cologne: Wissenschaft und Politik, 1970); Autorenkollektiv, *Die Schule und ihre Verbündeten: Erziehung—Sache der ganzen Gesellschaft* (Berlin: Volk und Wissen, 1976); and Walter Hoyer, *Betrieb und Schule—eng verbunden* (Berlin: Tribüne, 1986).

16. Klein, *Bildung in der DDR,* 75.

17. See, for example, the comments by Frank Hörnigk, a leading GDR German literature professor, on working in a factory before becoming a university student, in *Literary Intellectuals and the Dissolution of the State: Professionalism and Conformity in the GDR,* ed. Robert von Hallberg (Chicago: University of Chicago Press, 1996), 78ff.

18. For an example of such internal discussions see "Erfahrungen bei der Gestaltung der produktiven Arbeit der Schüler im Betrieb unter den Bedingungen des wissenschaftlich-technischen Fortschritts. Referat von Heinz Frankiewicz auf dem VII. Internationalen Polytechnischen Seminar in der DDR vom 26. bis 30. Oktober 1981," in Hans-Jürgen Fuchs and Eberhard Petermann, eds., *Bildungspolitik in der DDR, 1966–1990: Dokumente* (Wiesbaden: Harrassowitz, 1991), 161–65.

19. Jürgen Kuczynski, *Ein Leben in der Wissenschaft der DDR* (Münster: Westfälisches Dampfboot, 1994), 127.

20. See Merle Krueger and Carol Poore, " 'Ein Schaffender am Menschen': The Image of the Teacher in Recent GDR Fiction," in *Studies in GDR Culture*

and Society 4, ed. Margy Gerber et al. (New York: University Press of America, 1984), 199–212. On the disjunctures between schools and the working world in the GDR, see the documents reproduced in Ruth Reiher, ed., *Mit sozialistischen und anderen Grüßen: Porträt einer untergegangenen Republik in Alltagstexten* (Berlin: Aufbau, 1995), particularly the section entitled "Nicht für die Schule, für das Leben lernen wir," 35–86.

21. Freya Klier, *Lüg Vaterland: Erziehung in der DDR* (Munich: Kindler, 1990), 109–10.

22. See the entry on "Sozialistischer Wettbewerb" in *DDR Handbuch,* 2:1192–1208.

23. See the entries on "Brigade" and "Brigadetagebuch" in *DDR Handbuch,* 1:246. It would be an extremely important project to collect these brigade diaries in archives today.

24. See the following entries in the *DDR Handbuch:* "Erziehung, politisch-ideologische bzw. Staatsbürgerliche" (1:365–66); "Erziehung zu bewußter Disziplin" (1:366–67); "Kollektiv, Sozialistisches" (1:731–32); "Kollektiv- und Arbeitserziehung" (1:732–33); "Lebensweise, Sozialistische" (1:817–18); "Persönlichkeitstheorie, Sozialistische" (2:981–82).

25. Heiner Müller, "Der Lohndrücker," in his *Geschichten aus der Produktion I* (Berlin: Rotbuch, 1972), 43. See also "Lohndrücker 88. Heiner Müller inszeniert Heiner Müller: 'Der Lohndrücker' am Deutschen Theater," *Theater der Zeit* 4 (1988): 49–51.

26. This quote was repeated in many forms by the speakers at the first Bitterfeld Conference. See *Greif zur Feder Kumpel: Protokoll der Autorenkonferenz des Mitteldeutschen Verlages Halle (Saale) am. 24. April 1959 im Kulturpalast des elektrochemischen Kombinats Bitterfeld* (Halle: Mitteldeutscher Vlg., 1959).

27. See Alfred Kurella, "Vom neuen Lebensstil," in ibid., 10.

28. On the relationship of the Bitterfeld Program to the classical heritage, see Frank Trommler, "DDR-Erzählung und Bitterfelder Weg," in Reinhold Grimm and Jost Hermand, eds., *Basis* 3 (1972): 61–97. See also Zimmermann, *Industrieliteratur der DDR,* which contains an extensive bibliography on the Bitterfeld Program.

29. See, for example, the speeches by Fritz Bressau, head of the "Mitteldeutscher Verlag," and by miner Hans Busch in *Greif zur Feder,* 6 and 27.

30. David Bathrick, *The Powers of Speech: The Politics of Culture in the German Democratic Republic* (Lincoln: University of Nebraska Press, 1995), 120ff.

31. For a detailed discussion of some of these earlier industrial novels, see Trommler, "DDR Erzählung," 89, and Zimmermann, *Industrieliteratur der DDR,* 87ff.

32. Karl Mundstock, *Helle Nächte* (Halle: Mitteldeutscher Vlg., 1952), 238.

33. See Heiner Müller's prologue to "Der Lohndrücker," which states: "My play does not seek to portray the struggle of the new against the old (which a playwright cannot decide anyway) as a victory of the new brought to completion before the closing of the final curtain; it seeks rather to displace this struggle into the audience, which will decide for itself." Translation taken from Bathrick, *Powers of Speech,* 114.

34. See Zimmermann, *Industrieliteratur der DDR,* 10ff., and Bathrick, *Powers of Speech,* 120ff.
35. Heiner Müller, *Krieg ohne Schlacht,* 2nd ed. (Cologne: KiWi, 1994), 143.
36. See Helen Fehervary, "Heiner Müllers Brigadenstücke," in Reinhold Grimm and Jost Hermand, eds., *Basis* 2 (1971): 103–40.
37. Müller, *Krieg ohne Schlacht,* 153. See also the interview with Erwin Strittmatter, who gives essentially the same assessment of the Bitterfeld Program and denies that his novel *Ole Bienkopp* was influenced by this direction of cultural politics, in Grimm, *Was von den Träumen blieb,* 63ff.
38. Speech by Willi Bredel in *Greif zur Feder,* 65.
39. Speeches by Alfred Kurella, 17; Walter Ulbricht, 99; and Erwin Strittmatter, 52; all in *Greif zur Feder.*
40. Speech by Erwin Strittmatter in ibid., 51ff.
41. Speech by Walter Ulbricht in ibid., 109.
42. Ibid., 100ff.
43. Regina Hastedt, *Die Tage mit Sepp Zach* (Berlin: Tribüne, 1959), 158. Further page references will be given in the body of the text.
44. Biographical information on Hastedt is taken from Günter Albrecht et al., eds., *Schriftsteller der DDR* (Leipzig: VEB Bibliographisches Institut, 1975), 199.
45. On these gender stereotypes in the Red-One-Mark novels of the Weimar Republic, see Michael Rohrwasser, *Saubere Mädel, starke Genossen* (Frankfurt: Roter Stern, 1975).
46. See the discussion of Hastedt's text in Trommler, "DDR-Erzählung," 92. On the dynamics of representing those in traditionally subordinate positions, see Edward Said, *Orientalism* (New York: Pantheon, 1978), 160.
47. In this sense, Hastedt's characters recall the images of workers in earlier right-wing and Nazi texts. However, even in Hastedt's text, great emphasis is placed on workers' intellectual development—a fundamental difference from Nazi ideology.
48. Speech by Inge von Wangenheim in *Zweite Bitterfelder Konferenz 1964: Protokoll der von der Ideologischen Kommission beim Politbüro des ZK der SED und dem Ministerium für Kultur am 24. und 25. April im Kulturpalast des Elektrochemischen Kombinats Bitterfeld abgehaltenen Konferenz* (Berlin: Dietz, 1964), 500.
49. Christa Wolf, "Vorwort," in *Proben junger Erzähler,* ed. Wolf (Leipzig: Reclam, 1959), 3.
50. Zimmermann, *Industrieliteratur der DDR,* 190.
51. Compare Henry Schmidt, "What Is Oppositional Criticism? Politics and German Literary Criticism from Fascism to the Cold War," *Monatshefte* 79 (1987): 292–307.
52. For an incisive discussion of these earlier GDR narratives, see Trommler, "DDR-Erzählung."
53. Biographical information on Brigitte Reimann is taken from Albrecht et al., *Schriftsteller der DDR,* 444.
54. Biographical information on Christa Wolf is taken from Bernd Lutz, ed., *Metzler Autoren Lexikon* (Stuttgart: Metzler, 1994), 861.

55. Marc Silberman, *Literature of the Working World: A Study of the Industrial Novel in East Germany* (Bern: Lang, 1976), 38.
56. Biographical information on Adolf Endler is taken from Albrecht et al., *Schriftsteller der DDR*, 133. Endler's wife is the poet Elke Erb, who was born in 1938 in Scherbach/Eifel and moved to the GDR in 1949, also working in the Wische area in 1958–1959.
57. For a discussion of the poetry debate, see Bathrick, *Powers of Speech*, 72, and the references given there.
58. Adolf Endler, *Weg in die Wische* (Halle: Mitteldeutscher Vlg., 1960), 49. Further page references are indicated in the body of the text.
59. See Hans Mayer, *Der Turm von Babel: Erinnerung an eine Deutsche Demokratische Republik* (Frankfurt: Suhrkamp, 1991), 67–69. In Mayer's evaluation, "until about 1961 the Free German Youth was an independent, strong, critical association of young Germans." However, Mayer is also extremely critical here of the militarism and authoritarianism that became more and more entrenched along the lines of Soviet models: "And so the imitation of the Soviet Komsomol in Germany led unavoidably to the revival of former Hitler Youth rituals . . . . Such ceremonial events, which the European world correctly laughed at, drew on Germany's bad traditions: the imperial Germany of Wilhelm II and the Third Reich of the Führer and Reich Chancellor. These were the traditions of Heinrich Mann's 'loyal subject'."
60. Of course, the participation in these FDJ youth projects was partly voluntary and partly coerced, whereby published accounts emphasize the former. If diaries or archives are ever uncovered on this topic, they would be valuable documents of how these young people experienced this effort to give up class privilege.
61. Brigitte Reimann, *Ankunft im Alltag* (Berlin: Neues Leben, 1961), 24. Further page references will be given in the body of the text. For another novel that depicts a student learning discipline through work, see Paul Schmidt-Elgers, *Es begann im Sommer* (Rudolstadt: Greifenvlg., 1960).
62. See the discussion in Chapter 2 above of the connections between some groups within the Youth Movement and proponents of a national labor service. The "revolutionary romanticism" that these early GDR writers so often refer to is reminiscent of the mood in some sectors of the earlier Youth Movement. It is interesting that Alfred Kurella, one of the formulators of the Bitterfeld Program, was involved in the Youth Movement as a young man before he joined the Communist Party. See Kurella's "Deutsche Volksgemeinschaft: Offener Brief an den Führerrat der freideutschen Jugend," written in 1918 and reprinted in Werner Kindt, ed., *Grundschriften der deutschen Jugendbewegung* (Düsseldorf: Diederichs, 1963), 163–79.
63. See the discussion in Chapter 5 below of the West German student movement and the novel by Uwe Timm entitled *Heißer Sommer.*
64. See Reimann, *Ankunft im Alltag*, 228, and Mayer, *Turm von Babel*, on the early possibilities for liberation in the GDR.
65. Christa Wolf, *Der geteilte Himmel* (Munich: dtv, 1963), 30. Further page references will be given in the body of the text.
66. Speech by Heinz Sachs in *Zweite Bitterfelder Konferenz 1964*, 169.

67. Christa Wolf, "Dienstag, der 27. September 1960," in *Neue deutsche Literatur* 7 (July 1974): 20. Ellipses appear in the original.

68. Klaus Sauer, "Der lange Weg zu sich selbst: Christa Wolfs Frühwerk," in *Christa Wolf: Materialienbuch,* ed. Sauer (Darmstadt: Luchterhand, 1983), 91ff.

69. Wolf, "Dienstag," 13.

70. Biographical information on Franz Fühmann is based on Franz Fühmann, *Im Berg: Texte und Dokumente aus dem Nachlaß* (Rostock: Hinstorff, 1991); and Sigrid Damm, " 'Am liebsten tät ich auf die Straße gehn und brüllen': Zu Franz Fühmanns *Im Berg,*" *Sinn und Form* 45, no. 2 (March–April 1993): 349–59.

71. Fühmann, *Im Berg,* 5.

72. Franz Fühmann, *Kabelkran und Blauer Peter* (Rostock: Hinstorff, 1962), 6. Further page references will be given in the body of the text.

73. See Klaus Bogdal, *Schaurige Bilder: Der Arbeiter im Blick des Bürgers am Beispiel des Naturalismus* (Frankfurt: Syndikat, 1978).

74. Silberman, *Literature of the Working World,* 42.

75. On the Nazis' "Beauty of Labor" Office, see Tim Mason, *Social Policy in the Third Reich: The Working Class and the "National Community"* (Providence: Berg, 1993), 162ff. See also Karl Neurieg, "Bitterfelder Seitenwege," in *Alternative* 7, nos. 38–39 (October 1964): 12, who states: "No matter how well intended it may be, 'poeticizing' work eliminates its concrete, transformative, historical significance. By doing this, art could be degraded once again in the name 'of the Volk' to a strength-through-joy project."

76. See the chapter entitled "Genre mit Pensionsberechtigung: Die Reportage der DDR" in Michael Geisler, *Die literarische Reportage in Deutschland: Möglichkeiten und Grenzen eines operativen Genres* (Königstein: Scriptor, 1982), 294–305.

77. Fühmann, *Kabelkran und Blauer Peter,* 126ff.

78. Franz Fühmann's open letter appears in Erwin Kohn, ed., *In eigener Sache: Briefe von Künstlern und Schriftstellern* (Halle: Mitteldeutscher Vlg., 1964), here quoting from 38–39.

79. Christa Wolf, "Arbeitsbedingungen: Interview mit Richard A. Zipser," in her *Die Dimension des Autors* (Darmstadt: Luchterhand, 1987), 861.

80. See also the following statement by Brigitte Reimann about her impressions of the workers she had met: "I found the heroism I had expected in their work, in their eight or more hours in the factory hall or in the countryside. But gradually I noticed that many were only thinking about their wages, that they argued about bonuses, that they didn't try to understand the solidarity donations . . . . I noticed that people who I first thought were sacrificing their evenings for the cause were actually hoping for material gain. I noticed that people talked one way in meetings and another way in private . . . . And I noticed that the wishes and goals of many amounted to nothing more than collecting the objects necessary for a higher standard of living. They had to have a television set, a refrigerator, and, to top it all off, a Trabant. How is it possible that people who are activists and innovators at work can be satisfied to sit at home in their house slippers?" Quoted in Günther Rüther, *"Greif zur*

Feder, Kumpel": Schriftsteller, Literatur, und Politik in der DDR, 1949–1990 (Düsseldorf: Droste, 1991), 92.

81. "Gespräch mit Heiner Müller," in Müller, *Geschichten aus der Produktion I,* 140.

82. Zimmermann, *Industrieliteratur der DDR,* 270–71.

83. Volker Braun, "Der Schlamm," in Braun, *Texte in zeitlicher Folge* (Halle: Mitteldeutscher Vlg., 1989–1990), 1:43. Further page references will be given in the body of the text.

84. Fühmann, open letter in Kohn, *In eigener Sache,* 37–38.

85. Trommler, "DDR-Erzählung," 82.

86. Jay Rosellini, *Volker Braun* (Munich: Beck, 1983), 163, notes that this is Braun's own genre designation.

87. Ibid., 40, my translation.

88. Ibid., 164. See also Braun's poem "Bericht der Erbauer der Stadt Hoywoy," in Braun, *Texte,* 1:77–80.

89. Wolfgang Emmerich, "Volker Braun," in Lutz, *Metzler Autoren Lexikon,* 90.

90. Rosellini, *Volker Braun,* 42–43, my translation.

91. Compare the description of the workers at the site of the "Schwarze Pumpe" in Müller, *Krieg ohne Schlacht,* 152ff.: "There we met a group of adventurers, of gold-diggers—they called themselves gold-diggers. Criminals, asocial people, a shady bunch, nomadic figures who moved from one construction site to the next, old Nazis who were paid a lot of money to build the thing, anarchists . . . . No domesticated factory workers, but rather uprooted farmers or members of the petty bourgeoisie."

92. See Bahro, *The Alternative,* who quotes historian Rudolf Herrnstadt on the importance of popular initiative at the beginning of the Jacobin dictatorship: "He emphasized above all how the Jacobins managed to get everyone *working,* and moreover with a 'devotion never previously seen, even by people who had never been inclined to work.' (Subbotniks are in no way specifically socialist or communist, except in a very broad sense.) 'Some may have joined in from fear, others from curiosity, but the great majority worked enthusiastically because they finally felt at one with the course of world history. The Jacobin dictatorship had the young people on its side. The problem of the positive hero was unknown to it; it was generally seen as contemptible not to be a hero'" (383).

93. Braun lived through the bombing of Dresden as a child, and "Der Schlamm" refers to the ruins of this city.

94. For a discussion of the Nazis' "shovel cult" in the Reich Labor Service, see Chapter 2 above.

95. Braun, "Der Schlamm," 36. The reference here is clearly to Marx's famous statement in his "Contribution to the Critique of Hegel's *Philosophy of Right:* Introduction": "But in Germany every class lacks the logic, insight, courage and clarity which would make it a negative representative of society. Moreover, there is also lacking in every class the generosity of spirit which identifies itself, if only for a moment, with the popular mind; that genius which pushes material force to political power, that revolutionary daring which throws at its adversary the defiant phrase: *I am nothing and I should be everything*"

(emphasis in original, which was written in 1843). Quoted here from Tucker, ed., *Marx-Engels Reader*, 63.

96. Volker Braun, "Unvollendete Geschichte," in Braun, *Texte*, 4:66.

97. Franz Fühmann, "Im Berg: Bericht eines Scheiterns (Fragment 1983)," in Fühmann, *Im Berg*, 5–131. Further page references will be given in the body of the text.

98. See Damm, "Am liebsten tät ich auf die Straße gehn und brüllen."

99. Fühmann's open letter in Kohn, *In eigener Sache*, 40, refers to Tolstoy's "Herr und Knecht" as a great literary model that he wants to emulate.

100. Landolf Scherzer, *Fänger und Gefangene: 2386 Stunden vor Labrador und anderswo*, 2nd ed. (Rudolstadt: Greifenvlg., 1990). Further page references will be given in the body of the text.

101. See Geisler, *Die literarische Reportage*, 294ff.

102. See, for example, Gabriele Eckart, "Bauplatz: Ein Protokoll" and "Bei Schrubbke," in her *Per Anhalter: Geschichten und Erlebnisse aus der DDR* (Cologne: Kiepenheuer und Witsch, 1986), 47–81 and 111–21 (first published in the GDR in 1982). These short texts recount Eckart's experiences working as an unskilled laborer and a street-sweeper. See also the well-known examples of "Protokoll-Literatur" published in the GDR, including Sarah Kirsch's *Die Pantherfrau* (1973) and Maxie Wander's *Guten Morgen Du Schöne* (1977).

103. See Scherzer's next, much more sensational reportage, entitled *Der Erste* (Cologne: KiWi, 1989), which was published in the GDR in 1988. Scherzer accompanied a First Party Secretary of the SED through his daily routine and reported on *this* unknown side of the working world with a new openness and frankness.

104. See Annette Simon, " 'Kluge Kinder sterben früh': Die Achtundsechziger der DDR," *Die Zeit*, June 13, 1997, 16, who states, regarding the refusal of some in the GDR to go along with the prevailing ideology: "To refuse to hang out the flag, to vote, to make the required contribution to discussion in the trade union meeting. These were the dropouts, the cemetery workers, the bathhouse workers, the engine stokers with high school and university degrees. . . . The dropout movement was so large that the GDR leaders felt compelled to expand Paragraph 249 ('Endangering public order by asocial behavior') in 1979. After that, it was asocial not to hold down a regular job. In 1980, 10,714 people were sentenced under this law."

105. A look at the short story by Plenzdorf entitled "kein runter kein fern," which was written in 1973, the year *Die neuen Leiden des jungen W.* was published, confirms the suspicion that Plenzdorf muted many of his real criticisms in order to have the latter work published in the GDR. The short story was published in the Federal Republic in 1978, but it was never published in the GDR and was only produced there as a play in January 1990. In a graphically ironic twist on the earlier efforts to bridge the chasm between social classes, the short story centers around the figure of a young boy who wants to become a skilled carpenter or woodworker but who encounters barriers at every turn. Placed in a "special school" because of what is presumably a learning disability, the boy suffers from his father's low esteem for the world of manual labor

and consequent efforts to push his son in a more upwardly mobile direction. Plenzdorf lets this boy's thwarted journey to the working world stand in realistic, unresolved contradiction with the loudspeakers that are blaring out around him: "The socialist community is our greatest success!" The story appears in Manfred Behn, ed., *Geschichten aus der Geschichte der DDR, 1949–1979,* 2nd ed. (Darmstadt: Luchterhand, 1985), 164–80. See also Gerhard Ebert, "Tragisches Kinderschicksal als Spiegel einer unheilen Welt: Spiel 'Kein Runter kein Fern' von Ulrich Plenzdorf am DT uraufgeführt," in *Neues Deutschland,* January 16, 1990, 46.

106. Ulrich Plenzdorf, *Die neuen Leiden des jungen W.* (Frankfurt: Suhrkamp, 1976), 88. See also the discussion of Karl-Heinz Jakobs's novel *Die Interviewer* (1973) in Silberman, *Literature of the Working World,* 78–85. In this novel, a young dropout rejects the ideology of performance and intends to become an unskilled worker.

107. Jurek Becker, *Schlaflose Tage* (Frankfurt: Suhrkamp, 1978), 76–77. Further page references are given in the body of the text. The pressures on GDR teachers to encourage hypocrisy among their pupils had been such a source of dissatisfaction to them that since the early 1970s teachers had been pressured to stay on the job by a directive that barred them from taking any other kind of employment (see Klier, *Lüg Vaterland,* 133). It was one of the first demands of the New Forum's call for renewing the educational system in 1989 that teachers should be given more individual responsibility and not be compelled to pledge a lifelong commitment to their profession. See "Erste Positionen zur Erneuerung im Bildungswesen, bestätigt in der Vollversammlung des Neuen Forum am 28. November 1989" in Fuchs and Petermann, *Bildungspolitik,* 328.

108. See Lützeler, "Von der Arbeiterschaft zur Intelligenz," 252ff., on the theme of demotions.

109. Christa Wolf's *Was bleibt* (Frankfurt: Luchterhand, 1990), written in 1979 but not published then, contains the figure of the young woman writer who visits the narrator and tells her about being expelled from the university, being imprisoned, and becoming ill from the effects of prison work.

110. For a literary treatment of the experiences of the generation who protested against the invasion of Czechoslovakia, see Act 5 of Heiner Müller's *Wolokolamsker Chaussee,* entitled "Der Findling," in his *Shakespeare Factory 2.*

111. See Andrea Jäger, *Schriftsteller aus der DDR: Ausbürgerungen und Übersiedlungen von 1961 bis 1989: Autorenlexikon* (New York: Lang, 1995), 609ff.

112. Ibid., 119ff.

113. Thomas Brasch, *Vor den Vätern sterben die Söhne* (Berlin: Rotbuch, 1990), 53. Further page references are given in the body of the text.

114. Braun, "Unvollendete Geschichte," 69.

115. Quoted from the poem by Volker Braun, "Mein Terrortorium," in Braun, *Die Zickzackbrücke: Ein Abrißkalender* (Halle: Mitteldeutscher Vlg., 1992), 92.

116. See Frauke Meyer-Gosau, "Outing to Jurassic Park: 'Germany' in Post-Wall Literature: An Essay against Tiredness," in *Contentious Memories: Looking Back at the GDR,* ed. Jost Hermand and Marc Silberman (New York: Lang, 1998), 223–46; and my response to this article in the same volume, 247–51.

117. Brigitte Burmeister, *Unter dem Namen Norma* (Stuttgart: Klett-Cotta, 1994), 81ff.
118. Volker Braun, "Die Leute von Hoywoy II," in Braun, *Zickzackbrücke*, 63–64. All quotations are from these pages.
119. For twenty-five years, Hoyerswerda had been designated a "model socialist city." See Erich Wiedemann, " 'Eine liebenswerte, freundliche Stadt,' " *Spiegel*, August 8, 1994, 33. On the outbreaks of racist violence, see the cover story "Gewalt gegen Fremde," *Spiegel*, September 30, 1991, 30–51; and " 'Deutschland den Deutschen,' " *Spiegel*, December 9, 1991, 93–99.
120. Volker Braun, "Die Leute von Hoywoy," in Braun, *Es genügt nicht die einfache Wahrheit: Notate* (Frankfurt: Suhrkamp, 1976), 100–1 (originally published in the GDR in 1975).
121. On a visit to Leipzig in 1993, I saw the following piece of graffiti that responded to the outbreaks of racist violence: "Gewalt ist die Wut über ungelebtes Leben." [Violence is anger at unlived life.]
122. See Braun's poem "Mein Terrortorium": "Der Lehrer auf dem Marktplatz im reißenden Rudel der Schüler/ICH HABE IN VIERZIG JAHREN NICHTS GELEHRT /Ich vor meinen Lesern Helm im Gesicht/Den Plexiglasschild in Händen Tränengas," [My Terrortory: The teacher in the marketplace in the raging horde of pupils/ I TAUGHT NOTHING IN FORTY YEARS /I before my readers helmet over my face/ The plexiglass shield in my hands tear gas] in Braun, *Zickzackbrücke*, 92.
123. See also Braun's poem "Das Eigentum," ibid., 84.
124. Volker Braun, *Die vier Werkzeugmacher* (Frankfurt: Suhrkamp, 1996), 51.
125. See Volker Braun, "3. Oktober 1990," in Braun, *Zickzackbrücke*, 49: "We will work like the Turks, but our unemployed souls will remember the future, an old common cause that no longer has a name."

Chapter 5

1. See Jost Hermand, *Kultur im Wiederaufbau: Die Bundesrepublik Deutschland, 1945–1965* (Munich: Nymphenburger, 1986), 31–36.
2. On the situation of German students who needed to work after 1945 to support themselves, see Konrad Jarausch, *Deutsche Studenten, 1800–1970* (Frankfurt: Suhrkamp, 1984).
3. These statistics are taken from ibid., 217.
4. See Robert Alt, *Das Bildungsmonopol* (Berlin: Akademie, 1978).
5. See Jarausch, *Deutsche Studenten*, 216–17; and also Jost Hermand, *Die Kultur der Bundesrepublik Deutschland, 1965–1985* (Munich: Nymphenburger, 1988), 34, which points out that by 1979, approximately 15.4 percent of West German students were from working-class families.
6. Hermand, *Kultur im Wiederaufbau*, 40.
7. On the changing structure of poverty in the Federal Republic, see Stephan Leibfried et al., *Zeit der Armut: Lebensläufe im Sozialstaat* (Frankfurt: Suhrkamp, 1995).
8. Hermand, *Kultur im Wiederaufbau*, 255ff.
9. Quoted in Hermand, *Kultur der Bundesrepublik*, 36.
10. See Klaus L. Berghahn, "Dokumentarische Literatur," in *Neues Handbuch der*

Literaturwissenschaft: Literatur nach 1945 II, ed. Jost Hermand (Wiesbaden: Athenaion, 1979), 227, which interprets documentary prose as a literary expression of the economic difficulties of the mid-1960s.

11. See Merle Krueger, *Authors and the Opposition: West German Writers and the Social Democratic Party from 1945 to 1969* (Stuttgart: Hans-Dieter Heinze, 1982).

12. The reaction to Hochhuth's essay is discussed in detail in ibid., 273ff.

13. The reaction to Erhard's speech is discussed in detail in ibid., 283ff.

14. Günter Wallraff, *"Wir brauchen Dich": Als Arbeiter in deutschen Industriebetrieben* (Munich: Rütten + Loening, 1966), 73–74.

15. Helmut Gollwitzer, in *Die Welt des Arbeiters: Junge Pfarrer berichten aus der Fabrik,* ed. Horst Symanowski and Fritz Vilmar (Frankfurt: Stimme, 1963), 6–7.

16. Krystyna Nowak, *Arbeiter und Arbeit in der westdeutschen Literatur, 1945–1961* (Cologne: Pahl-Rugenstein, 1977).

17. Reinhard Dithmar, *Günter Wallraffs "Industriereportagen"* (Kronberg: Scriptor, 1973), 13.

18. The factories where Wallraff worked are named in ibid., although they are not identified in Wallraff's book.

19. Quoted in Ulla Hahn and Michael Töteberg, *Günter Wallraff* (Munich: Text + Kritik, 1979), 26.

20. Oskar Negt, "Wallraffs Untersuchungsarbeit in Bereichen der 'unterschlagenen Wirklichkeit': Literarische Sprachlosigkeit als Ende und Anfang," in *In Sachen Wallraff,* ed. Christian Linder (Cologne: KiWi, 1986), 277 and 288.

21. Wallraff, *Wir brauchen Dich,* 7. Wallraff published the diary that he kept while in the army in his *Von einem der auszog, und das Fürchten lernte* (Munich: Willi Weismann Vlg., 1970).

22. Wallraff, *Von einem,* 98.

23. Wallraff, *Wir brauchen Dich,* 10. Further page references will be given in the body of the text.

24. Hahn and Töteberg, *Günter Wallraff,* 46, point out Wallraff's emphasis on portraying workers as victims in contrast to other writers of documentary literature who brought out more strongly how workers resisted oppressive conditions.

25. On the response of workers to Wallraff's reportages, see, for example, Alfred Schüler, "Eulenspiegeleien, die gefährlich sind," 106, and Tita Henke-Gaehme and Rolf Henke, "Schwierigkeiten beim Befahren der Linkskurve," 120, both in Linder, *In Sachen Wallraff.* See also Negt, "Wallraffs Untersuchungsarbeit," 277 and 288.

26. Wallraff, *Von einem,* 71.

27. See, for example, Wallraff's "Anmerkungen" to his *Industriereportagen: Als Arbeiter in deutschen Großbetrieben* (Reinbek: Rowohlt, 1970), 113, which describes his leafletting with IG Metall, the Metalworkers' Union.

28. Günter Wallraff, "Einige Erfahrungen mit den Schwierigkeiten beim Veröffentlichen der Wirklichkeit hinter Fabrikmauern," in *Die Tabus der bundesdeutschen Presse,* ed. Eckart Spoo, 2nd ed. (Munich: Hanser, 1973), 29.

29. Wallraff, *Von einem,* 98.

30. Wallraff, "Einige Erfahrungen," 31.

31. Ibid., 33.

32. Negt, "Wallraffs Untersuchungsarbeit," 292.

33. This point is made by Raoul Hübner in "Antiautoritäre Aktionskunst: Aus Anlaß einer neueren Wallraff-Reportage," *Basis* 3 (1972): 131–72.

34. Wallraff, *Von einem*, 43–44.

35. Ibid., 71.

36. Hübner, "Antiautoritäre Aktionskunst," 158.

37. Roland Lang, *Ein Hai in der Suppe oder das Glück des Phillipp Ronge* (Munich: AutorenEdition, 1975), 189.

38. For a good general overview, see Paul Michael Lützeler, "Von der Intelligenz zur Arbeiterschaft: zur Darstellung sozialer Wandlungsversuche in den Romanen und Reportagen der Studentenbewegung," in *Deutsche Literatur in der Bundesrepublik seit 1965*, ed. Paul M. Lützeler and Egon Schwarz (Königstein: Athenäum, 1980), 115–35.

39. Hermand, *Kultur der Bundesrepublik*, 384.

40. Peter Mosler, *Was wir wollten, was wir wurden: Studentenrevolte—zehn Jahre danach* (Reinbek: Rowohlt, 1977), 20.

41. Henke-Gaehme and Henke, "Schwierigkeiten," 123–24.

42. Peter Schneider, "Günter Wallraff und seine Fertigmacher," *Die Weltwoche*, October 22, 1987, 6.

43. By contrast, see Rüdiger Safranski, *Ein Meister aus Deutschland: Heidegger und seine Zeit* (Munich: Hanser, 1994). Safranski attempts to defame the West German student movement here by equating it with Nazi student groups. See also Chapter 2 above on Heidegger and the Nazi Labor Service.

44. Uwe Timm, *Heißer Sommer* (Munich: Bertelsmann, 1974), 192.

45. These texts are discussed in some depth in Lützeler, "Von der Intelligenz," 125ff.

46. Peter Schneider, "Die Frauen bei Bosch," in Peter Schneider, *Die Botschaft des Pferdekopfs und andere Essais aus einem friedlichen Jahrzehnt* (Darmstadt: Luchterhand, 1981), 59–95. This reportage appeared first in *Kursbuch* 21 (1970). Further page references will be given in the body of the text.

47. Peter Schneider, *Lenz* (Berlin: Rotbuch, 1973), 88.

48. Michael Schneider, "Gegen den linken Dogmatismus, eine Alterskrankheit des Kommunismus," and "Peter Schneider: Von der Alten Radikalität zur Neuen Sensibilität," both in Michael Schneider, *Die lange Wut zum langen Marsch: Aufsätze zur sozialistischen Politik und Literatur* (Reinbek: Rowohlt, 1975), 51–100 and 317–30.

49. M. Schneider, "Gegen den linken Dogmatismus," 51–52.

50. M. Schneider, "Peter Schneider," 326–27.

51. Ibid., 327.

52. M. Schneider, "Gegen den linken Dogmatismus," 61.

53. So, for example, the student named Ullrich in Timm's *Heißer Sommer* is deeply impressed upon learning about Communist workers who resisted the Nazis and vows to follow what he takes as being their pure example of self-sacrifice.

54. Christina Thürmer-Rohr, *Vagabundinnen: Feministische Essays* (Berlin: Orlanda, 1987), 15.

55. Günter Wallraff, "Die Angst, feige zu sein: Gespräch mit Günter Wallraff über sein neues Buch *Ganz unten*," in *Süddeutsche Zeitung*, October 23, 1985, 15.

56. Henke-Gaehme and Henke, "Schwierigkeiten," 134–35.

57. Günter Wallraff, " 'Gastarbeiter' oder der gewöhnliche Kapitalismus," in Wallraff, *Die Reportagen* (Cologne: KiWi, 1976), 489–516. This was first published in Wallraff's *Neue Reportagen* (1972). The title recalls Reinhard Lettau's *Täglicher Faschismus* (1971).

58. John Howard Griffin, *Black Like Me* (New York: New American Library, 1961). One predecessor of Griffin, though without his existentialist overtones, was reporter Ray Sprigle, who also darkened his skin and traveled through the South. Sprigle described his experiences in the pamphlet "I Was a Negro in the South for 30 Days" (Pittsburgh: Post-Gazette, 1948) and in a longer form in *In the Land of Jim Crow* (New York: Simon and Schuster, 1949). See Paul Peters, "Ritter von der wandelbaren Gestalt: Zu Günter Wallraffs *Ganz unten*," *Frankfurter Hefte/Die neue Gesellschaft*, November 11, 1986, 1011, which maintains that Griffin and Wallraff can be compared in terms of the "authenticity" of their experiences and roles.

59. See Norman Mailer, "The White Negro," in his *Advertisements for Myself* (New York: Putnam, 1959).

60. See Eric Lott, "White Like Me: Racial Cross-Dressing and the Construction of American Whiteness," in *Cultures of United States Imperialism*, ed. Amy Kaplan and Donald E. Pease (Durham, N.C.: Duke University Press, 1993), 474ff.

61. Griffin, *Black Like Me*, 5 and cover. The 1976 edition notes that five million copies had been sold to date.

62. *Black Like Me* was serialized in the magazine *Sepia* before it appeared as a book. This magazine was a kind of *Life* magazine directed at black readers, and many letters to the editor praised Griffin for his undertaking. The book is still for sale at the memorial to Martin Luther King, Jr., in Atlanta.

63. Lott, "White Like Me," 475. Lott gives numerous examples of this tradition of "racial mimicry."

64. Ibid. gives the following quote from the minstrel Ben Cotton: "I used to sit with them in front of their cabins, and we would start the banjo twanging, and their voices would ring out in the quiet night air in their weird melodies. They did not quite understand me. I was the first white man they had seen who sang as they did, but we were brothers for the time being and were perfectly happy" (477–78).

65. Ibid., 485.

66. See ibid., 490.

67. For an earlier German example, see Hans Paasche, *Die Forschungsreise des Afrikaners Lukanga Mukara ins innerste Deutschland* (Berlin: Jakobsohn, 1980 reprint of 1912 first edition). Paasche, who was an important figure in the youth movement and the "Lebensreform" movement, used the voice of a "noble savage" to criticize German "civilization."

68. Günter Wallraff, *Ganz unten* (Cologne: Kiepenheuer und Witsch, 1985), 12. Further page references are indicated in the body of the text.
69. Wallraff, "Die Angst, feige zu sein," 15.
70. "Ich glaube an Veränderung," *WAZ*, October 30, 1985. In this interview, Wallraff stated: "Outwardly I'm a German again, but inside I'm still Ali."
71. Thus, *Ganz unten* is the only example of a journey to the working world in which the role contains elements of humor, whereby the source of the humor lies in Wallraff's concept of his Turkish persona as childlike and foolish.
72. See Anna Kuhn, "Bourgeois Ideology and the (Mis)Reading of *Ganz unten*," *New German Critique* 46 (Winter 1989): 191–202.
73. Gerhard Kromschröder's reportage was published in book form as *Als ich ein Türke war* (Frankfurt: Eichborn, 1983), which included readers' letters about the book and information about foreign workers in Germany. See also his *Ich war einer von ihnen* (Frankfurt: Eichborn, 1987). And see the interview with Kromschröder entitled "Wallraff hat die Oper geschrieben, Von mir stammt die Ouvertüre," *Welt der Arbeit,* January 9, 1986, 13. Another brief account of a West German student who posed as a Turk in order to try to do sociological research is "Als Türkin unterwegs: Was Frau Keskin erlebte—Eine Studentin untersucht die Ausländerphobie," *Die Zeit* (Hamburg edition), March 2, 1984, 67.
74. Max Weber, "Zur Rechtfertigung Göhres," *Christliche Welt* 6 (1892), cols. 1104–9.
75. Quoted in Hübner, "Antiautoritäre Aktionskunst," 158.
76. See, for example, Kromschröder's dedication of his *Ich war einer von ihnen* to "everyone in the antifascist resistance of yesterday and today," 4; as well as numerous examples throughout *Ganz unten*.
77. See Arlene Teraoka, "Talking 'Turk': On Narrative Strategies and Cultural Stereotypes," *New German Critique* 46 (Winter 1989): 104–28, which discusses some of these flaws in *Ganz unten* and contrasts Wallraff's reportage to the ethnographic studies of Paul Geiersbach, including his *Bruder, Muß zusammen Zwiebel und Wasser essen: Eine türkische Familie in Deutschland* (Berlin: Dietz Nachf., 1982).
78. A pamphlet that describes one of these large meetings is "Vor unseren Augen—Im Schatten der Öffentlichkeit: Veranstaltung mit Günter Walraff und Aras Ören" (Cologne: Hilfsfonds "Ausländersolidarität," 1985). The pamphlet refers to Stenbock-Fermor's *Deutschland von unten* as a forerunner of Wallraff's project. See also Cafer Kosova and Tayfun Demir, "Türkische Literatur," *Literatur Konkret* 11 (1986/1987): 97, who state that the Turkish translation of *Ganz unten* had sold approximately fifty thousand copies in the Federal Republic to date.
79. Peters, "Ritter von der wandelbaren Gestalt," 1012.
80. "Deutsche Linke im Beißkrampf," *Die Tageszeitung,* October 8, 1987, quoted in *Konkret* 11 (1987): 16.
81. Peters, "Ritter von der wandelbaren Gestalt," 1010.
82. See Bodo Rollka, *Die Reise ins Souterrain: Eugène Sue und Günter Wallraff* (Berlin: Arsenal, 1987), which analyzes Sue's *Mysteries of Paris* and Wallraff's *Ganz unten* as phenomenal best-sellers in the tradition of journeys to the

social abyss and also refers to Paul Göhre. See also Sven Papcke, "Ganz oben, oder: Der Charme des Elends," *L '80* 37 (1986): 5–9.

83. For examples of the investigations that *Ganz unten* provoked, see the pamphlet "Günter Wallraffs *Ganz unten* und die Folgen" (Cologne: Kiepenheuer und Witsch, n.d.); and also the 1988 edition of *Ganz unten* (Cologne: Kiepenheuer und Witsch), which contains an extensive section on "Die Folgen: Reaktionen—Wirkungen—Veränderungen."

84. For material on the controversies around *Ganz unten,* see Gremliza's attacks on Wallraff in *Literatur Konkret* 11 (1986/1987) and in *Konkret* 11 (1987). For defenses of Wallraff, see Peter Schneider, "Günter Wallraff und seine Fertigmacher"; Heiner Müller's statement quoted in "Deutsche Linke im Beißkrampf"; and "Mit Wallraff solidarisch," *Konkret* 11 (1987): 22.

85. Lutz Tantow, quoted in "Der Held mit doppeltem Gesicht," *Die Brücke* 38 (August–September 1987): 7.

86. Dursun Sekeroglu, "Ist 'Ganz unten' nichts anderes los als Schrecken?" *Die Brücke* 29 (February–March 1986): 18.

87. Gesine Lassen, "Günter-Wallraff-Debatte," *Die Brücke* 39 (October–November 1987): 8. See also the interview with one of Wallraff's important Turkish collaborators, "Vielleicht seinen Feinden ähnlich geworden," *Spiegel,* June 15, 1987, 188ff.

88. See Sekeroglu, "Ist 'Ganz unten' nichts anderes los als Schrecken?" For an earlier statement that criticizes the practice of drawing too direct parallels between the Nazi period and the Federal Republic, see Gino Chiellino, "Die Ausländerfeindlichkeit braucht keine Nazivergangenheit," *Kürbiskern* 1 (1983): 81–89.

89. "Streit mit Wallraff: Die Abrechnung mit der Ideologie der Inschutznahme: Kurzinterview mit Taner Aday," *Die Brücke* 39 (October–November 1987): 11. See also Aysel Özakin, "Ali hinter den Spiegeln," *Literatur Konkret* 11 (1986/1987): 6ff. Here, this Turkish author who was living and writing in the Federal Republic criticizes the one-sidedly negative image of Turks created by Wallraff in *Ganz unten.*

90. "Die Geschäfte der Firma Wallraff. Cumali Yabanci sprach mit Levent Sinirlioglu, dem wahren Ali in 'Ganz unten,' " *Die Brücke* 38 (August–September 1987): 9.

91. See the immigration researcher Stephen Castles's response in Kromschröder's *Als ich ein Türke war:* "The way people in the FRG talk about the problems of integrating foreigners is misleading. At present they are hardly given a chance to integrate themselves. This could only be possible with a clear and secure legal status, together with the readiness of Germans to accept new citizens as people with their own culture." (48).

92. Sekeroglu, "Ist 'Ganz unten' nichts anderes los als Schrecken?" 18.

93. Cf. Edward Said, *Orientalism* (New York: Vintage, 1979), 160: "The Orientalist can imitate the Orient without the opposite being true. What he says about the Orient is therefore to be understood as description obtained in a one-way exchange: as *they* spoke and behaved, *he* observed and wrote down."

94. For statements in defense of Wallraff, see note 84 above.

95. Thus, in various interviews about *Ganz unten,* Wallraff often mentioned the

positive things he had experienced in the community of Turkish foreign workers during his project, but he did not include these in his book. For example, Wallraff stated the following in *Marabo*, December 1985, 19: "And then I learned what hospitality really is from the Turkish families who invited me, the strange Ali, into their homes. I found out a lot about the culture and way of life of the Turkish people. How they treat their old people and children. I saw that we can learn a lot from them." This interview is entitled "Ausländer rein!"

96. For Wallraff's reaction, see " 'Dieses Buch ist wie ein Fluch für mich': Der Schriftsteller Günter Wallraff und die Folgen seines Super-Bestsellers Ganz unten," *Spiegel,* June 15, 1987, 182ff. See also Klaus-Michael Bogdal, "Wer darf sprechen? Schriftsteller als moralische Instanz—Überlegungen zu einem Ende und einem Anfang," *Weimarer Beiträge* 37, no. 4 (1991): 579–602, which mentions Wallraff's silencing after *Ganz unten* in the context of the later controversy around Christa Wolf's *Was bleibt* (1990).

97. Günter Wallraff, "Schreiben ist nicht alles," *Die Zeit,* August 18, 1989, 12.

Conclusion

1. Herbert Heckmann and Gerhard Dette, eds., *Erfahrung und Fiktion: Arbeitswelt in der deutschen Literatur der Gegenwart* (Frankfurt: Fischer, 1993).

2. Quoted in Jeremy Rifkin, *The End of Work* (New York: Putnam, 1996), 8. This book contains a wealth of useful statistics documenting the decline in manufacturing jobs. On the German situation in particular, see Jeremy Rifkin, "Die dritte Säule der neuen Gesellschaft," *Die Zeit,* May 9, 1997, 11.

3. Uwe Heuser, "Wohlstand für wenige," *Die Zeit,* October 31, 1997, 8.

4. See the special issue of *Argument* entitled "Auf der Suche nach der verlorenen Arbeit," 36, no. 6 (November–December 1994).

5. Nikolaus Piper, "Arme Reiche, reiche Arme?" *Die Zeit,* June 3, 1994, 11.

6. See Muzaffer Perik et al., *Arm dran: Armut—sozialer Wandel—Sozialpolitik* (Marburg: Schüren, 1995), 16; and Arne Daniels, "Das Desaster am Arbeitsmarkt," *Die Zeit,* February 5, 1998, 21.

7. See, for example, Rainer Butenschön et al., eds., *Gegen die soziale Lüge: Armut und Verelendung im reichen Deutschland* (Braunschweig: Steinweg, 1993), 16; and Walter Hanesch et al., eds., *Armut in Deutschland* (Reinbek: Rowohlt, 1994), 13ff.

8. See the interview with Walter Jens entitled " 'Die Tragödie ist das Bleibende,' " *Der Spiegel,* February 16, 1998, 183.

9. See Linda Alcoff, "The Problem of Speaking for Others," *Cultural Critique,* no. 20 (Winter 1991–1992): 5–32; and Jochen Vogt, "Have the Intellectuals Failed? On the Sociopolitical Claims and the Influence of Literary Intellectuals in West Germany," *New German Critique,* no. 58 (Winter 1993): 3–24.

Selected Bibliography

Primary Texts

Becker, Jurek. *Schlaflose Tage*. Frankfurt: Suhrkamp, 1978.

Braun, Volker. "Die Leute von Hoywoy (1)." In *Es genügt nicht die einfache Wahrheit*, by Volker Braun, 100–101. Frankfurt: Suhrkamp, 1975.

———. "Die Leute von Hoywoy (2)." *Argument* 36, no. 2 (March–April 1994): 167–68.

———. "Der Schlamm." In *Texte in zeitlicher Folge*, by Volker Braun, 1:7–49. Halle: Mitteldeutscher Verlag, 1989.

———. "Unvollendete Geschichte." In *Texte in zeitlicher Folge*, by Volker Braun, 4:7–70. Halle: Mitteldeutscher Verlag, 1990.

Brecht, Bertolt. *Furcht und Elend des Dritten Reiches*. Frankfurt: Suhrkamp, 1979.

Endler, Adolf. *Weg in die Wische*. Halle: Mitteldeutscher Verlag, 1960.

Flex, Walter. "Wolf Eschenlohr." In Walter Flex, *Gesammelte Werke*, ed. Konrad Flex, 1:185–257. Munich: Beck, n.d.

Fuchs, Hans-Jürgen, and Eberhard Petermann, eds. *Bildungspolitik in der DDR, 1966–1990: Dokumente*. Berlin: Harrassowitz, 1991.

Fühmann, Franz. *Im Berg: Texte und Dokumente aus dem Nachlaß*. Rostock: Hinstorff, 1991.

———. *Kabelkran und Blauer Peter*. Rostock: Hinstorff, 1962.

Goebbels, Joseph. *Michael: Ein deutsches Schicksal in Tagebuchblättern*. 6th ed. Munich: F. Eher Nachf., 1935 (first published in 1929).

Göhre, Paul. *Drei Monate Fabrikarbeiter und Handwerksbursche: Eine praktische Studie*. Leipzig: Grunow, 1891.

———. *Drei Monate Fabrikarbeiter und Handwerksbursche: Eine praktische Studie*. Ed. Joachim Brenning and Christian Gremmels. Gütersloh: Mohn, 1978.

———. *Three Months in a Workshop*. Trans. A. B. Carr. New York: Scribner, 1895.

———. *Wie ein Pfarrer Sozialdemokrat wurde*. Berlin: Verlag der Expedition der Buchhandlung Vorwärts, 1900.

Griffin, John H. *Black Like Me*. New York: New American Library, 1961.

Grünberg, Karl. *Brennende Ruhr: Roman aus der Zeit des Kapp-Putsches*. Berlin: Aufbau, 1959 (first published in 1928).

Hadamovsky, Eugen. *Hilfsarbeiter Nr. 50 000*. Munich: Zentralverlag der NSDAP, 1938.

Hastedt, Regina. *Die Tage mit Sepp Zach*. Berlin: Tribune, 1959.

Heidegger, Martin. "Political Texts, 1933–34." *New German Critique* 45 (Fall 1988): 96–115.

Jünger, Ernst. *Der Arbeiter: Herrschaft und Gestalt*. In Ernst Jünger. *Werke*, vol. 6. Stuttgart: Klett, 1960.

Körber, Lili. *Eine Frau erlebt den roten Alltag: Ein Tagebuch-Roman aus den Putilowwerken*. Berlin: Rowohlt, 1932.

Kromschröder, Gerhard. *Als ich ein Türke war*. Frankfurt: Eichborn, 1983.

Leitner, Maria. *Eine Frau reist durch die Welt*. Berlin: Agis, 1932.

———. *Elisabeth, ein Hitlermädchen: Erzählende Prosa, Reportagen, und Berichte*. Berlin: Aufbau, 1985.

Metropolis. Dir. Fritz Lang. 1927.

Mitgau, J. Hermann, ed. *Erlebnisse und Erfahrungen Heidelberger Werkstudenten: Eine Sammlung von Berichten*. Heidelberg: Hörning, 1925.

Nebe, Klaus Hermann. *Schippen aufnehmen! Im Gleichschritt—marsch! Ein Roman vom Arbeitsdienst*. Berlin: Westermann, 1934.

Plenzdorf, Ulrich. *Die neuen Leiden des jungen W.* Frankfurt: Suhrkamp, 1976 (first published in 1973).

Reimann, Brigitte. *Ankunft im Alltag*. Berlin: Neues Leben, 1961.

Richter, Hans. *Hochofen I: Ein oberschlesischer Roman*. Leipzig: Keil, 1923.

Riemkasten, Felix. *Stehkragenproletarier*. Leipzig: Gerstenberg, 1920.

Rohrbach, Paul. *The German Work-Student*. Dresden: Wirtschaftshilfe der deutschen Studentenschaft, 1924.

Scherzer, Landolf. *Fänger und Gefangene: 2386 Stunden vor Labrador und anderswo*. Rudolstadt: Greifenvlg., 1983.

Schneider, Michael. *Die lange Wut zum langen Marsch. Aufsätze zur sozialistischen Politik und Literatur*. Reinbek: Rowohlt, 1975.

Schneider, Peter. *Die Botschaft des Pferdekopfs und andere Essays aus einem friedlichen Jahrzehnt*. Darmstadt: Luchterhand, 1981.

———. *Lenz*. Berlin: Rotbuch, 1973.

Stenbock-Fermor, Alexander Graf von. *Deutschland von unten: Reise durch die proletarische Provinz*. Stuttgart: J. Engelhorns Nachf., 1931.

———. *Meine Erlebnisse als Bergarbeiter*. Stuttgart: J. Engelhorns Nachf., 1929.

———. *My Experiences as a Miner*. Trans. Frances, Countess of Warwick. London: Putnam, 1930.

———. *Der rote Graf: Autobiographie*. Berlin: Verlag der Nation, 1973.

Symanowski, Horst, and Fritz Vilmar. *Die Welt des Arbeiters: Junge Pfarrer berichten aus der Fabrik*. Frankfurt: Stimme, 1963.

Timm, Uwe. *Heißer Sommer*. Munich: Bertelsmann, 1974.

Triumph des Willens. Dir. Leni Riefenstahl. 1936.

Waldeyer-Hartz, Hugo von. *Werkstudent und Burschenband: Roman aus dem deutschen Studentenleben der Nachkriegszeit*. Leipzig: Koehler, 1924.

Wallraff, Günter. *Ganz unten*. Cologne: Kiepenheuer und Witsch, 1985.

———. *"Wir brauchen Dich": Als Arbeiter in deutschen Industriebetrieben*. Munich: Rütten + Loening, 1966.

Wettstein-Adelt, Minna. *Dreieinhalb Monate Fabrik-Arbeiterin: Eine practische Studie.* Berlin: J. Leiser, 1893.

Winter, Max. *Arbeitswelt um 1900: Texte zur Alltagsgeschichte.* Ed. Stefan Riesenfellner. Vienna: Europavlg., 1988.

———. *Im dunkelsten Wien.* Vienna: Wiener Vlg., 1904.

Wolf, Christa. *Der geteilte Himmel.* Berlin: Weiss, 1964 (first published in 1963).

Secondary Works

Alcoff, Linda. "The Problem of Speaking for Others." *Cultural Critique,* no. 20 (Winter 1991–92): 5–32.

Alt, Robert. *Das Bildungsmonopol.* Berlin: Akademie, 1978.

Anweiler, Oskar, et al., eds. *Bildungspolitik in Deutschland, 1945–1990: Ein historisch-vergleichender Quellenband.* Bonn: Bundeszentrale für politische Bildung, 1992.

Aronowitz, Stanley, and Jonathan Cutler, eds. *Post-Work.* New York: Routledge, 1997.

Bajohr, Stefan. "Weiblicher Arbeitsdienst im 'Dritten Reich.' " *Vierteljahreshefte für Zeitgeschichte* 28, no. 3 (1980): 331–57.

Bathrick, David. *The Powers of Speech: The Politics of Culture in the German Democratic Republic.* Lincoln: University of Nebraska Press, 1995.

Benz, Wolfgang. "Vom freiwilligen Arbeitsdienst zur Arbeitsdienstpflicht." *Vierteljahreshefte für Zeitgeschichte* 16 (1968): 317–46.

Bergmann, Klaus, et al., eds. *Abhauen: Flucht ins Glück.* Reinbek: Rowohlt, 1981.

Bogdal, Klaus-Michael. *Schaurige Bilder: Der Arbeiter im Blick des Bürgers am Beispiel des Naturalismus.* Frankfurt: Syndikat, 1978.

Brantlinger, Patrick. "Victorians and Africans: The Genealogy of the Myth of the Dark Continent." In *"Race," Writing, and Difference,* ed. Henry Louis Gates, Jr., 185–223. Chicago: University of Chicago Press, 1986.

Brenning, Joachim. "Christentum und Sozialdemokratie. Paul Göhre: Fabrikarbeiter—Pfarrer—Sozialdemokrat. Eine sozialethisch-historische Untersuchung." Diss., Marburg, 1980.

Butenschön, Rainer, et al., eds. *Gegen die soziale Lüge: Armut und Verelendung im reichen Deutschland.* Braunschweig: Steinweg, 1993.

Campbell, Joan. *Joy in Work, German Work: The National Debate, 1800–1945.* Princeton: Princeton University Press, 1989.

Canning, Kathleen. *Languages of Labor.* Ithaca: Cornell University Press, 1996.

Clifford, James, and George Marcus, eds. *Writing Culture: The Poetics and Politics of Ethnography.* Berkeley: University of California Press, 1986.

Croteau, David. *Politics and the Class Divide: Working People and the Middle-Class Left.* Philadelphia: Temple University Press, 1995.

Dithmar, Reinhard. *Günter Wallraffs Industriereportagen.* Kronberg: Scriptor, 1973.

Dudek, Peter. *Erziehung durch Arbeit: Arbeitslagerbewegung und Freiwilliger Arbeitsdienst, 1920–1935.* Opladen: Westdeutscher Vlg., 1988.

Eggerstorfer, Wolfgang. *Schönheit und Adel der Arbeit: Arbeitsliteratur im Dritten Reich.* New York: Lang, 1988.

Emmerich, Wolfgang. *Proletarische Lebensläufe*. Reinbek: Rowohlt, 1974 (Vol. 1), 1975 (Vol. 2).

Fishman, Sterling, and Lothar Martin. *Estranged Twins: Education and Society in the Two Germanys*. New York: Praeger, 1987.

Friedrichsmeyer, Sara, et al., eds. *The Imperialist Imagination: German Colonialism and Its Legacy*. Ann Arbor: University of Michigan Press, 1998.

Fülberth, Georg. *Proletarische Partei und bürgerliche Literatur*. Neuwied: Luchterhand, 1972.

Geisler, Michael. *Die literarische Reportage in Deutschland*. Königstein/Ts.: Scriptor, 1982.

Gerlach, Ingeborg. *Bitterfeld: Arbeiterliteratur und Literatur der Arbeitswelt in der DDR*. Kronberg: Scriptor, 1974.

"Greif zur Feder, Kumpel!" Protokoll der Autorenkonferenz des Mitteldeutschen Verlags am 24. April 1959 in Bitterfeld. Halle: Mitteldeutscher Vlg., 1959.

Greiner, Bernhard. *Von der Allegorie zur Idylle: Die Literatur der Arbeitswelt in der DDR*. Heidelberg: Quelle + Meyer, 1974.

Grimm, Reinhold, and Jost Hermand, eds. *Arbeit als Thema in der deutschen Literatur vom Mittelalter bis zur Gegenwart*. Königstein: Athenäum, 1979.

Grimm, Thomas. *Was von den Träumen blieb: Eine Bilanz der sozialistischen Utopie*. Berlin: Siedler, 1993.

Günter Wallraffs "Ganz unten" und die Folgen. Cologne: Kiepenheuer und Witsch, n.d.

Hahn, Ulla, and Michael Toteberg. *Günter Wallraff*. Munich: Beck Autorenbücher, 1979.

Hanesch, Walter, et al., eds. *Armut in Deutschland*. Reinbek: Rowohlt, 1994.

Heckmann, Herbert, and Gerhard Dette, eds. *Erfahrung und Fiktion: Arbeitswelt in der deutschen Literatur der Gegenwart*. Frankfurt: Fischer, 1993.

Hermand, Jost. "Carl Fischer: *Denkwürdigkeiten und Erinnerungen eines Arbeiters*." In *Unbequeme Literatur*, by Jost Hermand, 87–107. Heidelberg: Stiehm, 1971.

———. *Die Kultur der Bundesrepublik Deutschland 1965–1985*. Munich: Nymphenburger, 1988.

———. *Kultur im Wiederaufbau: Die Bundesrepublik Deutschland, 1945–1965*. Munich: Nymphenburger, 1986.

———. *Old Dreams of a New Reich: Volkish Utopias and National Socialism*. Bloomington: Indiana University Press, 1992.

Hertling, Viktoria. "Abschied von Europa: Zu Lili Körbers Exil in Paris, Lyon, und New York." *Germanic Review* 62, no. 3 (1987): 118–29.

———. *Quer durch*. Königstein/Ts.: Forum Academicum, 1982.

Hosfeld, Rolf, and Helmut Peitsch. " 'Weil uns diese Aktionen innerlich verändern, sind sie politisch': Bemerkungen zu vier Romanen über die Studentenbewegung." *Basis* 8 (1978): 92ff.

Hübner, Raoul. "Antiautoritäre Aktionskunst: Aus Anlaß einer neueren Wallraff-Reportage." *Basis* 3 (1972): 131–72.

Jarausch, Konrad. *Deutsche Studenten, 1800–1970*. Frankfurt: Suhrkamp, 1984.

Kater, Michael. "The Work Student: A Socio-Economic Phenomenon of Early

Weimar Germany." *Journal of Contemporary History* 10, no. 1 (1975): 71–94.

Keating, Peter, ed. *Into Unknown England: Selections from the Social Explorers.* Manchester: Manchester University Press, 1976.

Kelly, Arthur, ed. and trans. *The German Worker: Working-Class Autobiographies from the Age of Industrialization.* Berkeley: University of California Press, 1987.

Kohler, Henning. *Arbeitsdienst in Deutschland.* Berlin: Duncker und Humblot, 1967.

Kuhn, Anna. "Bourgeois Ideology and the (Mis)Reading of *Ganz unten*." *New German Critique* 46 (Winter 1989): 191–202.

Lesser, Wendy. *The Life below the Ground: A Study of the Subterranean in Literature and History.* Boston: Faber and Faber, 1987.

Lindner, Christian, ed. *In Sachen Wallraff.* Cologne: Kiepenheuer und Witsch, 1986.

Lott, Eric. *Love and Theft: Blackface Minstrelsy and the American Working Class.* New York: Oxford, 1993.

———. "White Like Me: Racial Cross-Dressing and the Construction of American Whiteness." In *Cultures of United States Imperialism,* ed. Amy Kaplan and Donald Pease, 474–98. Durham, N.C.: Duke University Press, 1993.

Low, Gail C. *White Skins/Black Masks: Representation and Colonialism.* New York: Routledge, 1996.

Lützeler, Paul Michael. "Von der Arbeiterschaft zur Intelligenz: Zur Darstellung sozialer Mobilität im Roman der DDR." In *Literatur und Literaturtheorie in der DDR,* ed. Patricia Herminghouse and Peter Hohendahl, 241–80. Frankfurt: Suhrkamp, 1976.

———. "Von der Intelligenz zur Arbeiterschaft: Zur Darstellung sozialer Wandlungsversuche in den Romanen und Reportagen der Studentenbewegung." In *Deutsche Literatur in der Bundesrepublik seit 1965,* ed. Paul Michael Lützeler and Egon Schwarz, 115–35. Königstein: Athenäum, 1980.

Markham, Sara. *Workers, Women, and Afro-Americans: Images of the U.S. in German Travel Literature from 1923 to 1933.* New York: Lang, 1986.

Mason, Timothy. *Sozialpolitik im Dritten Reich: Arbeiterklasse und Volksgemeinschaft.* Opladen: Westdeutscher Vlg., 1977.

Maynes, Mary Jo. *Taking the Hard Road: Life Course in French and German Workers' Autobiographies in the Era of Industrialization.* Chapel Hill: University of North Carolina Press, 1995.

Morrison, Toni. *Playing in the Dark: Whiteness and the Literary Imagination.* New York: Vintage, 1992.

Nord, Deborah E. "The Social Explorer as Anthropologist: Victorian Travellers among the Urban Poor." In *Visions of the Modern City,* ed. William Sharpe and Leonard Wallock, 118–30. New York: Columbia University Press, 1983.

Nowak, Krystyna. *Arbeiter und Arbeit in der westdeutschen Literatur, 1945–1961.* Cologne: Pahl-Rugenstein, 1977.

Oberschall, Anthony. *Empirical Social Research in Germany, 1848–1914.* Paris: Mouton, 1965.

Pelz, Annegret. *Reisen durch die eigene Fremde: Reiseliteratur von Frauen als autogeographische Schriften.* Cologne: Böhlau, 1993.

Pierson, Stanley. *Marxist Intellectuals and the Working-Class Mentality in Germany, 1887–1912.* Cambridge: Harvard University Press, 1993.

Riesenfellner, Stefan. *Der Sozialreporter: Max Winter im alten Österreich.* Vienna: Verlag für Gesellschaftskritik, 1987.

Rifkin, Jeremy. *The End of Work.* New York: Putnam, 1995.

Rollka, Bodo. *Die Reise ins Souterrain: Notizen zur Strategie des aufklärerischen Erfolgs: Eugène Sues "Geheimnisse von Paris" und Günter Wallraffs "Ganz unten."* Berlin: Arsenal, 1987.

Rosellini, Jay. *Volker Braun.* Munich: Beck, 1983.

Said, Edward. *Orientalism.* New York: Vintage, 1979.

Silberman, Marc. *Literature of the Working World: A Study of the Industrial Novel in East Germany.* Bern: Lang, 1976.

Teraoka, Arlene. "Talking 'Turk': On Narrative Strategies and Cultural Stereotypes." *New German Critique* 46 (Winter 1989): 104–28.

Trommler, Frank. "DDR-Erzählung und Bitterfelder Weg." *Basis* 3 (1972): 61–97.

———. "Die Kulturpolitik der DDR und die kulturelle Tradition des deutschen Sozialismus." In *Literatur und Literaturtheorie in der DDR,* ed. Patricia Herminghouse and Peter Hohendahl, 13–72. Frankfurt: Suhrkamp, 1976.

Zantop, Susanne. *Colonial Fantasies: Conquest, Family, and Nation in Precolonial Germany, 1770–1870.* Durham, N.C.: Duke University Press, 1997.

Zimmermann, Peter. *Industrieliteratur der DDR: Vom Helden der Arbeit zum Planer und Leiter.* Stuttgart: Metzler, 1984.

Zweig, Arnold. "Bericht aus dem Unbekannten." *Der Klassenkampf* 1, no. 1 (1927): 26–27.

Zweite Bitterfelder Konferenz 1964. Protokoll der von der Ideologischen Kommission beim Politbüro des ZK der SED und dem Ministerium für Kultur am 24. und 25. April im Kulturpalast des Elektrochemischen Kombinats Bitterfeld abgehaltener Konferenz. Berlin: Dietz, 1964.

Index

Books in Series

By the Rivers of Babylon: Heinrich Heine's Late Songs and Reflections, by Roger F. Cook, 1998

Reconstituting the Body Politic: Enlightenment, Public Culture, and the Invention of Aesthetic Autonomy, by Jonathan M. Hess, 1999

The School of Days: Heinrich von Kleist and the Traumas of Education, by Nancy Nobile, 1999

Walter Benjamin and the Corpus of Autobiography, by Gerhard Richter, 2000

Heads or Tails: The Poetics of Money, by Jochen Hörisch, trans. by Amy Horning Marschall, 2000

Dialectics of the Will: Freedom, Power, and Understanding in Modern French and German Thought, by John H. Smith, 2000

The Bonds of Labor: German Journeys to the Working World, 1890–1990, by Carol Poore, 2000